CW01394356

"In this fascinating and incisive re-reading of cheap printed sources, Charlotte-Rose Millar restores two vital elements to a conception of witchcraft that early modern people understood implicitly, but which many historians either overlook or underplay. The first of these is the devil, the second is emotion. This book's importance lies mainly in its compelling portrayal of witchcraft accusations as critical moments when rage and fear and envy boiled over, and its expert analysis of how emotion fused with suspicion and belief to give physical shape and substance to the witch. Seen thus, witches emerge as enemies to the community who were not merely malicious and magical but in intimate and deadly league with Satan."

—*Professor Malcolm Gaskill, The University of East Anglia*

"Charlotte-Rose Millar's insightful study of 66 pamphlets spread over almost 200 years offers a revisionist reading of these fascinating and vivid accounts. This includes a greater focus on diabolism and on newly-emergent topics such as animal familiars and emotional history. Millar's broad and detailed survey demonstrates both continuities and changes across the period, and deepens understanding of the pamphlets' context and major themes because of its long historical reach. The book includes a very useful bibliography and it is beautifully illustrated with images from the pamphlets."

—*Professor Marion Gibson, The University of Exeter*

"Charlotte-Rose Millar's Witchcraft, the Devil, and Emotions in Early Modern England is an original, and important contribution to English witchcraft studies. This is the first book to offer an exhaustive analysis of English witchcraft pamphlets, an unusually rich source. She uses these pamphlets to emphasise the diabolic aspects of English witchcraft beliefs, and offers exciting new insights into such topics as sex with the devil, the role of the familiar, and the place of witchcraft accusations in the history of the emotions."

—*Professor James Sharpe, The University of York*

Witchcraft, the Devil, and Emotions in Early Modern England

This book represents the first systematic study of the role of the Devil in English witchcraft pamphlets for the entire period of state-sanctioned witchcraft prosecutions (1563–1735). It provides a re-reading of English witchcraft, one which moves away from an older historiography which underplays the role of the Devil in English witchcraft and instead highlights the crucial role that the Devil, often in the form of a familiar spirit, took in English witchcraft belief. One of the key ways in which this book explores the role of the Devil is through emotions. Stories of witches were made up of a complex web of emotionally implicated accusers, victims, witnesses and supposed perpetrators. They reveal a range of emotional experiences that do not just stem from malefic witchcraft but also, and primarily, from a witch's links with the Devil. This book, then, has two main objectives. First, to suggest that English witchcraft pamphlets challenge our understanding of English witchcraft as a predominantly non-diabolical crime, and second, to highlight how witchcraft narratives emphasised emotions as the primary motivation for witchcraft acts and accusations.

Charlotte-Rose Millar is a Postdoctoral Fellow in the Institute for Advanced Studies in the Humanities at the University of Queensland and an Associate Investigator with the ARC Centre of Excellence for the History of Emotions (1100–1800). She obtained her PhD from the University of Melbourne in 2015. Millar has published numerous articles and book chapters on witchcraft, diabolism, emotions and sexual practices and has won two prizes for her published work. Her 2015 article on sexual relations between witches and devils has been labelled as the definitive piece on the issue.

Routledge Research in Early Modern History

For a full list of titles in this series, please visit www.routledge.com

Witchcraft, the Devil, and Emotions in Early Modern England

Charlotte-Rose Millar

Routledge
Taylor & Francis Group

LONDON AND NEW YORK

First published 2017
by Routledge
2 Park Square, Milton Park, Abingdon, Oxon OX14 4RN

and by Routledge
711 Third Avenue, New York, NY 10017

Routledge is an imprint of the Taylor & Francis Group, an informa business

© 2017 Charlotte-Rose Millar

The right of Charlotte-Rose Millar to be identified as author of this work has been asserted in accordance with sections 77 and 78 of the Copyright, Designs and Patents Act 1988.

All rights reserved. No part of this book may be reprinted or reproduced or utilised in any form or by any electronic, mechanical, or other means, now known or hereafter invented, including photocopying and recording, or in any information storage or retrieval system, without permission in writing from the publishers.

Trademark notice: Product or corporate names may be trademarks or registered trademarks, and are used only for identification and explanation without intent to infringe.

British Library Cataloguing-in-Publication Data
A catalogue record for this book is available from the British Library

Library of Congress Cataloging-in-Publication Data
A catalog record for this book has been requested

ISBN: 978-1-4724-8549-6 (hbk)
ISBN: 978-1-315-54701-5 (ebk)

Typeset in Sabon
by Apex CoVantage, LLC

MIX
Paper from responsible sources
FSC
www.fsc.org   FSC® C013056

Printed and bound in Great Britain by
TJ International Ltd, Padstow, Cornwall

Contents

Figures

Acknowledgments

I am greatly indebted to a number of people for their help and support in writing this book. First and foremost I would like to thank my doctoral supervisor Charles Zika for his kindness, generosity, intellectual rigour and encouragement, both during my PhD and while I was preparing the manuscript for publication. This book could not have been completed without him. I would also like to thank Jenny Spinks for her kindness, her support and her ceaseless encouragement. I am very grateful to my examiners, Malcolm Gaskill and Brian Levack for their ongoing support, and for their invaluable assistance in transforming the thesis into a book. I would also like to thank James Sharpe, Marion Gibson, Ronald Hutton, Darren Oldridge, Phil Almond, Clive Holmes and Catherine Kovesi, all of whom provided invaluable feedback on the manuscript as a whole or in part. I am also very grateful for the wonderful editorial support and guidance I received from Max Novick and Jennifer Morrow at Routledge. More generally, I have benefitted enormously from discussions with my colleagues at the University of Melbourne and, more recently, the University of Queensland, as well as the wonderful comradery and intellectual energy of my fellow members of the ARC Centre of Excellence for the History of Emotions.

Research towards this book has been supported by a number of scholarships and awards. I am very grateful to the ARC Centre of Excellence for the History of Emotions for a Research Support Scholarship, as well as a number of smaller grants, and to the University of Melbourne for an Australian Postgraduate Award. I would also like to thank the Australian and New Zealand Association for Medieval and Early Modern Studies (ANZAMEMS) for a number of travel and research bursaries, as well as the Network for Early Modern European Research, The M.A. Bartlett Travel Grant Scheme and the Melbourne Abroad Travelling Scholarships Scheme for the same. I also received a Gilbert Postdoctoral Career Development Fellowship from the University of Melbourne and a Humanities Strategic Investment Grant from the University of Manchester and the University of Melbourne, both of which were invaluable in the final stages of the project.

My greatest thanks go to those closest to me. I would like to thank my parents Carol Ryan and Ron Millar and my brothers Paul and Alex for their invaluable support, both emotional and intellectual. Without their encouragement, support and belief this book would not exist. My mother in particular has been a constant source of understanding, comfort and advice, both throughout this project and my life. I would also like to thank Elliott Hobbs, for his unwavering emotional support, encouragement and love.

Introduction: Rethinking English Witchcraft

In 1566 a sensational pamphlet was published in London which described the crimes of three women accused of witchcraft in Chelmsford, Essex.[1] Elizabeth Francis, Mother Agnes Waterhouse and Jone Waterhouse all confessed to possessing a familiar spirit whom they identified as 'Sathan'.[2] This creature, first described as a 'whyte, spotted Catte,' then a toad and, finally, 'a thynge lyke a blacke dogge with a face like an ape, a short tail, and a peyre of hornes on his head,' was said to 'require a drop of bloude' which he sucked from the accused witches.[3] In return for this blood Sathan brought his mistresses riches and revenge. He killed children and made several men impotent. He also forced the accused witches to 'say [their] pater noster [and all other prayers] in laten'.[4] After performing these acts, the familiar spirit betrayed his mistresses to the authorities. One hundred and fifty years later, in 1712, Jane Wenham became the last person to be found guilty of witchcraft in England. Though Jane was later pardoned, her story was immortalised in eight different pamphlet narratives, all published in 1712. Despite being published in a very different world to that inhabited by the Chelmsford witches (in 1712 Jane Wenham's witchcraft was linked to her connections with Dissenters rather than her supposed Catholicism), pamphlet accounts of the case described many similar beliefs to those seen in 1566. Witchcraft was still described as a diabolical crime, the witch was still said to be acting out of a desire for revenge, and non-conformity was still allied with witchcraft. By 1735, the date that James I's witchcraft statute was repealed, England was almost unrecognisable from the country that, one hundred and seventy years earlier, passed the 1563 witchcraft statute. It had also changed dramatically from the date of the second witchcraft statute in 1604. Yet, throughout this one hundred and seventy year period, witchcraft remained a concern, witchcraft belief continued and, even up until as late as 1717, witchcraft trials were held. Across this entire period, pamphleteers emphasised the importance of the Devil in witchcraft. In this book I will examine all extant witchcraft pamphlets from this period – of which sixty-six remain – and provide a re-reading of English witchcraft: a reading which emphasises the crucial role that the Devil played in popular depictions of English witchcraft, and the way in which emotions were portrayed in print as key motivators for witchcraft acts and accusations.

Sixty-six witchcraft pamphlets form the core body of sources for this book – a group of sources that have never before been studied in tandem. Although their content varied, many of these narratives followed a familiar form. Take, for example, the 1646 case of Ellen Shepherd. Ellen was unhappy with her life and was approached by the Devil in the shape of a rat. After some persuasion, Ellen agreed to give her soul to this rat. Ellen was promised 'all happinesse' in exchange for her soul and for allowing the devilish rat to suck her blood. Unfortunately, the Devil did not keep his promise and Ellen claimed that she had not experienced any happiness.[5] Such narratives are omnipresent in English witchcraft pamphlets and normally emphasise a witch's desire for revenge against the (sometimes imagined) slights of his or her neighbours. It is only in the last forty years that such witchcraft narratives have been the focus of more detailed study by historians and, in recent years, interest has only increased. The concept of a witch's revenge is well-documented in English historiography, but work that explicitly deals with the role of the Devil is harder to come by. European witchcraft studies have long been concerned with the relationship between witchcraft and the Devil, but it is only recently that witchcraft historians have suggested that English witchcraft may also include the involvement of the Devil. Some of these same historians have started to focus on the role of emotion in witchcraft narratives.[6]

This book is about the links between English witchcraft and the Devil in popular pamphlets. It focuses on the emotional interactions between witches and devils and a witch's supposed motivations for succumbing to Satan and performing witchcraft. In exploring these relationships, I aim to present an alternative perspective on English witchcraft, one that is based almost entirely on printed primary sources. This reading emphasises the diabolical elements of English witchcraft and moves away from the older historiographical view of English witchcraft as predominantly non-diabolic and malefic. Instead, this book explores how the Devil was viewed as a crucial component of a witch's ability to perform harmful magic or, as I will refer to it, *maleficium*.[7] The book will focus on the ways in which pamphleteers portrayed witches, how their readers viewed witches' motivations for succumbing to the Devil and how the accused witches told their stories. Stories of witches were made up of a complex web of emotionally implicated accusers, victims, witnesses, and supposed perpetrators. They reveal a range of emotional experiences that do not just stem from malefic witchcraft but also, and primarily, from a witch's links with the Devil. Examining this web of relationships allows a unique insight into the mentalities of early modern people. It also demonstrates that there were sections of English society that understood witchcraft as a diabolical activity. This book, then, has two main objectives. First, to suggest that English witchcraft pamphlets challenge our understanding of English witchcraft as a predominantly non-diabolical crime, and second, to highlight how witchcraft narratives emphasised emotions as the primary motivation for witchcraft acts and accusations.

Witchcraft in the Early Modern English Context

Although England saw relatively low numbers of witchcraft prosecutions, the centrality of witchcraft beliefs to English society should not be underestimated. Early modern English witchcraft beliefs were formed against the background of the Reformation, constant imagined and actual Catholic plots, a potentially shaky succession and a Civil War that culminated in the deaths of over 190,000 people and the legally sanctioned beheading of a king. Even though England had been officially established as a Protestant country by the 1559 religious settlement, tensions between Protestants and Catholics remained ever-present. Many English Protestants came to fear the presence of secret Catholics, and Reformation polemic helped create a strong imaginative association between Catholicism, magic and diabolical power.[8] As well as increasing tensions between Catholics and Protestants, reformers in newly Protestant England promoted belief in the ever-growing power of the Devil. In the words of Keith Thomas, the Reformation 'did nothing to weaken [belief in the Devil]; indeed it almost certainly strengthened it'.[9] Many men and women were disarmed by the Reformation. As will be discussed in the first chapter, the Reformation simultaneously emphasised the danger of the Devil and also forbade the use of relics, amulets and other Catholic objects used as safeguards against the Devil's power.

It was against this background of magic, the Devil and a fear of underground Catholicism that the Elizabethan witchcraft statute was published in 1563. Although a previous witchcraft statute had been enacted under Henry VIII in 1541 this was essentially a dead letter and was repealed under Edward VI in 1547. Elizabeth's Act began by condemning those who 'practised Invocacons and Conjuracons of evill and wicked Spirites', as well as those who used 'Wytchecraftes, Enchantementes Charms and Sorceries', to destroy the 'P[er]sons and Goodes of their Neighebours, and other Subjectes of this Realme'.[10] The Act not only condemned harming or killing others through witchcraft, but also created a state-sanctioned link between witchcraft and evil spirits. It prescribed death for any person who killed another through witchcraft or evil spirits and, unusually for the period, a one-year prison sentence for anyone who harmed but did not kill a person through witchcraft or for anyone who damaged somebody's goods. This prison sentence only applied to the first offence; for later offences the death penalty was enforced. In 1604, one year after James VI and I's ascension to the English throne, the king replaced Elizabeth's act with his own harsher version. As well as legislating against conjuring and using evil spirits, James's act made it illegal to keep, feed or reward these spirits. The Jacobean statute also increased the penalties for *maleficium*, and increased the list of offences punishable by death.[11] This meant that it became theoretically easier to prosecute witchcraft, as all that was now needed was a witness who claimed that a witch was keeping evil spirits, rather than, as was the case under Elizabeth, proof that witches were using these spirits to harm others.

Although it seems that the Jacobean witchcraft statute would have engendered higher prosecution rates in England, this is not reflected in trial records. After a peak in the 1580s, prosecutions continued to decline until the 1640s.[12] This is not to say that public fear of witchcraft declined; it may have even increased precisely because the law no longer seemed committed to rooting out witches.[13] Through its focus on the suckling of the familiar, the Jacobean witchcraft statute emphasised the role of the Devil. However, this had little effect on pamphlets, as narratives from both before and after the 1604 Act constantly referred to the work of the Devil and to familiar spirits. It would seem that the effect of both statutes was to recognise that witchcraft, both malefic and diabolical, was of real concern to the Crown and that both Elizabeth and James supported its suppression.

Although it appeared that witchcraft prosecutions were on the decline, this trend was halted by the events of the 1640s. This decade has often been treated differently by witchcraft historians. Several factors combined to make the 1640s particularly virulent for witchcraft accusations, trials and executions. The chaos of the Civil War period, combined with the anxiety that such a conflict produced, made people warier of witches, and more sure that they were acting in the world to destroy society. The terror that this conflict unleashed cannot be underestimated: 190,000, or 3.7 per cent, of the English population died, a greater proportion, as Malcolm Gaskill has noted, than during the First World War.[14] The breakdown of the state, including the abolition of episcopal authority and the Court of the Star Chamber (both effective institutions for dealing with witchcraft allegations), may well have 'removed a powerful brake on systematic witch-hunting'.[15] The removal of censorship and licensing laws (discussed below) meant that the trials that did occur were more likely to be publicised and circulated in print for the masses, thus increasing the sense that witches were everywhere. Finally, the emergence of the self-styled Witch-finder General Matthew Hopkins in Essex in the mid-1640s (himself a product of the seemingly apocalyptic times in which he lived) meant that during the Civil Wars England experienced its biggest ever witch-hunt. Between 1645 and 1647 as many as three hundred men and women were interrogated under suspicion of witchcraft, one hundred of whom were executed.[16]

There is no doubt that the 1640s were an exceptional period in England's history; a period which bred higher witchcraft trials and executions than had previously been seen in England. But it is going too far to see these trials as an 'aberration', or as something completely different from what came before or after, as so many have done before.[17] As much as the trials of the 1640s were unusual, they did not contain material that had not previously been included in witchcraft print. As this book will discuss in depth, ideas of demonic copulation, sabbaths and devil worship were all notable features of witchcraft pamphlets well before Hopkins, and continued to be so well after his death. One of the aims of this book, therefore, is to reshape the way in which the 1640s are viewed in historical scholarship – as a decade in which witchcraft intensified but was not reinvented.

Witchcraft belief and witchcraft pamphlets continued well after the 1640s, although securing a conviction did become more difficult. As Clive Holmes has noted, post-1660 the criteria for a witchcraft indictment became far more demanding than previously, with many magistrates and lawyers refusing to frame an indictment unless *maleficium* had resulted in the death of the victim or, more rarely, the accused was directly involved in diabolical practises.[18] As Holmes also notes, though, this change did not indicate any fundamental change in popular belief about witchcraft; rather, it instead demonstrated a new reading of the Jacobean witchcraft statute, a reading borne out of a growing reluctance on the part of many legal elites to prosecute witches.[19] Peter Elmer has also noted a revival in witchcraft belief in the 1660s, stemming, he argues, from the political and religious turmoil of the time.[20] Despite a growing decrease in prosecutions, witchcraft belief continued in the second half of the seventeenth century, with the 1680s producing more witchcraft pamphlets than any other decade (see Appendix B).

It was not until 1735, under George II, that the Jacobean statute was repealed and replaced by another that described witchcraft as a superstitious, fanciful activity. Instead of legislating against witchcraft, the Georgian statute legislated against people who pretended to practise forms of witchcraft such as fortune-telling, often for financial gain. This final statute marked an official end to state-sanctioned witchcraft prosecutions. In practice, however, prosecutions for witchcraft were already a thing of the past. The last execution for witchcraft took place in 1685, the last conviction occurred in 1712 (although the sentence was overturned by the trial judge) and the last trial transpired in 1717. By 1735, therefore, the witchcraft statute was effectively obsolete.[21] This did not mean, of course, that witchcraft belief ceased to exist, as is all too apparent from the horrific 1751 case that saw a mob attack and ultimately kill a 70-year-old couple who they suspected as witches. By 1751, however, these beliefs were no longer sanctioned by law and the ringleader of the group, Thomas Colley, was hanged for leading the mob.[22]

In the witchcraft cases that did appear during the late seventeenth and early eighteenth centuries, there was much that was reminiscent of earlier trials. As Peter Elmer has argued, 'one of the most notable features of the [later trials of 1682, 1702 and 1712] is the complete lack of originality that characterises both the evidence brought against the accused witches and the arguments subsequently adopted by those who debated the merits of the individual cases'.[23] Elmer points out that, as in previous years, most accused women were old, poor and situated on the fringe of their community and, in all of these cases there was a concern that these women had used witchcraft to harm their neighbours.[24] Crucially, the Devil's role in pamphlets also survived much unchanged. Throughout the entire early modern period, fear of the Devil and a witch's reliance on the Devil to perform harmful magic remained at the forefront of popular narratives. There were, of course, important differences in later pamphlets, many of which were influenced by the strong religious and political context from which they emerged. Although older trials also sometimes originated from periods of community tension or upheaval, these tensions had different resonances. From the mid-seventeenth century, for example, fears of underground Catholics became supplemented with new concerns about non-conformist sects, particularly Quakers, who became the subject of a number of pamphlets linking their practices with witchcraft.[25] But in my analysis of all sixty-six pamphlets, what is really striking are the similarities in pamphlet narratives across such a broad period.

The state-sanctioned prosecution of witches led to approximately 1,000 men and women being tried in English secular courts.[26] Although it is extremely difficult to estimate numbers, particularly due to loss of records, James Sharpe has suggested that rather less than five hundred people were executed for witchcraft in England between 1542 and 1735.[27] This relatively low rate of trials and executions has been widely attributed to the prohibition of torture and the absence of inquisitorial procedure.[28] There were a number of factors that contributed to England's low levels of prosecutions. English witchcraft trials could not be initiated at a government level; all indictments and bills had first to be approved by the grand jury. Additionally, once a case went to trial, the accused had to be found guilty by a jury, not just a judge. Finally, nearly all witchcraft cases took place at the county assizes and were overseen by a centrally appointed judge. This meant that trials did not take place in the witch's own community but, on the other hand, were administered by a judge who, in theory, had no personal knowledge of or investment in the case.[29] These legal processes served to lessen the number of witches accused and convicted in England. Surviving records from the Home Circuit Assizes demonstrate that less than a quarter of all accused witches were hanged.[30] Sharpe has noted that relatively small numbers of witchcraft accusations and executions should be viewed as part of a broader trend in the early modern English justice system to acquit far more often than European courts.[31] Sharpe warns us, therefore, that these numbers should not be taken as a reflection of the strength of witchcraft belief in England. Thomas' finding that, at the Essex Assizes in the 1580s witchcraft cases constituted 13 per cent of all criminal cases, is just one reminder of the prevalence of witchcraft prosecutions.[32] Others such as Alan Macfarlane have argued for the prevalence of witchcraft beliefs in every facet of village life, despite relatively low rates of prosecution.[33] These prosecutions and executions were not equal across genders and, as in much of Western Europe, women made up a large proportion of those under suspicion. From his study of court records, Macfarlane has estimated that 90 per cent of accused witches were female.[34] My own analysis of all early modern English witchcraft pamphlets demonstrates that 87 per cent of witches represented in these texts were also female. When we break this down by century, we see that in the sixteenth century 94 per cent of accused pamphlet witches were female, in the seventeenth-century this figure was 85 per cent and in the eighteenth it was 100 per cent. These high percentages position English witchcraft as an almost exclusively female crime.

At the same time as witchcraft beliefs were being incorporated into daily life, printing was becoming more prevalent than ever before. Witchcraft beliefs were not only expressed in secular trials or royal acts, but also circulated in popular pamphlets, ballads, broadsheets and plays. As noted above, sixty-six witchcraft pamphlets remain from the early modern period, and many more pamphlets on possession, ghosts and other supernatural activity have also survived.[35] Still more pamphlets remain which reference witchcraft in passing or were part of an ongoing debate about the reality of witchcraft. These pamphlets were part of a general increase in print production during the early modern period. This increase, relatively steady in the first half of the seventeenth century, underwent a massive surge between 1640 and 1660.[36] In England in 1640, only twenty-two pamphlets were published.[37] In 1642 this number increased to 1,996, a jump of almost 9,000 per cent.[38] As we might expect, the number of witchcraft pamphlets published during this time also rose dramatically, particularly given the corresponding rise in witchcraft prosecutions under Matthew Hopkins in the mid-1640s.[39] Of the sixty-six pamphlets included in this study, twenty-two were published between 1640 and 1660, the period between the decline of censorship in the early 1640s and its reinstatement in 1662.[40] The 1662 Licensing Act lapsed in 1695, causing pre-publication censorship and control of copyright to disappear, with only the latter reinstated by the 1710 Statute of Anne. This meant an end to formal pre-publication censorship from 1695 onwards, after which time eight of the pamphlets included in this study were published.[41] Unsurprisingly, the lapse of the Licensing Act was followed by an ever-growing surge of new cheap publications, most notably newspapers.[42] Approximately half of the witchcraft pamphlets in this study were printed under times of strict licensing laws. Appendix B shows the chronological spread of these pamphlets. These pamphlets are a key vehicle for tracing the spread of witchcraft beliefs throughout England.

English Witchcraft and the Devil: The Story So Far

The interpretation of English witchcraft as predominantly malefic harks back to the very early days of witchcraft scholarship.[43] As has already been made clear, this book aims to reinterpret the traditional historiographical view of English witchcraft as a predominantly malefic crime and to emphasise the key importance of the Devil. Given this emphasis, a review of the relevant historiography becomes crucial. Although historians are starting to become more sympathetic to the idea of diabolism in English witchcraft, there still remains a strong tendency to downplay the role of the Devil. To understand the long-held interpretation of English witchcraft as predominantly malefic, it is necessary to return to the beginnings of modern witchcraft scholarship, starting with the work of Wallace Notestein, Cecil L'Estrange Ewen and George Kittredge.

Wallace Notestein's 1911 book focused on English witchcraft from 1558 until 1718, thus covering nearly the entire period of state-sanctioned witchcraft accusations.[44] As one of the first modern scholars working on witchcraft, Notestein examined a large number of sources including pamphlets, local records, memoirs, diaries, newspapers, works by local historians and antiquarians, theological writings and state papers. Notestein's main focus was on tracing the development of English witchcraft, a task that had not previously been attempted. He defined the learned, theological, European concept of witchcraft as an inherently diabolical activity, but this was not his focus in examining English material. Indeed, when speaking about contracts between witches and devils, Notestein declared: 'this loathsome side of witch belief we cannot go into'.[45] For Notestein, the Devil could quite easily be sidestepped in a study of English witchcraft.

Perhaps most well-known of the early scholars is C.L. Ewen, whose use of Assize records produced vast numbers of new sources.[46] Ewen's second book is the most discursive, with his first being primarily an annotated guide to witchcraft documents such as indictments and depositions. In his second book Ewen supplemented his initial statistical analysis with an enquiry into the nature of magical practices.[47] For Ewen, medieval concepts of witchcraft were innately connected with Devil worship, particularly on the Continent. He devoted almost thirty pages of his 1933 book to an exploration of the Devil in both Continental and English witchcraft, but much of this was part of a discussion of how unlikely it would have been for witches to actually interact with demons. Ewen explored the confusion between the Devil and familiar spirits and also traced the development of the demonic pact.[48] Despite these thoughts on the Devil, Ewen, like Notestein, left his reader with the strong impression that diabolical witchcraft was far more prevalent in Europe than in England. The idea of English witchcraft as fundamentally different from its European equivalent was, even at this early stage, attributed to the supposedly smaller role of the Devil.

George Lyman Kittredge, another seminal historian writing on witchcraft in the late 1920s, chose to focus his 1929 study on both Old and New England. Kittredge succinctly summed up his position on the nature of English witchcraft:

> we should never forget that the essence of witchcraft is *maleficium*. The hatred and terror which a witch evokes is due to her will and her power to inflict bodily injury. Compacts with the devil, the suckling of imps, the violation of graves, the abomination of the Witches Sabbath – these are mere incidentals, the paraphernalia of the art.[49]

Kittredge went on to argue that the diabolical elements of English witchcraft did not stem from popular belief, but rather, were inserted into witchcraft narratives by learned judges, philosophers and divines.[50] He described the witch as a terrifying figure, one whose revenge for imagined or tiny slights was supported through legions of evil spirits. Thus, although Kittredge highlighted the role of the diabolical in English witchcraft, he saw witches' associations with evil spirits as secondary to the fear they bred by their very nature. Although I agree with Kittredge's assessment of witches as sources of fear, I contend that a witch's ties to the diabolical were crucial in fuelling the fear that people felt towards him or her. It is, therefore, not possible (or productive) to separate witches' *maleficium* from their diabolical ties.

Notestein, Ewen and Kittredge were all pivotal in developing witchcraft as a serious field for historical study. Their highlighting of previously unknown sources provided an excellent platform on which to base further studies. It was not until the 1970s that a new paradigm of witchcraft emerged, one that fundamentally defined how future historians would interpret English witchcraft. I refer, of course, to the work of Keith Thomas and Alan Macfarlane, scholars who were essential in cementing the idea that English witchcraft was primarily malefic and not, like its Continental equivalent, diabolical.[51] The studies of Thomas and Macfarlane are often referred to in tandem (often because of their emphasis on neighbourly charity – a concept further explored in chapter 3, this volume), and it is difficult to overestimate the influence of their work on more recent witchcraft historians. James Sharpe, in an introduction to the second edition of Macfarlane's work, reminds us that for at least a quarter of a century after it was written, Macfarlane's work (read with Thomas' study) was the 'standard interpretation' of English witchcraft.[52] Thomas and Macfarlane gave great weight to popular mentalities and provided detailed studies of beliefs about witches and their practices. In exploring popular belief, Thomas echoed Kittredge:

> sixteenth- and seventeenth-century England thus knew not one concept of witchcraft but two. On top of the popular belief in the power of maleficent magic was imposed the theological notion that the essence of witchcraft was adherence to the Devil.[53]

Thomas' argument that concerns about the Devil stemmed from a learned tradition, whereas village witchcraft was primarily malefic, was extremely influential. Like Ewen and Notestein before him, Thomas encouraged a strong distinction between the more malefic English witchcraft and its diabolical, Continental counterpart. This is a concept that has dominated English witchcraft history. Thomas suggested that demonic familiars and other diabolical elements were 'not the staple constituents of English witch-trials'.[54] He did, however, state that 'they appear often enough in the seventeenth century to demand some explanation'.[55] Although Thomas emphasised the malefic elements of English witchcraft, he was, of course, aware of the influence of diabolical ideas. The further exploration of these ideas is one of the key aims of this book.

Like his mentor, Macfarlane also emphasised the importance of studying witchcraft beliefs 'from below,' an approach that situated witchcraft firmly within its social context. Macfarlane's focus on village dynamics led him to argue strongly (like Thomas and Kittredge) for the importance of *maleficium* to English witchcraft beliefs. Macfarlane's statistical work and emphasis on social relationships helped create an understanding of English witchcraft as based firmly within neighbourhood conflicts. Both Thomas and Macfarlane were instrumental in cementing a view of English witchcraft as an activity far removed from belief in the Devil and his power. Barbara Rosen, another influential scholar, also subscribed to this view. In her excellent study of popular pamphlets, Rosen claimed that *maleficium* was the primary characteristic of English witchcraft, arguing that pamphlets in which the Devil was particularly prominent could be explained through the influence of Continental ideas.[56] Rosen described English witchcraft in completely different terms from that on the Continent, arguing that 'the absolutely basic adjunct of the Continental idea of a witch was [the] pact, entailing attendance at the Sabbath, sexual orgies and worship of the Devil'.[57] Despite her dismissal of the Devil's importance to English witchcraft, Rosen did, however, examine the figure of the familiar, a creature she described as 'a tame devil'.[58] Rosen claimed that the familiar was 'indispensable' to English witch-beliefs and firmly grounded in popular belief.[59] She also acknowledged that the familiar formed a pact between itself and the witch.[60] This apparent conflict between acknowledging the familiar as a devil and viewing English witchcraft as predominantly malefic is a curious commonplace in many English witchcraft studies.

Thomas, Macfarlane and Rosen, as well as highlighting the importance of village dynamics and popular mentalities, also helped to draw attention to the emotional factors in witchcraft acts and accusations. All three scholars highlighted a desire for revenge as a key motivator in performing witchcraft and pushed for an understanding of witchcraft belief "from below".[61] They also all highlighted the fear that people would have felt towards witches. By the early 1970s English witchcraft scholarship had constructed an 'English model' of witchcraft, which differed from the supposedly more demonic beliefs in 'Continental Europe'. This view, although changing, is extremely difficult to dislodge.

Few modern-day witchcraft historians will deny that there was a link between witchcraft and gender. Since the 1970s, and especially during the 1990s, an immense amount of work has been done on the links between gender, sex and witchcraft, so much so that it is impossible to summarise it in detail here.[62] Amongst this plethora of studies are two which take a more psychological approach by examining the lives, emotions and concerns of accused witches and, as such, are most relevant for this book. Deborah Willis and Diane Purkiss, both of whom published in 1995, argued for an understanding of the witch as a bad mother, one who used her maternal powers against her neighbours.[63] Purkiss, who labelled the witch an 'antimother', reinforced the agency of women in witchcraft narratives and attempted to understand women's anxieties and fears. Purkiss argued that for women, 'a witch was a figure who could be read against and within her own social identity as housewife and mother'.[64] Willis' book expressed many of the same ideas. Like Purkiss, Willis sought to understand the links between witchcraft and women by looking at the concerns of women themselves. She argued that 'witches were women . . . because women are mothers'.[65] Willis went on to explain that many village-level arguments that could lead to witchcraft accusations were often based around feeding, childcare, struggles to control household boundaries and other issues normally seen as part of the female sphere.[66] Willis' study was primarily concerned with this female sphere and the concept of the witch as a bad mother, one who was 'perverse' and who 'used her powers of nurture malevolently against neighbours'.[67] More than just highlighting the personal side of witchcraft accusations, Willis also emphasised the demonic through her focus on the familiar. Her argument that these imps often performed the role of surrogate demonic children to childless women had two main effects. First, it represented an attempt to recognise the importance of the Devil in English witchcraft belief and, second, it highlighted the critical role that emotions played in shaping the relationship between witch and Devil. Not only did Willis suggest a new way of understanding the links between women and witchcraft, but she was also one of the first historians to study the familiar in detail. Willis' work will be explored in greater depth in chapter 4 and will provide a starting point for exploring the emotions expressed between female witches and their devils.

In this book, female witches have been given their own chapter to explore the belief that witches engaged in sex with the Devil – something that we do not see with male witches in early modern England. Although male witches have not been singled out in this way, they still form an important part of this study.[68] Earlier works, such as those by Alan Macfarlane, Keith Thomas, E.W. Monter and Eric Midelfort, viewed the male witch as an aberration, something not worth particular attention.[69] Of the more recent scholars of male witchcraft, I align myself most closely with Malcolm Gaskill.[70] Gaskill believes that the category of "witch" should be taken just as seriously as "gender" because as witch accusations were relatively rare, anyone accused of witchcraft must have had traits in common regardless of sex. I view male and female witches as very similar in their practices and behaviour. Both these groups were believed to be malicious, to own familiars and to work with other witches and the Devil to wreak havoc on society. Although not implicated in sexual relationships with devils, male witches were still believed to form intimate relationships with the Devil in the form of a familiar spirit.

It was not until the mid-1990s that historians began to consider a paradigm of English witchcraft that moved away from the work of Thomas and Macfarlane and started to more fully explore the role of the Devil. There have also been concerted efforts to break down the idea of "Continental witchcraft" by highlighting regional differences between European countries and also through demonstrating that there are many examples of malefic witchcraft in countries other than England.[71] The trend for historians to no longer overlook the role of the Devil in English witchcraft owes much to James Sharpe's excellent studies on English witchcraft, the most influential of which was published in 1996.[72] Sharpe's reappraisal of the diabolical features of English witchcraft allowed historians to begin to move away from the malefic paradigm set by Thomas and Macfarlane. In 1998, Barry Reay referred to Sharpe's work:

> it is becoming evident that the characterisation of English witchcraft as non-demonological has been overdrawn. From an early stage, the figure of the Devil was present in the discourses of witchcraft found in the pamphlet literature. English demonology may not have been identical to Continental demonology – the pact is stronger and the sabbath is weaker – but it was important nonetheless.[73]

Through studies on the familiar, the period of trials associated with Matthew Hopkins in the 1640s and, most recently, the possibility of English sabbaths, Sharpe has suggested that English witchcraft was not the unique, predominantly malefic phenomenon that so many historians have claimed it was.[74] Sharpe's work provided much of the initial inspiration for this study. Although the presence of the diabolical is beginning to be acknowledged, far more work remains. There has yet to be a comprehensive study on the links between witchcraft and the role of the Devil in English pamphlet literature. My book attempts to fill this gap.

The Sources

Sixty-six witchcraft pamphlets make up the core group of sources used throughout this book. This number represents all early modern pamphlets that I have characterised as 'witchcraft pamphlets'. It has not always been easy to decide what constitutes a witchcraft pamphlet. For the purposes of this book a witchcraft pamphlet is defined as a pamphlet that describes a witchcraft trial or series of trials and is designed to be read or absorbed by a popular audience (as much as one can tell).[75] This definition has meant that I have excluded learned treatises and demonologies, as well as those pamphlets which refer to witchcraft in passing or talk generally about the nature and reality of witchcraft. Some broader pamphlets have been included because of their description of a specific witchcraft trial.[76] Possession pamphlets have been excluded as these constitute a distinct genre of their own.

Length has not played a part in these decisions; it is content that is the key. This definition is not perfect and, no doubt, there are some pamphlets that I have excluded which others will believe should have been included. What I have tried to do is to focus on these pamphlets as a genre which continues throughout the entire early modern period. These pamphlets, although divergent in length, authorship and style, all place specific witchcraft acts and accusations as their central focus. As such, my core group of sources is made up of sixty-six witchcraft pamphlets: ten from the sixteenth century, forty-eight from the seventeenth, and eight from the eighteenth. These sources form the basis for my analyses throughout the book. Any statistics are based on this group. A full list can be found in Appendix A.

There are multiple reasons for my decision to focus on popular print rather than trial records (or a mixture of both). Apart from the obvious limitation of space (an important concern given the chronological breadth of this study), first and foremost is the fact that there has not yet been a sustained study that analyses the content of all early modern English witchcraft pamphlets.[77] Very few of the pamphlets included in this book have been the subject of sustained scholarship; some have simply been transcribed and others referred to in passing.[78] In 1996, James Sharpe reminded us that 'these printed sources . . . have not been analysed systematically for many years'.[79] Although Marion Gibson has gone a long way towards undoing this neglect, witchcraft pamphlets have not yet been studied as an entire group as part of an argument about the fundamental nature of English witchcraft belief.[80] In addition, many historians of English witchcraft, particularly those who focus on printed culture or pamphlet literature, often confine themselves to the period between 1560 and 1620 or 1640.[81] The adoption of this time frame suggests that English pamphlet literature stops abruptly in the second half of the seventeenth century. Consequently, the pamphlets from the second half of the seventeenth century have been largely overlooked, or have been studied separately from those that came before.[82] My focus on the entire early modern period is part of an attempt to create a broader picture of witchcraft beliefs during this period. It also helps to place the 1640s more appropriately in a continuum of English witchcraft belief and not, as so many have suggested, as a decade which depicts a fundamentally different set of beliefs about witchcraft in England.

Another reason for my decision to focus on popular print stems from the importance of these sources. Popular pamphlets provide an excellent insight into witchcraft beliefs. They allow access to details that are sometimes missing from court proceedings and often support the accuracy of trial records. We can never know from pamphlets what actually occurred between accused witches and their supposed victims, but my focus is instead on what was believed to have happened, what was represented in print, what influence accused witches may have had on the narrative, and what pamphlet writers wanted their readers to believe. In this way, pamphlets form a solid basis for an analysis of early modern attitudes towards and beliefs about witchcraft.

This book takes pamphlets as its core sources in order to argue for a new interpretation of English witchcraft. The almost omnipresent references to devils in popular witchcraft print throughout the entire early modern period encourage an alternative reading of English witchcraft, one that provides a more central role for the Devil.

Several historians have remarked on the importance of pamphlets for witchcraft studies. Macfarlane has argued convincingly, claiming that witchcraft pamphlets are 'a vital and reliable source providing otherwise inaccessible material and correcting the somewhat narrow impression of witchcraft prosecutions given by indictments'.[83] He believes that court records are not a sufficient source for the study of witchcraft and has also done substantial work to demonstrate that court records often support the accuracy of pamphlets.[84] Writing forty years before Macfarlane, Ewen also argued for the importance of pamphlets to witchcraft studies, arguing that these documents 'are rarely fabrications, and, in general, bear the stamp of genuine attempts to record accurately the acts of the witch'.[85] Others have argued that court records often 'contain the barest essentials of a case', whereas pamphlets 'allow us to see what lay behind formal court records'.[86] Gibson, Rosen and Sharpe also all believe that popular print provides an excellent platform for understanding English witchcraft beliefs.[87] Recently, Frances Dolan has added her voice to these historians and highlighted the importance of pamphlets for the study of English witchcraft.[88] Dolan emphasises the 'role of stories' in interpreting English witchcraft beliefs and embraces Gibson's understanding of pamphlets as a genre which illuminates what people at the time believed happened or, at the very least, what they wanted us to believe happened.[89] Gibson has done the most work on these pamphlets and has demonstrated the impossibility of attempting to separate the different influences that go into each pamphlet.[90] Dolan is also aware of the limitations of pamphlets and reminds us that it is difficult to 'distinguish cleanly between how cases actually unfolded and how witnesses or pamphleteers chose to tell that story'.[91] Despite these problems, pamphlets remain one of the most valuable sources for the study of English witchcraft. Even those who have criticised the accuracy of pamphlet accounts feel that they are still important for 'what they have to tell us about the beliefs' of the time.[92]

Witchcraft pamphlets were able to reach a larger readership than may at first be supposed. The pamphlets analysed in this book, although all published in London, were also distributed to rural regions by chapmen, thus allowing witchcraft narratives to 'reach the public domain'.[93] Not only did pamphlets transcend geographical boundaries, they were also able to reach seemingly illiterate villagers. David Cressy has argued that at the accession of Elizabeth I, 20 per cent of men and 10 per cent of women in rural England were literate; that is, at the very least able to sign their name.[94] However, a number of scholars including Keith Thomas, Margaret Spufford and Heidi Brayman Hackel, have argued that these figures should be taken as a bare minimum.[95] Keith Thomas has gone so far as to suggest that they may be 'not just an underestimate . . . but a spectacular underestimate'.[96] Reading was taught before writing across all classes and was also taught separately, often within the home.[97] Measuring literacy by people's ability to sign their name also largely ignores women, 'since writing was frequently omitted from the school curricula for girls', whereas reading was included.[98] Literacy rates were not just affected by gender but also geography. Sandra Clark has estimated that approximately half of the male population in London could read, a much higher percentage than estimates for rural England.[99] Therefore, it is not accurate to judge people's ability to read by the ability to sign their name. Of course, reading ability leaves far fewer tangible signs than writing and, as such, is much harder to measure. This makes it very difficult to accurately judge how many people had access to books and pamphlets. It is easier to make this judgement, however, if we understand how early modern men and women engaged with written texts. Rather than reading privately, 'most [early modern people] experienced reading primarily aurally rather than visually'.[100] It was common for literate people to read broadsides and ballads to their illiterate neighbours.[101] It was also common for some people to be able to read print but not handwriting and this would have allowed them to access witchcraft pamphlets.[102] Taking all of these factors into account provides us with a sense of a much larger reading community than might otherwise have been assumed. It also demonstrates that many more people than those who could sign their names would have had access to witchcraft narratives. This allows us to view witchcraft print as a medium that was able to reach a broad social and geographical strata of the population of early modern England.

Studying popular pamphlets allows insights into the thoughts and beliefs of pamphleteers, accusers, witnesses, victims and witches. Witchcraft pamphlets contain a mixture of learned and popular beliefs about witchcraft and the Devil. Returning to Thomas's seminal study, we are reminded that historians have often talked about a divide between popular and learned belief in witchcraft.[103] Although Thomas acknowledges that these two ideas 'were to be found side by side, sometimes apart, sometimes intermingled', he is still keen to make a distinction between them.[104] Clive Holmes has suggested that the relationship between popular and elite concerns was 'symbiotic'.[105] He has explored how learned culture influenced popular and vice versa and has been keen to stress that 'the traffic was not entirely in one direction'.[106] Carlo Ginzburg has also made this point, arguing that 'relations between learned and popular culture are rarely a one-way process'.[107] More recently, Peter Burke has outlined some of the problems with categories such as "learned" and "popular" culture. Although these terms are inherently difficult to define, Burke believes that they should be retained. To avoid being overly simplistic, however, he suggests that it is best to use them 'without making the binary opposition too rigid'.[108] Burke suggests that 'the elites of Western Europe were "bicultural", participating in what historians call "popular culture" as well as in a learned culture from which ordinary people were excluded'.[109] This concept applies to pamphlets. As Frances Dolan has noted, 'at the height of witch prosecutions in England, popular and elite cultures were not discrete . . . each influenced and was shaped by the other. Witchcraft discourses reside at an intersection of the two; for instance, some "popular" pamphlets were written by legal personnel.'[110] Sharpe has also commented on the differing influences in witchcraft narratives:

> [Pamphlets] provide an alternative view of witchcraft which falls, as it were, between the theological abstractions of William Perkins and the all too concrete concerns of a villager worrying about the bewitchments of his cattle.[111]

Pamphleteers were often familiar with other works on witchcraft, including many learned demonological treatises. Thomas Potts' 1613 pamphlet, discussed at length in chapter 5, contains references to James VI and I's *Daemonologie*. The anonymous 1619 pamphlet on the Flower family mentions works by James VI and I, Alexander Roberts, John Cotta and George Gifford, as well as Potts' pamphlet and another popular pamphlet from 1612.[112] When describing the sabbath, a 1666 pamphlet quotes Scot's *Discoverie of Witchcraft* which, in turn, is actually quoting Jean Bodin.[113] It is clear that at least some pamphleteers read learned English and European witchcraft treatises and that ideas from these sources sometimes became entangled with views expressed in evidence from English witchcraft trials. In turn, popular narratives could influence learned treatises. For instance, Scot's famously sceptical treatise on witchcraft referenced over two hundred foreign and thirty-eight English works.[114] In many witchcraft narratives, there is a clear exchange between popular and learned ideas.[115]

   As is clear from this brief survey, witchcraft pamphlets betray a multiplicity of influences ranging from the testimony of often illiterate witches to the narrative voice taken by the pamphleteer.[116] Although the majority of pamphleteers were anonymous, they were obviously literate and some were ministers, lawyers or clerks, making them much more educated than the average witch.[117] Pamphleteers were able to shape narratives and to choose what they included or emphasised. But it was not just the pamphleteer who shaped the content of a witchcraft pamphlet. These narratives were also influenced by the proceedings of the court, the remarks of the magistrate, the notes of the clerk, the testimony of witnesses and victims and the confession of the witch. All of these elements helped to construct a witchcraft pamphlet, but it was the pamphleteer who chose which elements to emphasise or include. Pamphlets were marketable texts; they were designed to sell. The pamphleteer constructing the text, then, can be assumed to have selected and emphasised material that he (or in one rare case, she) felt would be most appealing to a popular audience.[118]

This emphasis on the powerful role of the pamphleteer is not intended to remove agency from accused witches, or their supposed victims. As mentioned above, most pamphlets were based on trial records, including examinations by magistrates and the confessions of accused witches. Lyndal Roper is just one of a number of historians who has stressed the witch's agency in witchcraft narratives.[119] Roper argues that by telling her story to authorities a witch was able to 'perform her own diabolical theatre'.[120] Even if witches confessed under pressure, Roper argues that they were able to construct their experiences and participate in the process of 'creating the narrative of the witch anew'.[121] In fact, Roper goes so far as to claim that witchcraft trials are one of the few places in the early modern world in which women ' "speak" at greater length and receive more attention than perhaps any other'.[122] Roper suggests then, that many witchcraft narratives involve collusion between subject and questioner, with the accused drawing on their own beliefs, experiences and fantasies. Malcolm Gaskill has described these numerous voices as a 'circularity of influences', one that is very difficult to define.[123] It is worth remembering that contemporaries gave enormous agency to the witch: as presenting witches as beings who chose to join with the Devil to enact revenge on their enemies, pamphleteers portrayed witches as men and women who were in charge of their own agency. Those who doubted the reality of witchcraft, as Dolan has noted, denied witches this agency, insisting that they were instead poor, uneducated victims of zealous magistrates.[124] Although we can never be sure of who influenced each element of a witchcraft pamphlet, we cannot claim that they are simply the uninfluenced work of one writer. Instead, pamphlets represent a complex web of often-competing narratives and, as such, are places in which we can locate many differing influences.

Witchcraft and Emotion

Throughout this book, popular pamphlets will be analysed not just for their insights into English witchcraft and the role of the Devil but also for what they can tell us about the emotional experiences of witches, victims, accusers, readers and authors. English witchcraft pamphleteers did not just portray witchcraft as inherently diabolical; they also emphasised the role of anger, malice, a desire for revenge, greed, hatred, love and lust in how a witch was believed to interact with the Devil. Anger, malice, fear or a desire for revenge often compelled witches to make a pact with the Devil. It was not just the initial pact that was understood in these terms. After the making of the pact, witches often developed loving, sexualised relationships with the Devil. Alternatively, some witches came to fear their devils. Within the context of these relationships with the Devil, witches used their newfound demonic powers to take revenge upon their hated neighbours, to acquire wealth and other possessions that they desired and to spread evil and discord. In the vast majority of pamphlets, all of these actions are described as taking place with diabolical assistance and are motivated by emotion.

The history of emotions is a relatively new field, one that is still being defined by historians, and is a field that is not without debates.[125] Nonetheless, at the heart of their shared endeavour, emotions scholars emphasise the role of emotions in driving historical action and social change.[126] Anger, malice, fear and other strong emotions were all crucial in witchcraft narratives. Without these strong emotions many of these narratives would not exist. Early modern ideas about witches' malice fuelled witchcraft accusations and shaped how they were portrayed in pamphlet literature, and witches' desires shaped their confessions. In recent years, key emotions historians have theorised different ways of looking at emotions. Peter and Carol Stearns, writing in the 1980s, coined the term 'emotionology', describing it as the 'attitudes or standards that a society, or a definable group within a society, maintains towards basic emotions and their appropriate expression'.[127] William Reddy, writing more recently, has suggested the paradigm of 'emotional regimes' and has suggested that emotion words such as 'I am angry' should be viewed as 'emotives' which alter the state of the person expressing them.[128] Reddy claimed that in articulating an emotion a person attempts to translate their inner feeling into language or action. Moreover, as emotives create a change in a person's state, they also become important sources for understanding historical change. Barbara Rosenwein has argued that the concept of 'emotional regimes' is flawed as it leaves us with a 'bipartite society'; one in which an individual is in one of two groups.[129] Instead, Rosenwein has suggested the term 'emotional communities' and argued that an individual can be part of more than one emotional community, that is, they can express and perform emotions differently in different contexts, thus being part of different communities that prioritise differing emotions.[130]

Although they take different approaches, Rosenwein, Reddy and the Stearnes have all stressed that emotions are 'culturally malleable', that is, they change over time and are dependent on the cultures in which they exist.[131] Not only do particular communities influence the expression and construction of emotions but, conversely, emotions influence society. A consideration of past emotions allows historians to understand the different facets of past societies more deeply. My book explores how emotions "work" in witchcraft narratives. Within it I embrace an understanding of emotions as key drivers of historical action through my exploration of the types of emotions that drive witchcraft acts and accusations. Through the testimony of witches, witnesses, accusers and victims, the commentary of pamphleteers and the influence of trial officials such as judges and clerks, witchcraft pamphlets construct a way of understanding witchcraft that is based on specific forms of emotional interaction and behaviour between witches and devils, witches and victims and witches and readers. Tracking key 'emotion words' in witchcraft narratives allows us to see how pamphleteers, witches, accusers and victims described witchcraft acts and demonstrates the types of emotions most commonly ascribed to these encounters. Through highlighting the types of emotions common in witchcraft cases (such as a witch's desire for revenge against a neighbour or her sexual desire for the Devil), we are able to explore: the importance of emotions in witchcraft narratives; which emotions were most commonly associated with witchcraft; and how pamphlets could act as cautionary tales about the danger of certain uncontrolled emotions. Through their testimonies, accused witches and supposed victims demonstrated how they viewed an emotion as "working" in their society. In this way, pamphlets created a framework for emotional responses to witchcraft narratives and normalised certain emotions while demonising others. These emotional responses were then immortalised in print, thus allowing even more people to participate. This book draws attention to the importance of anger, malice, fear, rage, hatred, love, lust and a desire for revenge in understanding witchcraft narratives.

Although the history of emotions can be used to shed light on any aspect of history, it is particularly fruitful for the study of witchcraft. Witchcraft accusations did not simply stem from particular beliefs; they were also motivated by strong emotions. Malcolm Gaskill has stressed this point and drawn heavily on the history of emotions and mentalities in his work on English witchcraft:

> Witchcraft accusations were never the inevitable or logical outcomes of . . . social paradigms; rather they were the product of an accumulation of factors, among which the emotions are often overlooked.[132]

The same can be said of a witch's supposed motivations for joining with the Devil and his or her desire for wealth, happiness or revenge.[133] Lyndal Roper has echoed Gaskill's remarks:

> without an understanding of the emotional dynamics of witchcraft, we cannot comprehend the intensity and bitterness of the witch trials that seized so many German communities in the early modern period.[134]

For Roper 'if ever a subject were concerned with the emotions, it is witchcraft'.[135] Gaskill and Roper have both demonstrated the importance of studying emotions in witchcraft history in order to fully understand this phenomenon.

Throughout this book the emotions of fear, envy, a desire for revenge, malice, anger, lust and love will be continually referenced, particularly regarding a witch's relationship with the Devil, a witch's motivations in joining with the Devil and performing malefic magic, and the way in which witches were perceived by pamphleteers and the reading public. This book presents witchcraft pamphlets as a genre in which these emotions were highlighted, discussed and explored. In doing so, I hope to remind readers of the importance of emotions in understanding perceived motivations for witchcraft and to demonstrate how certain emotions such as love, lust, hate, anger, malice and fear were common to most witchcraft narratives. It is partly in recognising the inherently emotional nature of witchcraft acts, beliefs, and accusations that this book attempts to understand the links between witchcraft and the Devil.

The current study is divided into five chapters. The first explores attitudes to the Devil in late medieval and early modern England. It looks at how earlier medieval beliefs about the Devil were affected and modified by the Reformation and the mix of pre- and post-Reformation ideas that formed the beliefs about the Devil held by many early modern men and women. This mixture of beliefs is visible in English witchcraft pamphlets. Chapter 1 also explores how fear of the Devil increased after the Reformation and then demonstrates how this newfound fear became a key part of witchcraft stories. This chapter highlights the close association between the Devil, witches and fear throughout the early modern period and demonstrates how witchcraft pamphlets do not present one view of the Devil but actually contain many different beliefs.

The second chapter focuses specifically on the figure of the familiar, a specifically English phenomenon. The familiar is a much understudied element of English witchcraft belief and represents one of the critical ways in which witches' practices were described and understood as diabolical. This chapter explores the diabolical nature of the familiar and examines the role of familiars in witchcraft pamphlets. It looks at where familiars came from, what they did, what form they took and how they entered into pacts with witches. Chapter 2 argues that the presence of the familiar spirit in English witchcraft pamphlets introduces a personal element to the relationship between witch and Devil. The third chapter explores the supposed motivations behind a witch's decision to join with the Devil and perform witchcraft. It revisits the role of malice, anger and a desire for revenge in witchcraft narratives, and demonstrates that the familiar was crucial in allowing the witch to act on her malicious tendencies. It will also explore how, in some witchcraft cases, the Devil was believed to lie in wait to snare potential witches who gave in to their anger or malicious desires. Finally, it will speculate on how the familiar spirit can be viewed as a conduit for a witch's own emotions.

Chapter 4 continues to discuss the personal relationship between witches and familiar spirits and focuses on the form this relationship took with female witches. In doing so, it re-evaluates and re-emphasises the importance of sex in English witchcraft narratives. It argues that English witchcraft pamphlets portrayed English witches as sexually deviant women who chose to engage in penetrative and non-penetrative acts with devils. In considering the emotions that a witch was believed to feel towards her familiar spirit, it suggests that, in many cases, female witches were believed to develop strong feelings of sexual or romantic love for their devils. This chapter goes against much previous scholarship which has viewed English witchcraft as a predominantly asexual crime and argues that English witches were believed to engage in sexual acts with devils. Finally, Chapter 5 explores how witches acted together as a group to wreak havoc on the world. It demonstrates that many witches were believed to work with each other and the Devil and that some of these witches even supposedly attended a form of sabbath or witches' assembly. Rather than exploring the personal relationship between witch and Devil, this chapter takes a step back to look more broadly at the fear that groups of witches were designed to engender in pamphlet readers. The witches' supposedly close links with the Devil are the key reason for this fear. Both chapters 4 and 5 take a chronological approach to showcase key changes and continuities across the early modern period.

Notes

1 John Phillips, *The Examination and Confession of Certaine Wytches at Chelmsforde in the Countie of Essex* (London: Willyam Powell for Willyam Pickeringe, 1566).
2 Ibid., sig. 1A6 r.
3 Ibid., sigs. 1A6 r and 2A4 v.
4 Ibid., sig. 3A2 r.
5 John Davenport, *The Witches of Huntingdon, Their Examinations and Confessions Exactly Taken by His Majesties Justices of Peace for That County* (London: Printed by W. Wilson for Richard Clutterbuck, 1646), 9–10.
6 See for example, Malcolm Gaskill, *Crime and Mentalities in Early Modern England* (Cambridge: Cambridge University Press, 2000), 30–119; Malcolm Gaskill, "Witchcraft, Emotion and Imagination in the English Civil War," in *Witchcraft and the Act of 1604*, eds. John Newton and Jo Bath (Leiden: Brill, 2008), 161–178; Deborah Willis, *Malevolent Nurture: Witch-hunting and Maternal Power in Early Modern England* (Ithaca: Cornell University Press, 1995); Diane Purkiss, "Women's Stories of Witchcraft in Early Modern England: The House, the Body, the Child," *Gender and History* 7 (1995): 408–432.
7 For more on *maleficium* and for *maleficium's* relationship to diabolism, particularly in a European context, see Brian Levack, *The Witch-Hunt in Early Modern Europe*, 3rd edn. (Harlow: Longman, 2006), 4–9. For witchcraft in England as primarily malefic rather than diabolic, see this same text, 10.
8 For more on the continuity of Catholicism in England, see Christopher Haigh, "The Continuity of Catholicism in the English Reformation," *Past and Present* 93 (1981): 37–69. For the supposed links between magic, the Devil and Catholicism, see: Norman Jones, "Defining Superstitions: Treasonous Catholics and the Act Against Witchcraft of 1563," in *State, Sovereigns & Society in Early Modern England: Essays in Honour of A.J. Slavin*, ed. Charles Carlton (London: Sutton, 1998); Emma Wilby, *Cunning Folk and Familiar Spirits: Shamanistic Visionary Traditions in Early Modern British Witchcraft and Magic* (Brighton: Sussex Academic Press, 2005), 13; Owen Davies, *Popular Magic: Cunning Folk in English History* (London: Hambledon Continuum, 2007), 170; and Nathan Johnstone, *The Devil and Demonism in Early Modern England* (Cambridge: Cambridge University Press, 2006), 5.
9 Keith Thomas, *Religion and the Decline of Magic: Studies in Popular Beliefs in Sixteenth- and Seventeenth-Century England* (London: Weidenfeld and Nicolson, 1971), 470.
10 "An Act Against Conjurations, Enchantments and Witchcrafts," 1563 5 Eliz. I c. 16, in *Witchcraft and Society in England and America, 1550–1750*, ed. Marion Gibson (Ithaca: Cornell University Press, 2003), 4.

11 For a useful chart which outlines punishments for particular witchcraft acts by statute, see Alan Macfarlane, *Witchcraft in Tudor and Stuart England: A Regional and Comparative Study*, 2nd edn. (London: Routledge, 1999), 15.

12 Marion Gibson, ed., *Witchcraft and Society in England and America 1550–1750* (London: Continuum, 2003), 5–6; James Sharpe, *Instruments of Darkness: Witchcraft in Early Modern England*, paperback edn. (Philadelphia: University of Pennsylvania Press, 1997), 109–110; Malcolm Gaskill, *Witchfinders: A Seventeenth-Century English Tragedy* (London: John Murray, 2005), 31–33.

13 Gaskill, *Witchfinders*, 32.

14 Ibid., 285.

15 Ibid., 239.

16 Ibid., 283.

17 A word used by Malcolm Gaskill, when summarising the traditional view of the Matthew Hopkins trials. Malcolm Gaskill, "Witchcraft, Emotion and Imagination in the English Civil War," 164.

18 Clive Holmes, "Women: Witnesses and Witches," *Past and Present* 140 (1993): 49–50 and Brian P. Levack, "The Decline and End of Witchcraft Prosecutions," in *Witchcraft and Magic in Europe*, eds. Bengt Ankarloo and Stuart Clark, *Volume Five, the Eighteenth and Nineteenth Centuries*, eds. Marijke Gijswijt-Hofstra, Brian Levack and Roy Porter (London: Athlone, 1999), 56.

19 Holmes, "Women: Witnesses and Witches," 49–50.

20 Peter Elmer, *Witchcraft, Witch-Hunting and Politics in Early Modern England* (Oxford: Oxford University Press, 2016), 11.

21 Levack, "The Decline and End of Persecutions," in *Witchcraft and Magic in Europe: Volume Five, the Eighteenth and Nineteenth Centuries*, 77, see entire chapter for more on the decline of witch-hunting.

22 For more on this case, see W.B. Carnochan, "Witch-Hunting and Belief in 1751: The Case of Thomas Colley and Ruth Osborne," *Journal of Social History* 4 (1971): 389–403.

23 Peter Elmer, ed., *The Later English Trial Pamphlets, Volume Five, English Witchcraft 1560–1736*, eds. James Sharpe and Richard Golden (London: Pickering and Chatto, 2003), vii.

24 Elmer, *The Later English Trial Pamphlets*, xvi.

25 See, for example, Anon., *Strange & Terrible Newes from Cambridge, Being a true Relation of the Quakers Bewitching of Mary Philips out of the Bed from Her Husband in the Night, and Transformed Her into the Shape of a Bay Mare, Riding Her from Dinton, Towards the University* (London: Printed for C. Brooks, 1659).

26 Levack, *The Witch-hunt in Early Modern Europe*, 22.

27 Sharpe, *Instruments of Darkness*, 125.

28 Brian Levack, "Patterns and Dynamics of Decline: Five Case Studies," in *Witchcraft and Magic in Europe*, eds. Bengt Ankarloo and Stuart Clark, *Volume Five, The Eighteenth and Nineteenth Centuries*, eds. Marijke Gijswijt-Hofstra, Brian Levack and Roy Porter (London: The Athlone Press, 1999), 53.

29 Levack, "Patterns and Dynamics of Decline: Five Case Studies," 54.

30 See chapter 3 of Macfarlane, *Witchcraft in Tudor and Stuart England*, for an analysis of these figures.

31 Sharpe, *Instruments of Darkness*, 125, 113.

32 Keith Thomas, *Religion and the Decline of Magic: Studies in Popular Beliefs in Sixteenth- and Seventeenth-Century England*, 2nd edn. (London: Penguin Books, 1991), 536.

33 Macfarlane, *Witchcraft in Tudor and Stuart England*, 113. Macfarlane demonstrated that in three Essex villages between 1560 and 1599 witchcraft accusations

were more common than those of murder, and in two of the villages, witchcraft cases were prosecuted in similar numbers to assault. Macfarlane, *Witchcraft in Tudor and Stuart England*, 2nd edn., 98.

34 Ibid., 160.

35 For a discussion of how I arrived at this number, see 'The Sources' section in this introduction.

36 The Civil War period saw 'complete freedom of the press' for the first time in England. Christopher Hill, *Some Intellectual Consequences of the English Revolution* (Madison: University of Wisconsin Press, 1980), 7. This was predominantly due to the removal of the Court of Star Chamber, the High Commission and the Archbishop of Canterbury, William Laud, which caused censorship and pre-publication licensing to cease almost entirely. See also Sabrina A. Baron, "Licensing Readers, Licensing Authorities in Seventeenth-Century England," in *Books and Readers in Early Modern England: Material Studies*, eds. Jennifer Andersen and Elizabeth Sauer (Philadelphia: University of Pennsylvania Press, 2002), 218.

37 Hill, *Some Intellectual Consequences*, 49.

38 Ibid.

39 See Appendix B.

40 Officially known as the *Act for Preventing Abuses in Printing Seditious, Treasonable and Unlicensed Books and Pamphlets, and for Regulating of Printing and Printing-Presses*. For more on this Act and printing laws in the late seventeenth and early eighteenth centuries, see Raymond Astbury, "The Renewal of the Licensing Act in 1693 and Its Lapse in 1695," *The Library* s5 – XXXIII, 4 (1978): 296–322.

41 This number does not include a number of eighteenth-century treatises on the reality of witchcraft, nor does it include all eight of the pamphlets published about the Jane Wenham case. See below under 'The Sources' for an explanation of why I have chosen to exclude some pamphlets about witchcraft from my core group of sources.

42 Jeremy Black, "The Eighteenth-Century British Press," in *The Encyclopedia of the British Press, 1422–1992*, ed. Dennis Griffiths (Basingstoke: MacMillan Press, 1992), 13–23.

43 For a recent summary of English witchcraft historiography, see Malcolm Gaskill, "Witchcraft Trials in England," in *The Oxford Handbook of Witchcraft in Early Modern Europe and Colonial America*, ed. Brian Levack (Oxford: Oxford University Press, 2013), 283–299.

44 Wallace Notestein, *A History of Witchcraft in England from 1558 to 1718* (Washington: The American Historical Association, 1911).

45 Ibid., 99.

46 Cecil L'Estrange Ewen, *Witch Hunting and Witch Trials: The Indictments for Witchcraft from the Records of 1373 Assizes Held for the Home Circuit A.D. 1559–1736* (London: Kegan Paul, Trench, Trubner & Co., Ltd, 1929).

47 Cecil L'Estrange Ewen, *Witchcraft and Demonianism: A Concise Account Derived from Sworn Depositions and Confession Obtained in the Courts of England and Wales* (London: Heath Cranton Limited, 1933).

48 Ibid., 50 and 62.

49 George Lyman Kittredge, *Witchcraft in Old and New England*, 3rd edn. (New York: Atheneum, 1972).

50 Ibid., 6.

51 Keith Thomas, *Religion and the Decline of Magic* (London: Weidenfeld and Nicolson, 1971); Thomas, *Religion and the Decline of Magic* (London: Penguin Books, 1991); and Macfarlane, *Witchcraft in Tudor and Stuart England*, 2nd edn.

52 James Sharpe, "Introduction," in *Witchcraft in Tudor and Stuart England*, 2nd edn., by Alan Macfarlane, xvi.
53 Thomas, *Religion and the Decline of Magic*, 1st edn., 449.
54 Ibid., 616.
55 Ibid.
56 Barbara Rosen, *Witchcraft* (London: Edward Arnold, 1969); Barbara Rosen, *Witchcraft in England 1558–1618*, 2nd edn. (Amherst: University of Massachusetts Press, 1991), 28.
57 Rosen, *Witchcraft in England*, 2nd edn., 15.
58 Ibid., 19.
59 Ibid., 26.
60 Ibid., 30.
61 Ibid., 35.
62 See, for example, Christina Larner, "Was Witch Hunting Women Hunting?," *New Society* 58 (1991): 11–12 reprinted in Christina Larner, *Witchcraft and Religion: The Politics of Popular Belief* (New York: Blackwell, 1984), 84; Clive Holmes, "Women: Witnesses and Witches," 45–78; J.A. Sharpe, "Witchcraft and Women in Seventeenth-Century England: Some Northern Evidence," *Continuity and Change* 6 (1991): 179–199; Levack, *The Witch-Hunt in Early Modern Europe*, 141–149; Willis, *Malevolent Nurture*; Purkiss, "Women's Stories of Witchcraft in Early Modern England"; Carol F. Karlsen, *The Devil in the Shape of a Woman: Witchcraft in Colonial New England*, 2nd edn. (London: Norton, 1998); Diane Purkiss, *The Witch in History: Early Modern and Twentieth Century Representations* (London: Routledge, 1996); Louise Jackson, "Witches, Wives and Mothers: Witchcraft Persecution and Women's Confessions in Seventeenth-Century England," *Women's History Review* 4 (1995): 64; Marianne Hester, *Lewd Women and Wicked Witches: A Study of the Dynamics of Male Domination* (London: Routledge, 1992), 107; Lyndal Roper, *Oedipus and the Devil: Witchcraft, Sexuality and Religion in Early Modern Europe* (London: Routledge, 1994); Lyndal Roper, *Witch Craze: Terror and Fantasy in Baroque Germany* (New Haven: Yale University Press, 2004).
62 Larner, *Witchcraft and Religion*, 87.
63 Willis, *Malevolent Nurture*; Diane Purkiss, "Women's Stories of Witchcraft in Early Modern England."
64 Purkiss, "Women's Stories of Witchcraft in Early Modern England," 411.
65 Willis, *Malevolent Nurture*, 6.
66 Ibid., 13.
67 Ibid., 14.
68 Although not discussed in detail in this study, my thoughts on how male witches were represented in English pamphlet literature will form the basis of a forthcoming article.
69 Macfarlane, *Witchcraft in Tudor and Stuart England*, 2nd edn., 160–161; Thomas, *Religion and the Decline of Magic*, 2nd edn., 678–679; Eric Midelfort, *Witch Hunting in Southwestern Germany, 1562–1684: The Social and Intellectual Foundations* (Stanford: Stanford University Press, 1972), 179–188; and E.W. Monter, *Witchcraft in France and Switzerland: The Borderlands During the Reformation* (New York: Cornell University Press, 1976), 23–24.
70 Malcolm Gaskill, "Masculinity and Witchcraft in Seventeenth-Century England," in *Witchcraft and Masculinities in Early Modern Europe*, ed. Alison Rowlands (Basingstoke: Palgrave Macmillan, 2009); Malcolm Gaskill, "The Devil in the Shape of a Man: Witchcraft, Conflict and Belief in Jacobean England," *Historical Research* 71 (1998): 142–171. See also Lara Apps and Andrew Gow, *Male Witches in Early Modern Europe* (Manchester: Manchester University

Press, 2003); Alison Rowlands, " 'Not the "Usual Suspects?' Male Witches, Witchcraft and Masculinities in Early Modern Europe," in *Witchcraft and Masculinities*, ed. Alison Rowlands; Elizabeth Kent, "Masculinity and Male Witches in Old and New England, 1593–1680," *History Workshop Journal* 60 (2005): 69–92; E.J. Kent, *Cases of Male Witchcraft in Old and New England, 1592–1692* (Turnhout: Brepols, 2013); and Alison Rowlands, "Witchcraft and Gender in Early Modern Europe," in *The Oxford Handbook of Witchcraft in Early Modern Europe and Colonial America*, ed. Brian Levack (Oxford: Oxford University Press, 2013), 449–467.

71 See, for example, Willem de Blécourt, "Sabbath Stories: Towards a New History of Witches' Assemblies," in *The Oxford Handbook of Witchcraft in Early Modern Europe and Colonial America*, ed. Brian Levack (Oxford: Oxford University Press, 2013), 84–100; Richard Kieckhefer, "The First Wave of Trials for Diabolical Witchcraft," in *The Oxford Handbook of Witchcraft in Early Modern Europe and Colonial America*, ed. Brian Levack (Oxford: Oxford University Press, 2013), 159–178; Robin Briggs, *Witches and Neighbours: The Social and Cultural Context of European Witchcraft* (London: HarperCollins, 1996).

72 Sharpe, *Instruments of Darkness*.

73 Barry Reay, *Popular Cultures in England, 1550–1750* (London: Longman, 1998), 116.

74 James Sharpe, "The Witch's Familiar in Elizabethan England," in *Authority and Consent in Tudor England: Essays Presented to C.S.L. Davies*, eds. George W. Bernard and Steven J. Gunn (Burlington, VT: Ashgate, 2002); James Sharpe, "The Devil in East Anglia: The Matthew Hopkins Trials Reconsidered," in *Witchcraft in Early Modern Europe: Studies in Culture and Belief*, eds. Jonathan Barry, Marianne Hester and Gareth Roberts (Cambridge: Cambridge University Press, 1996), 237–254 and James Sharpe, "In Search of the English Sabbat: Popular Conceptions of Witches' Meetings in Early Modern England," *Journal of Early Modern Studies* 2 (2013): 161–183.

75 For more on how witchcraft pamphlets were marketed towards a popular audience see Carla Suhr, *Publishing for the Masses: Early Modern English Witchcraft Pamphlets* (Helsinki: Société Néophilologique, 2011).

76 See, for example, the description of the witchcraft of Johane Harrison included in a 1606 pamphlet about a murder, Anon., *The Most Cruell and Bloody Murther* (London: Printed for William Firebrand, 1606).

77 Carla Suhr has published a linguistic study of English witchcraft pamphlets. She did not comment on witchcraft beliefs and confined herself to a study of the genre of witchcraft pamphlets. She gave particular attention to how these pamphlets were marketed for a popular audience. While this is a useful study, it is not designed to further our understanding of witchcraft belief. Carla Suhr, *Publishing for the Masses: Early Modern English Witchcraft Pamphlets* (Helsinki: Société Néophilologique, 2011).

78 For works which transcribe and introduce some sixteenth- and seventeenth-century witchcraft pamphlets see Rosen, *Witchcraft in England 1558–1618* and Marion Gibson, *Early Modern Witches: Witchcraft Cases in Contemporary Writing* (London: Routledge, 2000).

79 Sharpe, *Instruments of Darkness*, 95.

80 See Gibson, *Early Modern Witches;* Gibson, ed., *Witchcraft and Society in Early Modern England;* and Gibson, *Reading Witchcraft: Stories of Early English Witches* (London: Routledge, 1999).

81 See, for example, works by Marion Gibson and Barbara Rosen.

82 See, for example, Elmer, *The Later English Trial Pamphlets, Volume Five, English Witchcraft 1560–1736*.

83 Macfarlane, *Witchcraft in Tudor and Stuart England*, 2nd edn., 86.
84 Ibid., 81–86 and Alan Macfarlane, "Witchcraft in Tudor and Stuart Essex," in *Articles on Witchcraft, Magic and Demonology: A Twelve Volume Anthology of Scholarly Articles: Volume Six: Witchcraft in England*, ed. Brian Levack (New York: Garland Publishing Inc., 1992),18.
85 C.L. Ewen, *Witchcraft and Demonism*, 7.
86 Wilby, *Cunning Folk and Familiar Spirits*, 46 and Macfarlane, "Witchcraft in Tudor and Stuart Essex," 7.
87 Gibson, *Reading Witchcraft*, 6; Sharpe, *Instruments of Darkness*, 105 and Rosen, *Witchcraft in England*, 20.
88 Frances E. Dolan, *True Relations: Reading, Literature and Evidence in Seventeenth-Century England* (Philadelphia: University of Pennsylvania Press, 2013), chapter 2.
89 Dolan, *True Relations*, 55. Gibson, *Reading Witchcraft*, 75. See also David Cressy, *Travesties and Transgressions in Tudor and Stuart England: Tales of Discord and Dissension* (Oxford: Oxford University Press, 2000), 25.
90 See Gibson, *Reading Witchcraft*.
91 Dolan, *True Relations*, 61.
92 Frederick Valletta, *Witchcraft, Magic and Superstition in England 1640–70* (Burlington: Ashgate, 2000), 6.
93 Gibson, *Early Modern Witches*, 6.
94 David Cressy, *Literacy and the Social Order: Reading and Writing in Tudor and Stuart England* (Cambridge: Cambridge University Press, 1980), 176.
95 Keith Thomas, "The Meaning of Literacy in Early Modern England," in *The Written Word in Translation*, ed. Gerd Baumann (Oxford: Oxford University Press, 1986), 103; Margaret Spufford, *Small Books and Pleasant Histories: Popular Fiction and Its Readership in Seventeenth-Century England* (London: Methuen, 1981), 22 and Heidi Brayman Hackel, *Reading Material in Early Modern England: Print, Gender and Literacy* (Cambridge: Cambridge University Press, 2005), 58.
96 Thomas, "The Meaning of Literacy," 103.
97 Hackel, *Reading Material in Early Modern England*, 57.
98 Spufford, *Small Books and Pleasant Histories*, 22.
99 Sandra Clark, *The Elizabethan Pamphleteers: Popular Moralistic Pamphlets 1580–1640* (London: Athlone Press, 1983), 19.
100 Hackel, *Reading Material in Early Modern England*, 46.
101 Ibid.
102 Thomas, "The Meaning of Literacy," 103.
103 Thomas, *Religion and the Decline of Magic*, 2nd edn., 534. Kittredge, *Witchcraft in Old and New England*, 6.
104 Thomas, *Religion and the Decline of Magic*, 2nd edn., 534.
105 Clive Holmes, "Witches, Magistrates and Divines in Early Modern England," in *Understanding Popular Culture: Europe from the Middle Ages to the Nineteenth Century*, ed. Steven L. Kaplan (Berlin: Mouton, 1984), 105.
106 Ibid., 94.
107 Carlo Ginzburg, "The Witches' Sabbat: Popular Cult or Inquisitorial Stereotype?," in *Understanding Popular Culture: Europe from the Middle Ages to the Nineteenth Century*, ed. Steven L. Kaplan (Berlin: Mouton, 1984), 48.
108 Peter Burke, *What Is Cultural History?* (Cambridge: Polity Press, 2004), 28.
109 Ibid.
110 Dolan, *Dangerous Familiars*, 179. Some of the most interesting examples of elite influences in popular pamphlets include how: Justice Fenner commissioned *The Most Strange and Admirable Discoverie of the Three Witches of Warboys* (1593); Brian Darcy, a JP, almost definitely wrote *A True and Just Recorde* (1582); and

Thomas Potts, author of *The Wonderfull Discoverie of Witches* (1613) was a London lawyer and clerk commissioned by justices. Dolan has also explored this mingling of influences in her 2013 book: Dolan, *True Relations*, 53.

111 Sharpe, *Instruments of Darkness*, 95.
112 Anon., *The Wonderful Discoverie of the Witchcrafts of Margaret and Phillip Flower* (London: Printed by G. Eld for I. Barnes, 1619), sig. B4 v-C1 r.
113 Anon., *The Shee-Devil of Petticoat-Lane* (London: Printed by Peter Lillicrap,1666), 8.
114 Sharpe, *Instruments of Darkness*, 51–55.
115 For an exploration of the mingling of learned and popular belief in the Jane Wenham case see Holmes, *Women: Witches and Witnesses*, 50–51.
116 Brian Levack has found that 'the great majority of those prosecuted [for witchcraft] came from the lower levels of society'. Levack, *The Witch-Hunt in Early Modern Europe*, 3rd edn., 157.
117 There are very few pamphleteers for which any information survives. Known professions amongst pamphleteers include: lawyer and clerk (Thomas Potts, 1613), cleric (James Bower, 1653), ordinary to Newgate, author and minister (Henry Goodcole, 1621), minor gentlemen (Matthew Hopkins, 1647 and John Stearne, 1648), bookseller and author (Nathaniel Crouch, 1688), and clergyman and Congregationalist teacher (Samuel Petto, 1693). Dates refer to witchcraft pamphlets published by these men, see Appendix A for full details.
118 For an excellent breakdown of the role of the pamphleteer see Marion Gibson's exploration of Thomas Potts' 1612 pamphlet, *A Wonderful Discoverie of Witches*, in Gibson, *Reading Witchcraft*, 1–10, especially page 4.
119 Roper, *Oedipus and the Devil*, 19–20. For others see Purkiss, *The Witch in History*, 145–176; Kirilka Stavreva, "Fighting Words: Witch-Speak in Late Elizabethan Docu-Fiction," *Journal of Medieval and Early Modern Studies* 30 (2000): 309–38; and Jackson, "Witches, Wives and Mothers."
120 Roper, *Oedipus and the Devil*, 20.
121 Ibid.
122 Ibid.
123 Gaskill, *Crime and Mentalities*, 40.
124 Dolan, *Dangerous Familiars*, 194–195.
125 "AHR Conversation: The Historical Study of Emotions: Participants: Nicole Eustace, Eugenia Lean, Julie Livingston, Jan Plamper, William M. Reddy and Barbara H. Rosenwein," *American Historical Review* (2012): 1487–1531 and Jan Plamper, "The History of Emotions: An Interview with William Reddy, Barbara Rosenwein, and Peter Stearns," *History and Theory* 49 (2010): 237–265.
126 A note on terminology: This book uses the term 'emotions' rather than 'affect,' 'passions,' 'sentiments,' or 'feelings.' This term has been chosen based on its widespread acceptance in historical scholarship as an effective way to classify how past people felt about their environment, how they reacted to it and to events, and how what they felt could be the impetus for social or political change. For more on the emotions as a psychological category (a question outside the scope of this book) see Thomas Dixon, *From Passions to Emotions: The Creation of a Secular Psychological Category* (Cambridge: Cambridge University Press, 2003) and Paul Griffiths, *What Emotions Really Are: The Problem of Psychological Categories* (Chicago: The University of Chicago Press, 1997).
127 Peter N. Stearns with Carol Z. Stearns, "Emotionology: Clarifying the History of Emotions and Emotional Standards," *American Historical Review* 90 (1985): 813.
128 William Reddy, "Against Constructionism: The Historical Ethnography of Emotions," *Current Anthropology* 38 (1997): 327. See also William Reddy,

The Navigation of Feeling: A Framework for the History of Emotions (Cambridge: Cambridge University Press, 2001).

129 Barbara Rosenwein, *Emotional Communities in the Early Middle Ages* (Ithaca: Cornell University Press, 2006), 23.

130 Ibid., 2.

131 *AHR Conversation*, 1507, 1510, 1515.

132 Gaskill, *Crime and Its Mentalities*, 65.

133 For the European context compare Lyndal Roper, "Forum. History of Emotions," (with Alon Confino, Ute Frevert, Uffa Jensen, Lyndal Roper and Daniela Saxer) *German History* 28 (2012): 74.

134 Roper, "Forum. History of Emotions," 74.

135 Lyndal Roper, *The Witch in the Western Imagination* (Charlottesville: University of Virginia Press, 2012), 91.

1   The Devil in Early Modern England

Early modern witchcraft was a diabolical crime. This new form of diabolical heresy which first took root during the 1430s was explained through the Devil's very real presence in the world and his effect upon it. The Devil, an omnipresent force of evil in early modern Europe, was fundamental to how witchcraft was explained by theologians and witchcraft theorists. Witches did not act alone; their malicious actions were only possible with the Devil's assistance. The emergence of a diabolical witchcraft paradigm in the mid-fifteenth century and its ensuing development over the early modern period coincided with the religious upheavals instigated in part by the Reformation. In England, as in wider Europe, the Reformation not only created religious conflicts and tensions, it also changed many people's perception of the Devil and emphasised his presence. Some people retained purely pre-Reformation beliefs, particularly concerning the physicality of the Devil; others adopted the new, emerging Protestant emphasis on the Devil as an incorporeal force of evil who exercised his greatest power and danger through mental temptations. Many, however, straddled these two understandings and retained a pre-Reformation understanding of the Devil that was tempered by new doctrines. The proliferation of debate about the limits of diabolical power served to remind many that the Devil was everywhere. Although the strength of the Devil's power had waned for many by the early eighteenth century, the Devil continued to play a key role in witchcraft narratives throughout the entire period of state-sanctioned accusations and prosecutions.

Witchcraft pamphlets highlight concerns about the rise of diabolical power and act as an outlet for ongoing debates about the limits of the Devil's influence, the physical forms the Devil could assume and how best to ward off Satan. In this chapter, I argue that witchcraft pamphlets from across the entire period of witchcraft prosecutions demonstrate a continuing connection between witchcraft and the Devil in the minds of contemporaries. The Devil's vital presence in witchcraft pamphlets is highly suggestive and, as such, encourages us to re-evaluate the importance of diabolical ideas to English witchcraft belief. But before expanding on this idea, it is necessary to outline some of the key ways in which the Devil was perceived in early modern England.

This chapter begins by exploring the changing nature of beliefs about the Devil during the fifteenth, sixteenth, seventeenth and eighteenth centuries. In early modern England, the Protestant Reformation and the subsequent polarisation of faiths, combined with the unmasking of the Pope as Antichrist and the very real sense that the last days were coming, created a sense of war between the faiths. As Philip Almond has eloquently summarised, 'the issue of demonic activity [was] linked with that of the end of the world, and the conviction that, as history drew to a close and Christ's return in judgement became imminent, Satan would be all the more active'.[1] This fear was linked to the prophecy in Revelation 12.12 that Satan's rage would increase as his time became shorter.[2] In early modern England, this fear of the last days and sense of being at war caused fear of the Devil's power to greatly increase. Throughout the entire early modern period, political and religious crises were linked with the Devil's growing power in the world. As such, this chapter will emphasise the growing fear of the Devil that coincided with the Protestant Reformation in England and explore the increased emphasis on the Devil as a source of mental temptations. The primary focus will be on popular belief. The chapter will then turn to an exploration of the different concepts of the Devil that appeared in early modern English witchcraft pamphlets and demonstrate how these narratives incorporated an ambiguous set of beliefs about the Devil. It will then discuss the links between an increasing awareness of the Devil's intervention in the everyday world and the rise of the witch hunt. In its entirety, this chapter is concerned with the changing nature of Devil beliefs in post-Reformation England and argues that witchcraft pamphlets do not highlight just one understanding of the Devil, but are made up of the many differing beliefs about the Devil that were circulating in early modern England. Through examining the types of beliefs present in witchcraft narratives, we can see how these sources were at the forefront of changing ideas of demonic power and fear of demonic influence in the world.

Changing Conceptions of the Devil in Late Medieval and Early Modern England

Beliefs about the Devil in late medieval and early modern Europe have been the focus of study by numerous scholars, most notably Philip Almond, Darren Oldridge, Nathan Johnstone, Robert Muchembled, Jeffrey Burton Russell and Brian Levack. Darren Oldridge's excellent books on the Devil in early modern England explore both pre- and post-Reformation attitudes to the Devil including those of godly divines and the populace more broadly. When discussing popular medieval conceptions of the Devil, Oldridge reminds us that for many in the late Middle Ages, the Devil's existence as a physical being was assumed.[3] During this period the Devil was believed capable of assuming the form of a corporeal creature, one who could walk the earth and torment anyone unlucky enough to meet him.[4] This concept of the Devil, largely based on popular tales, plays, ballads and biblical stories, presented him as a tangible being, as someone who could inflict physical harm and who must be avoided at all costs. Although this view of the Devil was more prevalent before the Reformation, many traditional beliefs about the Devil remained in circulation until the 1700s and beyond. While traditional beliefs in the Devil as a physical being could inspire great fear, they also reminded men and women of the Devil's limits. It was possible to physically outrun the Devil and there are many medieval tales of men and women evading the Devil by running and hiding. A physical Devil was not just capable of walking the Earth; he was also, in some ways, bound to it. Far from being an all-powerful force, the Devil was presented in many late medieval and early modern tales as a fiend who, while dangerous, was essentially limited.[5]

Not only could the Devil be physically avoided, he could also be tricked. Through trickery men and women were given a fighting chance to prevail against demonic forces. One popular tale that highlights a person's ability to outwit the Devil described a man who agreed to give his soul to the Devil after a certain candle had guttered out. The Devil helped the man in exchange, but was cheated of the man's soul because he blew out the candle before it was able to burn itself out.[6] Another similar tale described how Jack and the Devil built a bridge; the Devil helped with the understanding that he would obtain the soul of the first living creature to cross. Jack outwitted the Devil by throwing a bone over the bridge so that a dog followed it and was the first living creature to cross.[7] Tales of ordinary people beating the Devil through wit alone allowed men and women to believe that they could combat the Devil. Perhaps unsurprisingly, these tales of the Devil being deceived were 'hugely popular'.[8] In medieval folklore, as Jeffrey Burton Russell argues, the emphasis on the physicality and ubiquity of the Devil was muted by seemingly contradictory representations of him as someone to be mocked rather than feared.[9] Robert Muchembled, when looking at medieval fabliaux and tales as well as the works of theologians, has also commented on the limited nature of the Devil's power, arguing that 'far from calling the tune, Satan was both constrained by divine will and challenged by human mischievousness'.[10] Through the knowledge that the Devil was essentially limited and able to be outmanoeuvred by human ingenuity, late medieval people were able to temper their fear. The Devil was not an omnipresent force of evil at this time but, according to medieval folklore, someone who could be outwitted, outrun, tricked and mocked.

As well as being physically limited, the dangers of the Devil were also muted by comic representations. Oldridge has explored comic depictions of the Devil from the early sixteenth century and argues that these tales were an occasion for laughter and mirth and were 'not presented as a warning against sin or a call to virtuous living'.[11] Jeffrey Burton Russell has also focused on the Devil as a comic figure or fool.[12] Both Oldridge and Russell believe that humorous tales about the Devil did not just exist in the medieval period but survived into the early modern.[13] Russell notes the tension between popular religion and folklore in the middle ages and argues that popular Christianity tended to present a tangible, 'vivid, frightening' Devil, whereas medieval folklore made the Devil 'ridiculous or impotent'.[14] He argues that the practice in folklore of presenting the Devil as someone to be laughed at helped to relieve the tension felt by many who feared the Devil's influence over human beings.[15] Both late medieval and early modern tales often associated the Devil with scatological or bawdy humour. Compare for instance two tales, one from 1530 and the other from 1661. The first tells the story of a man who dreamt he met the Devil who then led him into a field to dig for gold. The man finds the gold but the Devil will not let him take it and instructs the man to 'shyte over' the place so as to discourage others from going near it.[16] The man wakes to find that he has 'foule defyled his bedde'.[17] Undeterred, he jumps out of his bed to find his riches and puts on his hat 'wherein also the same nighte the catte hadde shyt . . . Thus his golden dreame turned all to dyrt'.[18] In this tale the Devil's mischief is a source of amusement. Early modern tales have similar themes. A poem from 1661 described how a baker tricked the Devil into being gelded.[19] Unsurprisingly, the Devil was angry and swore to castrate the Baker 'next Market day'.[20] Worried and afraid, the baker rode home and told his wife. Ingeniously, the wife put on her husband's clothes and went to meet the Devil:

'The Bakers wife to the devil did say,
Sir, I was gelded yesterday:
O' quote the devil, I mean to see;
And pulling her coats above the knee,
And so looking upward from the ground,
O there he spy'd a terrible wound.

O quote the devil, now I see
That he was not cunning that gelded thee,
For when that he had cut out the stones,
He should have closed up the wounds,
But if thou wilt stay but a little space
I'll fetch some salve to cure the place.

He had not run but a little way,
But up her belly crept a Flea:
The little devil seeing that,
He up with his paw and gave her a pat,
Which made the good wife for to start,
And with that she let go a rowsing fart.

O, quote the devil, thy life is not long
Thy breath it smells so horrible strong,
Therefore go thy way, and make thy will,
Thy wounds are past all humane skill;
Be gone, be gone, make no delay,
For here thou shalt no longer stay.'[21]

This amusing rhyme turns the Devil into a figure of fun. He is tricked into being gelded and then thwarted in his revenge. Not only does he fail to geld the Baker he actually offers help and sympathy and the reader is invited to laugh at his foolishness. In the early modern world comic depictions performed a similar function to those in the late middle ages. They were used to alleviate fear of the Devil and can be viewed as a reaction to an increasing Protestant emphasis on the very real dangers of the Devil.

At the same time that these comic depictions were circulating in folklore, theologians and godly divines were placing new stress on the Devil's power. The Protestant Reformation did not introduce an entirely new concept of the Devil. In fact, as Brian Levack reminds us, many Protestant reformers subscribed to the beliefs of late medieval Catholic demonologists.[22] The main differences between traditional conceptions of the Devil and those of the Protestant reformers were the latter group's tendency to emphasise the Devil's increasing activity and to encourage a more pervasive fear of his powers.[23] The Reformation did not weaken belief in the Devil; it strengthened it.[24] In 1564 the English theologian Thomas Becon warned of the Devil's advances:

> There is no ravening wolfe that so earnestly seeketh greedelye to devoure his praye as this enemye of mankynde, that olde serpent, [who] hunteth and studyeth every moment of an hour howe he maye destroy & brynge to everlasting damnaction mortall menne.[25]

Although Protestantism placed 'unprecedented stress upon the reality of the Devil and the extent of his earthly dominion' it also preached that steadfast faith in God was the only infallible protection against Satan.[26] So whilst many men and women were made newly aware of the Devil's power, they were simultaneously stripped of traditional ways of warding him off. As Kathleen Sands has argued:

> the common people of early modern England had been disarmed by the Reformation. In the face of evil, they were no longer allowed to take holy communion, cross themselves, wear amulets containing consecrated herbs or holy relics, petition the saints, make pilgrimages to the shrines, repeat ritual prayers, or be touched by a holy person.[27]

Writing in 1619, William Gouge mocked the 'egregious folly [of] superstitious Papists, who thinke to drive the Divell away with Holy-water, Holy-oyle, Crosses [and] Crucifixes'.[28] The polarisation of Protestantism and Catholicism went a long way to empowering the Devil; the tension between faiths left many with the feeling of being at war; a war in which the Devil was a key player.

As well as discouraging the use of charms, saints, pilgrimages and ritual prayers, Protestant doctrine also challenged belief in the powers of other supernatural beings such as fairies, demons and imps.[29] During the medieval period, the Devil was forced to compete with other supernatural tricksters such as fairies or monsters.[30] The battle for human souls was not waged between God and the Devil as two superior beings, but instead took place in a far more complex and well-populated supernatural world.[31] In this pre-Reformation world the Devil was one of many supernatural beings and, as such, did not command the same fear that he did in the sixteenth and seventeenth centuries. The Protestant emphasis on God's absolute power changed this dynamic and elevated the role of both God and the Devil. As Oldridge explains, 'by asserting the absolute authority of God, Protestants effectively abolished the influence of all other entities, and condemned any attempt to exploit their knowledge or power as "superstition." '[32] The Devil's power was emphasised from the period of the Reformation onwards by a growing preoccupation with the Devil as the ultimate force of evil.

Another way in which the Reformation stressed the power of the Devil was through the 'turning inwards of the Christian conscience', which emphasised the role of men and women as participants in an individual struggle with Satan.[33] Traditional interpretations of the Devil depicted him as an enemy of the world, one who sought to overthrow Christian society.[34] This view remained prevalent in early modern society. However, there was an increasing emphasis on the individual's struggle with the Devil.[35] Rather than being part of a community that could ward off the Devil through invoking the saints, going on pilgrimages, or touching holy relics, the early modern English Protestant was left alone to examine his or her soul for any weaknesses that might allow the Devil a way in. Russell has argued that this 'isolation provoked terror' and only enhanced an already growing fear of the Devil.[36] In practice then, Protestant theology emphasised the power of the Devil and 'placed the struggle against him at the centre of religious life'.[37] As well as emphasising the Devil's power, Protestant theology also emphasised humankind's innate sinfulness.[38] Protestant writers on witchcraft emphasised people's individual responsibility for allowing the Devil to corrupt them.[39] According to William Perkins 'if the devill were not stirred up, and provoked by the Witch, he would never do so much hurt as he doth'.[40] The Puritan author Thomas Cooper took a similar approach and claimed that because of '*our owne cursed nature . . . wee are Sathan's slaves naturally*'.[41] Despite folkloric depictions of the Devil as a comic figure, new Protestant emphases heightened awareness and fear of Satan as well as men and women's natural tendency to become slaves of the Devil. For many Protestants, the Devil was a central figure of fear in the early modern world, one whom only strong faith in God could defeat.

Part of the newly amplified fear of the Devil stemmed from an increasing Protestant emphasis on Satan's powers of mental temptation. Although the work of the Devil in late medieval belief was to tempt and torment men and women, the 'central focus' of Protestant divines was, in the words of

Nathan Johnstone, to 'emphasise the Devil's power of temptation, especially his ability to enter directly into the mind and plant thoughts within it that led people to sin'.[42] As Johnstone goes on to explain, 'whereas the medieval remit of the Devil had included temptation as one of a variety of activities with which he might afflict mankind, Protestants elevated it into the single most important aspect of his agency, which virtually eclipsed all others'.[43] For Martin Luther for instance, the Devil was constantly present, eager to tempt men and women into sin.[44] Similarly, Jean Calvin believed that 'the power of Satan was so strong and pervasive that the true Christian saint had to engage in an "unceasing struggle against him"'.[45] This is not to say that Protestant demonology denied that Satan had the power to appear in physical form; it simply asserted that the Devil's ability to tempt and torment his potential victims was more common and more dangerous'.[46] Not only did the Devil attempt to draw men and women away from God, he inevitably did this through lies and broken promises. The biblical understanding of the Devil as both a tempter and the Father of Lies was a powerful belief that circulated widely in the early modern world. According to one contemporary, the Devil used 'crafty persuasions, deceatefull and false illusions' to win followers.[47] It is hardly surprising then, that the belief in the Devil as a liar is prominent in English witchcraft pamphlets.

The Devil in Early Modern Witchcraft Pamphlets

The understanding of the Devil promoted by Protestant theologians never entirely triumphed in early modern England. Instead, Protestant beliefs were only partially assimilated into English society and a 'diverse and ambiguous set of beliefs about Satan came to be accepted by the majority of the English population by the end of the seventeenth century'.[48] Despite the best efforts of godly divines, pre-Reformation ideas 'continued to flourish in the sixteenth and seventeenth centuries'.[49] In witchcraft narratives, these older ideas even survived into the eighteenth century. Nowhere is the continuation and conflation of belief more apparent than in witchcraft pamphlets. English witchcraft narratives most commonly portrayed the Devil as a familiar spirit – a physical being who often took the form of an animal or, more rarely, a man. The familiar spirit (a phenomenon almost unique to England) highlights the multi-faceted nature of beliefs about the Devil circulating in early modern England.[50] Oldridge has argued that the familiar demonstrates the 'unreformed' nature of ideas about the Devil in popular witch belief:

> Instead of a powerful, pervasive force for spiritual evil, [the Devil] was often a limited and essentially physical creature who could assume various guises but preferred to appear as a small animal. He busied himself mainly by harming the health and property of innocent Christians, who could defend themselves with magical objects like bottles and shoes.[51]

While this is absolutely true, the familiar also embodies new Protestant emphases on the Devil's power, most noticeably as a source of mental temptation. Familiars, devils in animal form, were determined to tempt men and women into joining with Satan. These demonic creatures created a personal bond between themselves and the witch. Through this bond, familiars acted as personal tempters, perhaps mirroring in some ways the Protestant emphasis on a person's own individual struggle with Satan. Through the physical form of the familiar, the witch's internal struggle against the Devil and his temptations was externalised and made manifest in a small, tangible, demonic creature.

This set of beliefs about the Devil was highlighted not only through accounts of witches' activities, but also introductory material at the beginning of pamphlet narratives. Most witchcraft pamphlets were introduced by a prologue or note to the reader which warned of the Devil's increasing presence in the world. In these prologues authors sometimes warned readers to repent and turn to God less they too be tricked by the Devil. Witchcraft pamphlets, then, simultaneously presented two different understandings of the Devil: one that emphasised the Devil's corporeality and another that focused on the Devil as a source of mental temptations and growing influence in the world. These two seemingly conflicting beliefs coexisted and intermingled in witchcraft pamphlets and mirrored the diverse nature of beliefs about the Devil circulating in early modern England. Their presence allows us an insight into the fluidity of beliefs about the Devil in England and highlights how these beliefs were integrated into witchcraft narratives.

In 1996 James Sharpe suggested that there is 'a serious gap in our knowledge' about the role of the Devil in English witchcraft.[52] Since then there has been some attempt by historians to comment on how the Devil was portrayed in English witchcraft pamphlets. Johnstone, who considers witchcraft pamphlets atypical of Devil beliefs in England more broadly, argues that 'the physical Satan retained an absolute hold in narratives of witchcraft'.[53] Oldridge has also stressed the lack of impact Protestant conceptions of the Devil had on witchcraft pamphlets, by reminding us that 'the Devil as a single, powerful entity was . . . compromised by popular beliefs about individual demons and wicked spirits'.[54] The presence of multitudes of familiar spirits in witchcraft pamphlets certainly reinforces Oldridge's remarks. Despite prologues that emphasised the centrality of a powerful Satan figure (a phenomenon which will be explored later in this chapter), the presence of familiars in witchcraft trials and pamphlets illustrates the struggling nature of the Protestant concept of the Devil as a unitary force for evil. It would be wrong to suggest, however, that witchcraft pamphlets presented a wholly pre-Reformation concept of the Devil. While it is true that the Devil maintained a very physical presence in witchcraft narratives, it is also important to remember that this same physical Devil was nearly always portrayed as a tempter. Johnstone has argued that this physical concept of diabolical temptation marks witchcraft pamphlets as unusual in early modern English demonism. In these narratives pre- and post-Reformation concepts of the Devil do not just coexist; they complement each other, thus creating a new sense of how the Devil operates in the world.

There are many dozens of cases to draw on to highlight the diverse and ambivalent nature of the Devil in early modern English witchcraft. One particularly chilling tale which emphasises the physical temptation so common in witchcraft narratives appears in 1582 and describes the torments of accused witch Elizabeth Bennet. Elizabeth was approached by two spirits, 'one called *Suckin*, being blacke like a Dogge, the other called *Lierd*, beeing red like a Lion'.[55] This is one of the few cases in English witchcraft pamphlets in which a familiar is described as a lion and is perhaps a reference to the biblical understanding of the Devil as a roaring lion who prowls around looking for those he can devour.[56] According to the pamphlet, Suckin asked Elizabeth to go with him but Elizabeth refused while invoking God's name; Suckin and Lierd both disappeared. A short time later the same spirits reappeared and once again asked her to go with them; once again Elizabeth invoked God and refused, and the spirits vanished. On both of these occasions Suckin physically grabbed and held Elizabeth by her coats after which time Elizabeth was unable to move for two hours.[57] On the next day both spirits appeared on two separate occasions and urged Elizabeth to go with them, this time grabbing her by the leg. Once again, the spirits were unsuccessful.[58] Within half an hour of this last unsuccessful encounter Suckin reappeared:

> [Suckin] came unto [Elizabeth] & tooke this examinat by the hippes, and saide, seeing thou wilt not be ruled, thou shalt have a cause, & would have thrust this examinat into the burning Oven, & so had (as this examinat saith) but for the foresaide forke, but this examinat striving and dooing what shee coulde to her uttermost, the saide spirite burnt her arme, the which burning is apparaunt and evidently too bee seene[59]

This narrative demonstrates how witchcraft pamphlets portrayed the Devil as a physical tempter. Suckin and Lierd, two 'evil spirits' approach Elizabeth and tempt her to join with them; Elizabeth wards them off through prayer and invoking God.[60] This method of resisting the Devil is based on a Protestant emphasis on the importance of prayer in one's struggle with Satan. Elizabeth does not reach for a cross, invoke a saint or say a charm; she relies on prayer. However, through the physicality of Suckin and Lierd, Elizabeth's internal struggle against Satan becomes externalised. These demonic creatures grab at Elizabeth, at her coats, legs and hips. The pamphleteer's naming of each place that the familiars touch reinforces their physical nature. In this encounter, the Devil does not just try to tempt Elizabeth; he literally tries to drag her away. When Suckin and Lierd fail to convert Elizabeth, they take a purely physical form of revenge, pushing her into a burning oven. Despite having failed to recruit Elizabeth to their cause, these devils leave a lasting physical impression: a burnt arm that is visible to all.

It was very common in English witchcraft pamphlets for devils to leave physical marks on their victims. These marks generally took the form of teats as tangible reminders of the blood pact (a phenomenon which will be discussed in depth in chapter 2). There are, however, other cases (such as the above) in which men and women were otherwise marked by their encounters with Satan. One narrative that demonstrates the Devil's physical impact comes from 1582 and describes the witchcraft of Henry and Cysley Cilles, a married couple. John, their six-year-old son, testified that one night when he was in bed a 'blacke thing . . . [took him] by the legge'.[61] Later in the testimony it emerges that this creature, also called John, was one of his mother's imps. The testimony concludes by noting that 'there is a scarre to bee seene of this examinats legge where it was taken, and also the naile of his little Toe is yet unperfect'.[62] John has been permanently scarred by his encounter with Satan. For both Elizabeth Bennet and John Cilles, the Devil is a physical creature whose touch causes physical damage.

In some witchcraft narratives, differing perceptions of the Devil were combined through the use of an abstract concept (giving one's soul to the Devil) described as a physical act (a blood pact). This understanding of the Devil is apparent in the first English witchcraft pamphlet of 1566. This pamphlet describes accused witch John Walsh's relationship with his familiar, a creature who appeared sometimes 'lyke a gray blackish Culver, and sometime lyke a blended Dog, and somtimes lyke a man in all proportions, saving that he had cloven feete'.[63] John recounts how he had to pay the familiar for services rendered; sometimes he gave living things like chickens or cats, but other times he had 'to deliver . . . one drop of his blud, whych bloud the Sprite did take away upon hys paw'.[64] It was common for witches to seal their pact with Satan through blood; however, in this narrative the physical exchange of this act is emphasised. The spirit does not suck John's blood, but carefully carries away the blood and, with it, John's soul. This physical exchange through the performance of the blood pact, an act that symbolises giving one's soul to Satan, illustrates a combination of pre-and post-Reformation beliefs about the Devil. English witchcraft pamphlets took a multi-faceted approach to these beliefs. Abstract concepts such as personal temptation and the blood pact were made manifest through the physicality of the familiar spirit. In the above cases we see a construction of a diverse set of sometimes contradictory and ambivalent claims that are found in pamphlets throughout the entire period of witchcraft prosecutions.

The Devil and the Rise of the Witch Hunts

Many historians have drawn links between the rise of witchcraft accusations and the Devil's newfound influence in early modern Europe. Attitudes towards these links have changed substantially in the last three decades. Writing almost thirty years ago, Jeffrey Burton Russell labelled the 'witch craze' as 'both cause and result of the revival of the idea of the Devil, who had been flagging but now returned to his kingdom in full pomp and regalia'.[65] Like most historians, Russell defines the witch craze as a phenomenon which had roots in the Middle Ages but only came to full maturity during the sixteenth and seventeenth centuries.[66] He argues that the emphasis on the witch as a servant of Satan and the growing numbers of witch trials throughout Europe heightened fear and awareness of the Devil. This is a rather difficult statement to prove. Could it also be that a growing awareness of the Devil's power encouraged witchcraft persecutions? This is the view taken by Robert Muchembled, who argues that 'the sudden intensification of the witch hunt in the last quarter of the sixteenth century is proof that fear of the devil greatly increased at this period'.[67] In either case, rising numbers of witchcraft cases and an increasing fear of the Devil coexisted during the fifteenth, sixteenth and seventeenth centuries. Brian Levack, when writing on the sixteenth century, takes a different perspective from both Russell and Muchembled. Rather than suggesting that witchcraft trials grew out of an increasing emphasis on diabolical power, he instead argues that a greater awareness of the Devil's activities changed the tenor and frequency of witchcraft accusations:

> the heightened consciousness of diabolical activity certainly made early modern European communities – and not just the members of the ruling elite – more eager to prosecute these witches as agents of the Devil whenever accusations of *maleficium* surfaced.[68]

For Muchembled, witchcraft trials gave weight to diabolical ideas and provided a practical setting in which to prove a theoretical construct:

> The witchcraft trials put flesh on the bones of demonology. They proved it was true. They turned a complex theological theory into an observable reality. They incarnated the devil, essentially as unknowable as God, in the person of the accused, man or woman. In doing so, they transported the struggle between good and evil from heaven to the human heart, raising the terrible spectre of the personal guilt of each individual. The devil moved from the outside to the inside.[69]

Muchembled's reading is convincing and shows the strong link between a theoretical belief in the Devil and his very real presence in the world. Given the emphasis on diabolical power in the sixteenth and seventeenth centuries, it is not surprising that English witchcraft pamphlets focused on diabolical spirits and sought to explore how a witch made contact and interacted with the Devil. These pamphlets placed the witch's relationship with the Devil as paramount and, as such, must be part of any re-evaluation of the role of the Devil in English witchcraft belief.

Contemporary authors make it very clear that they believed that the Devil's increasing power in the world was directly related to increasing numbers of witches. For these authors, witches represented a 'manifestation of Satan's activity on earth' and, as such, needed to be wiped out.[70] Both sixteenth- and seventeenth-century English witchcraft pamphlets often started with an epistle, preface, prologue, note to a patron or note to the reader; it was in these preambles that pamphleteers often emphasised their belief in Satan's power. Although epistles do exist in eighteenth-century witchcraft pamphlets, they are rare and do not focus on the Devil's increasing power. This is a preoccupation that is most common amongst sixteenth and seventeenth century authors. One pamphleteer, writing in 1579, believed 'that old Serpent Sathan, suffred to be the scourge for our sinns, hath of late yeares, greately multiplyed the broude of [witches], and muche encreased their malice'.[71] This anonymous author emphasises that Satan is particularly active in the current age and, as such, spends his time creating ever more witches to plague humanity with their newly increased malice. A second pamphleteer, this time writing in 1597, claimed that in this current age Satan corrupts more 'mens minds by his wicked suggestions' than in any previous time.[72] This author focuses on Satan's ability to turn men and women away from God and suggests that this is a more common occurrence than ever before. A third sixteenth-century author explained that he wrote his 1579 pamphlet 'to discover the Ambushementes of Sathan, whereby he would surprise us lulled in securitie, and hardened with contempte of Gods vengeance threatened for our offences'.[73] Like the previous pamphleteer, this writer is keen to describe the Devil's habit of lying in wait for men and women who have lost their fear of God. These ambushes, as the pamphleteer goes on to explain, have been placed by Satan in 'moste partes of this realme . . . to undermine and spoile the states of suche as God permitteth him to have power over'.[74] The impression from all three of these pamphleteers is that the populace is at ever-increasing risk from Satan's growing influence in the world. The link between Satan's increasing power and larger numbers of witches is clear in the minds of these men.

Seventeenth-century pamphleteers also believed in the link between the Devil's growing power and increasing numbers of witches. One author, whilst introducing a 1649 witchcraft pamphlet, referred to the Devil as the 'Old Serpent' who was set upon 'the enlarging of his territories; by strengthening of himself upon the weaknesse of his subjects, relapsed men and women'.[75] This declaration served as a warning to readers to avoid the temptations of Satan. Another pamphleteer, who also referred to Satan as the 'Old Serpent', warned his readers in 1645 of the 'cunning subtilties' of Satan who 'labours daily to insnare soules, and [attempts] to bring them to utter ruine'.[76] This writer also called Satan a 'grand impostor', thus highlighting his deceitful nature.[77] A third pamphleteer, this time writing in 1658, claimed that in 'our dayes' we find the Devil 'daily subverting, ensnaring men and women, his policies and devices are many, his temptations subtle'.[78] This author goes on to comment on the intense activity of the Devil in pursuing his objectives: 'the following Relation doth further manifest in these days, How busy the devil is to gain the persons, nay the soules of people'.[79] These comments highlight a belief in the increased powers of the Devil, but they are rare in seventeenth-century pamphlets and seemingly non-existent in eighteenth century materials. Instead, many later authors emphasised the power of the Devil by stressing the reality of both devils and witches.

Many seventeenth-century pamphleteers began by addressing those who did not believe in witchcraft.[80] These authors were keen to combat the kind of scepticism found, for example, in Reginald Scot's *Discoverie of Witch-craft*. In the later seventeenth and early eighteenth centuries, this engagement with and attempt to quell scepticism about witchcraft became even more pronounced. As one 1716 pamphlet began 'it hath been a great Controversie among Learned Men, about the possibility of Men and Women being *Wizards Witches* or no, some affirming such they may be, and others to the contrary'.[81] Pamphleteers typically addressed those 'many that remain yet in doubt whether there be any Witches, or no, or any such spirits, who offer their service unto them, or rather who by fained service doe tyrannize over them.'[82] These pamphleteers employed ancient, biblical and legal examples to suggest that anyone who does not believe in witchcraft believes more in the 'singularity of their owne opinions, then the certainty of Reason or Judgement'.[83] Many authors tempered their warnings of the Devil's power with such comments on the doubtful intelligence of those who refused to believe in witchcraft and the power of the Devil. But perhaps the set of pamphlets that most embodies the debate between the sceptics and the believers are the eight pamphlets published in 1712 in the wake of the Jane Wenham case. Jane Wenham was the last witch found guilty of witchcraft in England. Despite her conviction, Jane was not executed as the presiding judge, Sir John Powell, obtained a pardon for her from Queen Anne.[84] Perhaps unsurprisingly, this case sparked heated debate over the fundamental nature of witchcraft. Of the eight pamphlets, four (three written by Francis Bragge), stressed the reality of witchcraft and hoped that this case would change the minds of those 'slow Believers' and force 'their Prejudices [to give way] to the Testimony of their Reason and Senses'.[85] On the other side of this debate were those who condemned the 'Waste of Humane Blood in every Village, upon the wild Testimonies of a parcel of Brain-sick People'.[86] Through emphasising the reality and power of both witches and devils, pro-witchcraft authors used their introductory preambles to fight against increasing scepticism and, in doing so, stressed the Devil's very real power in the world.

Many sixteenth and seventeenth-century prologues, and even some from the eighteenth century, also mention the Devil's cunning and deceit. For these authors the Devil is a trickster, a creature sent to snare men and women into witchcraft. For earlier authors he is also an ever-growing force of evil in the world, someone whose power is increasing daily. The tone of these introductions differs quite dramatically from the witchcraft narrative itself, suggesting that educated Protestant concepts of the Devil may have differed significantly from those at a village level expressed through the testimonies of victims, witches and accusers. In such narratives the emphasis on the physicality of the Devil and less explicit concern for the Devil's growing presence in the world, suggests that the witches, accusers, victims and witnesses whose stories are being recorded did not share the same sense and understanding of the Devil as that espoused by many pamphleteers. This discrepancy appears to reinforce the view that Protestant ideas were not widely accepted among the populace.

The Decline of the Devil's Power

In 1550, in the words of Philip Almond:

> It was as impossible not to believe in the Devil as it was impossible not to believe in God. By the middle of the eighteenth century, intellectual conditions had changed sufficiently for at least some among the "literate" elite, both religious and non-religious, to contemplate the non-existence of the Devil, or at least to question whether he any longer had a role in history or could actually act in the world.[87]

We see this change in the epistles to early modern witchcraft pamphlets. Between the sixteenth and the eighteenth centuries, references to the Devil's growing power become increasingly rare. What endures, however, are the devilish aspects of the witchcraft narratives themselves; references to familiar spirits, devilish compacts and selling one's soul remain common in pamphlets right through the seventeenth and early eighteenth century. This discrepancy between the more learned prologues and the witchcraft narrative, composed of village testimonies from witnesses, victims and accused witches, reinforces the growing disconnect between learned and popular beliefs about the Devil in the later early modern period.

It was in a world of declining witchcraft accusations, prosecutions and pamphlets that Daniel Defoe writing in the 1720s was able to reflect on the death of the Devil:

> we don't find our Houses disturb'd as they used to be, and the Stools and Chairs walking about out of one Room into another, as formerly; that Children don't vomit crooked Pins and rusty stub Nails, as of old, the Air is not full of Noises, nor the Church-Yard full of Hobgoblins; Ghosts don't walk about in Winding Sheets, and the good old scolding Wives visit and plague their Husbands after they are dead, as they did when they were alive. The Age is grown too wise to be agitated by these dull scare-crow Things which their Fore-Fathers were tickled with; Satan has been obliged to lay by his Puppet-shews and his Timblers, those things are grown stale; his morrice-dancing Devils, his mountebanking and quacking won't do now.[88]

By the middle of the eighteenth century 'for an educated elite at least, the Devil had become a figure *of* history – one of the past rather than the present or future – and not a participant *within* it'.[89] However, the same cannot be said for the majority of the population. Just two years before Defoe wrote his *History of the Devil*, Newcastle-upon-Tyne curate Henry Bourne reflected on the stories he heard of commoners telling each other how they had seen fairies, spirits and 'even the Devil himself, with a cloven Foot'.[90] The Devil remained a force for evil in the popular imagination well into the eighteenth century and even beyond.[91] As Owen Davies has argued, 'the Devil's grip on society was firmer, more pervasive and lasted longer than it is usually thought. The idea of the Devil stalking the country promoting mischief continued to be held [in the eighteenth century] by not a few Anglican clergymen and was certainly widespread in popular culture.'[92] As will be discussed in depth in the next chapter, the Devil remained a key element of witchcraft narratives, particularly so as an explanation for how a witch was able to hurt others. Despite growing scepticism about witchcraft and the Devil's role in the world, witchcraft narratives, although dwindling, continued to suggest that the Devil was a very real threat.

Early modern England did not have one clear notion of how the Devil acted or how he should be warded off. Rather than having one, or even two well-defined concepts of the Devil, post-Reformation English witchcraft pamphlets included a multitude of ambiguous and often apparently contradictory understandings of the Devil. In the three-hundred-year period between the fifteenth and eighteenth centuries, ideas about the Devil changed significantly: the Protestant Reformation emphasised the power of the Devil and, in so doing, helped to create a growing awareness and fear of Satan's presence in the world. It also emphasised the Devil as a source of mental temptations. Rather than displacing traditional concepts of the Devil, these new views of the Devil's power existed side by side. In witchcraft narratives, old and new ideas about the Devil complemented one another; physical devils tempted men and women and they reacted through prayer. Increasing fear of the Devil and growing numbers of witchcraft trials existed side by side, in England as well as in Europe. Even as scepticism grew in the later seventeenth and early eighteenth centuries, the Devil remained a key actor in witchcraft narratives. In order to understand English witchcraft, one must examine the role of the Devil. This chapter has explored how a growing fear of the Devil, combined with changing conceptions of Satan, came together in English witchcraft narratives to present an ambiguous and multi-faceted view of the Devil. This view was not wholly Catholic, nor wholly Protestant, but somewhere in between. This conflation of beliefs is fundamental to an understanding of the Devil in early modern English witchcraft pamphlets.

Notes

1 Philip Almond, *The Devil: A New Biography* (Ithaca: Cornell University Press, 2014), 168.
2 Ibid.
3 Darren Oldridge, *The Devil in Early Modern England* (Stroud: Sutton, 2000), 17. This work has been republished in revised form as *The Devil in Tudor and*

Stuart England (Stroud: The History Press, 2010). As there are significant differences between the texts, both versions will be referred to throughout this volume.

4   Ibid., 2. Robert Muchembled has argued that the belief in the Devil as a physical being, capable of turning into bestial or human form, originated in the twelfth century. Robert Muchembled, *A History of the Devil: From the Middle Ages to the Present*, trans. Jean Birrell (Cambridge: Polity Press, 2003), 27–34.

5   Oldridge, *The Devil in Early Modern England*, 21.

6   Jeffrey Burton Russell, *Lucifer: The Devil in the Middle Ages* (Ithaca: Cornell University Press, 1984), 74.

7   Ibid.

8   Muchembled, *A History of the Devil*, 20.

9   Russell, *Lucifer*, see chapter 4, especially 72–77.

10   Muchembled, *A History of the Devil*, 20.

11   Oldridge, *The Devil in Tudor and Stuart England*, 35.

12   Russell, *Lucifer*, 63.

13   Oldridge, *The Devil in Early Modern England*, 66 and Russell, *Lucifer*, 63.

14   Russell, *Lucifer*, 63.

15   Ibid.

16   Anon., *Tales and Quicke Answers Very Merry, and Pleasant to Rede* (London: Printed in the house of Thomas Bethelet, 1532), sig. C2 r.

17   Ibid.

18   Ibid.

19   W.N., *The Second Part of Merry Drollery, or, a Collection of Jovial Poems, Merry Songs, Witty Drolleries, Intermix'd with Pleasant Catches Collected by W.N., C.B., R.S., J.G., Lovers of Wit* (London: Printed by J.W. for P.H., 1661), 12–15.

20   Ibid., 13.

21   Ibid., 14–15.

22   Brian Levack, *The Witch-hunt in Early Modern Europe*, 3rd edn. (Harlow: Longman, 2006), 112.

23   Ibid.

24   Keith Thomas, *Religion and the Decline of Magic: Studies in Popular Belief*, 1st edn. (London: Weidenfeld and Nicolson, 1971), 470.

25   Thomas Becon, *The Worckes of Thomas Becon Whiche He Hath Hitherto Made and Published, with Diverse Other Newe Books Added to the Same, Heretofore Never Set Forth in Print, Divided into Thre Tomes or Parts and Amended This Present [sic] of Our Lord 1564; Perused and Allowed, Accordyng to Thorder Appointed in the Quenes Majesties Injunctions* (London: Printed by John Day, 1564), I 390 v.

26   Thomas, *Religion and the Decline of Magic*, 1st edn., 494, 495.

27   Kathleen Sands, *Demon Possession in Elizabethan England* (London: Praeger, 2004), 146.

28   William Gouge, *The Whole Armour of God: Or a Christians Spirituall Furniture, to Keep Him Safe from All the Assaults of Satan: The Second Edition Corrected & Inlarged: Whereunto Is Added a Treatise of the Sin Against the Holy Ghost* (London: John Beale, 1619), II, 21.

29   Oldridge, *The Devil in Early Modern England*, 7.

30   Muchembled, *A History of the Devil*, 20.

31   Ibid., 21.

32   Oldridge, *The Devil in Early Modern England*, 7.

33   Jeffrey Burton Russell, *Mephistopheles: The Devil in the Modern World* (Ithaca: Cornell University Press, 1986), 31.

34 Ibid.
35 Ibid.
36 Ibid., 33.
37 Oldridge, *The Devil in Tudor and Stuart England*, 19.
38 James Sharpe, *Instruments of Darkness: Witchcraft in Early Modern England*, paperback edn. (Philadelphia: University of Pennsylvania Press, 1997), 84.
39 Ibid.
40 William Perkins, *A Discourse of the Dammed Art of Witchcraft so Farre Forth as It Is Revealed in the Scriptures, and Manifest By True Experience* (Cambridge: Cantrel Legge, 1608), 253.
41 Thomas Cooper, *The Mystery of Witch-craft* (London: Printed by Nicholas Okes, 1617), 31.
42 Nathan Johnstone, *The Devil and Demonism in Early Modern England* (Cambridge: Cambridge University Press, 2006), 2.
43 Ibid., 16.
44 Russell, *Mephistopheles*, 40.
45 Levack, *The Witch-hunt in Early Modern Europe*, 113.
46 Johnstone, *The Devil and Demonism*, 7.
47 John Olde, *A Short Description of Antichrist Unto the Nobilitie of Englande, and to All My Brethren and Contreymen Borne and Dwelling Therin, with a Warnynge to See to, That They Be Not Deceaved By the Hyposcrise and Crafty Conveyance of the Clergie* (1555), 2 v.
48 Oldridge, *The Devil in Tudor and Stuart England*, 80.
49 Ibid., 8.
50 The Basque country was the only geographical region other than England in which familiars were common in early modern Europe. Sharpe, *Instruments of Darkness*, 71.
51 Oldridge, *The Devil in Tudor and Stuart England*, 176.
52 James Sharpe, "The Devil in East Anglia: The Matthew Hopkins Trials Reconsidered," in *Witchcraft in Early Modern Europe: Studies in Culture and Belief*, eds. Jonathan Barry, Marianne Hester and Gareth Roberts (Cambridge: Cambridge University Press, 1996), 252.
53 Johnstone, *The Devil and Demonism*, 7.
54 Oldridge, *The Devil in Tudor and Stuart England*, 84.
55 W.W., *A True and Just Recorde, of the Information, Examination and Confession of All the Witches* (London: Printed by Thomas Dawson, 1582), sig. B7 r.
56 1 Peter 5: 8.
57 W.W., *A True and Just Recorde*, sigs. B7 r and B7 v.
58 Ibid., sig. B7 v – B8 r.
59 Ibid., sig. B8 r.
60 Ibid., sig. B7 v.
61 Ibid., sig. D2 r.
62 Ibid., sig. D2 v.
63 Anon., *The Examination of John Walsh Before Maister Thomas Williams* (London: Printed by John Awdely, 1566), sig. B1 v.
64 Ibid., sig. B2 r.
65 Russell, *Mephistopheles*, 30.
66 Ibid., 28.
67 Robert Muchembled, *A History of the Devil*, 53.
68 Levack, *The Witch-hunt in Early Modern Europe*, 114.
69 Muchembled, *A History of the Devil*, 60.
70 Oldridge, *The Devil in Early Modern England*, 10. Oldridge has rephrased this in the second edition and suggested that, for some, witches were a type of

'satanic fifth column' within their communities. Oldridge, *The Devil in Tudor and Stuart England*, 21.

71 Anon., *A Rehearsal Both Straung and True, of Heinous and Horrible Actes Committed by Elizabeth Stile alias Rockingham, Mother Dutten, Mother Devell, Mother Margaret, Fower Notorious Witches* (London: Printed by J. Kingston for Edward White, 1579), sig. A2 r.

72 I.D., *The Most Wonderfull and True Storie, of a Certaine Witch Named Alse Gooderige of Stapen hill, Who Was Arraigned and Convicted at Darbie at the Assises There as Also a True Report of the Strange Torments of Thomas Darling, a Boy of Thirteene Yeres of Age, That was Possessed by the Devil, with His Horrible Fittes and Apparitions by Him Uttered at Burton upon Trent in the Countie of Stafford, and of His Marvellous Deliverance* (London: Printed for I.O., 1597), sig. A2 r.

73 Anon., *A Detection of Damnable Driftes, Practized by Three Witches Arraigned at Chelmisforde in Essex at the Last Assizes There Holden, Whiche Were Executed in Aprill, 1579* (London: Printed by J. Kingston for Edward White, 1579), title page.

74 Ibid., sig. A2 v.

75 B. Misodaimon. *The Divels Delusions or a Faithfull Relation of John Palmer and Elizabeth Knott Two Notorious Witches Lately Condemned at the Sessions of Oyer and Terminer in St. Albans* (London: Printed for Richard Williams, 1649), 1. The author's full name is unclear.

76 H.F., *A True and Exact Relation of the Several Informations, Examinations, and Confessions of the Late Witches, Arraigned and Executed in the County of Essex* (London: Printed by M.S. for Henry Overton and Benj. Allen, 1645), 2.

77 Ibid.

78 Anon., *The Snare of the Devil Discovered: Or, a True and Perfect Relations of the Sad and Deplorable Condition of Lydia the Wife of John Rogers* (London: Printed for Edward Thomas 1658), 1.

79 Ibid., 2–3.

80 Many post-1700 witchcraft pamphlets are only one or two pages in length and do not include a prologue or epistle. These include Anon., *A True and Full Account of the Apprehending and Taking of Mrs Sarah Moordike* (London: Printed for John Alkin, 1701); Thomas Greenwel, *A Full and True Account of the Discovering, Apprehending, and Taking of a Notorious Witch* (London: Printed by H. Hills near the Waterside, 1704); Anon., *A Full and True Account of the Tryal, Examination, and Condemnation of Mary Johnson, a Witch* (London: Printed by J. Bland, 1706); and Anon., *The Whole Trial and Examination of Mrs Mary Hicks and Her Daughter Elizabeth* (London: Printed by W. Matthews in Long-Acre, 1716).

81 Anon., *The Whole Trial and Examination of Mrs Mary Hicks and Her Daughter Elizabeth*, 2. For other pamphlets which condemn growing scepticism, see, for example, Anon., *A Trial of Witches at the Assizes* (London: Printed for D. Brown, J. Walthoe and M. Wotton, 1716), 'to the reader' and Francis Bragge, *Witchcraft Farther Display'd* (London: Printed for E. Curll, 1712), 'introduction'.

82 Anon., *The Witches of Northampton-shire* (London: Printed by Tho: Parfoot, for Arthur Johnson, 1612), sig. A3 v.

83 Ibid.

84 Phyllis J. Guskin, "The Context of Witchcraft: The Case of Jane Wenham (1712)," *Eighteenth-Century Studies* 15 (1981), 48.

85 Francis Bragge, *A Full and Impartial Account of the Discovery of Sorcery and Witchcraft Practis'd by Jane Wenham of Walkerne in Hertfordshire* (London: Printed for E. Curll, 1712), second page of preface.

86 Anon., *A Full Confutation of Witchcraft: More Particularly of the Depositions Against Jane Wenham* (London: Printed for J. Baker, 1712), 5.
87 Almond, *The Devil*, 196.
88 Daniel Defoe, *A History of the Devil* (London, 1727), 388–389.
89 Almond, *The Devil*, 220.
90 Henry Bourne, *Antiquitates Vulgares* (1725) quoted in Margaret Spufford, *Small Books and Pleasant Histories: Popular Fiction and Its Readership in Seventeenth-Century England* (London: Methuen, 1981), 5.
91 For a study which provides an overview of changing historiographical attitudes towards the decline of magic and the 'disenchantment of the world' and, in doing so, reinforces the importance and continuation of "supernatural" beliefs in the eighteenth and nineteenth centuries, see Alexandra Walsham, "The Reformation and 'The Disenchantment of the World' Reassessed," *The Historical Journal* 51 (2008): 497–528.
92 Davies, "Talk of the Devil: Crime and Satanic Inspiration in Eighteenth-Century England," (2007), 2.

2   The Role of the Familiar

The familiar spirit is one of the most important yet understudied aspects of English witchcraft belief. These creatures, almost entirely unique to England, went by many names: familiar spirits, imps, sprites, devils and demons. They were bestial, tangible creatures which were most often described as domestic or common animals such as dogs, cats, chickens, toads, rats or ferrets although they could, on occasion, appear as mythological animals such as dragons. These creatures, which featured in nearly all English witchcraft pamphlets, were very often described as or conflated with the Devil. Through their bonds with accused witches, familiar spirits created a demonic pact between themselves and the accused witch and, in doing so, added a strong diabolical element to English witchcraft belief. This chapter focuses on exactly what function the familiar performed in witchcraft narratives and explains the link between it and the diabolical. By emphasising the importance of the familiar spirit and its diabolical associations, this chapter argues that the prevalence of these creatures encourages us to re-evaluate the importance of diabolical ideas to English witchcraft belief.

More than a decade ago James Sharpe declared that a 'detailed investigation into the phenomenon of familiars is currently one of the most urgent items on the agenda for future research into English witchcraft history'.[1] Some work has been done since; much more remains.[2] The familiar has been labelled as 'a small household-demon',[3] 'a privately owned Devil in animal form'[4] or as an 'incarnation of the Devil'.[5] It has been called a 'famously distinct feature of English witch beliefs',[6] one that was 'central' to an English understanding of witchcraft.[7] It is indisputably key to English witch belief, as has been noted by historians as wide-ranging as Alan Macfarlane, James Sharpe, Robin Briggs, Marion Gibson, Clive Holmes and Emma Wilby.[8] As early as 1970, Macfarlane argued that the familiar was so integral to English witchcraft that 'an unnatural mark on the body of a suspected witch [supposedly caused by a familiar] was seen as sufficient proof of witchcraft'.[9] Although historians do refer to the familiar and suggest that it performs the role of the Devil, the implications of this claim and the specific nature of familiars have yet to be given the attention they deserve. In 1996, Sharpe argued that 'the widespread belief in familiars takes us away from a model of witchcraft which is based on village *maleficium* into one where something very like a diabolical element is present'.[10] This chapter takes Sharpe's assertion as its starting point and explores how beliefs about familiars contributed to the diabolical elements of early modern English witchcraft belief. The fundamental importance of the familiar, when understood as a diabolical agent, creates an image of English witchcraft that contains strong diabolical elements and, as such, encourages us to rethink the paradigm of English witchcraft as a primarily non-diabolical activity.

In the last two decades work on the familiar has flourished. Sharpe has written at length about the familiar's demonic nature, as well as having written more broadly on the familiar's role in early modern England.[11] Crucially for this chapter, Sharpe believes that familiars 'offer a challenge to the argument that in England popular ideas about witchcraft in the early modern period were largely innocent of diabolical elements'.[12] Other work on the familiar, while extremely valuable, has been less preoccupied with these diabolical features. Emma Wilby's work on the possible links between familiars and fairies in England and Scotland makes a case for this conflation – although as I will discuss later, the theory is not entirely convincing, particularly as many of Wilby's strongest examples are Scottish.[13] Wilby's examination of the 'working relationship' between witch and familiar is fascinating and represents one of the first attempts to understand the emotions present within these relationships. Deborah Willis has, of course, also worked on the relationship between witch and familiar, particularly in terms of inverted maternity.[14] James Serpell and Greg Warburton have also added their voices to those studying the familiar.[15] Serpell's study provides a quantitative analysis of the frequency of certain familiar forms and names. He also focused on the idea of the familiar as a cross between a type of pet and a shamanistic guardian spirit. Warburton's article focused on his belief that women used the familiar to resist diabolical narratives imposed from above. Although other historians have referred to the familiar spirit, often in passing, these works, all of which emerged during the past fifteen to twenty years, represent some of the most sustained discussions on the subject.

Although all of these works contribute valuably to our understanding of the familiar spirit, this creature's demonic characteristics have yet to be systematically explored. This book continues the work I began in a 2010 article, which, based on seven sixteenth-century witchcraft pamphlets, argued that the familiar spirit was understood as a sexualised demonic creature who transformed women into sexually deviant witches who had been tricked or tempted into selling their soul to the Devil.[16] The current book takes this argument further by looking at all sixty-six remaining witchcraft pamphlets from the entire period of state-sanctioned witchcraft accusations. Of these sixty-six witchcraft pamphlets only three fail to mention witches' reliance on the Devil to help them inflict *maleficium*.[17] In all but five of these sixty-three remaining pamphlets the Devil is represented as a familiar spirit.[18] This representation is usually explicit through the description of animalistic creatures acting as the Devil but, in a handful of pamphlets, becomes more implicit through references to hidden teats found on the body of the witch.

References to familiars are one of the most unchanging aspects of early modern witchcraft pamphlets. Even as witchcraft trials declined in the late seventeenth and early eighteenth centuries and fewer pamphlets were published, familiars remained a crucial element of witchcraft narratives. The high percentage of familiars visible in pamphlet narratives appears to be significantly greater than those in trial records.[19] This suggests that pamphleteers chose to publish cases in which the role of the Devil was a key concern, either as a warning against the trappings of Satan (as is clear in many epistles) or out of the belief that stories of demonic animals would sell. Pamphlets were a powerful vehicle for spreading beliefs about witchcraft to the masses. As Keith Thomas has argued, 'contemporaries . . . were dependent for their knowledge of the subject [of witchcraft] upon the chance appearance of a pamphlet account of a notable trial'.[20] The apparent preference given to diabolical narratives would have created a very specific understanding of witchcraft amongst English readers and positions pamphlets as a key source for understanding the connection between witchcraft and diabolism in early modern England. Eight of the ten extant sixteenth-century witchcraft pamphlets refer to familiar spirits, as do forty of the forty-eight remaining seventeenth-century pamphlets and six of the eight remaining from the eighteenth century. This means that between 1566 and 1735 fifty-four of sixty-six witchcraft pamphlets (or over 80 per cent) include references to familiar spirits.

As well as highlighting the prevalence of familiar spirits in pamphlet literature, these statistics also remind us that familiars were not, as has frequently been suggested, simply a feature of the Civil War period. Although the trials overseen by Matthew Hopkins during the 1640s are often seen as atypical of English witchcraft, Sharpe has argued that 'whatever was untypical in the Hopkins trials, the familiar was not'.[21] Sharpe has discovered that of one hundred and ten Hopkins narratives, seventy-eight involved familiar spirits.[22] These figures, particularly when added to my own findings (as described above) reinforce the centrality of the familiar spirit within pamphlet literature not just in the 1640s but throughout the entire period of early modern witchcraft belief in England. Through analysing all sixty-six extant witchcraft pamphlets from this period, it becomes clear that the familiar provided a crucial diabolical element to English witchcraft beliefs. As such, it is not possible to understand the important role of the Devil in English witchcraft without a thorough understanding of the familiar spirit.

The Origins of the Familiar

The origins of the familiar spirit remain elusive. As Sharpe has noted, it is difficult to understand how the seemingly well-developed concept of the familiar entered popular print in 1566 but was hardly ever mentioned in earlier witchcraft cases.[23] As early as the sixteenth century the familiar appeared in pamphlets as an easily recognisable, bestial, demonic creature. In fact, from the very first witchcraft pamphlet, the idea of the familiar was fully formed and remained remarkably stable throughout the entire period of witchcraft accusations. The Witchcraft Acts of both 1563 and 1604 criminalised interaction with spirits.[24] Although it does not mention familiars by name, the 1563 Witchcraft Act specifically forbade the 'use practise or exercise [of] any Invocations or Conjurations of evill and wicked Spirites'.[25] The punishment for conjuring evil spirits was death.[26] It is hard to know whether these 'Spirites' referred to familiars as well as to conjured demons. Garthine Walker has suggested that legal references to ritualistic magic may have been 'a remnant of the late medieval discourses of sorcery and magic which were better known among the literate elite than ordinary people'.[27] Beliefs about familiars were certainly circulating when this act was passed. As Sharpe and C.L. Ewen have noted, belief in familiar spirits predated both witchcraft statutes; Ewen, for example, cites a 1510 Yorkshire case as the first reference to a familiar (in this case, a bee) sucking blood from its owner.[28] By the time of the 1604 statute, familiars were clearly visible in anti-witchcraft legislation. The 1604 act criminalised the keeping of familiar spirits as well as the mere conjuring of them. As well as repeating the Tudor warning against using or conjuring evil and wicked spirits, the act also forbade anyone to 'consult covenant with entertaine employ feede or rewarde any evill and wicked Spirit to or for any intent or purpose'.[29] Pamphlet descriptions of familiar spirits did not change significantly between the passing of these two acts. As Walker has pointed out, the emphasis on diabolism in the relationship between witch and familiar was present both before and after the 1604 statute.[30] Instead of the law dictating the types of beliefs about spirits circulating in England, it seems that, in the 1604 act, the law was catching up with popular belief.

Most historians will agree that the idea of the familiar stemmed from popular English beliefs rather than those of theologians. As Oldridge argues:

> The presence of familiars in English witchcraft cannot . . . be attributed to the influence of continental demonology, as these creatures appeared less frequently in European sources. Still less can it be traced to the work of those English theologians who wrote on the subject. Indeed, reports of witches' imps were problematic for many demonologists, as they departed in their appearance and behaviour from the reformed understanding of the Devil: it is unlikely that they would have featured in published accounts of the crime unless they appeared in the original allegations. They were also described at length by writers profoundly critical of popular witch beliefs, such as Gifford and Reginald Scot. All this suggests that the belief was rooted in popular traditions that probably predated the Reformation.[31]

For many Protestants, the idea of the devil as a small, tangible, domestic creature that did jobs for its mistress, sat uncomfortably with a learned understanding of the Devil's role in the world. Some attempted to explain away the familiar's appearance by referring to Satan's role as a trickster. As one pamphleteer writing in 1619 explained, the Devil attends the potential witch 'in such prety formes of dog, cat, or Rat that [his victims] should neither be terrified, nor any body else suspicious of the matter'.[32] But as clear as it is that familiars arose from popular rather than learned belief, it is still unclear exactly from where these beliefs stemmed.

There are two main theories concerning the origins and development of the familiar and both of these argue that belief in the familiar was grounded in popular culture. For some historians, the familiar may have been 'a form of household fairy, or hob'.[33] Although there is much that is convincing about this theory, beliefs about fairies and familiars coexisted separately throughout the early modern period. This is clear when looking at popular plays, ballads and pamphlets which depict beliefs about fairies and the fairy kingdom. Rather than arguing for a direct link between fairies and familiars, I would suggest that these two groups of supernatural creatures were occasionally confused in the minds of contemporaries.

Proponents of the fairy/familiar theory have focused on the names given to both creatures, on their bodily form and on their behaviour and relationship with humans. These links are not without their problems. As Wilby has noted, fairies 'were believed to resemble humans in appearance and behaviour'.[34] However, familiars nearly always took the shape of animals. In her comprehensive book on fairy lore, Diane Purkiss has suggested that 'the animal form of the English familiars recalls the English hob's fondness for animal-skin clothing, and for suits of leather, also animal hide'.[35] We also know that fairies were believed able to shape shift between human and animal form so it may be possible to view the familiar as a shape-shifted fairy. Another point raised to support a connection between fairies and familiars is their sometimes-similar names. Peter Marshall and Darren Oldridge have reflected on the fairy-like names, such as "Puckle", "Robin" or "Hob" that some familiars possessed; but these are just three of many, many different names that we see attributed to familiars. As Serpell has demonstrated, the vast majority of familiar names were either diminutives such as Jack, John, Bunne, Tibb or standard pet names such as Pusse, Gibb or Ball. They could also have descriptive names such as White, Blew or Calico and, of course, they could go by far more diabolically suggestive names such as Sathan or Beelzeebub.[36] As Purkiss has pointed out, the varied names of familiars point to the 'multiplicity of identities' attributed to them.[37] For Purkiss, perhaps the main lesson from these names is that they all suggest the smallness of the familiar and the affectionate nature of the relationship between them and the accused witch who named them. As Purkiss has argued, even though it is difficult to know how many of these names were assigned by the accused, by pamphleteers and by examiners, it seems unlikely that learned officials would give affectionate names to what they viewed as demonic creatures. Instead, Purkiss suggests that familiars' names form a 'central part' of women's fantasies about their familiars.[38]

Rather than look to a familiar's name to understand its origin, we need to look at what it actually did. Unlike fairies, familiars appeared as small animals and fed on teats from a witch's body. They obeyed human commands and were inherently wicked – all characteristics that cannot easily be attributed to fairies.[39] Historians of fairy beliefs have pointed out the tendency for both fairies and familiars to be fed milk.[40] However, familiars were far more likely to be fed blood instead of milk.[41] Purkiss, after suggesting possible links between fairies and familiars, concludes that 'none of this is to suggest that all familiars are fairies'.[42] Instead, she argues that the two beliefs may have been occasionally conflated in the minds of contemporaries.

There are only four narratives in printed accounts of English witchcraft which suggest confusion between fairy and familiar beliefs. The first textual account appears in the very first English witchcraft pamphlet. This narrative, from 1566, details the ecclesiastical trial of accused witch John Walsh. On being asked whether he had a familiar, John vehemently denied it, claiming that he 'has none about hym, neyther in anye other place of this worlde, eyther above the ground, or under the ground, either in any place secrete or open'.[43] He did, however, admit to talking to fairies.[44] Throughout the examination John frequently confused the terms "fairy", "sprite", "familiar sprite" and "familiar." On being asked how long he had possessed his familiar spirit, John told the court that:

> his familiar would sometime come unto hym lyke a gray blackish Culver [a type of dove or pigeon], and sometime lyke a blended Dog, and sometimes lyke a man in all proportions, saving that he had cloven feet.[45]

John's description of his familiar includes some bestial and demonic attributes which are suggestive of a familiar, and also human qualities which may have been inspired by contemporary fairy beliefs. Another example of this confusion does not appear until the 1619 account of the witchcraft of Joan Willimott:

> shee hath a Spirit which shee calleth *Pretty*, which was given unto her by *William Berry* of *Langbolme* in *Rutlandshire*, whom she served three yeares; and that her Master when hee gave it unto her, willed her to open her mouth, and hee would blow into her a Fairy which should doe her good; and that shee opened her mouth, and he did blow into her mouth; and that presently after his blowing, there came out of her mouth a Spirit, which stood upon the ground in the shape and forme of a Woman, which Spirit did aske of her her Soule, which shee then promised unto it, being willed thereunto by her Master.[46]

The 1635 version of this pamphlet repeats the confession. Joan's spirit, despite its appearance as a woman rather than an animal, behaves very similarly to a familiar, most notably in its request for Joan's soul, a key part of the witch/familiar interaction.

These two examples are well-known to witchcraft historians. Two other examples that do not seem to have been remarked upon appear in the second half of the seventeenth century. In his 1688 publication *The Kingdom of Darkness*, Nathanial Crouch wonders whether it 'may be proper to inquire into the nature of those large dark Rings in the Grass, which they call Fairy Circles, whether they be the Randezvous of Witches, or the dancing places of those little Puppet Spirits which they call Elves or Fairies'.[47] He then relates a story from Germany, and includes an image of women dancing with cloven-footed, horned beasts in a ring. These are described as 'satyrs'.[48] This reference shows a clear conflation between ideas of witches' sabbaths and fairy gatherings. A second reference, this time from a ballad of 1682, depicts an image of what appears to be a giant horned Devil standing at the centre of a group of dancing witches. However, this image is also common throughout the early modern period in depictions of Robin Goodfellow, a character commonly associated with mischievous elves and fairies.[49]

The confessions of John Walsh and Joan Willimott as well as visual representations in two texts from the 1680s, appear to be the only examples in English witchcraft print that imply a relationship between fairies and familiars. They suggest that fairies and familiars were not always clearly differentiated within the minds of contemporaries and that these folkloric beliefs could be confused. However, this seems to have been an uncommon confusion, as so few pamphlets from the early modern period mention it.[50]

Putting fairies to one side, we come to a second possible explanation for how beliefs about familiars originated. Sharpe has suggested that the familiar may have been 'a folklorised version of the demons and other denizens of the spiritual world that the learned magicians of the Middle Ages were meant to be able to raise'.[51] Sharpe does not argue in favour of either this explanation or for the one concerning fairies, pointing out that there is too little evidence to reach a conclusion. Instead, he suggests that both could have played a part. It is certainly possible that the 1563 Witchcraft Act may have been referencing this type of medieval, learned magic. We also see occasional references to learned magic being used to conjure familiar spirits in popular pamphlets. Returning to the example of John Walsh from 1566, we learn that John raised his familiar spirit with the help of wax candles and ritualistic circle magic.[52] In this one pamphlet both possible explanations for the origin of the familiar are visible: the familiar as a type of fairy and the familiar as a demonically conjured spirit. The occasional English pamphlet witch who supposedly conjured spirits was described differently from other witches and was seen to be performing a different type of magic. Doctor

John Lambe, for example, was indicted for conjuring and invoking evil and wicked spirits but it is never made clear whether or not these are familiars.[53] Lambe is atypical of most accused in that he acts more like a sorcerer or learned magician than a village witch. Lambe's supposed apprentice, Anne Bodenham, who was arrested for witchcraft in 1653, also engaged in learned magic and was believed to conjure her spirits with the aid of a book, circle magic and a crystal glass.[54] Anne's spirits, named Belzebub, Tormentor, Sathan and Lucifer, are decidedly devilish, eat crumbs sprinkled by Anne, dance in a circle with a cat and a dog, and, later, are transformed into the shape of animals. Although these creatures are conjured, they embody many of the traits attributed to familiar spirits. These isolated examples are the only ones in English pamphlet literature that suggest that familiars may have stemmed from beliefs about learned magic and conjuration. In the vast majority of pamphlets familiars are not conjured at all; they tend either to appear independently, to appear in reaction to witches losing control of their emotions or to be gifts or trades from other witches. They are nearly always described as tangible domestic or common animals.

Although both of the theories explained above have merit, neither appears wholly convincing, particularly given the lack of evidence in pamphlets, one of the key sources for understanding witchcraft belief. The answer may lie in the form of the familiar. The emphasis on the bestial nature of the familiar seems likely to stem from a much older understanding of the Devil's ability to take animal form. As Oldridge reminds us, the concept that the Devil could appear in corporeal form was not new but one that predated, and was challenged by, the Reformation.[55] Sharpe considers a similar explanation and suggests that the 'half-animal, half-demon' form of the familiar may have been inspired by classical stories of animal demons.[56] The belief that the Devil could appear in animal form was common during the late Middle Ages.[57] Both Judeo-Christian and pagan traditions depicted the Devil as a wide variety of animals: adders, apes or monkeys, asps, basilisks, bats, bears, bees, boars, bulls, camels, cats, centaurs, chimaeras, crocodiles, crows, deer, dogs, dragons, eagles, fish, flies, foxes, gnats, lizards, moles, ostriches, owls, phoenixes, pigs, ravens, roosters, salamanders, serpents, sheep, sparrows, spiders, stags, swallows, tigers, toads, tortoises, vultures, wasps, whales, wolves or worms.[58] Serpents (or dragons), goats and dogs were the most common of these.[59] The varied nature of these depictions may have, in some ways, inspired early modern descriptions of familiars. The belief that the Devil commonly took the form of a dog reminds us of the frequent references to dog familiars in early modern England. In the following sections I shall focus on the animalistic form of the familiar as well as its role in witchcraft narratives. The familiar's frequent appearance as an animal, combined with its definite role as a devil or agent of the same reinforces the possibility that its origins lie in the belief that the Devil was able to assume animal form.

The Familiar and the Demonic Pact

From the first writings on witchcraft as a new type of diabolical heresy in the early fifteenth century, the demonic pact was a fundamental element of early modern European witchcraft theology. In his 1437 *A Letter to all Inquisitors of Heretical Depravity*, Pope Eugenius IV stressed the importance of the satanic pact to a witch's ability to perform evil.[60] Johannes Nider's 1437 *Formicarius* followed similar lines as did other key works from the 1430s.[61] Although the diabolical pact stemmed from European witchcraft demonology, the concept was also circulating widely in England. The Protestant divine William Perkins devoted a chapter of his 1608 *Discourse of the Damned Art of Witchcraft* to the 'ground of witchcraft' in other words the 'league or covenant made between the Witch and the Devill'.[62] John Stearne expressed similar views in 1648 when he argued that 'before any [witches] can have power to doe any thing, against, or for any party, or have any desired ends effected, the league expresse or implicit is first made'.[63] But, in English witchcraft belief, the pact was not conducted strictly according to theology. Although English witches did meet with the Devil and enter into a pact with him (in doing so giving up their souls for magical, malefic powers), this Devil was not the fiend of the learned imagination but, rather, the familiar spirit of popular belief.

Stories of witches making pacts with small, tangible devils who often took the form of domestic animals highlight a merging of learned theology with popular belief. One pamphlet from 1589 underlines the importance of the familiar in forming the demonic pact and, in doing so, makes it clear how the pact was understood by many in early modern England. According to the anonymous pamphleteer, at about ten o'clock at night accused witch Joan Prentice was approached in her home by Bidd, a 'dunnish cullored ferret, having fiery eyes'.[64] Bidd tells Joan that he is Satan and that she must give him her soul.[65] Joan hesitates and asks how she can give away her soul when 'her soule is appertained onely unto Jesus Christ, by whose precious blood shedding it was bought'.[66] Unfazed, Bidd explains that if Joan gives him some of her blood Christ's claim will be overridden. Apparently satisfied, Joan agrees, and after Bidd sucks blood from Joan's finger, the pact is complete.

In this narrative, the demonic pact acts as a transformative moment, one in which Joan becomes a witch in league with the Devil. The familiar, as an agent of the Devil, performs the Devil's role and convinces Joan to stray away from Christ and give her soul to Satan. It is only through her agreement with a demonic agent that Joan is able to access supernatural powers. The making of the pact is a cornerstone of witchcraft narratives. In pamphlets, the pact was nearly always made at the first meeting between witch and Devil and was viewed as a necessary prerequisite for becoming a witch. In many narratives the pact is explicit but in others it is implied by the Devil's presence, by teats on the witch's body and by the witch's reliance on the Devil's assistance. A case from 1612 highlights a typical pact narrative:

> comming homeward from begging, there met her this Examinate [Elizabeth Sowtherns] neere unto a Stonepit in *Gouldshey*, in the sayd Forrest of *Pendle*, a Spirit or Devill in the shape of a Boy, the one halfe of his Coate blacke, and the other browne, who bade this Examinate stay, saying to her, that if she would give him her Soule, she should have any thing that she would request.[67]

This devil, whose name was Tibb, continued to visit Elizabeth to ask 'what she would have' and to suck her blood.[68] Although Tibb originally appeared in the shape of a boy, in later years he takes on the appearance of a brown dog.[69] The encounter between Elizabeth and the Devil, and Tibb's attempt to create a pact based on exchange, is seen as the catalyst for Elizabeth's turning to witchcraft.

A similar case, this time from 1645, also betrays the witch's initial hesitancy to abandon Christ. Joan Williford confessed:

> That the divell about seven yeeres agoe did appeare to her in the shape of a little dog, and bid her to forsake God and leane to him: who replied, that she was loath to forsake him. Shee confessed also that shee had a desire to be revenged upon *Thomas Letherland* and *Mary Woodrafe* now his wife. She further said that the divell promised her, that she should not lacke, and that she had money sometimes brought her she knew not whence, sometime one shilling, sometimes eight pence, never more at once; she called her Divell by the name of *Bunne* . . . She further saith, that neere twenty yeeres since she promised her soule to the divell. She further saith, that she gave some of her blood to the Divell, who wrote the covenant betwixt them. She further saith that the Divell promised to be her servant about twenty yeeres.[70]

Although this confession refers to a written covenant between witch and Devil (a relative rarity in English witchcraft pamphlets), the conditions of the pact remain the same.[71] Joan is initially loath to forsake Christ but is persuaded to do so through the Devil's promises of revenge and money. Pamphlets from 1658 and 1684 also label a witch's desire for wealth as a key motivator for her decision to join with the Devil.[72] Joan's confession not only highlights the role of the familiar as a demonic agent but also underlines a witch's reliance on the Devil. Joan explains that it has been twenty years since the Devil offered to be her servant for twenty years. As this time has now elapsed, the Devil has withdrawn his protection from Joan and, for this reason, she has been arrested for witchcraft. Without the Devil, Joan is powerless.

Many witches were described as being persuaded to enter into a demonic pact because of a desire for power, revenge or wealth.[73] In return for allegiance, the familiar spirit offered the witch the ability to have power, revenge, property, money or livestock. All of these rewards were made possible because of the witch's access to supernatural powers through a newly acquired familiar spirit. Accused witch Ellen Greene chose to give up her soul in order to have her familiar spirits carry out revenge:

> shee gave her soule to the Divell to have these spirits at her command; for a confirmation whereof, she suffered them to suck her alwayes as aforesaid about the change and full of the Moone.[74]

Instead of being approached directly by these spirits, Ellen was offered two familiars by fellow accused witch Joan Willimott. Ellen related that Joan persuaded her to forsake God and join with the Devil because she promised her two spirits.[75] Ellen agreed and was given a Kitlin called pusse and a Moldiwarp (a European mole) named hisse hisse.[76] Ellen did not make a pact with the Devil directly but with another witch who then gave her some spirits. Ellen's decision to give up her soul for these imps highlights the importance she placed on them, and suggests she viewed them as powerfully magical. Ellen allows the familiars to suck blood from her neck and then sends them to 'bewitch to death' two people who unwisely called her a witch.[77] The familiars are then sent to kill another two people.[78] Ellen kills these men and women instantly on receiving the familiars, suggesting that she had precisely this purpose in mind when she gave up her soul. Ellen's confession highlights the fundamental link between being able to perform witchcraft and owning familiar spirits.

   Pamphlets did not always describe the first meeting between witch and Devil or the making of a pact. Despite this, the pact was viewed as a necessary prerequisite for owning familiars and performing witchcraft. Although witches were often portrayed as beings whose power was firmly tied to familiars, many pamphleteers believed that witches had been tricked by the Devil and, rather than controlling a demonic creature, were actually servants of Satan:

> It seems to me that these vilde Spirits, which Witches have at command, and by their imployment are suffred to have power to hurt the bodyes of others, have a greater Power over them that set them a worke, for they doe not onely feed uppon them participating with the blood of humane flesh, for the redemption wherof Christ shed his owne precious blood, But it appeares that they have also power even over their Soules . . . [the witches] are lost for ever.[79]

Brian Levack has explored the changing nature of magic and witchcraft between the medieval and early modern periods and argued that 'the magician who was gradually being transformed into the witch became much more the servant than the master of the Devil'.[80] In giving their souls to Satan witches were believed to become his servants, or in the words of King James VI and I, his 'slaves'.[81] Not all pamphleteers referred explicitly to the demonic pact. However, nearly all witchcraft pamphlets refer to it implicitly through their references to familiars and to the Witch's Mark.[82] When looking for external signs of the demonic pact, examiners often looked for the Witch's Mark on the body of the witch. This mark is sometimes confused with the Devil's Mark, a spot on a witch's body thought to be insensible and incapable of bleeding. In certain parts of Europe the Devil's Mark was believed to be the sign of a witch and witches could be pricked to try and find this elusive spot.[83] This mark is hardly ever described in English witchcraft pamphlets.[84] Instead, witches were typically searched for the Witch's Mark, a teat-like protrusion that the familiar spirit was believed to suckle. This subtle change highlights the importance of the familiar in witchcraft beliefs. The Witch's Mark was a crucial part of the pact between familiar and witch as it allowed the familiar to easily suck the witch's blood in return for diabolical assistance.[85] Any person found with this mark was associated with familiars and, in turn, labelled a witch.

Familiar spirits were fundamental to witches' ability to hurt their neighbours and in many cases acted as agents of witches' wrath. This concept will be explored in depth in chapter 3 and so will be outlined only briefly here. One case from 1613 clearly demonstrates the link between the demonic pact and the witch's power to hurt others through a familiar spirit. In this narrative Master Enger's seven-year-old son enraged Mother Sutton and Mary Sutton by throwing rocks at Mary and calling her a witch. The two women vowed revenge:

> To effect their divellish purpose to the young childe of Master Enger, they called up their two Spirits whom [the witch] called Dicke and Jude and having given them sucke at their two Teats which they had on their thighs (found out afterwards by enquirie, and search of women) they gave them charge to strike the little boy, and to turne him to torment.[86]

This narrative makes it very clear that familiars willingly hurt people on behalf of witches, provided that those witches offer them blood in return. The witch's power is not her own but is supplied through her relationship with the familiar spirit.

It is important to take a step back and think about how these stories would have been interpreted by early modern men and women. The early modern culture of covenant theology and oath-taking can perhaps provide an insight. Given the post-Reformation English monarch's role as the head of the Church, loyalty to God and to the monarch were closely linked. As such, making a pact with the Devil did not only demonstrate a religious failing but also a political one. In a world in which declarations of allegiance to the monarch and to God were frequent, stories of witches swearing allegiance to the Devil would have been viewed as a complete rejection of Christian society.

Covenant theology, the belief in a conditional agreement or covenant between God and man which was entered into at baptism, was a key, hotly debated element of Puritan thought in early modern England.[87] Pacts with the Devil were a dark inverse of this godly theology. At least two witchcraft pamphlets from the seventeenth century and another two from the eighteenth referred to the demonic pact as a covenant.[88] Although demonic pacts are present in witchcraft narratives throughout the entire early modern period, the use of the word 'covenant' seems confined to pamphlets from the 1640s and beyond. This is not to say that these ideas and associations would not have been circulating earlier. James' 1604 Witchcraft Act specifically forbade men and women to 'consult covenant with entertaine employ feede or rewarde any evill and wicked Spirit to or for any intent or purpose'.[89] Perkins' treatise, appearing just four years later, warned of the dangers of making a league or covenant with the Devil.[90] Although covenant theology had been debated in England since the reign of Henry VIII, enshrined in English theology since the years of Edward VI, and further developed in the 1580s and 1590s, it was in the 1640s during the upheaval caused by the Civil Wars that its key role in official doctrine was really emphasised.[91] Similarly, although state oaths were common throughout the entire early modern period, they proliferated during the periods of the Civil Wars and the Restoration.[92] Out of the many, many religious debates between break-away religious and political groups during the 1640s, there emerged the notion that what was really key was a person's own agency in freely entering into a contract or covenant with God.[93] It is perhaps this emphasis on oaths and covenants throughout the early modern period, and especially during the 1640s, that inspired some accused witches or, indeed, encouraged certain pamphleteers to use words such as 'covenant', 'contract' or 'league' when describing witches entering into demonic pacts. For an early modern reader, these stories would have been intrinsically tied to ideas of loyalty to God and to the state and would have been read as the ultimate rejection of both religious and secular society.

The Shape of the Familiar

In his study of English trial records from 1530 to 1705, James Serpell found that familiars most commonly took the form of cats, dogs, toads, wild birds, poultry, moles and rats.[94] These forms, with the exception of wild birds and poultry, were all common to English witchcraft pamphlets. In pamphlet illustrations from 1566, 1579 and 1589, familiars were depicted as normal animals such as dogs, cats, lizards, toads and ferrets (figures 2.1, 2.2, 2.3 and 2.4). In one 1619 image, a woodcut depicts a cat, owl, rat and dog as

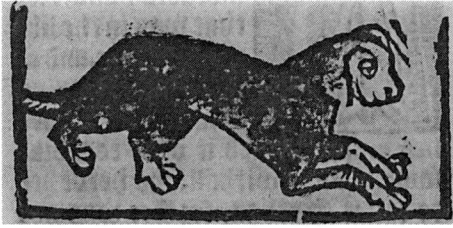

Figure 2.1 A dog, depicted in John Phillips, *The Examination and Confession of Certaine Wytches at Chelmsford in the Countie of Essex* (London: Printed by Willyam Powell for Willyam Pickeringe, 1566), sig. B3 v. © Lambeth Palace Library, 1587.12.03 f.11v.

Figure 2.2 A cat, depicted in John Phillips, *The Examination and Confession of Certaine Wytches at Chelmsford in the Countie of Essex* (London: Printed by Willyam Powell for Willyam Pickeringe, 1566), sig. A6 v. © Lambeth Palace Library, 1587.12.03 f.6v.

Figure 2.3 A lizard, depicted in John Phillips, *The Examination and Confession of Certaine Wytches at Chelmsford in the Countie of Essex* (London: Printed by Willyam Powell for Willyam Pickeringe, 1566), sig. B2 r. © Lambeth Palace Library, 1587.12.03 f.10r.

familiar spirits (figure 2.5). In a later 1655 pamphlet, the title page portrays familiars in the shape of an owl, a black bird and a cat (figure 2.6).

Although familiars generally appeared in the shape of normal, domestic animals, some were more exotic. A talking familiar with a head like an ape appeared at the foot of one witch's bed in 1618.[95] Another, although initially

Figure 2.4 Toad and ferret familiars, depicted in John Phillips, *The Examination and Confession of Certaine Wytches at Chelmsford in the Countie of Essex* (London: Printed by Willyam Powell for Willyam Pickeringe, 1566), title page, © Lambeth Palace Library, 1587.12.03.

Figure 2.5 Owl, dog, rat and cat familiars, depicted in Anon., *The Wonderful Discoverie of the Witchcrafts of Margaret and Phillip Flower, Daughters of Joan Flower Neere Bever Castle: Executed at Lincolne, March 11. 1618* (London: Printed by G. Eld for I. Barnes, 1619), title page. © The British Library Board, C.27.b.35, title pg.

described as a hedgehog, was complicated by the description that it was 'as soft as a Cat'.[96] Two more familiars, Grissell and Greedigut, were described as being 'in the shapes of dogges with great brisles of hogges haire upon their backs'.[97] One mole-like familiar appeared normal until it spoke in a hollow voice.[98] Similarly, cats tormenting a woman appeared rather mundane until they cried out like young children.[99] Others portrayed distinctly devilish characteristics, such as a dog with cloven feet.[100] Perhaps most sensational was the creature who chose to appear as a bear, horse, cow and even a dragon.[101] Some images also depicted these odd creatures. In 1566 the first ever witchcraft pamphlet included an image of a demonic dog with horns (figure 2.7). The frontispiece of Hopkins' *Discoverie of Witches* included an image of Vinegar Tom, a long, skinny dog-like creature with horns (figure 2.8). However, these hybrid creatures were not the norm and the vast majority of familiars hid their demonic nature by masquerading as everyday animals.

The familiar continued to be represented as an animalistic creature throughout the entire early modern period. But, from the 1640s onwards, there was more of a trend towards human devils. These man-like apparitions did not replace animal familiars but, instead, existed side-by-side, and were remarkably fluid (as will be discussed below). For an indication of this trend compare, for example, two pamphlets, one from 1619 and one

THE
Witch of the Woodlands :
Or, The
Coblers New Tranſlation ;
Written by *L. P.*
Here Robin the Cobler for his former evils,
Was puniſht worſt then Fauſtus was with de-
(vils.

London, Printed for *John Stafford*, dwelling at the Signe
of the *George* at *Fleet-bridge.* 1655.

Figure 2.6 Owl, black bird and cat familiars, depicted in L.P., *The Witch of the Woodlands: Or, The Coblers New Translation* (London: Printed for John Stafford, 1655), title page. © The Bodleian Libraries, The University of Oxford, Wood_704_ Tpage.

Figure 2.7 A demonic dog, depicted in John Phillips, *The Examination and Confession of Certaine Wytches at Chelmsford in the Countie of Essex* (London: Printed by Willyam Powell for Willyam Pickeringe, 1566), sig. 2A1 r. © Lambeth Palace Library, 1587.12.03 f. 13r.

Figure 2.8 A familiar in the shape of a long, skinny demonic dog, depicted in Matthew Hopkins, *The Discovery of Witches: In Answer to Severall Queries, Lately Delieved to the Judges of Assize for the County of Norfolk* (London: Printed for R. Royston, 1647), title page. © The Provost and Fellows of the Queen's College, Oxford, Sel.b.138(8) frontis.

from 1645. The 1619 pamphleteer writes that the Devil 'himselfe will attend [witches] in some familiar shape of Rat, Cat, Toad, Birde, Cricket etc'.[102] The 1645 pamphlet, on the other hand, explains that witches:

> ordinarily have a familiar, or spirit, which appeareth to them; sometimes in one shape, sometimes in another, as in the shape of a Man, Woman, Boy, Dogge, Cat, Foale, Fowle, Hare, Rat, Toad etc.[103]

It is not just these two pamphlets that suggest a change. Pamphlets from 1645, 1646, 1648, 1652, 1682, 1687, 1693, 1705 and 1712 also refer to familiars appearing in the shape of a man.[104] Even though these familiars take the shape of men, they are still very much conflated with familiars within these pamphlets. Although descriptions of the Devil as a man in English witchcraft were not especially frequent, they appear to have existed throughout the 1640s, 1650s, 1680s, 1690s and into the eighteenth century.

These devilish men are described as handsome, black, deformed, or a combination of all three. One exception to this is the 1652 pamphlet which, rather strangely, describes the Devil as appearing in the likeness of a lawyer with a long gown.[105] It was not unusual in medieval and early modern tales for the Devil to be described in human form.[106] A pamphlet from 1648 describes the Devil appearing 'in the shape of a young black man, standing by [the witch's] bed side'.[107] Another, published in 1693 but concerning a trial from 1664, explains how the Devil appeared to Alice Huson as a black man on a black horse, whereas a 1705 pamphlet simply referred to him as a 'tall Black man'.[108] Pamphlets from 1682 and 1687, both of which focus on the same three witches (Temperance Floyd, Mary Trembles and Susanna Edwards), also record descriptions of the Devil as a black man.[109] Temperance Floyd explains that a magpie who fluttered at her window was actually 'the black Man in the shape of the Bird'.[110] She also confesses to having 'familiarity' with the Devil in the shape of a black Man'.[111] Susanna Edwards refers to the Devil as 'a gentleman with black clothes'.[112] In some narratives it is difficult to tell whether witches are referring to the blackness of the Devil's skin or to his clothes. A 1648 pamphlet records Joane Wallis's confession that the Devil 'came to her in the likenesse of a man, in blackish cloathing . . . which she called Blackman'.[113] This confession was initially recorded in a 1646 Huntingdonshire pamphlet in which the Devil was said to introduce himself to Joane as 'Blackeman'.[114]

The description of the Devil as a black man is not confined to the 1640s, but seems to have first appeared in English witchcraft pamphlets during this decade. Representations of the Devil as a black man, or simply as a man with black clothes, were common in many European tales in the medieval and early modern periods.[115] It seems that witchcraft narratives incorporated these popular conceptions of the Devil. During the 1640s and in later decades, the Devil was sometimes described not only as black but also as having cloven feet. Joane Wallis confessed that Blackman had cloven feet and was 'more uglier then man'.[116] Alice Huson, whose devil appeared to her as a black man on a black horse also described the fiend's cloven feet.[117] In these confessions the Devil did not hide his true form beneath an animalistic or even human-like form; his demonic nature was openly displayed. Alice Huson was so overcome by the Devil's appearance on a horse that she 'fell down, and did Worship him upon my Knees'.[118] One of the strangest depictions of the Devil describes him as a tiny and playful man-like creature. This portrayal comes from Temperance Floyd who, in 1682, described her familiar as a black man who 'was about the length of her Arm: And that his Eyes were very big; and that he hopt or leapt in the way before her'.[119] In a second pamphlet Temperance builds on her earlier description. She claims that the first time the Devil appeared to her he was in the 'Shape of a comly Black Man' and his feet 'resemble those of an Oxe'.[120] Although these two descriptions differ, it was very common for witches to describe the Devil in numerous forms, a fact which points to the prevalence of beliefs about shape-shifting devils and familiar spirits. A second witch, whose confession was printed in 1693, similarly described the Devil as good-looking. Abre Grinset, alias Thrower, confessed that the first time she met the Devil he was 'in the form of a Pretty handsom Young Man [who] spake to her with a hollow Solemn Voice'.[121] In later encounters this Devil took the shape of a 'blackish Gray Cat or Kitling'.[122] Descriptions of familiars as both animals and men emphasise the mutability with which familiar spirits were described in popular witchcraft narratives.

The Fluidity of the Familiar

In popular pamphlets, the line between familiars and devils is extremely fine and difficult to navigate. It is often unclear whether a familiar in the shape of a man is a devil or a familiar. And if familiars are devils, what is the difference? Are familiars simply animals that perform the role of the Devil, are they the Devil himself or are they some form of lesser devil? These are questions that seem to bother modern historians far more than they ever did contemporaries. Witchcraft pamphlets often refer to 'the Devil', 'a devil', 'devils', 'familiars', 'imps', 'sprites', 'spirits' and 'familiar spirits' interchangeably. The way in which a familiar or devil is described often changes depending on the pamphlet. In this book, I adopt contemporary terminology and label familiars according to how they are described in pamphlets. For this reason, familiars are described as 'devils', 'imps' or 'sprites' or sometimes as the Devil, but not as 'demons'. Oldridge, who aptly describes the distinction between these terms as 'blurred', has suggested that 'in all probability, the distinction between Satan, demons and familiar spirits was much less important to the witnesses and accused in witch trials than they are to contemporary theologians or modern historians'.[123] As Oldridge points out, this was not a phenomenon confined to witchcraft pamphlets but was also visible in witchcraft plays and treatises.[124] Both James Sharpe and Emma Wilby have also commented on this 'conflation' in witches' narratives between the Devil and familiar spirits.[125]

One narrative which highlights the fluidity of descriptions of devils and familiars comes from a pamphlet of 1652. One evening Giles Fenderlyn, a man accused of witchcraft and murder, was sitting up with three men, when at about midnight he experienced a strange sight:

> There was such a thundering in the chimney, as if there had been a Drum beating: whereupon one *Rob Bull* looked out of the window,

and saw a man to his thinking walk up & down in the Ward-yard, who thinking it had been one of the servants in the house, called to him; but received no answer: and being Moon-light . . . he could perfectly discern the proportion of a man; save onely it had neither head nor armes.[126]

On seeing this apparition one of the men said, '*Certainly, this is a familiar*'.[127] The following night Giles was sitting up with three different men, when at midnight another apparition appeared, this time 'in the shape and likeness of a Dog, who leapt up on the said *Giles*: but he renounced it, saying, '*Avoid Sathan*'.[128] In this pamphlet, not only is the dog clearly identified as the Devil, but the more man-like apparition, which appears demonic, is labelled a familiar. This narrative reminds us that for many contemporaries the lines between devil and familiar spirit were not fixed but malleable. Familiar spirits were simultaneously viewed as demonic, as agents of the Devil and as the Devil himself.

Although familiars and devils were interchangeable in the vast majority of pamphlets, some pamphleteers did make a distinction between the Devil and familiars. In these rare cases, familiars were viewed as agents of the Devil. One 1612 Northamptonshire pamphlet demonstrates this distinction:

[Arthur Bill had] three Spirits to whom hee gave three speciall names, the Divell himself sure was godfather to them all, The first hee called Grissill, The other was named Ball, and the last Jacke, but in what . . . shapes they appeered unto him I cannot learne.[129]

In this narrative we see familiar spirits as decidedly demonic but as servants or minions of the Devil. In a similar case from 1705, Mary Phillips and Elinor Shaw confessed that when they were living together they made a contract with the Devil, who then sent them three imps. At the same time as the imps appeared the Devil also materialised in the shape of a tall black man and said that the imps would always be at the witches' service provided that they allowed them to 'Suck their Flesh every Night'.[130] The witches agreed and then had sexual intercourse with the man-like Devil.[131] Oldridge has pointed out that during the 1645 East Anglian trials, witches confessing to Matthew Hopkins sometimes drew distinctions between the Devil and their familiars. As is clear from these other narratives, this was not a phenomenon confined to the 1640s. In these rare cases the imps are very clearly agents of the Devil but are described as distinct from the Devil himself.

In the majority of witchcraft narratives, the Devil and the witch were viewed as separate but cooperating entities. However, in a small number of pamphlets the line between witch and familiar became blurred. In 1652 a pamphlet described how accused witch Joan Peterson bewitched a child and 'rock'd the Cradle in the likenesse of a Cat'.[132] While still in the shape of this cat, Joan terrified a baker who claimed that 'he never saw such a cat before, and hoped in God he should never see the like again'.[133] The pamphlet makes it clear that this animal is not meant to be a familiar but Joan herself in animal form. This is not an isolated occurrence. One pamphlet from 1693 describes the crimes of Alice Huson, a woman who was tried for witchcraft in 1664. During her confession, Alice explains that she overheard two women plotting while she was under the window in the form of a cat.[134] A third witch, Anne Bodenham, is described in a pamphlet of 1653 as being able to change into a cat as well as a mastiff, a black lion, a white Bear, a wolf, a horse, a bull and a calf.[135] In Nathanial Crouch's 1688 *The Kingdom of Darkness*, Anne is once again imagined as a cat.[136] Although Anne appeared in many shapes, the black cat seems to be her animal of choice.[137] In two 1712 pamphlets, both results of the controversy surrounding the last-minute reprieve of Jane Wenham, Francis Bragge describes Jane's frequent appearances as a cat. Anne Thorn and Anne Street, both of whom were tormented by Jane, repeatedly claim that Jane is appearing to them in the shape of a cat but with her own face.[138] To make this apparition worse, it frequently attempts to convince Anne Thorn to kill herself and even offers her a knife.[139] In this same preface, Bragge refers to the expectation from many that 'the Witch should turn herself into a Cat, that Cat into a Dog, that Dog into a Bear, that Bear into a Lion, and that Lion back into an Old Woman again'.[140] Although all of these narratives are from the late seventeenth or early eighteenth century, Edward Fairfax's *Daemonologia* demonstrates that this view was circulating much earlier. Fairfax claims that 'the changing of witches into hares, cats, and the like shapes, is so common as late testimonies and confessions approve unto us, that none but the stupidly incredulous can wrong the credit of the reporters, or doubt of the certainty'.[141] In just one example of this apparently common phenomenon, a 1579 pamphlet claims that accused witch Father Rosimonde 'can transforme himself by Divelishe meanes, into the shape and likenesse of any beaste whatsoever he will'.[142]

It was not just in England that witches were believed able to transform themselves into cats and other animals. This was a common trope in many European demonologies. Jean Bodin in his 1580 work retold the story of the witches of Vernon 'who usually gathered and assembled in an old ruined château, in the guise of a great number of cats'.[143] Four or five men who stayed the night in this place were attacked by the cats – one man was killed and the others injured – however, they did manage to maim some of their feline attackers. These cats were later found changed into wounded women. Similar accounts exist in the works of demonologists such as Martin del Rio, Nicolas Rémy and Francesco Maria Guazzo.[144] It is impossible to say whether these learned European ideas of witches transforming into cats influenced English witchcraft beliefs. In the above examples, the descriptions of feline transformations cannot be said to be wholly imposed by court officials. In the case of Alice Huson, the description seems to stem from her own confession. For Anne Bodenham it is her maid that claims she took this form and, in the case of Joan Peterson, three witnesses are all terrified by the appearance of a cat rocking the cradle but it is only in the pamphleteer's title page that this cat becomes the witch herself. It is impossible to ever be sure of the origins of these ideas, but it does seem that the concept that witches could turn into cats was circulating at a number of levels.

As Robert Darnton has famously demonstrated, cats took on a multiplicity of meanings in early modern Europe.[145] As is obvious from the numerous references in demonologies and witchcraft treatises, cats were suggestive of witchcraft and diabolism in the early modern period.[146] But they were also believed to possess occult powers independently of these ties, particularly in a French context.[147] Even today, cats are still associated with women and the feminine, often in terms of lewd, sexual metaphor as is demonstrated by the word "pussy," or "chat" in French.[148] There was also a culture of violence towards cats in early modern Europe, a practice definitely not unknown in England, and many believed that to maim or kill a cat was to strip it of its malevolent powers.[149] Keeping in mind these multiple associations, we can read the above narratives of English witches transforming into cats in multiple ways. They draw on learned demonologies but, given that many of those who claimed that witches appeared as cats were uneducated witnesses (three of the four are servants), these ideas were clearly also circulating at a popular level. Imagining the witch as a cat presented her as a malevolent, lewd creature that could legitimately be injured to protect oneself from evil.

It was not just cats into which witches were believed to transform. In 1648, John Stearne related the story of a dog that was beaten by a boy and then attacked by another dog. The boy beat the dog with 'two or three blowes over the back', and then the second dog 'bit [the first dog] on the neck, and gave him some shuckes'.[150] The injured dog ran away but, soon afterwards, an unnamed witch was 'found bitten on the neck, or bruised on the other parts in a most fearfull manner'.[151] A second case, reported in a 1693 pamphlet but taken from a Gloucester trial of 1649, also describes a witch who transformed herself into an animal. The pamphlet relates that a man in Teukesbury was concerned and confused because his Sow seemed 'to have great store of Milk, and yet the Pigs [were] almost Famished'.[152] The man concluded that something else must be drinking the sow's milk so he lay in wait to catch it. Sure enough, after some little time, the man saw 'a black Four-footed Creature like a Pole-Cat, come and beat away the Pigs, and suck the Sow'.[153] The farmer chased the cat and speared it through the thigh with a pitchfork. Soon after, a village witch was seen by neighbours, running from the farm while dripping blood. The neighbours caught her and, on searching, found that she was injured in exactly the same way as the polecat.[154] A third case from the 1640s describes John Palmer, a witch who transformed himself into a toad. While in toad form, John was kicked by a young man and 'immediately [John] *Palmer* complained of a sore shinne'.[155] In revenge for this mishap, John bewitched the man for many years to his 'great woe and torment'.[156] All three of these narratives not only demonstrate that some witches were believed to be able to turn themselves into animals but that any wounds delivered to the witch in animal form were believed to translate onto the body of the human witch.

The above narratives highlight that witches could be hurt while in animal form. In some pamphlets we see a related yet distinctly different belief: that the witch could be hurt when his or her familiar spirit was injured or killed. This sympathetic bond is rarely mentioned in pamphlets and, when it is, seems almost entirely confined to toad familiars.[157] In medieval and early modern Europe, toads were widely viewed as ugly, hateful and repulsive. They were believed to have powerful magical properties (not least because of the jewel or "toadstone" in their heads), they were sometimes thought of as malevolent spirits and they were commonly associated with evil, debauchery and sinful sexuality.[158] In relating stories of witches and toads, accused witches and witnesses were drawing on their understandings of toads and incorporating them into diabolical narratives of familiar spirits. A 1616 treatise on witchcraft tells the tale of Marie Smith who sent her familiars (a toad and several crabs) to Edmund Newton's shop, presumably to make mischief.[159] On seeing the toad, one of Edmund's servants picked it up and put it into the fire 'where it made a groaning noyse for one quarter of an houre before it was consumed'.[160] During this time '*Mary Smith* who sent it, did endure . . . torturing paines'.[161] Although Marie does not die, as her toad does, she is seriously injured and pained by the encounter. A pamphlet from the 1680s presents the act of throwing familiars in the fire as a common remedy against witchcraft. After angering Amy Duny, a woman who had the 'Reputation of a *Witch*', Dorothy Durent became concerned that her child was bewitched.[162] Dorothy consulted Doctor Jacob, a man reputed to be able to help the victims of witchcraft. Doctor Jacob advised Dorothy to hang the child's blanket in the chimney corner all day, and if anything appeared in it, she should not be afraid to throw it in the fire.[163] Dorothy followed Doctor Jacob's instructions, and on pulling down the blanket found a 'great Toad', which she held in the fire with tongs.[164] On being placed in the fire, the toad made a 'great and horrible Noise', and 'after a space there was a flashing in the Fire like Gun-powder, making a noise like the discharge of a Pistol', and the toad vanished.[165] The next day, Dorothy was told by a neighbour that Amy was in 'a most lamentable condition having her face all scorched with fire', as well as her legs and thighs.[166] Although these two cases are separated by almost seventy years, they are remarkably similar and suggest a blurring of the lines between witch and familiar spirit, and a belief in sympathetic magic.

The familiar spirit is omnipresent in pamphlet accounts of English witchcraft and was fundamental to a witch's ability to inflict harm on his or her neighbours. Through its association with the Devil, the familiar was able to capture a person's soul and convince them to pledge themselves to Satan. In return, these creatures gave the witch power, money and revenge, all of which witches were only able to access through their newly acquired supernatural powers. Familiars were an indispensable part of English witchcraft pamphlets. Their centrality encourages us to reconsider how important diabolical ideas were to contemporary understandings of English witchcraft. However, the ubiquity of the familiar in English witchcraft pamphlets does more than emphasise the role of the Devil; it also adds a personal element to the witch/Devil dynamic. In each of the above narratives, the witch has a personal relationship with the Devil, one that was changeable and often developed over many years. It was only through a witch's relationship with the Devil that he or she was able to act. Although many of the above narratives explore examples of *maleficium*, these vengeful actions would not have been possible without personal, diabolical assistance. This will be the focus of the next chapter. In the present chapter we have seen that the familiar, as the witch's personal helper, was able to provide demonic aid to help a witch take revenge. In doing so, I hope to have highlighted the centrality of familiar spirits to early modern English witchcraft, and to have encouraged a re-evaluation of the extent to which English witchcraft should be viewed as diabolical.

Notes

1 James Sharpe, *Witchcraft in Early Modern England* (Harlow: Longman, 2001), 64 and James Sharpe, "The Witch's Familiar in Elizabethan England," in *Authority and Consent in Tudor England: Essays Presented to C.S.L. Davies* (Farnham: Ashgate, 2002), 219–232.

2 This chapter builds on ideas first explored in a 2010 article, Charlotte Millar, "The Witch's Familiar in Sixteenth-Century England," *Melbourne Historical Journal* 38 (2010): 119–136. Other articles on the familiar include: Emma Wilby, "The Witch's Familiar and the Fairy in Early Modern England and Scotland," *Folklore* 111 (2000): 283–305; James A. Serpell, "Guardian Spirits or Demonic Pets: The Concept of the Witch's Familiar in Early Modern England, 1530–1712," in *The Human/Animal Boundary*, eds. A.N.H. Creager and W.C. Jordan (Rochester: University of Rochester Press, 2002), 157–190; Greg Warburton, "Gender, Supernatural Power, Agency and the Metamorphoses of the Familiar in Early Modern Pamphlet Accounts of English Witchcraft," *Parergon* 20 (2003): 95–118; Emma Wilby, *Cunning Folk and Familiar Spirits: Shamanistic Visionary Traditions in Early Modern British Witchcraft and Magic* (Brighton: Sussex Academic, 2005); Sharpe, "The Witch's Familiar in Elizabethan England," in *Authority and Consent in Tudor England* and James Sharpe, "Familiars," in *Encyclopedia of Witchcraft: The Western Tradition*, ed. Richard M. Golden (Santa Barbara, California: ABC-CLIO, 2006), 347–349. For a new piece which agrees with many of my conclusions and looks at the familiar spirit within a global context, see Chapter 10 in Ronald Hutton, *The Witch*, forthcoming with Yale University Press. I am grateful for the opportunity to read through this work prior to publication and for Professor Hutton's comments on this chapter.

3 Diane Purkiss, *Fairies and Fairy Stories: A History* (Stroud: Tempus, 2007), 165.

4 Barbara Rosen, *Witchcraft in England, 1558–1618*, 2nd edn. (Amherst: University of Massachusetts Press, 1991), 23.

5 Charles Zika, *The Appearance of Witchcraft: Print and Visual Culture in Sixteenth-Century Europe* (New York: Routledge, 2007), 188.

6 Garthine Walker, "The Strangeness of the Familiar: Witchcraft and the Law in Early Modern England," in *The Extraordinary and the Everyday in Early Modern England: Essays in Celebration of the Work of Bernard Capp*, eds. Angela McShane and Garthine Walker (New York: Palgrave Macmillan, 2010), 111.

7 Barry Reay, *Popular Cultures in England, 1550–1750* (London: Longman, 1997), 116.

8 James Sharpe, *Instruments of Darkness: Witchcraft in Early Modern England*, paperback edn. (Philadelphia: University of Pennsylvania Press, 1997); Robin Briggs, *Witches and Neighbours: The Social and Cultural Context of European Witchcraft* (London: HarperCollins, 1996); Marion Gibson, *Reading Witchcraft: Stories of Early English Witches* (London: Routledge, 1999); Clive Holmes, "Women, Witnesses and Witches," *Past and Present* 140 (1993): 45–78; Reay, *Popular Cultures in England*; and Wilby, *Cunning Folk and Familiar Spirits*. Keith Thomas is slightly more reticent about the role of familiars, warning that they were 'far from an indispensable feature of English witch-trials' but does, like later scholars, acknowledge their importance and peculiarity, *Keith Thomas, Religion and the Decline of Magic*, 1st edn. (London: Weidenfeld and Nicolson, 1971), 445–446.

9 Alan Macfarlane, *Witchcraft in Tudor and Stuart England: A Regional and Comparative Study*, 2nd edn. (London: Routledge, 1999), 18.

10 James Sharpe, "The Devil in East Anglia: The Matthew Hopkins Trials Reconsidered," in *Witchcraft in Early Modern Europe: Studies in Culture and Belief*, eds. Jonathan Barry, Marianne Hester and Gareth Roberts (Cambridge: Cambridge University Press, 1996), 248.

11 Sharpe, "The Witch's Familiar in Elizabethan England," in *Authority and Consent in Tudor England*; Sharpe, *Instruments of Darkness*, 71–74; Sharpe, *Witchcraft in Early Modern England*, 62–64.

12 Sharpe, "The Witch's Familiar in Elizabethan England," 220.

13 Wilby, "The Witch's Familiar and the Fairy," and Wilby, *Cunning Folk and Familiar Spirits*.

14 Deborah Willis, *Malevolent Nurture: Witch-Hunting and Maternal Power in Early Modern England* (Ithaca: Cornell University Press, 1995).

15 Serpell, "Guardian Spirits or Demonic Pets," and Warburton, "Gender, Supernatural Power, Agency and the Metamorphoses of the Familiar," 95–118.

16 Millar, "The Witch's Familiar in Sixteenth-Century England," 119–136. See also, Millar, "Sleeping with Devils: The Sexual Witch in Seventeenth-Century England," in *Supernatural and Secular Power in Early Modern England*, eds. Marcus Harmes and Victoria Bladen (Farnham: Ashgate, 2015), 207–231.

17 These are: Anon., *A Magazine of Scandall* (London: for R.H., 1642); Anon., *Strange and Wonderful News From Yowel in Surry* (London: Printed for J. Clarke, 1681); and Anon., *A Full and True Account of the Apprehending and Taking of Mrs Sarah Moordike* (London: Printed for John Alkin, 1701).

18 Pamphlets that mention the Devil but do not mention the presence of a familiar spirit are: Anon., *A Most Certain, Strange and True Discovery of a Witch* (London: Printed by John Hammond, 1643); Anon., *Signes and Wonders from Heaven* (London: Printed by I.H., 1645); Anon., *The Power of Witchcraft* (London: Printed for Charls Tyns, 1662); Anon., *Great News from the West of England* (London: Printed by T.M., 1689); and Anon., *A Full and True Account of the Tryal, Examination, and Condemnation of Mary Johnston, a Witch* (London: Printed by T. Bland, 1706).

19 It is extremely difficult to calculate the percentage of trials in which familiars featured given the loss of records. For more on this, see Cecil L'Estrange Ewen, *Witchcraft and Demonianism*, 2nd edn. (New York: AMS Press, 1984);

Macfarlane, *Witchcraft in Tudor and Stuart England*, 2nd edn. (London: Routledge, 1999), 25 and Sharpe, *Instruments of Darkness*, 107–119.

20 Thomas, *Religion and the Decline of Magic*, 2nd edn., 537.
21 Sharpe, "The Devil in East Anglia," 248.
22 Ibid.
23 Sharpe, "Familiars," in *The Encyclopedia of Witchcraft: The Western Tradition*, 348.
24 For a detailed examination of English witchcraft and the legal process, see Garthine Walker, "The Strangeness of the Familiar," in *The Extraordinary and the Everyday in Early Modern England: Essays in Celebration of the Work of Bernard Capp*, eds. Angela McShane and Garthine Walker (New York: Palgrave MacMillan, 2010), 105–124.
25 "An Act Against Conjurations, Enchantments and Witchcrafts," 1563 5 Eliz I c. 16, in *Witchcraft and Society in England and America, 1550–1750*, ed. Marion Gibson (Ithaca: Cornell University Press, 2003), 4.
26 For a useful chart which outlines punishments for specific witchcraft acts by statute see Macfarlane, *Witchcraft in Tudor and Stuart England*, 2nd edn., 15.
27 Walker, "The Strangeness of the Familiar," 111.
28 Sharpe, "The Devil in East Anglia," 250, fn. 37 and C.L. Ewen, *Witchcraft and Demonianism*, 73
29 "An Act Against Conjuration, Witchcraft and Dealing with Evil and Wicked Spirits," 1604, 1 Jas. I c. 12," in *Witchcraft and Society in England and America*, ed. Marion Gibson (Ithaca: Cornell University Press, 2003), 5.
30 Walker, "The Strangeness of the Familiar," 113.
31 Oldridge, *The Devil in Tudor and Stuart England*, 167.
32 Anon., *The Wonderful Discoverie of the Witchcrafts of Margaret and Phillip Flower* (London: Printed for G. Eld by I. Barnes, 1619), sigs. C4 v-D1 r. See also George Gifford, *A Dialogue Concerning Witches and Witchcraftes* (London: Printed by John Windet for Tobie Cook and Mihil Hart, 1593), 22–23.
33 Diane Purkiss, *Troublesome Things: A History of Fairies and Fairy Stories* (London: Penguin, 2000); Diane Purkiss, "Fairies," in *The Encyclopedia of Witchcraft: The Western Tradition*, ed. Richard M. Golden (Santa Barbara, California: ABC-CLIO, 2006), 346; Wilby, *Cunning Folk and Familiar Spirits*, 17–25; Sharpe, "Familiars," in *The Encyclopedia of Witchcraft*, 349; Peter Marshall "Protestants and Fairies in Early-Modern England," in *Living with Religious Diversity in Early-Modern Europe*, eds. Scott Dixon, Dagmar Freist and Mark Greengrass (Farnham: Ashgate, 2009), 139–159; and Darren Oldridge, "Fairies and Devils in Early Modern England," *The Seventeenth Century* (2016): 1–15.
34 Wilby, *Cunning Folk and Familiar Spirits*, 19.
35 Purkiss, *Fairies and Fairy Stories*, 168.
36 See the detailed data on names of familiars compiled by Barbara Rosen and James Serpell. Rosen, *Witchcraft*, 1st edn. (London: Edward Arnold, 1969), 396, reprinted in Rosen, *Witchcraft in England*, 2nd edn., 396; Serpell, "Guardian Spirits or Demonic Pets," 175.
37 Diane Purkiss, *The Witch in History: Early Modern and Twentieth-Century Representations* (London: Routledge, 1996), 135.
38 Purkiss, *The Witch in History*, 135.
39 Oldridge, "Fairies and Devils in Early Modern England," 7.
40 Wilby, "The Witch's Familiar," 295; Purkiss, *Fairies and Fairy Stories*, 165–169.
41 For a few rare examples of familiars being fed milk, see W.W., *A True and Just Recorde, of the Information, Examination and Confession of All the Witches* (London: Printed by Thomas Dawson, 1582) and Anon., *A Rehearsal Both Straung and True, of Heinous and Horrible Actes Committed By Elizabeth Stile*

   alias Rockingham, Mother Dutten, Mother Devell, Mother Margaret, Fower Notorious Witches (London: Printed by J. Kingston for Edward White, 1579).

42 Purkiss, *Fairies and Fairy Stories*, 169.

43 Anon., *The Examination of John Walsh Before Maister Thomas Williams* (London: Printed by John Awdely, 1566), sigs. A4 v-A5 r.

44 Ibid., sig. A5 r.

45 Ibid., sig. A5 v.

46 Anon., *The Wonderful Discoverie of the Witchcrafts of Margaret and Phillip Flower* (London: Printed by G. Eld for I. Barnes 1619), sig. E3 v.

47 Nathanial Crouch, *The Kingdom of Darkness* (London: Printed for Nath. Crouch, 1688), 56.

48 Ibid., 57.

49 See, for example, Anon., *The Merry Pranks of Robin Goodfellow* (London: Printed by and for W.Q, date unknown).

50 Emma Wilby has found additional evidence of this confusion in Scottish witch trials and pamphlets. This suggests that the link between witchcraft, familiars and fairies may have been stronger in Scotland than in England. Wilby, *Cunning Folk and Familiar Spirits*.

51 Sharpe, "The Witch's Familiar in Elizabethan England," 227.

52 Anon., *The Examination of John Walsh*, sig. A5 r.

53 See Anon., *A Brief Description of the Notorious Life of Doctor John Lambe* (Amsterdam [London]: G.E. Miller, 1628). For more on John Lambe's life, see Alastair Bellany, "The Murder of John Lambe: Crowd Violence, Court Scandal and Popular Politics in Early Seventeenth-Century England," *Past and Present* 200 (2008): 37–76; Karin Amundsen, "The Duke's Devil and Doctor Lambe's Darling: A Case Study of the Male Witch in Early Modern England," *Psi Sigma Journal* (2004): 29–60; Leba M. Goldstein, "The Life and Death of John Lambe," *Guildhall Studies in London History* 4 (1979): 19–32; Malcolm Gaskill, "Witchcraft, Politics, and Memory in Seventeenth-Century England," *The Historical Journal* 50 (2007): 289–308; and Charlotte-Rose Millar, "Witchcraft and Deviant Sexuality: A Case Study of Doctor Lambe," in *The British World: Religion, Memory, Society, Culture*, eds. Marcus Harmes, Lindsay Henderson, Barbara Harmes and Amy Antonio (Toowoomba: University of Southern Queensland, 2012), 51–62.

54 See Crouch, *The Kingdom of Darkness*, 10–18; Edmond Bower, *Doctor Lambe Revived or Witchcraft Condemned in Anne Bodenham* (London: Printed by T. W., 1653); James Bower, *Doctor Lambe's Darling* (London: Printed for G. Horton, 1653). See also Gaskill, "Witchcraft, Politics, and Memory in Seventeenth-Century England" and Elizabeth J. Kent, "Turning off the Witch," in *Hearing Places: Sound, Place, Time and Culture*, eds. Ros Bandt, Michelle Duffy and Dolly MacKinnon (Newcastle: Cambridge Scholars Publishing, 2007), 268–275.

55 Darren Oldridge, *The Devil in Early Modern England* (Stroud: Sutton, 2000), 16–17.

56 Sharpe, *Witchcraft in Early Modern England*, 62 and 63.

57 Oldridge, *The Devil in Early Modern England*, 17.

58 Jeffrey Burton Russell, *Lucifer: The Devil in the Middle Ages* (Ithaca: Cornell University Press, 1984), 67.

59 Ibid.

60 Pope Eugenius IV, *A Letter to All Inquisitors of Heretical Depravity* (1437) in *Witchcraft in Europe 400–1700: A Documentary History*, eds. Alan Charles Kors and Edward Peters, 2nd edn. (Philadelphia: University of Pennsylvania Press, 2001), 154.

61 Johannes Nider, "The Formicarius," in *Witchcraft in Europe 400–1700: A Documentary History*, eds. Alan Charles Kors and Edward Peters, 2nd edn.

(Philadelphia: University of Pennsylvania Press, 2001), 155–159; Claude Tholosan, "Ut Magnorum et Maleficiorum Errores," in *Witchcraft in Europe 400–1700: A Documentary History,* eds. Alan Charles Kors and Edward Peters, 2nd edn. (Philadelphia: University of Pennsylvania Press, 2001), 162–166 and Anon., "The Errores Gazariorum," in *Witchcraft in Europe 400–1700: A Documentary History,* eds. Alan Charles Kors and Edward Peters, 2nd edn. (Philadelphia: University of Pennsylvania Press, 2001), 159–162.

62 William Perkins, *A Discourse of the Damned Art of Witchcraft: So Far Forth as It Is Revealed in Scriptures and Manifest by True Experience* (Cambridge: Printed by Cantrel Legge, 1608), 41–42.

63 John Stearne, *A Confirmation and Discovery of Witchcraft,* 10. For more on the pact between witch and Devil, see chapter 2, this volume.

64 Anon., *The Apprehension and Confession of Three Notorious Witches* (London: E. Allde, 1589), sig. B1 r.

65 Ibid., sig. B1 v.

66 Ibid.

67 Thomas Potts, *The Wonderfull Discoverie of Witches in the Countie of Lancaster* (London: Printed by W. Stansby for John Barnes, 1613), sig. B2 v.

68 Ibid., sigs. B2 v–B3 r.

69 Ibid., sig. B3 r.

70 Anon., *The Examination, Confession, Triall, and Execution, of Joane Williford, Joan Cariden, and Jane Hott* (London: Printed for J.G., 1645), 1.

71 For other pamphlets which refer to written covenants, see, for example, the case of Mrs Mary Hicks who signed her covenant with the Devil in her own blood, Anon., *The Whole Trial and Examination of Mrs Mary Hicks and Her Daughter, Elizabeth* (London: Printed by W. Matthews, 1716), 3, or the story of Lydia Rogers who cut a vein in her right hand to make a pact with the Devil, Anon., *The Snare of the Devil Discovered: Or, a True and Perfect Relations of the Sad and Deplorable Condition of Lydia the Wife of John Rogers* (London: Printed for Edward Thomas, 1658), title page, or the tale of the male witch John Palmer who was commanded by the Devil to write his mark on the ground, B. Misodaimon, *The Divels Delusions* (London: Printed for Richard Williams, 1649), 4, or even the witch who made her written covenant with the Devil through a Jesuit, Anon., *The Tryal and Examination of Mrs Joan Peterson* (London: Printed for G. Horton, 1652), sigs. A2 r–A2 v.

72 Anon., *The Snare of the Devil Discovered,* title page; Anon., *Strange and Dreadful News* (London: Printed for D.W.), title page.

73 The importance of revenge in witchcraft narratives will be discussed in chapter 3, this volume.

74 Anon., *The Wonderful Discoverie of the Witchcrafts of Margaret and Phillip Flower,* sig. F2 v.

75 Ibid.

76 Ibid.

77 Ibid., sig. F2 r.

78 Ibid.

79 Anon., *The Witches of Northampton-shire* (London: Printed by Tho: Parfoot, for Arthur Johnson, 1612), sigs. C4 v–D1 r.

80 Levack, *The Witch-hunt in Early Modern Europe,* 3rd edn. (Harlow: Longman, 2006), 40, see also Philip Almond, *The Devil: A New Biography* (Ithaca: Cornell University Press, 2014), 97.

81 King James VI, *Daemonologie,* 1597, ed. G.B. Harrison (London: John Lane, 1924), 9.

82 For more on historical understandings of implicit and explicit pacts see Levack, *The Witch-hunt in Early Modern Europe*, 3rd edn., 37–40; Sarah Ferber, "Body of the Witch," in *The Encyclopedia of Witchcraft: The Western Tradition*, ed. Richard M. Golden (Santa Barbara, California: ABC-CLIO, 2006), 131–133; William Monter, "Devil's Mark," in *The Encyclopedia of Witchcraft: The Western Tradition*, ed. Richard M. Golden (Santa Barbara, California: ABC-CLIO, 2006), 275–277; Vincenzo Lavenia, "Witch's Mark," in *Encyclopedia of Witchcraft: The Western Tradition*, ed. Richard M. Golden (Santa Barbara, California: ABC-CLIO, 2006), 1220–1221.

83 See, for example, Nicolas Rémy, *Demonolatry: An Account of the Historical Practice of Witchcraft* (1595), trans. E.A. Ashwin, ed. Montague Summers (London: J. Rodker, 1930), Book 1, Chapter 5.

84 For a rare example, see Anon., *Great News from the West of England*, 2. For more on the conflation and distinction between the Witch's Mark and the Devil's Mark, see Almond, *The Devil*, 138–140.

85 Chapter 4, this volume, will explore the sexual and maternal connotations of this relationship.

86 Anon., *Witches Apprehended, Examined and Executed* (London: for Edward Marchant, 1613), sig. C1 v.

87 For more on covenant theology, see Leonard J. Trinterud, "The Origins of Puritanism," *Church History* 20 (1951): 37–57; Lyle D. Bierma, "The Role of Covenant Theology in Early Reformed Orthodoxy," *The Sixteenth Century Journal* 20 (1990): 453–462; Karl Gunther, "The Origins of English Puritanism," *History Compass* 4 (2006): 235–240; and David Weir, *The Origins of the Federal Theology in Sixteenth Century Reformation Thought* (Oxford: Clarendon Press, 1990).

88 Anon., *The Whole Trial and Examination of Mrs Mary Hicks*; Francis Bragge, *A Full and Impartial Account of the Discovery of Sorcery and Witchcraft Practis'd by Jane Wenham of Walkerne in Hertfordshire* (London: Printed for E. Curll, 1712); Anon., *A True Relation of the Arraignment of Eighteen Witches* (London: Printed by I. H., 1645); and Anon., *The Tryal and Examination of Mrs Joan Peterson*.

89 "An Act Against Conjuration, Witchcraft and Dealing with Evil and Wicked Spirits," 1604, 1 Jas. I c. 12," in *Witchcraft and Society in England and America*, 5.

90 Perkins, *A Discourse of the Damned Art of Witchcraft*, 41–42.

91 Trinterud, "The Origins of Puritanism," 38–39, 44, 48–49 and 51–52.

92 Caroline Robbins, "Selden's Pills: State Oaths in in England 1558–1714," *Huntington Library Quarterly* 35 (1972): 303 and 311–313 and John Spurr, "Perjury, Profanity and Politics," *The Seventeenth Century* 8 (1993): 29. See also David Martin Jones, *Conscience and Allegiance in Seventeenth Century England: The Political Significance of Oaths and Engagements* (New York: University of Rochester Press, 1999), especially chapter 3.

93 Trinterud, "The Origins of Puritanism," 53.

94 Serpell, "Guardian Spirits or Demonic Pets," 169.

95 Anon., *The Wonderful Discoverie of the Witchcrafts of Margaret and Phillip Flower*, sig. G1 r.

96 Anon., *The Examination, Confession, Triall, and Execution, of Joane Williford, Joan Cariden, and Jane Hott*, 4.

97 John Davenport, *The Witches of Huntingdon, Their Examinations and Confessions Exactly Taken by His Majesties Justices of Peace for That County* (Printed by W. Wilson for Richard Clutterbuck, 1646), 12.

98 John Stearne, *A Confirmation and Discovery of Witch-craft* (London: Printed by William Wilson, 1648), 28.

99 Bragge, *A Full and Impartial Account*, 17.

100 Stearne, *A Confirmation and Discovery*, 31.

101 Mary Moore, *Wonderful News from the North* (London: Printed by T.H., 1650), 5.

102 Anon., *The Wonderful Discoverie of the Witchcrafts of Margaret and Phillip Flower*, sigs. B3 r-v.

103 Anon., *The Lawes Against Vvitches, and Conivration* (London: Printed for R.W, 1645), 4.

104 H.F., *A True and Exact Relation of the Several Informations, Examinations, and Confessions of the Late Witches, Arraigned and Executed in the County of Essex* (London: Printed by M.S. for Henry Overton, and Benj. Allen, 1645); Anon., *The Lawes Against Witches*; Davenport, *The Witches of Huntingdon*; Stearne, *A Confirmation and Discovery of Witchcraft*; Anon., *The Tryall and Examination of Mrs. Joan Peterson*; Anon., *A True and Impartial Relation of the Informations Against Three Witches* (London: Printed by Freeman Collins, 1682); Anon., *The Life and Conversation of Temperance Floyd, Mary Lloyd, and Susanna Edwards* (London: Printed by J.W., 1687); Samuel Petto, *A Faithful Narrative of the Wonderful and Extraordinary Fits Which Mr. Tho. Spatchet (Late of Dunwich and Cookly) was under by Witchcraft* (London: Printed for John Harris, 1693); Matthew Hale, *A Collection of Modern Relations of Matter of Fact Concerning Witches and Witchcraft* (London: Printed for John Harris, 1693); Ralph Davis, *An Account of the Tryals, Examination and Condemnation of Elinor Shaw and Mary Phillip's (Two Notorious Witches)* (London: Printed for P. Thorn, 1705); and Bragge, *A Full and Impartial Account of the Discovery of Sorcery and Witchcraft*.

105 Anon., *The Tryal and Examination of Mrs Joan Peterson*, 5.

106 Russell, *Lucifer: The Devil in the Middle Ages*, 68.

107 Stearne, *A Confirmation and Discovery*, 29.

108 Hale, *A Collection of Modern Relations*, 58; Davis, *An Account of the Tryals*, 6.

109 Anon., *A True and Impartial Relation of the Informations Against Three Witches*; Anon., *The Life and Conversation of Temperance Floyd, Mary Lloyd, and Susanna Edwards*.

110 Anon., *A True and Impartial Relation of the Informations Against Three Witches*, 12.

111 Ibid., 13.

112 Ibid., 36.

113 Stearne, *A Confirmation and Discovery of Witchcraft*, 13.

114 Davenport, *The Witches of Huntingdon*, 12.

115 Russell, *Lucifer: The Devil in the Middle Ages*, 68–69.

116 Stearne, *A Confirmation and Discovery of Witchcraft*, 13.

117 Hale, *A Collection of Modern Relations*, 58. For the common belief that the Devil rode a black horse, see Russell, *Lucifer: The Devil in the Middle Ages*, 69.

118 Hale, *A Collection of Modern Relations*, 58.

119 Anon., *A True and Impartial Relation of the Informations Against Three Witches*, 15.

120 Anon., *The Life and Conversation of Temperance Floyd, Mary Lloyd, and Susanna Edwards*, 2.

121 Petto, *A Faithful Narrative*, 18.

122 Ibid.

123 Oldridge, *The Devil in Early Modern England*, 140.

124 Oldridge, *The Devil in Tudor and Stuart England*, 168–170.

125 Sharpe, *Instruments of Darkness*, 74; Wilby, "The Witch's Familiar," 284, 287.

126 Anon., *The Tryall and Examination of Mrs Joan Peterson*, 6.

127 Ibid.

128 Ibid.

129 Anon., *The Witches of Northampton-shire*, sig. C3 v.
130 Davis, *An Account of the Tryals*, 6.
131 Ibid. For more on the sexual relationship between witches and devils see chapter 4, this volume.
132 Anon., *The Witch of Wapping: Or an Exact and Perfect Relation, of the Life and Devilish Practices of Joan Peterson, That Dwelt in Spruce Island, near Wapping* (London: Printed for Th. Spring, 1652), title page.
133 Ibid., 6.
134 Hale, *A Collection of Modern Relations*, 58.
135 Bower, *Doctor Lamb's Darling*, 7.
136 Crouch, *The Kingdom of Darkness*, 14.
137 Ibid., 5.
138 Bragge, *A Full and Impartial Account*, 29, 32 and 36.
139 Bragge, *A Full and Impartial Account*, 36 and Bragge, *Witchcraft Farther Display'd*, introduction.
140 Bragge, *A Full and Impartial Account*, preface.
141 Edward Fairfax, *Daemonologia: A Discourse on Witchcraft as It Was Acted in the Family of Mr Edward Fairfax, of Fuyston, in the County of York, in the Year 1621*, ed. William Grainge (Harrogate: R. Ackrill, 1882), 97. Fairfax goes on to make it clear that this is not a real transformation but one that is an illusion through which the Devil tricks the witch and witnesses, see 97–98.
142 Anon., *A Rehearsal Both Straung and True*, sig. A5 r.
143 Jean Bodin, *On the Demon-Mania of Witches*, trans. Randy A. Scott, ed. Jonathan Pearl (Toronto: Centre for Reformation and Renaissance Studies, 1995), Book 2.6, 123–4.
144 Martin del Rio, *Investigations into Magic*, trans. P.G. Maxwell Stuart (Manchester: Manchester University Press, 2000), Book 2.18, 100; Nicolas Rémy, *Demonolatry*, trans. E.A. Ashwin, ed. Montague Summers (New York: University Books, 1974), Book 1. xiii, 51–2, Book 2. vii, 99 and Book 2.5, 108–109; and Francesco Maria Guazzo, *Compendium Maleficarum*, trans. E.A. Ashwin, ed. Montague Summers (New York: University Books, 1974), Book 2.18, 100.
145 Robert Darnton, "The Great Cat Massacre," *History Today* August (1984): 7–15.
146 For another example, see David Cressy, "Agnes Bowker's Cat: Childbirth, Seduction, Bestiality and Lies," chapter 1 in *Travesties and Transgressions in Early Modern England* (Oxford: Oxford University Press, 2000), 9–28.
147 Darnton, "The Great Cat Massacre," 12.
148 Ibid., 13.
149 Ibid., 10–12.
150 Stearne, *A Confirmation and Discovery of Witchcraft*, 19.
151 Ibid.
152 Hale, *A Collection of Modern Relations Concerning Witches and Witchcraft*, 51.
153 Ibid.
154 Ibid., 52.
155 B. Misodaimon, *The Divels Delusions*, 5.
156 Ibid.
157 Toads were also associated with witchcraft in early modern Normandy; see William Monter, "Toads and Eucharists: The Male Witches of Normandy, 1564–1660," *French Historical Studies* 20 (1997): 563–595. Fascinatingly, a 1914 article on magic in Kentucky details how witches were believed able to transform themselves into black cats and toads, and were able to be injured in these forms: Josiah Henry Combs, "Sympathetic Magic in the Kentucky Mountains: Some Curious Folk Survivals," *The Journal of American Folklore* 27 (1914): 328–330.

158 See Marty Crump, *Eye of Newt and Toe of Frog, Adder's Fork and Lizard's Leg: The Lore and Mythology of Amphibians and Reptiles* (Chicago: University of Chicago Press, 2015); Keith Thomas, *Man and the Natural World: Changing Attitudes in England, 1500–1800*, 2nd edn. (Oxford: Oxford University Press, 1996); and Martha R. Baldwin, "Toads and Plague: Amulet Therapy in Seventeenth-Century Medicine," *Bulletin of the History of Medicine* 67 (1993): 227–247.

159 Alexander Roberts, *A Treatise of Witchcraft: Wherein sundry Propositions are Laid Downe, Plainely Discouering the Wickednesse of That Damnable Art, with Diuerse Other Speciall Points Annexed, Not Impertinent to the Same, Such as Ought Diligently of Euery Christian to Be Considered* (London: Printed by N[icholas] O[kes] for Samuel Man, 1616), 57–61.

160 Ibid., 58.

161 Ibid.

162 Anon., *A Tryal of Witches at the Assizes Held at Bury St. Edmonds for the County of Suffolk; on the Tenth day of March, 1664* (London: Printed for William Shrewsbery, 1682), 4.

163 Ibid., 5–6.

164 Ibid., 6.

165 Ibid. Later in this pamphlet a child claims to have seen a mouse which no one else can see. On throwing this mouse into the fire, there is a flash of gunpowder. Anon., *A Tryal of Witches at the Assizes*, 28.

166 Ibid., 7–8. This narration is repeated in Francis Bragge's 1712 retelling of the case, Bragge, *Witchcraft Farther Display'd*, 2 and in a 1716 retelling, Anon., *A Tryal of Witches at the Assizes* (London: Printed for D. Brown, J. Walthoe, and M. Wotton, 1716), 80. Bragge relates that the affected child was well after the toad was burnt.

3 Anger, Malice and Emotional Control

In early modern England witches were viewed as malicious, dangerous men and women who failed to properly regulate their emotions. Accused witches were often portrayed in popular pamphlets as impoverished, once-powerless people who, through their pact with the Devil were able to draw on diabolical power to act on their desires. This chapter explores the importance of the Devil in allowing witches to act on their anger and malice. The first section will begin by revisiting the well-known trope of the malicious and vengeful English witch and, in doing so, emphasise the importance of the Devil's role in allowing witches to act on their vengeful desires. This will be combined with a discussion of women's anger and ideas of revenge in early modern England. The second section will continue this discussion of anger but focus on the importance of the control of one's anger in early modern England. In exploring six cases in which the Devil appears to a potential witch specifically because of her lack of emotional control, this chapter demonstrates the strong links between anger, lack of control, and diabolical association. Finally, the chapter ends with a discussion of how familiar spirits were portrayed in print as physical manifestations of a witch's rage, hatred and malice. Here I will explain how familiars performed a dual role, a duality related to their two origins: they were devils from hell sent *to* the witch to tempt her, and they were also external embodiments of witches' internal thoughts and desires, sent *from* her to act out those desires and thoughts in the world. Ultimately, this chapter stresses the links between witchcraft, the Devil, and emotional control and does so by describing how emotions led men and women to enter into a pact with the Devil; to draw on the aid of familiar spirits; and to use these spirits to take revenge on their neighbours.

The Vengeful and Malicious Witch

Of the twenty-three witchcraft pamphlets published between 1566 and 1645, only one fails to refer to witches as malicious, vengeful men and women and/or to label revenge, malice, rage, anger or hate as either the primary, or one of the primary reasons, for a witch's decision to perform *maleficium*.[1] With only three exceptions, every single one of these pamphlets links a witch's ability to take revenge on her neighbours to the power provided by her diabolical spirits.[2] Although references to vengeful and malicious witches exist throughout the entire early modern period, post-1645 these references begin to decrease. They are almost impossible to find in pamphlets from the 1650s and 1660s and it is not until the 1670s and 1680s that we again find the kinds of developed instances of rage, malice and revenge so prevalent in earlier decades – although these are by no means omnipresent.[3] Although revenge narratives are relatively uncommon in the third quarter of the seventeenth century, on entering the eighteenth century we find that they re-emerge strongly, so much so that every single eighteenth-century pamphlet references a witch's malice and desire for revenge as the primary, or one of the primary, motivations for witchcraft acts. It is possible that the decline in revenge narratives in the late seventeenth century could in part be attributed to changes in witchcraft prosecutions post-1660. As Clive Holmes has explained, post-1660 legal elites became hesitant to try any witchcraft case that did not involve death or diabolical practices.[4] This decrease in prosecutions could go some way to explaining why there are fewer narratives detailing revenge and malice from this period, particularly of those cases that did not result in death. But this does not explain their reoccurrence in the eighteenth century, particularly given the stabilisation of the Poor Law and the related decrease in moral duty towards the poor that, according to Keith Thomas, should have heralded the end of many guilt-induced witchcraft accusations.[5] Although witchcraft accusations, prosecutions and pamphlets definitely decreased during the later seventeenth and early eighteenth centuries, the pamphlets that do remain rely on the traditional trope of witchcraft: that of the witch maliciously taking revenge against the slights of her neighbours. This suggests that by the eighteenth century, there was a very strong idea of what a witchcraft act entailed and how a typical witchcraft narrative should be presented. As Peter Elmer has noted, many of the features of witchcraft pamphlets remained remarkably similar throughout the early modern period.[6] Malice, revenge, anger and hatred were all central to these narratives.

It is important to clarify at this point how I am using the term 'revenge narratives'. In his seminal study, Thomas highlighted the importance of malice and revenge in English witchcraft narratives, positing a 'charity-refused' model which saw the witch take revenge after she was refused alms from her neighbours. Thomas attributed the increase in these accusations to guilt on the part of the neighbour who refused the witch. As Thomas explained, the changing and ambiguous nature of parish relief during the Tudor and Stuart periods meant that many felt guilt after refusing a poor woman alms. When after their refusal misfortune invariably struck, their guilt led them to suspect the person to whom they had refused charity.[7] Alan Macfarlane, another famous proponent of the charity-refused model, gave the example of Mother Cunny who, after being refused a drink by her neighbour, went

away discontented. The next day Mother Cunny's neighbour experienced
terrible pain.[8] Years later Marion Gibson developed these ideas further by
providing in-depth analyses of denial narratives, charity-refused narratives
and, also, motiveless malignancy narratives.[9] This chapter is concerned with
all of these narratives, and, while categorising these interactions is extremely
valuable for our understanding of the construction of witchcraft narratives,
I have not distinguished between them here, instead referring to them all
as 'revenge narratives'. Instead of simply re-treading the ground so com-
prehensively explored by Thomas, Macfarlane, Gibson and others, all of
whom have established malice and revenge as central to English witchcraft
narratives, I want to focus instead on the role of the Devil in these emotional
interactions and argue that the Devil was crucial in allowing the witch to
act on her emotions.[10] Twenty years ago, Deborah Willis suggested that,
for some witches, familiars may have been seen as 'consoling allies' who,
in return for attention, were a means of getting even with hostile neighbours.[11] This idea will be explored in depth in this chapter. The vast majority of witchcraft pamphlets emphasised the anger, hatred, and malice of
the accused, something that did not pass unremarked by contemporaries.[12]
Through studying these emotional drivers, we can begin to understand how
pamphlets constructed a witch's motivations for performing witchcraft and
joining with the Devil.

In one of the last early modern pamphlets on witchcraft, an anonymous
author explained that 'it is by Evil Spirits that Witches do what they do . . .
under the government of a Prince that employs them in a continual Opposition to the Designs of God [who commands] vast Legions and Myriads of
Devils . . . by whom Witches do exert their divilish and malignant Rage
upon their Neighbours'.[13] The idea that witches resorted to devilish power
to hurt their neighbours remained strong throughout the entire early modern period, although, as mentioned, references to this concept were few in
pamphlets from the mid-to-late seventeenth century. This idea was strongly
gendered. In early modern England, approximately 90 per cent of accused
witches were women.[14] Although men do exist in English witchcraft pamphlet narratives, they are not usually associated with the types of revenge
narratives that are so typical in England. Of the few men accused of witchcraft in English pamphlets only two, Arthur Bill in 1613 and James Device
(also 1613), are accused of using their familiars to seek revenge.[15] In the vast
majority of narratives it is women, the supposedly vengeful sex, who draw
on their familiars to act on their malicious tendencies. This should not perhaps be surprising given that early modern discourse generally gendered the
emotions as feminine, while reason and intellect were deemed masculine.[16]
For early modern contemporaries, the threat of the uncontrolled and disordered woman was very real. David Underdown has argued that between
1560 and 1640, the peak period in England for witchcraft prosecutions,
court records demonstrate an increasing preoccupation with women who
represented a threat to the patriarchal system.[17] Cases of women scolding

and brawling with their neighbours, women refusing to enter service and women dominating or beating their husbands all appeared more frequently during this period than in those immediately before or after.[18] Martin Ingram, whilst disagreeing with many of Underdown's arguments, has also highlighted the importance of neighbourhood conflicts in prosecutions for scolding.[19] The most dangerous and feared manifestation of women's anger was the witch's *maleficium*. In witchcraft narratives, ideas of women as angry, uncontrolled creatures found a home. Witches were described as disordered, scolding, malicious and ill-natured women who lashed out at their neighbours. Crucially, these women did not act alone. Their malice was only made possible through their diabolical associations. In English witchcraft pamphlets, uncontrolled female witches and their dangerous emotions became fundamentally linked with the Devil.

In popular pamphlets witches were often described as 'spightfull and malitious', 'monstrous', of a 'revengfull nature' or simply 'ill-natured'.[20] The very first seventeenth-century depiction of witchcraft in print, published in 1606, cites the witch's vengeful nature and labels revenge as the primary driver for witchcraft. Marion Gibson has suggested that this account, published within a pamphlet about a murder, is 'pure fiction' a conclusion she reaches based on the 'knockabout vulgarity of the account, its detail, comic structuring and obvious gusto'.[21] However, she also points out that the explicit content of the story is less important than the 'instantly recognizable witch's revenge genre'.[22] In this pamphlet, accused witch Johane Harrison and her daughter, known only as A.H., are described as able to torture their victims through the help of their demonic spirits and a magical parchment.[23] Johane has two spirits, one to torture men and another to torture cattle.[24] Johane is called an 'old Hagge' by one of her neighbours, a yeoman, and instantly swears revenge, threatening that the man 'shalt feele more from me hereafter'.[25] The yeoman is struck down by 'continual aches & wracking of his limbs', and this eventually kills him.[26] So great is the yeoman's pain that he feels 'as if the Divell had set him on his Tentors to make broadcloth of him'.[27] Not only does this description emphasise the agony that witches can induce, it also links this pain with the Devil. The pamphlet presents a very clear narrative: Johane is a vengeful woman who has diabolical powers. A neighbour has insulted her and because of her vengeful nature she swears to have her revenge. Johane then draws on her demonic power (presumably through her familiar who can hurt men) to torture and eventually kill her neighbour. The pamphleteer does not place any blame on the yeoman who insulted Johane, nor does he imply that Johane might have any reason to be angry. Instead he portrays her as unnecessarily and overly vengeful.

In 1612 a pamphlet was published about the witchcrafts of Agnes Browne and her daughter Joane Vaughan. Agnes, we are told, was 'of an ill nature and wicked disposition, spightfull and malitious'.[28] Not surprisingly given this description, Agnes was feared and hated among her neighbours. Joane, the daughter, was apparently of a similar nature to that of her mother. The pamphlet begins with a confrontation between neighbours:

> [Joane] whether of purpose to give occasion of anger to the said Mistris Belcher, or but to continue her vilde and ordinary custome of behaviour, committed something either in speech, or gesture, so unfitting, and unseeming the nature of woman hood, that it displeased the most that were there present: But especially it touched the modesty of this Gentlewoman, who was so much moved with her bold, and impudent demeanor, that she could not containe her selfe, but sodainely rose up and stroke her, howbeit hurt her not, but forced her to avoide the company.[29]

Joane was 'enraged' by this treatment and told Mistress Belcher that 'shee would remember this injury, and revenge it' to which Mistress Belcher 'bade her doe her worst'.[30] Joane returns home to her mother and tells her what has happened. The pamphleteer interjects here and tells his reader that had Joane and Agnes had 'an hundred Spirits at command, the worst, and the most hurtfull had been called to this counsel, and imployed about this businesse.'[31] The tense here makes it unclear as to whether the pamphleteer is suggesting that this actually happened or that this would have happened had it been a possibility. As it stands, Agnes and Joane wait three or four days before acting from 'rage and revenge' to cause Mistress Belcher 'intollerable paine'.[32] The delayed response from Agnes and Joane is described as a move designed to allay suspicion, but it also reflects contemporary ideas about the nature of women's anger. As both Natalie Davis and Kristi Gourlay have explored, humoral theory dictated that women's anger differed from men's in that it was colder and longer-lasting.[33] So while men were prone to bursts of temper, these were short-lived moments of loss of reason, and, as such, could often be used as a defence in court.[34] Women, on the other hand, experienced an enduring, all-encompassing anger, which was often linked to an insatiable desire for revenge. As Alexander Roberts wrote of women in his 1616 witchcraft treatise, 'this sex, when it conceiveth wrath or hatred against any, is unplacable, possessed with unsatiable desire of revenge, and transported with appetite to right (as they thinke) the wrongs offered unto them'.[35] This anger, if left unchecked, could lead to madness or bodily illness.[36] Women's anger often took much longer to be acted upon. We see this belief in the witchcraft narrative above. In this 1612 narrative the sequence of events is very clear, as are Joane's motives for hurting the gentlewoman and her method of doing so. Joane desires revenge and this revenge is directly linked to assistance from demonic spirits. Throughout the entire narration, Joane and her mother's malicious temperaments and their extreme anger at what the pamphleteer classifies as a non-hurtful and well-deserved blow for bad behaviour have been emphasised.

At the heart of both of these narratives is a preoccupation with women who are unable to control their emotions, specifically their anger, and who then draw on the Devil's assistance to maliciously act upon this anger to take revenge on those who have offended them. As Thomas Wright explained in his 1601 treatise on the passions, anger 'proceedeth from some injurie offered and therefore hateth the inflictor, and by all meanes possible seeketh revenge'.[37] The French writer Nicholas Caussin also linked anger with a desire for revenge and cast women's anger as extremely dangerous, noting that 'the anger of potent women is above all dreadfull, when they are not withheld by considerations of conscience, because they have a certaine appetite of revenge, which exceedeth all may be imagined'.[38] This common link between anger and revenge has a long history and derives from writings by Aristotle, Seneca and Aquinas, among others.[39] Senecan revenge tragedies even witnessed a resurgence in England in the 1560s and again in the 1580s, with many being performed and even rewritten to emphasise the supposedly causative links between the feminine, bodily, uncontrolled passion of anger and the desire for revenge.[40] This may help to explain why only one sixteenth-century English witchcraft pamphlet fails to link a witch's *maleficium* to her desire for revenge. Crucially, this pamphlet is about a male witch.[41] It is also possible that the decline of revenge tragedies during the seventeenth century, and the closing of the theatres between 1642 and 1660, may both have contributed to the decline of revenge narratives in witchcraft pamphlets during the third quarter of the seventeenth century. The link between anger and revenge continued (and still continues), of course, long after the sixteenth century. As late as 1712 we see it drawn upon anew in witchcraft pamphlets with one particularly enthusiastic author explaining that 'revenge is naturally the first New Thought that is excited by *Anger* in a wicked mind'.[42]

In comparison to the Latin originals, early modern English translations of Senecan revenge tragedies emphasised that a person must feel the all-encompassing pain of anger before being in the right state to take revenge.[43] In these translations uncontrolled anger was described as feminine. As Gwynne Kennedy has explained, women in early modern England were 'believed to get angry *more* often and *more* easily than men because of their physiological, intellectual and moral inferiority to men . . . an angry person of either sex surrenders to passions that are usually kept in check, but what for men is a momentary lack of self-restraint is for women a more serious character flaw'.[44] Witchcraft pamphlets from this same time period are littered with references to women losing control of their emotions and giving in to anger. In 1579, Mother Staunton, for example, went away from her neighbour's house in 'greate anger' after being denied alms and accused of stealing a knife, after which time a child sickened and died.[45] Joan Pechey in 1582 'seemed to be in a great anger' after being given hard bread as did Joan Robinson when she was denied cheese from a neighbour.[46] Another woman in this pamphlet, Ales Newman, sent one of her spirits to plague a man after she 'fell out with him very angerly'.[47] In another incident from 1579, accused witch Elizabeth Stile explained the link between anger and revenge in terms of witchcraft:

> They [witches] and every one of them, if any had angred them, they would go to their Spirites and saie suche a one hath angred me, goe dooe them this mischief, and for their hire, would give them a droupe of their owne blood, and presently the partie was plagued by some lamentable casualtie.[48]

Anger is clearly a strong motif throughout witchcraft narratives and, as we see in the cases of Elizabeth Stile and Ales Newman, was a catalyst for taking revenge with the assistance of the Devil.

Another early seventeenth-century narrative also stressed the link between anger, taking revenge and diabolical assistance. The anonymous author of this 1613 pamphlet tells us that Mother Sutton, a widow of declining years, is angry with Master Enger, a gentleman of worship.[49] No explanation as to the cause of this anger is recorded in the pamphlet but we are told that Mother Sutton 'had vowed to take a strange and actuall revenge for the discontent she had conceived against him'.[50] In revenge against Master Enger, Mother Sutton killed all of his horses. Gruesomely, we are told that some horses were strangled and some beat out their own brains. Mother Sutton also bewitched Master Enger's pigs so that some of them suddenly fell mad and violently tore out the guts and bowels of their fellows.[51] Mother Sutton's choice of revenge is extremely violent, torturous and deeply disturbing. In this narrative there is no account of how Mother Sutton was able to take revenge. However, all is still to be revealed. The pamphlet relates how after these disturbing attacks, Master Enger caught Mother Sutton's son, Henry, throwing stones near Master Enger's property and causing damage. After admonitions failed, Master Enger gave him 'a little blow or two' and Henry went home crying.[52] Here the pamphleteer emphasises that Master Enger has taken no revenge for the great hurts done to him by Mother Sutton (the pigs and the horses) and that this incident is entirely unrelated and caused by Henry's bad behaviour. He also emphasises that Master Enger only hit Henry as a last resort after words failed. The pamphleteer then states that 'though [Henry] had received no hurt, [Mother Sutton] vowed to take revenge' for this attack against her son.[53] Here we see Mother Sutton's anger and desire for revenge clearly articulated. We also see where the pamphleteer's sympathies lie – even though he relates that Henry has been struck and is crying, he insists that he has received no hurt. As with the pamphleteer who insisted that Mistress Belcher did not hurt Joan, this author is keen to emphasise the witch's unnecessarily vengeful nature.

For many pamphleteers, witches were vengeful creatures who reacted unnecessarily violently against those whom they perceived to have wronged them. Although these slights are downplayed in pamphlet narratives we must remember that, for at least some of these women, there appears to be a real sense of a grievance that must be avenged. We can be fairly confident that many of the accused did feel that they had been insulted or injured (Mistress Belcher's attack on Joan and Master Enger's attack on Henry are only two examples) and that they did feel the need to punish those who had wronged them. As such, after Henry has been hurt, Mother Sutton apparently uses her two devilish spirits, Dick and Jude, to 'strike' and 'turn to torment' the young son of Master Enger.[54] Although to modern readers Mother Sutton's reliance on evil spirits is dubious, her anger and desire for revenge on behalf of her son rings true. Mother Sutton is not portrayed as a wronged woman whose son has been attacked but as an unnecessarily vengeful and violent creature that uses the Devil to torment helpless children.

A much later pamphlet of 1645 also explains how witches were believed to use their familiars to take revenge on their neighbours. Accused witch Joane Williford confesses that the Devil first appeared to her twenty years ago and, seven years ago, the Devil appeared to her again in the shape of a little dog. She called this dog Bunne.[55] Although Joane was initially reluctant to forsake God, the pamphleteer implies that her confessed desire to 'be revenged upon' Thomas Letherland and his wife was one of the reasons for her decision to join with the Devil.[56] As has already been noted, it was not at all unusual for witches to be believed to have entered into a pact with the Devil out of a desire for revenge. It is unclear from this pamphlet whether or not Joane was able to take revenge on Thomas Letherland. She did, though, take revenge on Thomas Gardler. We are not told why Joane disliked Thomas Gardler, only that Bunne (the familiar) pushed him out of a window.[57] Joane was found guilty and at her execution she counselled the assembled crowds to 'take warning by her' and not 'be deceived by the Divell, neither for lucre of money, malice, or anything else, as she had done'.[58] Not only does this pamphlet highlight the devastating revenge that Joane's familiar took on her behalf, it also identifies revenge as the primary driver for entering into witchcraft and explores how Joane's desire for revenge persuaded her to create an alliance with the Devil. In this narrative, Joane's familiar acts directly on her behalf to take revenge, thus placing it as central to her malicious desires. Joane is not the only witch to act in this way; Joan Cariden and Elizabeth Harris, both fellow accused, also confessed to joining with the Devil in an attempt to take revenge on their neighbours.[59] Even though this pamphlet appears in the 1640s, a decade sometimes perceived as atypical of English witchcraft beliefs, these witches' narratives very closely resemble those of previous decades. For all three of these witches, their relationship with the Devil is what allows them to take revenge. For Mother Sutton, Joane Williford and Elizabeth Harris, their familiars are the direct cause of men's deaths.[60]

The women in these pamphlets are portrayed as overly emotional beings that are filled with anger and a desire for revenge. Not only were women believed to be more susceptible to anger; the type of anger they experienced was viewed by some contemporaries as 'a disease of a weake mind which cannot moderate it selfe but is easily inflamed'.[61] This anger, the purview of 'women, children, and weake and cowardly men' differed from more acceptable, masculine forms of anger and, according to one contemporary, was not anger but wrath, and, accordingly, one of the seven deadly sins.[62] Numerous other early modern writers such as Pierre Charron, Robert Burton, Richard Braithwaite and William Gouge all labelled women as more emotional and more given to anger than men.[63] Lisa Perfetti, when using the term "medieval" as an umbrella term for medieval and early modern experiences, has summarised pre-modern views by claiming that 'one might even say that in the medieval way of thinking, emotions *were* female'.[64] Even as these views changed in the late seventeenth century, a time when anger started to become more often associated with men than women, women who did give in to anger were still judged harshly; perhaps more so, given the new emphasis on the importance of a woman's gentleness of temper.[65] It is not surprising in this context that English witches, an almost exclusively female group, were viewed as overly emotional, angry and malicious.

We might wonder, though, why female witnesses and victims in these narratives are not also implicated in this understanding of women's emotional stability. Although women as a group in early modern England were believed to have less control over their emotions than men, in medieval and early modern texts 'noblewomen are more likely to be represented as emotionally stable and rational compared to women of lower birth'.[66] The same is true of the late seventeenth and eighteenth centuries during which time 'angry voices could now only be expected to be heard from a certain [lower] class of woman'.[67] If we return to the case of Joane Vaughan and Mistress Belcher, we see this theory in action. Mistress Belcher is a 'gentlewoman', while Joane is born of a woman of 'poore parentage and poorer education'.[68] This is not an isolated example. As Brian Levack has convincingly argued, 'we can be fairly certain that the great majority of those prosecuted [for witchcraft] came from the lower levels of society'.[69] Their gender, as well as their social status, ensured that the majority of English witches were described in print as women who were unable to control their emotions and who gave in to anger to take revenge on their neighbours.

The Devil's Victims: Emotionally Vulnerable Witches

As we have seen above, accused witches were only believed able to take revenge with the assistance of diabolical spirits. They drew on these spirits at moments of anger and vengeance. But in some rare narratives, the Devil actually chose to appear to potential witches precisely because he noted this propensity to anger.[70] Six narratives emerge from the early modern period in which the Devil chose to appear to potential witches at the exact moment in which they gave into anger and lost control of their emotions. At this moment of turmoil, the Devil was afforded a way in. These cases, which date from 1579, 1619, 1621, 1646, 1693 and 1712, highlight both the importance of emotional control in early modern England and the supposed links between giving in to anger and allowing the Devil a way in. Not only did these narratives stress the importance of malice and vengeance in witch-craft acts, they also portrayed the Devil as being aware of this precondition. The Devil was portrayed as an ever-present companion, a figure of tempta-tion who waited in the background for ordinary men and women to slip and succumb to his influence – an idea emphasised in many pamphlet epistles, as discussed in chapter 1. In portraying the Devil in this way, these pamphlets both reflected and encouraged a belief in the fundamental link between giv-ing in to overwhelmingly strong emotions and affording the Devil a way in.

During the medieval and early modern periods, numerous conduct books were written on the appropriate expression of anger.[71] The godly preacher (and later bishop of Norwich) Edward Reynolds in his 1640 treatise on the passions, counselled that anger 'must first be schooled before it is imployed, as men bridle their horses before they ride them'.[72] Women's anger, as Gwynne Kennedy and Kristi Gourlay have explained, was often viewed as an affront to male authority. Although, as Gourlay argues, there were appropriate times for a woman to become angry (such as during an affront to her chastity), she should rely on her male representatives to act on this anger. Women who expressed anger, therefore, were clearly viewed as an 'affront to male authority and a threat to social harmony'.[73] This is not to claim that women did not become angry. Linda A. Pollock's detailed study demonstrates that many elite women often acted on their anger and, as the above witchcraft narratives make very clear, many poorer women also indulged their anger.[74] Pollock encourages us to examine historical moments of anger or 'passion' in their situated context to determine whether or not the expression of anger was deemed appropriate.[75] In witchcraft narratives, the witch's anger is invariably described as all-encompassing, unjustified or unfeminine and, as such, further demonises the suspected witch.

The most common words used to refer to anger in early modern letters and memoirs were 'passion' and 'anger'.[76] With the addition of the word 'rage' this observation could easily be applied to early modern witchcraft pamphlets. Passion, as Pollock has noted,

> appeared to describe particularly strong anger, more like rage, which assailed and engulfed the will. Individuals gripped in passion's vice could do little to regulate the emotion and had to wait until it ebbed. Less extreme anger, though, was more firmly within an individual's control.[77]

For contemporaries, anger was an 'unruly Passion,' which by subverting Man's reason robbed 'a Man of the best part of himself'.[78] The idea that witches were more prone to anger and had unruly passions comes through strongly in witchcraft pamphlets from across the entire early modern period. As we have seen, anger was a cornerstone of witchcraft narratives, and references to anger as a passion exist in mid-to-late seventeenth- and early eighteenth-century pamphlets. In 1648, Matthew Hopkins' associate John Stearne explained that 'we [humanity] are as impatient, profane, and unconscionable as ever, having distempered passions, violent in affection, given to ill company, and vain curiosities, not having respect of Religion, by which occasions the Devill taketh advantage and works to have his will'.[79] Stearne then elaborated on how the Devil sits waiting, watching for any sign of these weaknesses such as a 'distempered passion' or being 'enraged with anger, plotting revenge' so that he may draw these men and women to witchcraft.[80]

The use of 'passion' to mean rage or extreme anger was not unknown in witchcraft narratives, particularly in those from the later period. When asked in 1682 whether or not she cursed a neighbour, Joan Buts pleaded 'I spake those words in passion, my Lord, but I intended no such thing'.[81] A woman mentioned in a witchcraft pamphlet but accused of murder, Prudence Lee, 'had been a very lewd liver, and much given to cursing and swearing . . . she further confessed that being jealous of her husband, and some unfitting words passing between them, in her passion she stabbed him'.[82] Another accused, this time from 1704, 'fell into a great Passion' because she thought a shopkeeper had said something 'to Ridicule her' so she 'ran out of the shop and threatned Revenge'.[83] Predictably, the next day the shop was turned 'topsy-turvy' and the shopkeeper came down with a strange disease.[84] Perhaps the most violent example comes from a 1706 broadsheet: after being refused ten shillings, the accused, Mary Johnson, 'went away in a great Passion' and swore revenge. That evening the neighbour's husband 'was siez'd with Contractions in his Face till his Eyes seem'd to start out of his Head, his Nose extended in several Forms, and his Mouth was drawn almost to his Ears; all which Disasters was follow'd with a violent Vomiting of Water and Blood, of which he died in three Hours'.[85] In these examples, 'passion' is used to describe a particularly violent and uncontrolled form of anger.

It is this uncontrolled, violent rage that, as Stearne was keen to point out, afforded the Devil a way in. It is worth noting that the concept of a manipulative Devil, lying in wait for his prey to fall, is by no means groundbreaking. As Oldridge has reminded us, in the early modern period devils 'typically . . . deceived the witch with illusory promises of success or wealth'.[86] But there is still more work to be done on how the Devil was believed to play on emotion as part of this process. As Lyndal Roper has so eloquently explained in a German context:

> The Devil whom witches encountered was not an abstract force or a symbolic figure of evil. Though he appeared in different guises he was, first and foremost, on each occasion a character with whom one had a relationship.[87]

For men and women in early modern England, losing control of one's emotions and giving in to anger, was only the first step in an ongoing relationship with the Devil.

In 1579 an anonymous pamphlet began by warning its readers of the 'Ambushementes of Sathan, whereby he would surprise us lulled in securitie, and hardened with contempt of Gods vengeance threatened for our offences'.[88] As was discussed in chapter 1, this epistle forms part of a common tradition in which witchcraft pamphlets began with a warning to their readers about the very real dangers of the Devil, specifically on how he will tempt men and women into his service. The author goes on to relate how Elizabeth Francis along with two other women from Chelmsford, Essex, was accused of witchcraft. The other two women in the pamphlet are described as malicious women who use their familiars to seek revenge against their neighbours, but it is only in Elizabeth's case that the Devil appears to her in a moment of extreme rage. This is not Elizabeth's first appearance in print. In 1566 she was the subject of one of the first witchcraft pamphlet accounts in England. In this first narrative Elizabeth's dealings with her familiar spirit are quite pragmatic. She asks her familiar for eighteen sheep, which he grants until they all disappear mysteriously, and she also asks for a husband.[89] Her familiar, a 'whyte spotted Catte', which she inherited from her grandmother, was called 'Sathan' and required Elizabeth's blood in return for its favours.[90] Sathan says that she can marry Andrew Byles, as she requests, but she must sleep with him first.[91] Elizabeth does so and falls pregnant but, when Andrew won't marry her, she has her cat, Sathan, kill him.[92] Sathan also helps Elizabeth to abort her illegitimate child and to find a second husband, with whom she has a child 'a quarter of a yere after they were married'.[93] However, Elizabeth lives unquietly with her child and husband so asks Sathan to kill the child and lame her husband which he does.[94] Elizabeth confesses and is given four sessions on the pillory and a year's imprisonment. Elizabeth was tried again for witchcraft in 1572 but, once again, evaded execution.[95]

This is all we know of Elizabeth until the 1579 pamphlet. In this narrative, Elizabeth's encounter with the Devil is described very differently. Elizabeth's cat familiar is not mentioned in the pamphlet; instead, this pamphlet describes how she met a shaggy dog straight after an altercation with a neighbour. Elizabeth confesses:

> about Lent last (as she now remembreth) she came to one Pooles wife her neighbour, and required some olde yest of her, but being denied the same, she departed towards one good wife Osbornes house a neighbour dwelling thereby of whome she had yest, and in her waie going towardes the saied goodwife Osbornes house, shee cursed Pooles wife, and hadde a mischief to light upon her, for that she would give her no yest, Whereuppon soddenly in the waie she hard a great noise, and presently there appeared unto her a Spirite of a white colour in seeming

like to a little rugged Dogge, standying neere her upon the grounde, who asked her whether she went? Shee aunswered for suche thinges as she wanted, and she told him therewith that she could gette no yeest of Pooles wife and therefore willed the same Spirite to goe to her and plague her, whiche the Spirite promised to doe, but first he had her give him somewhat, then she having in her hand a crust of white bread, did bite a peece thereof and threwe it upon the grounde, which she thinketh he tooke up and so went his waie, but before he departed from her she willed hym too plague Pooles wife in the head, and since then she never sawe him, but she hath harde by her neighbours that the same Pooles wife was grevoously pained in her head not longer ager, and remayneth very sore payned still, for on saterdaie last past this Examinate talked with her.[96]

This narrative is what we would think of as a typical exchange in English witchcraft cases. Elizabeth has begged for alms and been refused. Her anger has led her to walk away cursing Poole's wife. But there is more than this here. At the exact moment that Elizabeth allows her anger to take over, the Devil appears. James Sharpe has commented briefly on this case pointing out that these are the exact circumstances that many demonologists believed would make the Devil most likely to appear. Sharpe takes this example as evidence that the familiar performs the same function in witch-beliefs as did the devil of learned demonology.[97] Given that Protestant reformers stressed the concept of the Devil as a tempter and trickster, it is hardly surprising that these struggles with the Devil started to be incorporated into witchcraft print, as did the Protestant emphasis on the individual's struggle with Satan. But, given the pamphlet's clear links between anger, cursing and the Devil's appearance, we can also read this text as a warning of the dangers of uncontrolled emotion.

A second example comes from a 1619 pamphlet, which describes the witchcrafts of Joane Flower and her daughters Margaret and Philippa.[98] In 1618 Margaret Flower, a servant working for the Earl of Rutland, fell under suspicion of theft.[99] Margaret was well-known for her laziness, her malice and her association with base characters. Even more seriously, she was suspected of working with her mother, Joane Flower, a suspected witch, for unknown but undoubtedly evil purposes. Joane Flower was a 'monstrous malicious woman, full of oaths, curses, and imprecations irreligious' who had eyes which were 'fiery and hollow . . . speech fell and envious [and a] demeanour strange and exoticke', all of which 'gave great suspition that she was a notorious Witch . . . who dealt with familiar spirits'.[100] Here we see that Joane's malice is part of the reason for her neighbours' suspicion. Unsurprisingly, Joane's neighbours were terrified of her, particularly by her 'curses and threatening of revenge'.[101] Margaret Flower's base lifestyle and the suspicion that she was a thief who was plotting unnamed evil with her mother, Joane Flower, led to her dismissal from the Earl's household.

Margaret's dismissal enraged both herself and her mother. We are told that her dismissal turned her 'love and liking toward this honourable Earl and his family to hate and rancor'.[102] Joane was exceedingly angry on her daughter's behalf and 'grudged at it exceedingly, swearing in her heart to be revenged'.[103] In her anger over her daughter's mistreatment, Joane cursed the Earl's family.[104] At this exact moment, the pamphlet tells us, the Devil 'perceived the inficious disposition of this wretch, and that she and her Daughters might easily bee made instruments to enlarge his Kingdome'.[105] The pamphleteer emphasises Joane's anger and desire for revenge and presents her malicious disposition as key to her fall into witchcraft. Without it, Joane would not have lost control of her emotions and so attracted the Devil's attention. This same justification is given in a 1635 version of the case. In both of these works the Devil is portrayed as specifically targeting those whom he believes to have an appropriately malleable disposition. He also appears to be targeting those who experience a strong change in their emotional state that causes them to lose control.

Although not explicitly noted, the implication within this pamphlet is that the Devil has appeared at this woman's most vulnerable moment – at the point when his advances are most likely to succeed. The two women lose little time in using their newfound powers to act upon their malicious desires. From this time on, the Earl and the Countess are 'many times subject to sicknesse and extraordinary convulsions'.[106] The eldest son, Henry, 'sickened very strangely' and died, the next eldest son Francis was 'most barbarously and inhumanely tortured by a strange sicknesse' and, not long after, their daughter Katherine 'was set upon by their dangerous and divellish practises, and many times [was] in great danger of life, through extreame maladies and unusuall fits'.[107] The witches' familiar, a cat called Rutterkin, was instrumental in these attacks. In the death of Henry, for example, Rutterkin is rubbed on the back with a glove stolen from the child.[108] It is only after this ritual that Henry sickens and dies.[109]

In a pamphlet from 1621 an explicit link is made between a witch's anger, her uncontrolled emotions, and her cursing, blaspheming and swearing. This pamphlet was written by the minister Henry Goodcole who based it on an interview he had with Elizabeth Sawyer, the accused witch, when he was ordinary and visitor to Newgate jail. Goodcole explains that 'by Diabolicall help, and out of malice afore-thought, [Elizabeth] did witch unto death *Agnes Ratcleiffe*, a neighbour of hers' because she saw Agnes strike her sow.[110] Within four days of being threatened by Elizabeth, Agnes died, 'foaming at the mouth, and . . . extraordinarily distempered' according to her husband and neighbours.[111] Agnes did not die quietly and painlessly; she suffered a strange, terrifying and fast moving physical affliction. The unusual nature of Agnes' death, combined with Elizabeth's threats and the public knowledge that Elizabeth's 'malice [was] great', led Agnes's husband and neighbours to conclude that Elizabeth had killed Agnes by witchcraft.[112]

In questioning Elizabeth, Goodcole asked how she first came to know the Devil:

> By what meanes came you to have acquaintance with the Divell, and when was the first time that you saw him, and how did you know that it was the Divell?[113]

Elizabeth replied:

> The first time that the Divell came unto me was when I was cursing, swearing and blaspheming, he then rushed in upon me, and never before that time did I see him, or he me: and when he, namely the Divel, came to me, the first words that hee spake unto me were these: *Oh! Have I now found you cursing, swearing, and blaspheming? Now you are mine.*[114]

As in previous pamphlet examples, here the Devil is portrayed as someone who is forever lying in wait for men and women to fall prey to his influence. This point seems so crucial to Elizabeth's story that it even forms the title page of the 1621 play based on her story, *The Witch of Edmonton* (figure 3.1). Goodcole is keen to stress the dangers of blaspheming, cursing and bad language, claiming that Elizabeth's tongue, by its cursing, swearing and blaspheming, occasioned the Devil's access to her and, as such, was 'the meanes of her owne destruction, which had destroyed many before'.[115]

As well as emphasising the dangers of uncontrolled anger, Elizabeth Sawyer's case stresses the perils of cursing, swearing and blaspheming. In the case of both Elizabeth Sawyer and Joane Flower, the Devil appears immediately after they have cursed someone. Words and, more specifically, the mouth and tongue, were given enormous power in pre-modern England. As David Cressy has reminded us:

> early modern authors knew that words had consequences, that spoken utterance caused situation-altering effects. They knew . . . that speech could provoke violence, discord, unhappiness or sedition. An oath or a slur, an insult or a curse, a joke or a lie, could all intensify divisions within communities and erode the fabric of society. These "sins of the tongue" could damage reputations, set neighbour against neighbour, and undercut the authority of the crown.[116]

Witches used words, in the form of commands to spirits or inscrutable muttering, in order to take their revenge on those who had wronged them. As we see in the cases of Joane Flower and Elizabeth Sawyer, sinful or unguarded words could leave ordinary men and women open to the Devil's influence. From the victim's perspective, angry, threatening or blasphemous words had a dangerous power that often mutated into a vicious physical attack. Maleficent words and the power of the tongue were a fundamental part of witchcraft stories.

The Witch of Edmonton

A known true STORY.

Compofed into

A TRAGI-COMEDY

By divers well-efteemed Poets;

William Rowley, Thomas Dekker, John Ford, &c

Acted by the Princes Servants, often at the Cock-Pit in *Drury-Lane,*
once at Court, with fingular Applaufe.

Never printed till now.

Ho have I found thee Curfing.

Sanctabecetur nomen tuum

Mother Sawyer

Help, Help I am Drownd

Cuddy Banks

London, *Printed by* J. Cottrel, *for* Edward Blackmore, *at the Angel in*
Paul's *Church-yard.* 1658.

Figure 3.1 A familiar talking to a witch, depicted in William Rowley, Thomas Dekker and John Ford, *The Witch of Edmonton: A Known True Story* (London: Printed by J. Cottrel for Edward Blackmore, 1658), title page. Houghton Library, Harvard University, 14433.26.13.

For many Elizabethan and Jacobean writers, the tongue was a part of the body that needed to be governed, lest the abuse of it risked its owner's soul.[117] Vast numbers of tracts were published counselling their readers on how to control their dangerous tongues.[118] Authors warned against the dangers of cursing, swearing and blaspheming, but also grumbling, murmuring or defaming.[119] In witchcraft cases, witches often inflicted their punishments after going away dissatisfied and grumbling or muttering under their breath.[120] This mumbling often took on a sinister significance after the witch had inflicted punishment. The act of muttering, then, was a powerful act in and of itself.[121] Witches like Elizabeth Sawyer and Joane Flower opened themselves to the Devil's influence through their unruly tongues. Much of this early modern understanding of the sinful tongue was based on biblical references: 'the wicked is snared by the transgression of his lips' or 'for he that will love and see good days, let him refrain his tongue from evil'.[122] A witch's cursing had many different meanings. It gave the witch power, both through the Devil's offers of assistance and the fear of the victim, but it also condemned the witch to an ungodly life. Cursing, swearing and blaspheming were all sins of the tongue that helped a witch to take revenge against her enemies but also opened her up to the Devil's influence.

Elizabeth's inability to control her tongue goes hand-in-hand with her inability to control her emotions, notably her anger. As Kristine Steenberg has noted in her study of early modern English revenge tragedies, the emotion of anger possessed a 'bodily agency quite of its own, thereby diminishing self-control'.[123] Anger was believed to take control of the body, leaving the afflicted governed by an irresistible force. Pollock has also noted this phenomenon.[124] In a Spanish context, Maureen Flynn has demonstrated how men and women accused of blaspheming often claimed in their defence that their anger had overtaken them.[125] Goodcole seems keen to make the connection between anger, loss of control and diabolical influence in the minds of his readers. Elizabeth's inability to control her rage is portrayed as central to the Devil's interest in her. Elizabeth's confession draws this link clearly. The Devil appears to Elizabeth at the time of her emotional outburst when she was cursing, swearing and blaspheming which allowed the Devil to take control of her. Elizabeth's malice and anger, as we see in the narratives of Joane Flower and Elizabeth Francis, have made her a prime target for the Devil's advances – but it is her succumbing to anger that allows the Devil a way in.

Two further examples emerge from a 1646 pamphlet written by the Reverend John Davenport. Davenport begins by warning his readers 'how craftily and dangerously the Devill tempeth and seizeth on poore soules'.[126] He then goes on to warn against 'Hypocrisie, anger, malice, swearing, Idolatry, Lust, Covetousnesse, and other grievous sins, which occasioned [the witches'] downfall'.[127] Davenport makes an explicit link between uncontrolled emotions, witchcraft, and joining with the Devil. In a description reminiscent of Elizabeth Sawyer blaspheming and cursing in 1621, accused witch John Winnick is described as 'swearing, cursing, raging' about the loss of seven shillings, which he suspects a family member has stolen from him.[128] In a rage, John wishes that 'some wise body (or Wizzard) would helpe him'.[129] At this moment, a spirit 'blacke and shaggy, and having pawes like a Beare, but in bulk not fully so big as a Coney' appears to John.[130] The black, shaggy spirit asks John what is wrong, and on hearing about the lost money, replies: 'if you will forsake God and Christ, and fall down & worship me for your God, I will help you'.[131] John agrees and his money is restored. However, John is actually forced to worship two other, additional spirits (a white Cat and a grey Coney), to give the bear spirit his soul, and to allow all three spirits to 'suck of his body'.[132] John has been seduced into the Devil's service in a moment of weakness and need and the Devil has taken advantage of this. Rather than the initial agreement that John would just worship the bear spirit, he has now forfeited his soul. Although John has been tricked, he is promised by 'the Cat Spirit that it would hurt cattel when he would desire it' and by 'the Coney-like Spirit that it would hurt men when he desired'.[133]

Not only has John lost control of his temper, he has also lost control of his tongue and speech. Early modern authors were concerned that men and women were not doing enough to govern their tongues, a body part synonymous with 'the stearne of a ship by which the whole vessel is ruled and governed'.[134] For the godly divine William Perkins the tongue contained both 'the tongue of Christ' and 'the devil's language'.[135] In his treatise on the proper governance of the tongue, Perkins wrote of the daily abuse of the tongue noticeable throughout the country. He claimed that 'swearing, blaspheming [and] cursed speaking . . . overflow in all places' and are 'sinnes against God'.[136] The pamphleteer and moral reformer Edward Stephens agreed:

> *Prophane* SWEARING, is . . . A Crime so *Unnatural, and intirely Diabolical*, without any Natural Disposition to it, but merely of Diabolical Impression, that the Common Swearer may reasonably be reputed an Associate with that Cursed Prophane Company of Witches, and Confederates with the Devil.[137]

For Stephens, swearing, witchcraft and devilry were inseparable. This view was by no means confined to England; for hundreds of years the Church attempted to curtail blasphemy and prevent people from breaking the third commandment.[138] One Spanish Dominican complained in 1556 of those who rebelled against God through swearing and blaspheming: 'At the slightest frustration, peasants are ready to scream at their beasts of burden . . . and commend their souls to the Devil'.[139] For these authors, swearing and blaspheming were inarguably linked with turning away from God and giving oneself to the Devil. Both John Winnick and Elizabeth Sawyer are guilty of these abuses. Although women were believed to be more prone to unruly speech, 'the topic of the evil tongue cannot be reduced to gender issues'.[140] Both men and women were expected to control their speech, and in these two witchcraft narratives, both a man and a woman failed. Through their blaspheming, swearing, raging and cursing they abused God and invited the Devil into their lives.

John is not the only witch in this pamphlet who curses and blasphemes. Ellen Shepherd, a second witch from Davenport's 1646 pamphlet, was in her home 'swearing and cursing about the discords of her children, [when] there appeared unto her a Spirit, somewhat like a Rat, but not fully so big, of an iron-grey colour'.[141] The spirit asks Ellen to go with him, but Ellen refuses and says she must 'avoid Satan'.[142] The spirit leaves, but a short time after, Ellen goes into a field 'cursing, and fretting, and blaspheming' and the rat reappears; this time with two other rats, presumably as reinforcements.[143] On both occasions these rats appear directly after Ellen has lost control of her temper and her tongue. Her cursing, swearing and blaspheming, all products of her anger at her children, have encouraged the Devil to appear to her. The Devil tells Ellen that she 'must forsake God and Christ, and goe with me, and take those spirits for your Gods, and you shall have all happinesse'.[144] This time Ellen agrees.

The next witch for whom the appearance of the Devil was caused by her uncontrolled passions was described in a collection of witchcraft tales put together by Matthew Hale's son-in-law Edward Stephens in 1693.[145] The actual case is dateless but, we are told, hails from a case in Oxford during the reign of Charles I.[146] Nobody in the pamphlet is given a name but Stephens describes how an elder sister was jealous of the younger as the younger sister's marriage was a success, unlike her own. These circumstances 'moved great Envy against her in her Sister, who was reduced to great Straits. In her Passion the Devil appeared to her, and she made a Contract with him, and became a Witch'.[147] The Devil, having sensed this woman's highly emotional state, has chosen this moment to appear to her and, in doing so, turns her into a witch and persuades her to kill her sister's child.[148]

The final narrative which shows the links between uncontrolled anger and the Devil's appearance comes from one of the eight pamphlets written about the 1712 accusation, conviction and subsequent acquittal of Jane Wenham, the last witch convicted in England. In the first of his three publications about the case, Francis Bragge describes how Jane confessed that she left herself open to the Devil's influence because her neighbours 'vexed' and angered her.[149] When asked what had induced her 'to enter into this Familiarity with the Devil', Jane replied that it was a 'Malicious and Wicked Mind; for when any of the Neighbours vexed her she used horrid Curses, and Imprecations, on which the Devil took Advantage over her'.[150] As in the cases of Elizabeth Francis, Joane Flower, Elizabeth Sawyer, John Winnick and Ellen Shepherd, Jane Wenham's cursing and loss of emotional control has allowed the Devil access to her soul.

Of the six pamphlets referred to in this section, four have named authors. Henry Goodcole, an ordained minister and the author of the 1621 narrative about Elizabeth Sawyer; John Davenport, another ordained minister and the author of the 1646 narrative about witches from Huntington;

Matthew Hale's son-in-law, Edward Stephens (a.k.a Socrates Christianus), a moral reformer and prolific pamphleteer, who edited the 1693 collection of witchcraft narrations, including reprinting one of Hale's writings: and Francis Bragge, a young man 'destined for the Church' and the author of three pamphlets defending the trial of Jane Wenham, the last witch condemned in England.[151] Both Goodcole and Davenport were ordained ministers. Stephens was a deeply religious man who founded his own religious society and wrote against Catholics, Quakers, the 1552 Book of Common Prayer, Calvinists and numerous English bishops and clergy.[152] He was also a strong proponent of the reinstatement of monasticism. Although outspoken, Stephens was 'without a doubt a devout clergyman of the Church of England.'[153] Bragge, although no doubt interested in political point-scoring and sensationalism, may have, as a soon-to-be clergyman, seen it as his duty to draw attention to the dangers facing the church and the role of the clergy in protecting it.[154] The professions and interests of these men can, perhaps, shed some light on why these pamphlets and not others stress the Protestant emphasis on the Devil's powers of mental temptation and the dangers of leaving oneself open to his influence. However, it would be wrong to argue that these ministers were creating their own tradition of English witchcraft belief. As was made clear in the introduction, pamphleteers contributed to a vast genre of literature which labelled witches as emotionally unstable beings whose lack of emotional control, inability to control their tongues, and malicious and vengeful temperaments made them easy prey for the Devil. Across the entire early modern period, throughout a vast range of pamphlets, witches were portrayed as malicious, angry beings that joined with the Devil to fulfil their vengeful desires. In the next section, this chapter will explore exactly how witches used their familiar spirits to act on these malicious desires.

The Familiar as Emotional Conduit

Thus far, this chapter has explored the importance of the witch's anger, malice and desire for vengeance in witchcraft narratives, and the Devil's role in allowing witches to act on their malicious desires. In this section I would like to suggest that the familiar can be viewed as an external conduit for the witch's internal desires.[155] As Michael MacDonald has argued, 'demonology and witch beliefs provided ordinary men and women with a means to express their unconscious yearning to violate moral imperatives and a way to mitigate their guilt by attributing their sins to supernatural beings'.[156] In the below narratives, we see the Devil described as an outlet for malicious desires, as well as being used as a way to distance oneself from vengeful actions. Only through forming a personal bond with the familiar spirit was a witch believed able to act upon her overwhelming hatred, envy, malice and greed to maim or kill her neighbours, destroy livestock and kill children.

In order to provide an in-depth exploration of the familiar spirit as a physical manifestation of a witch's emotional desires, this section will focus on the events of 1582 in and around St. Osyth, Essex. In 1582, over ten women and men living in and just outside this village were accused of and indicted for witchcraft. At least two were hanged. This trial was recorded in a witchcraft pamphlet of over one hundred pages, the longest thus far to emerge in England.[157] The length and detailed nature of this pamphlet, most likely written by the presiding magistrate Brian Darcy, provides a tantalising glimpse into the social background of these witchcraft acts and accusations, and also highlights the key role of emotional conflicts in witchcraft narratives.[158] This is not unusual. Nearly all English witchcraft pamphlets demonstrate both a witch's emotional motivations for succumbing to the Devil and performing witchcraft, as well as highlighting the emotions that drove many men and women to accuse their neighbours of this crime. This 1582 Essex pamphlet, however, provides one of the clearest depictions of interpersonal village relationships and of how familiar spirits were supposedly shared amongst a community of witches. In analysing this particular pamphlet, this section focuses on how demonic creatures allowed witches the power to act on their emotional desires, how they were traded as a form of emotional exchange and, in turn, how familiars can be understood as physical manifestations of accused witches' hatred, desire and fear.

As discussed in the introduction, pamphlets provide one of the best sources for studying English witchcraft belief due to their accuracy compared to trial records and the amount of detail they provide. This is particularly true of the 1582 St. Osyth pamphlet. As has been demonstrated by Marion Gibson and Barbara Rosen, this pamphlet consists almost entirely of pre-trial examinations that would have been taken before a justice of the peace and certified to the Assizes.[159] At the Assizes these examinations would have formed a basis for deciding whether or not a case should be brought to trial. It is clear that Brian Darcy, the presiding magistrate and likely author, was extremely keen to showcase the trial procedure in as much detail as possible and he did this either through direct authorship or through supervising an unknown author. As such, this pamphlet provides one of the fullest accounts of the pre-trial legal process against witches and also includes the informations of witnesses and victims. This means that the accused witches' statements may be less altered in this pamphlet than they appear in other pamphlets in which the pamphleteer takes a more narrative approach. Through its attention to detail, reliance on pre-trial documents, length and the sheer number of witches investigated, the St. Osyth pamphlet provides a unique record of a community and the people involved in one of the biggest witch-scares in English history.

The first woman accused in Essex in 1582 was Ursley Kempe, a woman long suspected of witchcraft who was prone to falling out with her neighbours. Ursley was believed to have four familiar spirits, one called Tyffin, who was white like a lamb, another called Tittey, who was a little grey cat, the third called Pigine, who was black like a toad, and the fourth called Jacke, who was black like a cat.[160] Ursley had very clear ideas about the use of these spirits. She explained that the two he (or boy) spirits were to punish and kill to death and that the two she (or girl) spirits were to punish with lameness and other diseases of the body, and also to destroy cattle.[161] Ursley had much cause to draw on these spirits as she often 'fell out' with her neighbours. One of the first allegations against Ursley comes from her neighbour, Grace Thurlowe, who claims that after she would not allow Ursley to nurse her new baby, the baby fell from its cradle, broke its neck, and died.[162] Later, after being promised favour from Brian Darcy if she confessed, Ursley claims that it was the spirit Tiffey, shaped like a little grey cat, that caused the baby's death.[163] Here we see MacDonald's thesis in practice in Ursley's attribution of her malice to a demonic creature.

Ursley continued to squabble with her neighbours, falling out over numerous arguments and refusals of charity. In the same confession she claimed that she sent her familiar Jacke, who was black like a cat, to plague her sister-in-law because this woman had called her a witch and a whore.[164] In both of these narratives, Ursley is able to place her own malicious desires onto her demonic spirits. Although we can be fairly confident that Ursley did not actually cause the misfortunes of the baby or of her sister-in-law, it does seem clear from numerous witness statements and Ursley's own confession that she was angry with both the baby's mother, with whom she had argued and fallen out, and her sister-in-law who had called her names. Frances Dolan has argued that, through witchcraft, 'angry, powerless women [found] an alternative to their own limited physical, social and economic power'.[165] In other words, the ability to perform witchcraft gave otherwise powerless women agency. For Ursley, it is her familiar that is the conduit of her anger which, in turn, gives her the agency to take revenge on those who have wronged her.

In attempting to understand how accused witches may have viewed their relationships with their familiars and their interactions with their neighbours, I sympathise with the interpretations of both Lyndal Roper and Diane Purkiss of women's tales of witchcraft as fantasies.[166] For Purkiss, these fantasies 'enabled village women to negotiate the fears and anxieties of housekeeping and motherhood'.[167] This idea can be taken further; rather than looking just at the space of the household, we can ask what happens if we attempt to understand witchcraft narratives as stories that reflect accused witches' emotions and, more specifically, how the familiar can be seen to represent these emotions. As was mentioned in the introduction, Lyndal Roper has argued that witchcraft trials provided a genre that allowed women to "speak" and to transform their own life experience into the 'language of the diabolic'.[168] As she has eloquently explained, witches 'used elements of their culture to create narratives which made sense of their lives: of their unbearable hatreds, agonies, jealousies'.[169] Applying this reading of witchcraft narratives to an English context has implications for our

understanding of the use of emotion within witchcraft stories and, importantly, also asserts the importance of diabolical ideas to English witchcraft
narratives in an attempt to counter the traditional view of English witchcraft as an almost entirely non-diabolical crime. In witchcraft narratives,
we see men and women's anger, hatred, rage and vengeance given diabolical
power through the familiar spirit. We then see these confessions, influenced
to a greater or lesser extent by pamphleteers, judges, examiners and clerks,
printed and circulated as evidence of the growing danger of the Devil in the
world.

In her recent book on the emotions of women in pre-modern Europe, Lisa
Perfetti has argued that, in the pre-modern era, emotions were not inner
feelings that served to constitute a highly individuated self with a unique
personality. Instead, she argues, they were oriented outward and defined
an individual's relationship to a community.[170] This interpretation of emotions comes through strongly in witchcraft narratives. Ursley is defined, and
defines herself, in opposition to her community. She is clearly disliked, suspected of witchcraft, and prone to neighbourhood squabbles. In using her
familiars, and telling stories of sending them to do her revenge, Ursley uses
these demonic vessels to unleash her rage on her community. This understanding of emotions, when coupled with the interpretations of witch's
narratives put forward by Roper and Purkiss, helps us to understand how
English men and women accused of witchcraft understood and created their
own diabolical narratives to make sense of their malicious desires. In sending her spirits to torment those who have angered her, Ursley is using these
creatures as conduits for her own anger, hurt and pride. The use of demonic
proxies also, in some ways, allows Ursley to distance herself from her malicious intentions.

This distancing is developed further in Ursley's second confession when,
apparently, she requested an audience with Brian Darcy, the presiding magistrate, as she had forgotten to tell him something important.[171] Ursley
described how she had fallen out with Ales Newman who had called her
a witch but, after this incident, they had become friends.[172] In this second
examination, Ursley claims that she had actually asked Ales to send the familiar spirit Tiffey on her behalf to hurt Grace Thurlowe (the baby's mother) and
that Tiffey was actually owned by Ales.[173] Three months later, Ursley relates
how she was again insulted by a neighbour and called a witch so she, once
again, returned to Ales Newman and asked her to send Jacke, the familiar,
to hurt the neighbour, which she does.[174] On both of these occasions, Ursley
allowed the spirits to suck blood from her in return for their services. This
second confession is clearly an attempt by Ursley to implicate someone else
in her wrong doing – a tactic that works, as Ales is arrested and convicted,
although she avoids being hanged and is instead imprisoned for the following
six years.[175] Ursley, on the other hand, is found guilty and hanged.[176]

At this point in the narrative, it is very unclear whose spirits are whose as it seems that they are being traded and shared by at least two different women, a common occurrence throughout this pamphlet. In this second examination, Ursley is attempting to distance herself from the spirits, from the allegations against her, and from her malicious desires, by contradicting herself and claiming that she did not send the familiars but that they were sent on her behalf and that they were not her spirits. Even as Ursley does this, however, she does not challenge the idea that these spirits were the vehicles for her malicious desires. Returning to MacDonald, we remember his argument that it was common for medieval and early modern villagers to 'personify their unacceptable feelings and actions by ascribing them to the instigation of the Devil'.[177] By describing familiars as creatures that one borrowed when one felt a desire to inflict injury or revenge, Ursley is both highlighting the crucial role of the Devil in witchcraft stories and, also, presenting familiars as emotional conduits, creatures that allow these women to express and share their emotions and act on them together.

After being implicated by Ursley's testimony, Ales Newman is examined before Brian Darcy. Our knowledge of Ales's use of spirits comes predominantly from witness accounts rather than her own examination. Ursley claims that Ales fell out 'very angerly' with a neighbour and so sent her spirit (which she had borrowed from Ursley) to plague him.[178] Here we are reminded about the malleability of ownership of these creatures in this particular village, something uncommon in other narratives. Ursley also recounts that Ales was very angry after being refused a piece of meat so, once again, sent her spirit to punish her refuser.[179] Ursley's testimony against Ales may be explained by the fact that they had recently argued and so, when pressured to name other witches, Ursley turned on Ales; but it cannot just be dismissed out of hand. In the same way that Ursley was explaining her own malicious desires through her familiar spirits, she is doing the same to Ales's narrative. For Ursley, familiar spirits were clearly a key way of taking revenge and taking back power.

Mother Elizabeth Bennett, another accused witch in this pamphlet, used her familiars to injure a neighbour. Elizabeth was taken into custody after Ursley accused her of owning spirits. Ursley claims that when she went to visit Elizabeth, she saw a small ferret-like creature sticking its head out of a cloth-covered pot. When asked why the ferret was doing this, Ursley said it was hungry.[180] In her examination, it emerges that Elizabeth owns two familiars, Suckin and Lyerd, one of whom is like a black dog and the other is red like a lion (although neither resembles Ursley's description of a ferret-like creature).[181] Elizabeth at first denies all charges but confesses after Darcy produces the pot lined with wool that Ursley claims she saw. Elizabeth tells Darcy about her neighbour, William Byet, with whom she initially got on well but, after a year, constantly fell out and argued.[182] William calls Elizabeth names such as old witch and old trot and curses her and her cows.

In turn, Elizabeth threatens William. Soon after this fight, William's cows die although Elizabeth denies any involvement and says it is because William beats them. It is only after this first incident that Elizabeth meets her spirits. Over the following few years William continues to mistreat Elizabeth and her cows so, as a result, Suckin, one of Elizabeth's familiars, takes it upon himself to go and kill William's cows.[183] Elizabeth stresses that she did not do this, nor did she order her spirit to do it: it did it on her behalf. Soon after this incident, Suckin again comes to talk to Elizabeth and says that he has plagued William's wife to death.[184] Elizabeth once again stresses that the spirit did this on its own accord. There does come a point though, when Elizabeth takes responsibility for William's woes. On another occasion, Elizabeth, sick of William calling her lewd names, sends Suckin to go and plague him.[185] After reporting back, Suckin is fed milk by Elizabeth and put to bed in a pot lined with wool.[186]

Elizabeth's narrative demonstrates the convoluted nature of many village conflicts that end in witchcraft accusations. Elizabeth and her neighbour have been fighting for many years before this witchcraft trial occurs. In the wake of Elizabeth's arrest for witchcraft, her neighbour is able to provide years' worth of evidence of her malice, and of events supposedly caused by her familiar spirits. Elizabeth too is able to draw on these experiences and create her own diabolical narrative. Although Elizabeth and Ursley's accounts are some of the more developed in this narrative, there are many other similar examples of the St. Osyth witches using familiars to fulfil their emotional desires. Another pair of accused witches that appear to have traded spirits is Ales Mansfield and Mother Grevell. Ales confesses to owning four spirits, named Robin, Jack, William and Puppet.[187] Two were boys and two were girls and all took the form of black cats.[188] According to the witness statements, Ales is often falling out with her neighbours. One witness claims that Ales swore revenge at him after he was unable to fix something in her house for her. A little later, on passing Ales's house, the witness's cart got stuck, and he suspected witchcraft.[189] Other witnesses commented on the connection between Ales being refused milk by a neighbour because she only had enough to feed the calf and the same calf dropping dead after Ales left.[190] This same neighbour also refused Ales curds as she didn't have any. Ales later confesses that she sent her familiar Puppet to plague her neighbour's beasts after she was refused curds.

Ales does not just use her familiar spirits on her own behalf; she also allows others to use them to act on their desires. In her confession Ales implicates Mother Margaret Grevell who is later called in for questioning as a witch. Like Ales, Margaret is also implicated by numerous witness statements in small squabbles over food and alms. According to Ales's confession, Margaret came at least three times to her to borrow her familiar spirits. The first time Margaret asked to borrow the familiar Robin, specifically because she had fallen out with a neighbour and wanted to use the familiar to plague her beasts.[191] Two years later, Margaret borrows Robin again, this time to kill the neighbour by having Robin plague his big toe.[192] A few years after this incident, Margaret borrows Robin yet again, this time to slowly torture her husband to death.[193] Each time that Robin does something for Margaret she feeds him blood in return. In this narrative, Ales presents familiar spirits as immensely powerful creatures that can be lent out to devastating effects. She makes a direct connection between Margaret's anger and her need of the familiar.

The witchcraft beliefs expressed in this pamphlet are nearly entirely typical of those circulating in other pamphlets of this genre. The accused admit to feeling anger, hurt and a desire for revenge after a real or imagined slight. They also admit to entering into a pact with the Devil (in the form of a familiar spirit), to allowing these spirits to suck blood from their bodies and to using these spirits to maim or fatally injure their neighbours. This pamphlet does, however, showcase two beliefs that are not nearly as obvious in others. Many of the witches in these pamphlets claim that they fed their familiars milk and kept them in cosy pots filled with wool. These confessions stand side-by-side declarations by the accused that their familiars sucked blood from their bodies. Although the belief that familiars were fed milk does appear in other pamphlets, it is extremely rare and does not appear in pamphlets after the sixteenth century. Another key point in this pamphlet that is rare in other narratives is the tendency for witches to apparently trade familiars between themselves, and to lend their familiars to each other in times of need. This is, once again, quite an unusual phenomenon in witchcraft pamphlets. Both of these activities provide valuable insight into how accused witches viewed their familiars: as pet-like creatures to care for and protect, as supernatural beings that needed to be rewarded for jobs done and as powerful devils that could be borrowed or leant in times of need. As Ursley's testimony makes clear, familiars were believed to serve different purposes: some were to kill men and some were to injure cattle. In these narratives we see the trade in familiars as a form of emotional exchange, an exchange in which ordinary women were able to use these devils to act on their desires. For the owners of these creatures, for their friends and acquaintances, familiars were used to punish those who had wronged them and take revenge in situations in which the accused witch was otherwise powerless. The 1582 St. Osyth pamphlet not only reminds us of the fundamental role that village conflicts and tensions played in witchcraft allegations but, also, demonstrates how accused witches imagined the role of familiar spirits in these conflicts and how they used them as a conduit for their own desires.

Through an exploration of the links between witchcraft, the Devil, anger, malice, vengeance and lack of emotional control, this chapter has demonstrated the critical importance of emotion in witchcraft narratives. Not only that, but it has shown that witches were only believed able to take revenge or act on their (often uncontrolled) emotions, with the Devil's assistance, who most commonly appeared as a familiar spirit. By allowing their anger to overwhelm them, early modern men and women accused of witchcraft left themselves open to the Devil's influence. This influence could, however, be a powerful thing, with many witches drawing on the Devil's power to fulfil their own emotional desires. In the next chapter, this book will turn to a discussion of the more intimate relationships between witch and Devil, many of which had a sexual bent.

Notes

1　For the exception, see, Anon. *The Examination of John Walsh Before Maister Thomas Williams* (London: Printed by John Awdely, 1566).
2　For the exceptions, see, Anon. *The Severall Factes of Witch-Crafte* (London: Printed by John Charlewood, 1585); T.I., "A Memorial of Certaine Notorious Witches and of Their Dealings," in *A World of Wonders, a Masse of Murthers, a Covie of Cosenages: Containing Many of the Moste Notable Wonders, Horrible Murthers and Detestable Cosonages That Have Been Within This Land* (London: Printed for William Barley, 1595); Anon., *A Magazine of Scandall* (London: Printed for R.H., 1642). The 1595 pamphlet is a version of a lost pamphlet from 1574–75, see Marion Gibson, *Early Modern Witches: Witchcraft Cases in Contemporary Writing* (London: Routledge, 2000), 146–147 and Marion Gibson, "Mother Arnold: A Lost Witchcraft Pamphlet Rediscovered," *Notes and Queries* 243 (1998): 296–300.
3　For a rare but still under-developed example of witch's rage in the 1650s, see John Vicars, *Against William Li-Lie (alias) Lillie* (London, 1652).
4　Clive Holmes, "Women: Witnesses and Witches," *Past and Present* 140 (1993): 49.
5　Keith Thomas, *Religion and the Decline of Magic: Studies in Popular Beliefs in Sixteenth- and Seventeenth-Century England*, 2nd edn. (London: Penguin Books, 1991), 695. This will be further discussed below.
6　Peter Elmer, ed., *The Later English Trial Pamphlets*, vol. 5 of *English Witchcraft 1560–1736*, eds. James Sharpe and Richard Golden (London: Pickering and Chatto, 2003), vii.
7　Thomas, *Religion and the Decline of Magic*, 2nd edn., 652–680.
8　Alan Macfarlane, *Witchcraft in Tudor and Stuart England: A Regional and Comparative Study*, 2nd edn. (London: Routledge, 1999), 159.
9　See Marion Gibson, *Reading Witchcraft: Stories of Early English Witches* (London: Routledge, 1999), chapter 3. Although Gibson takes Thomas as her starting point, her interpretation differs, most notably in her development of 'motiveless malignancy' narratives, a category that Thomas rejects.
10　See also Malcolm Gaskill, *Crime and Mentalities in Early Modern England* (Cambridge: Cambridge University Press, 2000); Robin Briggs, *Witches and Neighbours: The Social and Cultural Context of European Witchcraft* (London: HarperCollins, 1996); Deborah Willis, *Malevolent Nurture: Witch-Hunting and Maternal Power in Early Modern England* (Ithaca: Cornell University Press, 1995) and Holmes, "Women: Witnesses and Witches," 57.
11　Willis, *Malevolent Nurture*, 77.
12　See, for example, Reginald Scot, *The Discoverie of Witchcraft* (Printed by Henry Denham for William Brome, 1584) and George Gifford, *A Dialogue Concerning Witches and Witchcraftes* (Printed by John Windet, 1593).
13　Anon., *The Whole Trial and Examination of Mrs Mary Hicks and Her Daughter Elizabeth* (London: Printed by W. Matthews in Long-Acre, 1716), 3–4.
14　Macfarlane, *Witchcraft in Tudor and Stuart England*, 2nd edn., 160. See also my analysis of witchcraft pamphlets by gender in the introduction, this volume.

15 Anon., *The Witches of Northampton-shire* (London: Printed by Tho: Parfoot, for Arthur Johnson, 1612); Thomas Potts, *The Wonderfull Discoverie of Witches in the Countie of Lancaster* (London: Printed by W. Stansby for John Barnes, 1613).

16 Gwynne Kennedy, *Just Anger: Representing Women's Anger in Early Modern England* (Carbondale: Southern Illinois University Press, 2000), 5.

17 David Underdown, "The Taming of the Scold: The Enforcement of Patriarchal Authority in Early Modern England," in *Order and Disorder in Early Modern England*, eds. Anthony Fletcher and John Stevenson (Cambridge: Cambridge University Press, 1985), 119.

18 Underdown, "The Taming of the Scold," 119. Martin Ingram has questioned some of Underdown's conclusions, most notably his declaration that cases of scolding rose rapidly from 1560 on by noting the prevalence of scolding cases pre-1560. Ingram does not, however, disagree that these legal cases decreased markedly post-1640. Martin Ingram, "'Scolding Women Cucked or Washed': A Crisis in Gender Relations in Early Modern England?," in *Women, Crime and the Courts in Early Modern England*, eds. Jenny Kermode and Garthine Walker (London: UCL Press, 1994), 52–53.

19 Ingram, "Scolding Women Cucked or Washed," 72.

20 Anon., *The Witches of Northampton-shire*, sig. B2 r; Anon., *The Wonderful Discoverie of the Witchcrafts of Margaret and Phillip Flower* (London: Printed by G. Eld for I. Barnes, 1619), sig. C3 r; B. Misodaimon, *The Divels Delusions* (London: Printed for Richard Williams, 1649), 3; and Anon., *Strange News from Shadwell* (London: Printed by E. Mallet, 1684), 1.

21 Marion Gibson, *Reading Witchcraft*, 97.

22 Ibid., 98.

23 Anon., *The Most Cruell and Bloody Murther* (London: Printed for William Firebrand and John Wright, 1606), sig. C3 r.

24 Ibid.

25 Ibid.

26 Ibid. Interestingly, this man decides to scratch Johane Harrison to try and reverse the bewitchment. This works but he is then sued by Johane's daughter for costs and is forced to pay. Ibid., sig. C3 v.

27 Ibid., sig. C3 r. 'Tenter, *n*.1 A wooden framework on which cloth is stretched after being milled, so that it may set or dry evenly and without shrinking'. Oxford English Dictionary. Available [Online]: www.oed.com.ezp.lib.unimelb.edu.au/view/Entry/199229?rskey=8GpMen&result=1&isAdvanced=false#eid [29 July, 2014].

28 Anon., *The Witches of Northampton-shire*, sig. B2 r.

29 Ibid., sig. B2 v.

30 Ibid.

31 Ibid., sigs. B3 r and B2 v.

32 Ibid., sig. B3 r.

33 Natalie Davis, *Fiction in the Archives: Pardon Tales and Their Tellers in Sixteenth-Century France* (Stanford: Stanford University Press, 1987), chapter 2 and Kristi Gourlay, "A Pugnacious Pagan Princess: Aggressive Female Anger and Violence in Fierabras," in *The Representation of Women's Emotions in Medieval and Early Modern England*, ed. Lisa Perfetti (Gainesville: University Press of Florida, 2005).

34 See also Elizabeth Foyster, "Boys Will Be Boys?: Manhood and Aggression, 1660–1800," in *English Masculinities, 1660–1800*, eds. Tim Hitchcock and Michèle Cohen (London: Longman, 1999), 166.

35 Alexander Roberts, *Treatise of Witchcraft* (London: Printed by N.O. for Samuel Man, 1616), sig. G2 r.

36 Linda A. Pollock, "Anger and the Negotiation of Relationships in Early Modern England," *The Historical Journal* 47 (2004): 570, 573, 582 and 586; Elizabeth Foyster, " 'Boys Will Be Boys?'," 154 and Yasmin Haskell, "Early Modern Anger Management: Seneca, Ovid, and Lieven De Meyere's 'De Ira libri' tres (Antwerp, 1694)," *International Journal of the Classical Tradition* 18 (2011): 50.
37 Thomas Wright, *The Passions of the Minde in Generall* (London: 1601), 262.
38 Nicolas Caussin, *The Holy Court: The Command of Reason over the Passions*, trans. T.H. Rouen (Printed by John Cousturier, 1638), 316.
39 Kennedy, *Just Anger*, 18; Gourlay, "A Pugnacious Pagan Princess."
40 Kristine Steenberg, "Emotions and Gender: The Case of Anger in Early Modern English Revenge Tragedies," in *A History of Emotions 1200–1800*, ed. Jonas Liliequist (London: Pickering and Chatto, 2012), 125.
41 The only sixteenth-century pamphlet that does not mention revenge or malice as a motivation for witchcraft is Anon., *The Examination of John Walsh*, 1566.
42 Francis Bragge, *A Full and Impartial Account of the Discovery of Sorcery and Witchcraft Practis'd by Jane Wenham of Walkerne in Hertfordshire* (London: Printed for E. Curll, 1712), sig. B2 r.
43 Steenberg, "Emotions and Gender," 125.
44 Kennedy, *Just Anger*, 3–4. See also Simon Shephard, *The Women's Sharp Revenge: Five Women's Pamphlets from the Renaissance* (London: Fourth Estate, 1985), 11 and Pollock, "Anger and the Negotiation of Relationships in Early Modern England," 579.
45 Anon., *A Detection of Damnable Driftes, Practized by Three Witches Arraigned at Chelmisforde in Essex at the Last Assizes There Holden, Whiche Were Executed in Aprill, 1579* (London: Printed by J. Kingston for Edward White, 1579), sig. A8 r.
46 W.W., *A True and Just Recorde, of the Information, Examination and Confession of All the Witches* (London: Printed by Thomas Dawson, 1582), sigs. A4 v and F7 v.
47 W.W., *A True and Just Recorde*, sig. B4 v.
48 Anon., *A Rehearsal Both Straung and True, of Heinous and Horrible Actes Committed by Elizabeth Stile alias Rockingham, Mother Dutten, Mother Devell, Mother Margaret, Fower Notorious Witches* (London: Printed by J. Kingston for Edward White, 1579), sig. A8 r-v. For another pamphlet on this case, this time written by the alleged victim, see Richard Galis, *A Brief Treatise* (1579). In this very strange first-person narration, Galis appears convinced that the witches are all against him and determined to torment him and that the magistrates are indifferent. For an analysis of the similarities and discrepancies between these two pamphlets, see Gibson, *Reading Witchcraft*, 96–97 and for more on the unusual nature of Galis's pamphlet, see Gibson, *Early Modern Witches*, 50–51.
49 Anon., *Witches Apprehended, Examined and Executed* (London: Printed for Edward Marchant, 1613), sig. A4 r.
50 Ibid., sig. A4 v.
51 Ibid.
52 Ibid., sig. B1 r.
53 Ibid.
54 Ibid., sigs. B1 r and C1 v.
55 Anon., *The Examination, Confession, Triall, and Execution, of Joane Williford, Joan Cariden, and Jane Hott* (London: Printed for J.G., 1645), 1.
56 Ibid.
57 Ibid. This appears to be a different man from the Thomas Letherland that Joan initially sought revenge upon.

58 Ibid., 2.
59 Ibid., 3 and 5.
60 Ibid., 1 and 5.
61 Helkiah Crooke, *Microcosmographia* (London: Printed by William Jaggard, 1615), 276.
62 Crooke, *Microcosmographia*, 276. See also Francis Bacon who, writing in 1597, believed that anger reigned in 'children, women, old folks, sick folks'. Francis Bacon, *The Essays, or Councils, Civil and Moral* (London, 1718), 150.
63 See Kennedy, *Just Anger*, 6–7 and Foyster, " 'Boys will be boys?'," 157.
64 Lisa Perfetti, "Introduction," in *The Representation of Women's Emotions in Medieval and Early Modern England*, ed. Lisa Perfetti (Gainesville: University Press of Florida, 2005), 4.
65 Foyster, 'Boys will be Boys?,' 156–158.
66 Perfetti, "Introduction," in *The Representation of Women's Emotions in Medieval and Early Modern England*, 7.
67 Foyster, " 'Boys Will Be Boys?'," 158.
68 Anon., *The Witches of Northampton-shire*, sig. B2 r.
69 Brian Levack, *The Witch-hunt in Early Modern Europe*, 3rd edn. (Harlow: Pearson Longman, 2006), 157.
70 Frances Dolan has noted this occurrence but does not expand upon it, Frances Dolan, *Dangerous Familiars: Representations of Domestic Crime in England, 1550–1700* (Ithaca: Cornell University Press, 1994), 199.
71 For a detailed study on different expressions of anger in the Middle Ages, see Barbara Rosenwein, ed., *Anger's Past: The Social Uses of an Emotion in the Middle Ages* (Ithaca: Cornell University Press, 1998) and for a short but useful summary, see Pollock, "Anger and the Negotiation of Relationships in Early Modern England," 570–571.
72 Edward Reynolds, *A Treatise of the Passions and Faculties of the Soule of Man* (London: Printed by R. H., 1640), 329.
73 Perfetti, "Introduction," in *The Representation of Women's Emotions in Medieval and Early Modern England*, 12. See also Gourlay, "A Pugnacious Pagan Princess" and Kennedy, *Just Anger*.
74 Pollock, "Anger and the Negotiation of Relationships in Early Modern England."
75 Ibid.
76 Ibid., 573.
77 Ibid., 574.
78 Lancelot Blackburne, *The Unreasonableness of Anger* (London: Printed by Tho. Warren for Thomas Bennet, 1694) quoted in Elizabeth Foyster, " 'Boys Will Be Boys?'," 154.
79 John Stearne, *A Confirmation and Discovery of Witchcraft* (London: Printed by William Wilson, 1648), 5.
80 Ibid.
81 Anon., *An Account of the Tryal and Examination* (London: Printed for S. Gardener, 1682), 2
82 Anon., *The Witch of Wapping* (London: Printed for Th. Spring, 1652), 7.
83 Thomas Greenwel, *A Full and True Account of the Discovering, Apprehending and Taking of a Notorious Witch* (London: Printed by H. Hill, 1704), 1.
84 Ibid.
85 Anon., *A Full and True Account of the Tryal, Examination and Condemnation of Mary Johnson, a Witch* (London: Printed by T. Bland, 1706), 1.
86 Darren Oldridge, *The Devil in Early Modern England* (Stroud: Sutton, 2000), 136.
87 Lyndal Roper, *Oedipus and the Devil: Witchcraft, Sexuality and Religion in Early Modern Europe* (London: Routledge, 1994), 234.

88 Anon., *A Detection of Damnable Driftes*, title page.
89 John Phillips, *The Examination and Confession of Certaine Witches* (London: Willyam Powell for Willyam Pickeringe, 1566), sigs. A6 v and A7 r.
90 Ibid., sigs. A6 r and A6 v.
91 Ibid., sig. A7 r.
92 Ibid.
93 Ibid., sig. A7 v.
94 Ibid., sig. A8 r.
95 James Sharpe, "The Witch's Familiar in Elizabethan England," in *Authority and Consent in Tudor England: Essays Presented to C.S.L. Davies*, eds. George W. Bernard and Steven J. Gunn (Burlington, VT: Ashgate, 2002), 223.
96 Anon., *A Detection of Damnable Driftes*, sigs. A4 r-v.
97 Sharpe, "The Witch's Familiar in Elizabethan England," 224.
98 This pamphlet was republished in 1635, Anon., *Witchcrafts Strange and Wonderfull* (London: Printed for M.F. for Thomas Lambert, 1635). There is also a ballad that describes this case, Anon., *Damnable Practices/Of three Lincolneshire Witches, Joane Flower, and Her Two Daughters,/Margret and Phillip Flower, Against Henry Lord Rosse, With Others the Children of the Right/Honourable the Earle of Rutland, at Beauer Castle, Who for the Same Were Executed at Lincolne the 11. of/ March Last* (Printed by G. Eld for John Barnes, 1619).
99 Anon., *The Wonderful Discoverie of the Witchcrafts of Margaret and Phillip Flower*. For two recent books on this case, see Tracy Borman, *Witches: James I and the English Witch-Hunts* (London: Vintage, 2014) and Michael Honeybone, *Wicked Practise & Sorcerye: The Belvoir Witchcraft Case of 1619* (Buckingham: Baron, 2008).
100 Anon., *The Wonderful Discoverie*, sig. C3 r.
101 Ibid., sigs. C3 r-v.
102 Ibid., sig. C4 v.
103 Ibid., sig. F4 r.
104 Ibid., sig. C4 v.
105 Ibid., sig. D1 r.
106 Ibid., sig. D1 v.
107 Ibid., sig. D2 r. As Gibson has explained, there is much confusion over the dates of these deaths. Henry died in 1613, years before this pamphlet was printed, but the pamphlet does not accurately depict this. There is also confusion about whether or not Francis was alive or dead at the time of the witches' arrest (Christmas 1618), as we know that Francis did not die until March 1620. The many contradictions and loss of legal records make it difficult to accurately date the events of this pamphlet. Gibson, *Early Modern Witches*, 276–278.
108 Anon., *The Wonderful Discoverie*, sig. F3 r.
109 Ibid., sig. G1 v.
110 Ibid. There is some confusion in the pamphlet about Agnes Ratclieffe's name. At one point the pamphleteer refers to Elizabeth Ratclieffe. This appears to be a mistake and, for clarity's sake, I assume that the neighbour's name was Agnes.
111 Ibid.
112 Henry Goodcole, *The Wonderfull Discoverie of Elizabeth Sawyer a Witch* (London: Printed for William Butler, 1621), sig. C1 r.
113 Ibid.
114 Ibid., sig. C1 r- C1 v.
115 Ibid., sigs. A4 v-B1 r.
116 David Cressy, *Dangerous Talk: Scandalous, Seditious and Treasonable Speech in Pre-Modern England* (Oxford: Oxford University Press, 2010), 6. For more

on the power of words in the early modern world, see Peter Burke and Roy Porter, eds., *The Social History of Language* (Cambridge: Cambridge University Press, 1987) and Maureen Flynn, "Blasphemy and the Play of Anger in Sixteenth-Century Spain," *Past and Present* 149 (1995): 29–56, especially 36–39.

117 Cressy, *Dangerous Talk*, 2.

118 See, for example, William Perkins, *A Direction for the Government of the Tongue According to Gods Word* (Edinburgh: Printed by Robert Waldegrave, 1593); Jean de Marconville, *A Treatise of the Good and Evell Tounge* (London: By J. Wolfe for John Perin, 1592); George Webbe, *The Araignement of an Unruly Tongue: Wherein the Faults of an Evill Tongue Are Opened, the Danger Discovered, the Remedies Prescribed, for the Taming of a Bad Tongue, the Right Ordering of the Tongue, and the Pacifying of a Troubled Minde Against the Wrongs of an Evill Tongue* (London: Printed by G. Purslowe for John Budge, 1619); John Abernethy, "The Poysonous Tongue," in *A Christian and Heavenly Treatise Containing Physicke for the Soule: Very Necessary For All That Would Enjoy True Soundnesse of Minde, and Peace of Conscience* (London: Printed by Felix Kyngston for John Budge, 1622), 463–485; Edward Reyner, *Rules for the Government of the Tongue: Together, with Directions in Six Particular Cases Added as a Supplement to The rules for Governing the Thoughts, the Affections in the Precepts for Christian Practice, or, the Rule of the New Creature, New Molded, by Edward Reyner* (London: Printed by R. I. for T. N, 1658).

119 Cressy, *Dangerous Talk*, 2.

120 See, for example, H.F., *A True and Exact Relation of the Several Informations, Examinations, and Confessions of the Late Witches, Arraigned and Executed in the County of Essex* (London: Printed by M.S. for Henry Overton, and Benj. Allen, 1645), 7.

121 See Dolan, *Dangerous Familiars*, 198.

122 The King James Bible, Proverbs 12: 13 and 1 Peter 3: 10.

123 Steenberg, "Emotions and Gender," 127.

124 Pollock, "Anger and the Negotiation of Relationships in Early Modern England," especially 569–570.

125 Flynn, "Blasphemy and the Play of Anger in Sixteenth-Century Spain," 44–45. This was often an effective defence.

126 John Davenport, *The Witches of Huntingdon, Their Examinations and Confessions Exactly Taken by His Majesties Justices of Peace for That County* (London: Printed by W. Wilson for Richard Clutterbuck, 1646), title page.

127 Ibid.

128 Ibid., 3.

129 Ibid.

130 Ibid.

131 Ibid.

132 Ibid., 4.

133 Ibid.

134 Claude Paradin, *The Heroicall Devises of M. Claudius Paradin Canon of Beauieu: Whereunto Are Added the Lord Gabriel Symeons and Others* (London: Imprinted by William Kerney, 1591), 138.

135 Nathalie Vienne-Guerrin, ed., *The Unruly Tongue in Early Modern England: Three Treatises* (Madison: Fairleigh Dickinson University Press, 2012), xviii.

136 William Perkins, *A Direction for the Government of the Tongue According to Gods Word* (Edinburgh: Printed by Robert Walde, 1593), preface.

137 Edward Stephens, *Phinehas, or, the Common Duty of All Men, and the Special Duty of Magistrates, to be Zealous and Active in the Execution of Laws Against Scandalous Sins and Debauchery: And of That in Particular Against*

prophane Cursing and Swearing (London: Printed for Richard Smith, 1695), 14, quoted in John Earl Joseph, *Language and Politics* (Edinburgh: Edinburgh University Press, 2006).

138 Flynn, "Blasphemy and the Play of Anger in Sixteenth-Century Spain," 29.

139 Luis de Granada, *Guia de pecadores* (1556) quoted in Flynn, "Blasphemy and the Play of Anger in Sixteenth-Century Spain," 31–32.

140 Vienne-Guerrin, ed., *The Unruly Tongue in Early Modern England*, xxii.

141 Davenport, *The Witches of Huntington*, 9.

142 Ibid.

143 Ibid.

144 Ibid.

145 For Stephens as editor see, Gilbert Geis and Joan Bunn, *A Trial of Witches: A Seventeenth-Century Witchcraft Prosecution* (London: Routledge, 1997), 157.

146 Sir Matthew Hale and Edward Stephens, *A Collection of Modern Relations Concerning Matters of Fact*, 48.

147 Ibid., 48–49.

148 Ibid., 49.

149 Bragge, *A Full and Impartial Account*, 16.

150 Ibid.

151 Phyllis J. Guskin, "The Context of Witchcraft: The Case of Jane Wenham (1712)," *American Society for Eighteenth-Century Studies* 15 (1981): 64.

152 See entry for 'Stephens, Edward, d. 1706' in the Oxford English Dictionary. Available [Online]: www.oxforddnb.com.ezproxy.library.uq.edu.au/view/article/263 80?docPos=2 [20 September, 2016].

153 Greg Peters, *Reforming the Monastery: Protestant Theologies of the Religious Life* (Oregon: Cascade Books, 2014), 61.

154 Guskin, "The Context of Witchcraft: The Case of Jane Wenham (1712)," 64. There is sometimes confusion between Francis Bragge and his father of the same name. The Reverend Francis Bragge was the Francis Bragge who wrote three witchcraft pamphlets in 1712. Bragge senior was vicar of Hitchin, rector of Cottered, and canon of Lincoln. His son, the witchcraft author, was ordained deacon at London in June 1712. Guskin, "The Context of Witchcraft," note 2, page 49. See also Orna Alyagon Darr, *Marks of an Absolute Witch: Evidentiary Dilemmas in Early Modern England* (Farnham: Ashgate, 2011), 132.

155 For an article in which I explore this concept using different sources see Charlotte-Rose Millar, "Over-Familiar Spirits: The Bonds Between English Witches and Their Devils," in *Emotions in the History of Witchcraft*, eds. Michael Ostling and Laura Kounine (London: Palgrave Studies in the History of Emotions, 2017.).

156 Michael MacDonald, *Mystical Bedlam: Madness, Anxiety and Healing in Seventeenth-Century England* (Cambridge: Cambridge University Press, 1981), 202.

157 W.W., *A True and Just Recorde.*

158 Gibson, *Early Modern Witches*, 72; Barbara Rosen, *Witchcraft in England 1558–1618*, 2nd edn. (Amherst: University of Massachusetts Press, 1991), 103–104; Holmes, "Women: Witnesses and Witches," 54.

159 Gibson, *Early Modern Witches*, 72–73, Rosen, *Witchcraft in England*, 103–104.

160 W.W., *A True and Just Recorde*, sig. A3 v.

161 Ibid., sig. A8 r.

162 Ibid., sig. A1 v.

163 Ibid., sig. A8 r.

164 Ibid.

165 Dolan, *Dangerous Familiars*, 197. For more on witchcraft as a way of taking back power, see Malcolm Gaskill, "Witchcraft and Power in Early Modern England: The Case of Margaret Moore," in *Women, Crime and the Courts in Early Modern England*, eds. Jenny Kermode and Garthine Walker (London: UCL Press, 1994) and James Sharpe, "Witchcraft and Women in Seventeenth-Century England: Some Northern Evidence," *Continuity and Change* 6 (1991): 179–199.

166 For a study which uses psychoanalytical theories to explore the persecutory fantasies of accusers, see Deborah Willis, *Malevolent Nurture: Witch-hunting and Maternal Power in Early Modern England* (Ithaca: Cornell University Press, 1995).

167 Diane Purkiss, "Women's Stories of Witchcraft in Early Modern England: The House, the Body, the Child," *Gender and History* 7 (1995): 410.

168 Roper, *Oedipus and the Devil*, 20.

169 Ibid.

170 Perfetti, "Introduction," in *The Representation of Women's Emotions*, 8.

171 W.W., *A True and Just Recorde*, sig. B1 v.

172 Ibid.

173 Ibid., sigs. B1v-B2 r.

174 Ibid., B2 r.

175 Marion Gibson, "Late Witchcraft Trials 1579–1589," in the Oxford Dictionary of National Biography.

176 Ibid.

177 MacDonald, *Mystical Bedlam*, 202.

178 W.W., *A True and Just Recorde*, sig. B4 v.

179 Ibid.

180 Ibid., sig. B3 r.

181 Ibid.

182 Ibid., sigs. B6 v-B7 r.

183 Ibid., sigs. B8 v-C1 r.

184 Ibid., sig. C1 r.

185 Ibid.

186 Ibid., sig. C1 v.

187 Ibid., sig. D5 v.

188 Ibid., sig. D6 r.

189 Ibid., sig. D7 r.

190 Ibid., sig. E2 v.

191 Ibid., sig. D6 r.

192 Ibid., sigs. D6 r-D6 v.

193 Ibid., sig. D6 v.

4   Sleeping with Devils

It is clear that witches in early modern England were believed to form strong bonds with the Devil in the shape of a familiar spirit.[1] But what form did these bonds take? In this chapter, I will emphasise an often-overlooked but important aspect of the witch/devil relationship: the erotic. The trope of the sexualised female witch is present from the very beginning of witch-craft pamphlets. In sixteenth-century pamphlets many pamphleteers refer to witches as 'lewd' or make sure to mention their illegitimate children or the fact that they engaged in pre-marital sex. During the seventeenth century, however, these references to dubious sexual morality develop into some-thing far more explicit. In seventeenth-century England, female witches were believed to engage in intimate, often sexual relationships with devils, relationships which can go some way to revealing ordinary women's hopes, fears and desires. In popular pamphlets there were two main beliefs about how witches and devils interacted sexually. The first involved the witch allowing her demonic (and nearly always animalistic) familiar to suck her in her 'privy parts'. The second involved the familiar appearing in the form of a devilish man and having sexual intercourse with the witch. These two different interactions can be linked to specific chronology; penetrative acts with man-like devils were confined to the 1640s and later, whereas non-penetrative acts with animalistic devils occurred most commonly in the first half of the seventeenth century; although they did continue after this time. Within these narratives, witches were often portrayed as willing participants in pleasurable sexual relationships with devils.

Much older historiography dismisses the idea that English witchcraft was sexualised. In relation to witchcraft trials, Alan Macfarlane once observed that 'English witchcraft . . . differed considerably from that on the Conti-nent [because there] did not seem to be any marked sexual element'.[2] Keith Thomas shared this view and commented that the 'blatantly sexual aspects of witchcraft were a very uncommon feature of the trials, save perhaps of the Hopkins period'.[3] Like Thomas, many authors acknowledged that English witchcraft in the 1640s involved 'a definite sexual element'.[4] There is, how-ever, a strong tendency to focus attention on this decade to the exclusion of others. Both Macfarlane and Thomas focused primarily on witchcraft trial records. But in focusing on witchcraft pamphlets, it becomes clear that sexual encounters between witches and devils were not confined to the 1640s, but were present in pamphlet narratives throughout the seventeenth century and beyond. This difference in source material provides an alternative perspective on English witchcraft, one which focuses on the centrality of sexual interactions between witches and devils. This sexual relationship allows us to explore the frequently-overlooked links between English witchcraft, the Devil and sexual deviancy.

Although the seventeenth century is the time in which ideas of sexually promiscuous witches really flourished, we can see the beginnings of these ideas in sixteenth-century pamphlets. If we return to Elizabeth Francis, an accused witch we met in chapter 3, we see an early preoccupation with emphasising accused witches' loose sexual morals. Elizabeth Francis engaged in pre-marital intercourse with two men. She killed the first (Andrew Byles) because he would not marry her after they had sex and then, finding herself pregnant, 'willed Sathan to destroye' the child.[5] She then slept with a second man out of wedlock and, as the pamphleteer pruriently points out, had a child 'borne within a quarter of a yere' after their marriage.[6] Eventually, Elizabeth calls on Satan again, this time to kill her living child and to lame her husband.[7] Not only is the Devil crucial in allowing Elizabeth to inflict harm on her family, he is instrumental in her sexual impropriety as it was the cat familiar Sathan that told Elizabeth that she could have Andrew Byles for a husband only if she slept with him first.[8] A 1579 pamphlet, while not going into nearly as much detail, described accused witch Elizabeth Stile as a 'lewd' woman and in another pamphlet from 1582, one accused witch was called 'old trot, old whore and other lewde speaches,' while another was described as 'a naughtie woman, yet another as a 'stinking whore' and one more as 'a light woman and a common harlot' a 'wicked harlot', a 'veild strumpet' and a 'harlot and witch'.[9] One particularly deviant witch in this same pamphlet was believed to have willed her son 'beeing of the age of xxiii years to lye in bedde with her'.[10] In 1589 accused witch Joan Cunny was said to be 'living very lewdly, having two lewde daughters [and] two Bastard Children'.[11] These references, interspersed with far more of witches killing children and hurting their husbands, depict witches as lewd, immoral and sexually deviant women. It is not, however, until the seventeenth century that these allusions to sexual immorality become far more explicit and start to point to a belief that witches engaged in sexual relationships with devils.

My analysis of the forty-eight witchcraft pamphlets that survive from the seventeenth century demonstrates that twenty-three (or 48 per cent) contain examples of sexual interactions between witches and devils. In ten of these pamphlets (or approximately 20 per cent) this interaction is described as 'carnal intercourse' between a witch and a devil. In the other thirteen pamphlets a range of sexual behaviour is described, the most common being devils sucking at teats in a witch's genitalia or anus. These descriptions are part of an ongoing English belief in the witch's pact with the Devil, a phenomenon discussed in chapter 2. The belief that familiars sucked blood from witches (often from teats) as part of the diabolical pact was well established in popular print from as early as the sixteenth century. The position of these teats varied but, as James Sharpe has argued, 'by the early seventeenth century, it was generally accepted that the [witch's] mark [in the form of a teat] would be on the witch's genitals or on her anus, thus adding a sexual dimension to the relationship between the female witch and her familiar'.[12] Sharpe's argument is a relatively new one in a field that has for so long viewed English witchcraft as asexual. In this chapter I argue that the Devil's frequent sucking at witches' genitalia, as well as accounts of sexual intercourse between witches and devils, provide strong evidence for understanding English witchcraft as a sexualised activity.

In seventeenth-century pamphlet accounts of sexual practices between witches and devils, devils take two main forms. The first is as we would typically think of a familiar: a small domestic or common animal such as a rat, cat, dog, bird, toad or ferret that performs the role of the Devil. The second is slightly more difficult to categorise. It can best be described as a devil that resembles a man, who may or may not be defined as a familiar, but is always demonic. The first category of devils (animalistic familiars) is more likely to engage in sexual activity that stops short of penetrative sex. These devils perform acts that resemble foreplay, cunnilingus or anilingus on witches by sucking at teats located on the breasts, genitalia or anus. The more man-like devils, although they too engage in these practices, are more often described as engaging in penetrative sex with their mistresses. Pamphlets do not just describe the physical acts between witch and devil; they also describe the witch's willingness to participate in them and emphasise their pleasurable nature.

These two main forms of sexual activity in witchcraft pamphlets are clearly limited to discrete chronological periods. Pamphlets from the first half of the seventeenth century focus primarily on non-penetrative sexual practices. These activities are described in pamphlets as late as the 1690s, but from the 1640s onwards they tend to be supplemented, and sometimes replaced, by references to witches engaging in intercourse with man-like devils. This change from familiar spirits to a mixture of familiar spirits and man-like devils represents a shift in beliefs about English witchcraft. Although familiar spirits very clearly perform the role of the Devil, and are often described in pamphlets as the Devil himself, their supplementation with man-like devils introduces a change to the way in which diabolical witchcraft was portrayed in England.

Is Everything about Sex? Some Ambiguous Narratives

Although the focus of this chapter is on the sexual nature of English witchcraft, it would be wrong to claim that all intimate interactions between witches and devils were sexual. Many narratives are ambiguous, and while they have definite sexual undertones, some hint at a more maternal relationship. As Philip Almond has recently summarised, 'in the English context, the sexual, demonic and maternal were complexly interwoven'.[13] Another recent work has commented on this conflation, noting that relationships between witches and familiars could take on many meanings: 'contractual, vampiric, maternal, demonic, and erotic'.[14] For one instance of this confusion, take, for example, Susanna Edwards's 1682 confession (discussed in greater detail as follows). Susanna confesses that her Devil 'had the carnal knowledge of her Body Four several times'.[15] She also admits, however, that this Devil took the form of a boy, lay with her in bed and sucked at her breasts.[16] This narrative perfectly encapsulates the ambiguity between sexuality and maternity found in some witchcraft narratives and in early modern society more generally. If it were not for the Devil's shape as a boy, we might assume that references to the Devil sleeping in the same bed as Susanna, as well as the sucking of her breasts, would be part of her sexual encounters with Satan. This could still be the case, and the Devil's shape might simply add an extra layer of deviancy to the encounter. Or this narrative may be referring to elements of both maternal and sexual affection.

The line between sexuality and maternity was blurred during the early modern period. As Walter Stephens has highlighted, 'the corporeal contact involved in suckling [a child] is about as intimate as sexual intercourse', not least because of the exchange of bodily fluids.[17] In witchcraft narratives, these associations become even more confused. Early modern medical thinking understood breast milk as a substance which came from blood. As one contemporary explained, 'the milk by which the infant is nourish, is but the blood of which it was framed in the womb, further concocted in thye breast, and turn'd white there'.[18] Deborah Willis suggests that witches (who were generally beyond their childbearing years) 'inverted this process, providing blood as a substitute for milk'.[19] Walter Stephens has added to this interpretation by pointing out that, because of this belief, 'there was no essential difference between suckling a familiar with blood and giving milk to one's child'.[20] Diane Purkiss disagrees, arguing that through the turning of her milk to blood a woman is turned 'from the giver of life to the giver of death'.[21] The problem with the suggestion that the witch is a giver of death is that witches were able to feed and sustain their familiars through blood. Deborah Willis and Diane Purkiss have both argued convincingly for an interpretation of the bonds between female witch and familiar as akin to mother and child. They interpret the witch as an anti-mother who disrupts familial or marital harmony.[22] Both scholars focus their analyses primarily on the sixteenth and early seventeenth centuries, but instances of witches disrupting marital or domestic harmony, killing children and harming livestock are a common thread of witchcraft pamphlets throughout the seventeenth century and even into the eighteenth. Take, for example, Jane Wenham who, in 1712, stroked a nurse child, causing its feet to become 'so distorted' that 'the Toes were turned back behind the Heel' eventually leading to fits and death, or Mary Johnson who, in 1706, killed a three-year-old boy by causing him to be taken with 'strange Convulsions, bleeding strangely at the Nose [and] Mouth' until he died, or even Amy Duny who, in 1682, being angry that she was not allowed to nurse a neighbour's child, caused the child to fit so severely that it became unable to suckle.[23] This chapter does not wish to take anything away from the interpretation of the witch as a disruptive anti-mother – a crucial theme of witchcraft narratives – rather, it seeks to shed light on another, far less explored aspect of the relationship between witch and Devil: the erotic.

The conflation between sexual and maternal affection is most obvious in narratives which describe familiars sucking at their mistresses' breasts. Breasts can be conceived of in different ways; they are a source of maternal nurture and also a stimulus of sexual attraction. It is not surprising that these uses can become blurred and untangling them from a distance of almost four hundred years is difficult, if not impossible. There are only three or four instances from the seventeenth century of familiars sucking at witches' breasts, and none from either the sixteenth or the eighteenth. The closest sixteenth-century example comes from an illustration in a 1589 pamphlet, in which Bidd (the 'dunnish culloured ferret having fiery eyes' who we met in chapter 2) is sucking blood from Joan's cheek (see figure 2.4 in chapter 2).[24] In the illustration, Joan cups her breast and rests her hand on her stomach while Bidd sucks, thus hinting at the ambiguous sexual and maternal undertones of the arrangement.[25]

For the first reference to familiars actually sucking their mistresses' breasts, we need to turn to Thomas Potts' famous Lancashire Witches pamphlet of 1613. In this narrative, Alizon Device describes how a black dog appeared to her and 'desir[ed] her to give him her Soule'.[26] Alizon agreed and, to seal the pact, the black dog 'did with his mouth . . . sucke at her breast, a little below her Paps, which place did remaine blew halfe a year'.[27] Alizon's black dog familiar goes on to lame a pedlar for her, but then vanishes after Alizon refuses to stay and talk to him.[28] The familiar's anger (or perhaps hurt) at being ignored characterises the relationship between familiar and witch as one that engendered emotional responses and did not just take the form of a business transaction. In this narrative there is no indication of a sexualised or maternal relationship between witch and Devil. The only hint of this is the familiar's decision to suck at Alizon's breast rather than at another part of her body. With so little context it is impossible to interpret this interaction clearly.

A more straightforward narrative appears in a pamphlet of 1619. In this pamphlet Philippa Flower attempts to trade the love of her familiar for the love of a man. Philippa's story is told in pamphlets from both 1619 and 1635. In the earlier pamphlet, Philippa describes how she 'hath a Spirit sucking on her in the forme of a white Rat, which keepeth her left breast, and hath so done for three or foure yeares'.[29] When questioned on the agreement between herself and the rat, Philippa explains that when her familiar 'came first unto her, shee gave her Soule to it, and it promised to doe her good, and cause *Thomas Simpson* to love her.'[30] The 1635 version of this story also recounts Philippa's confession. The continued sucking on Philippa's breast by her familiar over so many years is highly emotive, and perhaps acts as a substitute for the ongoing love she would like to share with Thomas Simpson. If this is the case, then the sucking of the familiar becomes rather more sexual than maternal and seems to indicate desire. Thomas Simpson does in fact fall in love with Philippa. Unfortunately, Thomas eventually leaves her, after claiming that he only stayed with her because 'shee had bewitched him: for hee had no power to leave her'.[31] Philippa explains that her reason for joining with the Devil was to make Thomas Simpson fall in love with her. Philippa's motivation for joining with the Devil (love) makes it seem more likely that her familiar's sucking at her breast symbolises a projection of her sexual desire rather than maternal affection.

Another narrative, this time from 1646, depicts a witch who, while wanting to have an intimate relationship with her devils, is unable to do so because of their refusal. Joane Wallis tells her examiner that 'she first would have had [her familiars] suck her breasts, but they would not, and chose the place [to suck] themselves'.[32] Joane's specific wish for her familiars to suck her breasts and not her genitalia or thighs (as appears in some other accounts) suggests that she has maternal feelings towards her devils and wishes them to act as surrogate children. During the early modern period, it was generally believed that mothers should breastfeed their own children rather than allow other women to do so. The importance of this task was emphasised by Protestant reformers as part of the latter sixteenth-century ideal of motherhood as a 'special vocation'.[33] This was partly due to the belief that maternal feeding allowed a mother's good qualities to be passed on to her children.[34] Joane's desire to nurse her familiars may suggest that she feels responsible for their welfare. Her familiars' refusal to conform to this wish could suggest that Joane's familiars have assumed the role of rebellious children who have rejected their mother. This instance, unlike many of its predecessors, seems to have a great deal more maternal than sexual relevance.

In 1648, John Stearne made a general statement about witches' teats. He claimed that these marks are 'much like the circle of a womans brest which hath been sucked' and argued that 'it is more easier to finde them on the brest then in any other place'.[35] This last comment appeared straight after Stearne's account of Ellen Greenliefe, a witch who confessed to sleeping with the Devil. Although Stearne's description of women's breasts is not overly sexual, its placement after a sexual confession is suggestive. Stearne does not offer any explanation for this phenomenon. A pamphlet of the following year simply states that Elizabeth Knott's familiar 'sucked upon her breast' and then disappeared.[36] This description involves no emotional descriptors; rather it is a statement of fact. It is possible, as this is the last early modern reference to this type of behaviour, that the concept was so ingrained in popular beliefs about witchcraft that an explanation of its significance had become unnecessary.

These examples from the 1640s mark the last printed references to animalistic familiars sucking at witches' breasts. In the second half of the century, pamphleteers appear to have lost interest in this phenomenon, only to replace it with more sexually explicit references. It is also less common to find references in the second half of the century to devils sucking at witches in their 'secret parts', a phenomenon that will be discussed below. But the ambiguities between sexuality and maternity still existed in witchcraft narratives from the second half of the seventeenth century. In one example, from 1682, the pamphlet describes the examination of Rose Cullender:

> they found in her Privy Parts three more Excrescencies or Teats . . . the long Teat at the end thereof there was a little hole, and it appeared unto them as if it had been lately sucked, and upon the straining of it there issued out white milkie Matter.[37]

Although this description seems sexual in its depiction of familiars sucking at Rose's genitalia, it describes the liquid coming from Rose's teats as milk rather than blood.[38] This apparent contradiction is perhaps less surprising when we remember the early modern belief that breast milk was formed from the conversion of blood inside a woman's body. The interchangeability of blood and milk during this period makes it hard to determine the exact meaning of this interaction between witch and familiar. Although this narrative does not appear to be overtly sexualised, as Julia M. Garrett has pointed out, the practice of searching for teats in witches' genitalia was an inherently sexualised process, one which provided a legitimate context for communal scrutiny and intimate investigation of women's bodies.[39] Even in those pamphlets that did not describe explicit sexual encounters, witches' bodies were still sexualised.

Sex with Devils: Cunnilingus, Anilingus and Other Sexual Practices

Of the seven popular witchcraft pamphlets published between 1606 and 1635 all but one describe familiars sucking the thighs or the 'secret' parts of their mistresses.[40] Although predominantly a seventeenth-century concept, the belief that witches could have teats on their thighs or secret parts also existed in one pamphlet from the sixteenth century. These descriptions are all very similar but some are more explicit than others. A 1582 pamphlet describes how Ursley Kempe and Annis Glascocke both had identical marks on their inner thighs. These spots have apparently been sucked, but the pamphlet does not say which familiars sucked them.[41] When Ursley is asked about where on her body her familiar sucked she says she doesn't know; it is the female searchers who suggest that the marks on Ursley's thighs have been sucked.[42] Here we see the pamphleteer and witnesses interpreting Ursley's relationship with her familiar in a sexual light. Another narrative, from 1619, refers to accused witch Margaret Flower, a woman who has two dog familiars, one white and one black. The pamphlet claims that 'the white [dog familiar] sucked under her left brest, and the blacke spotted [dog familiar] within the inward parts of her secrets'.[43] This narrative describes the witch as engaging in sexually explicit behaviour with her devil and is typical of the other pamphlets from this period. Although these pamphlets do not explicitly refer to sex with the Devil, they do describe cunnilingus between a witch and her demonic spirit. Geoffrey Quaife has argued that non-penetrative sex may have been extremely common during the early modern period. Although Quaife's study specifically focuses on Somerset, his conclusions allow us an insight into sexual practices in England. When attempting to reconcile low birth rates with a lack of contraception, Quaife argues that 'heavy petting' may have become 'an end in itself' rather than a precursor to intercourse.[44] He also suggests that digital penetration may have sometimes been preferred to penetrative sex and cites a number of assaults in which men only digitally penetrated their victims.[45] J.L. Flandrin, when looking at the French context, also suggests that men and women commonly engaged in non-penetrative sexual acts outside marriage and believes that many men and women would have engaged in oral sex.[46] Against a background of Christian morality these non-penetrative acts were viewed as 'illicit', as they did not take the form of sexual intercourse for the procreation of children within marriage.[47] Although the number of acts viewed as 'illicit' had contracted somewhat by the seventeenth century, many sexual practices still remained taboo in the eyes of Church authorities.[48] Fornication, for example, was punishable by three months jail and a good behaviour bond for a further year.[49] Sexual activities such as cunnilingus and fornication were incorporated into popular witchcraft print and made even more unnatural through the substitution of man and woman with Devil and witch.

The most explicit description of oral sex from the first half of the seventeenth century comes from a 1621 pamphlet narrating the supposed witchcrafts of the spinster Elizabeth Sawyer.[50] As we saw in chapter 3, this pamphlet takes the form of a question and answer interrogation that allows the reader to feel that they are hearing Elizabeth's version of events. Elizabeth tells her interrogator (Henry Goodcole, ordinary to Newgate and author) that her devil 'always [appeared] in the shape of a dogge, and of two collars, sometimes of blacke and sometimes of white'.[51] Goodcole asks Elizabeth: 'Whether did you pull up your coates or no when the Divell came to sucke you?' Elizabeth replies, 'No, I did not, but the Divell would put his head under my coates, and I did willingly suffer him to doe what hee would'.[52] Goodcole here has introduced a decidedly sexual element to Elizabeth's narrative. Tellingly, Elizabeth has not initiated this discussion of sexual practice. Goodcole's introduction of the question suggests that at least some pamphleteers believed that illicit sex was a normal element of witch-craft and concourse with the Devil. Goodcole's question about Elizabeth's coats reflects typical ideas about sexual practice during the early modern period. Quaife has suggested that when engaging in illicit sexual practices it was most common for a woman to simply pull up her dress to expose her lower body rather than for her to disrobe entirely. This, Quaife argues, was because of the nature of women's dress; the typical laced bodices worn by most women during this time made it more difficult to access a woman's upper body than her lower half.[53] The above description would seem to reflect this practice. Goodcole is also adopting the form of words used to describe sexual acts in a legal setting. Laura Gowing has commented on the formulaic way in which many early modern witnesses described sexual acts. The phrase 'taking up her coats' was a euphemistic and less embarrassing way for witnesses, particularly women, to describe sexual activity.[54] Eliza-beth, however, denies lifting up her skirts despite her testimony that she let the Devil do what he wanted. Elizabeth could, perhaps, be emphasising her initial reluctance to engage in illicit sexual activity. As we see from the rest of Elizabeth's testimony, however, this reluctance is quickly overcome. The erotic nature of her description strongly suggests to the reader that Elizabeth engaged in cunnilingus with the Devil.

It is impossible to know how common oral sex between men and women was during the early modern period. Flandrin believes that oral sex occurred commonly in early modern culture but Edward Shorter has suggested that although oral sex was practised, cunnilingus was one of the least common forms of sexual activity.[55] Richard Davenport-Hines has speculated that oral sex may have been unappealing to many early modern people because of low hygiene standards.[56] Quaife also highlights the rarity of cunnilingus, stating instead that 'the manual stimulation of the penis, clitoris and vagina' was one of the most common forms of sexual practice.[57] Tim Hitchcock, in his study of the eighteenth century, has argued that oral sex was almost com-pletely unheard of during this century.[58] Various pre-marital sexual activities were, not surprisingly, relatively common in early modern England, and although perhaps less common than other types of sexual practice (such as digital penetration or fellatio), cunnilingus was certainly not unknown to the early modern populace. If it was less common than other sorts of sexual practices, then its frequent inclusion in witchcraft pamphlets would seem to emphasise the unnaturalness of sexual acts between witches and devils. Of all possible illicit sexual practices, it was cunnilingus, an act designed specifically for female pleasure, which was referred to and incorporated into witchcraft print.

The way in which Goodcole describes Elizabeth's sexual encounter con-veys the impression that she is a willing participant. Goodcole relates that Elizabeth wanted the Devil to suck her (presumably in her genitalia), sug-gesting sexual desire. Elizabeth emphasises this apparent pleasure by sup-posedly telling Goodcole that 'when hee [the Devil] suckt mee, I then felt no paine at all'.[59] In this narrative there is no mention of the Devil sucking at Elizabeth for blood or any other gain. Instead, this action appears to be purely for pleasure. Historians such as Edward Shorter have controversially claimed that 'there is little evidence that women derived much pleasure' from sex within the traditional family.[60] There is a wealth of evidence that counters this argument. In the English context, Quaife's study of sexual practices among peasants in Somerset strongly suggests that at least some women in early modern society actively enjoyed sex and frequently engaged in pre-marital sex.[61] Although many church authorities disapproved of sexual desire and pleasure, it is clear that men and women still engaged in and sought out pleasurable, non-procreative sexual activities. In the English context it is clear that 'the Church's strict sexual code was never universally observed'.[62] Keith Thomas's finding that approximately one-fifth of brides were pregnant on their wedding day reminds us that many men and women engaged in pre-marital sex.[63] It is impossible to believe that women would have engaged in these interactions if they did not derive some pleasure from them.

Goodcole's 1621 pamphlet also outlines a more practical reason for the Devil sucking at Elizabeth's body. In reply to Goodcole's question, 'In what place of your body did the Devill sucke of your bloud, and whether did hee himselfe chuse the place or did you your selfe appoint him the place?'[64] Elizabeth replies:

> The place where the Divell suckt my bloud was a little above my fundi-ment, and that place chosen by himselfe; and in that place by continuall drawing, there is a thing in the forme of a Teate, at which the divell would sucke mee. And I asked the Divell why hee would sucke my bloud, and hee sayd it was to nourish him.[65]

In this example Elizabeth explicitly states that the Devil sucked her to nour-ish himself with her blood. This explanation, however, does not explain why the Devil has chosen to suck at a sexualised part of Elizabeth's body, namely, her anus. The above passage implies acts of both cunnilingus and anilingus and furthers the argument that English witchcraft was often described in sexual terms.[66] It also indicates a desire on behalf of the witch to enter into these types of liaisons.[67]

Less explicit but still sexualised are the repeated references during this period to familiars sucking at witches' thighs. The first of these appears in 1613, in which two witches, as payment for their familiars killing a young boy, Master Enger, allow their familiars (Dicke and Jude) to 'sucke at their two Teats which they had on their thighes'.[68] This practice is repeated in 1619 and 1635 in two pamphlets that recount the witchcraft of Margaret and Philippa Flower. The 1619 pamphlet tells us that Joane Willimot, one of the accused, 'had a spirit sucking on her, under the left flanke, in the likenesse of a little white Dogge'.[69] This description is repeated in the 1635 version of this pamphlet.[70] In both of these accounts it is impossible to tell how Joane feels about her familiars suckling her, as this description comes from another accused witch, Ellen Greene. In the first example from 1613, the familiars' sucking at their mistresses so that they can kill a child seems to adhere to a typical understanding of the witches' pact. And like the previous references to sucking at witches' genitalia, these acts demonstrate the sexual and innately personal nature of this agreement.

During the 1640s references to teats in genitalia and on thighs continue. Interspersed amongst these descriptions are examples of intercourse between witches and devils. There is also more of a preoccupation with man-like devils. Many pamphlets depicted both animalistic familiars sucking at witches' thighs and genitalia and also acts of sexual intercourse between witches and both animal and man-like devils. The descriptions of animalistic familiars sucking at witches' genitalia and thighs do not differ greatly from those in the decades before. In 1645 Elizabeth Clarke described her first encounter with her familiars:

> there came a white thing to her in the night, and the night after a gray one, which spake to this Examinant, and told her they would doe her no hurt, but would helpe her to an Husband, who should maintaine her ever after: And that these two things came into this Examinants bed every night, or every other night, and sucked upon the lower parts of her body.[71]

This passage presents these sexualised encounters as a ritual in which both parties willingly participate. Elizabeth's familiars always appear in her bed at night, suggesting that they and Elizabeth engage in regular and ongoing sexual activity. Both familiars explicitly state that they will not hurt Elizabeth and offer her a husband and a stable life. Elizabeth, an old woman who has only one leg and lives in poverty, accepts this offer of protection.[72] In the familiars' quest to find a husband for Elizabeth they take on elements of the role of husband themselves by regularly sharing Elizabeth's bed and engaging in sexual activity with her. As Frances Dolan has noted, this case is remarkably homely, and betrays Elizabeth's desire for emotional and financial support.[73] The familiars' promises to protect and support Elizabeth also echo the role of a husband in early modern society.

Throughout the 1640s there are nine references to familiars sucking at witches' genitalia or thighs.[74] After the 1640s these descriptions of cunnilingus-type activity seem to disappear from popular print apart from one mention during the 1650s.[75] They do not reappear until the 1680s and 1690s. A 1684 pamphlet implicitly refers to cunnilingus through its description of the examination of accused witch Alice Fowler's body. Alice was found 'stripped, dead and cold as *Clay* laying on the Floor on her Back, and having two great Toes ty'd together, and a *Blanket* flung over her'.[76] After neighbours made this grotesque discovery, they searched Alice's body and 'found in the private parts of the Corps five Teats; . . . and that they were all of them as black as a *Coal*'.[77] The suggestion that familiars sucked at teats in Alice's genitalia is very strong here.

The belief that devils sucked witches in their genitalia is a reoccurring motif throughout the seventeenth century. Earlier pamphlets (such as those from 1619 and 1621) are more explicit in describing how devils sucked at the genitalia of witches. The above 1684 pamphlet does not explicitly state why there are teats in Alice's genitalia; the author seems to be assuming that his readers will understand this reference to illicit sexuality. By the 1680s there appears to be a strong tradition of witches being portrayed in pamphlets as women who regularly engaged in illicit sexual practices with their devils. The assumption of deviant sexuality in witchcraft narratives is perhaps strongest in a frontispiece engraving from 1688. This image from Nathaniel Crouch's *The Kingdom of Darkness* clearly shows two female witches kneeling before the Devil and performing fellatio (figure 4.1). This extraordinary depiction is part of a montage of common witchcraft beliefs, including witches and devils dancing and feasting together, witches conjuring devils from a magic circle, and witches riding goats through the sky.[78] The witches fellating the Devil are very prominently depicted. The witches' kissing of the Devil's genitals, as well as having very clear sexual overtones, could also be viewed as a reversal of the obscene kiss, an act in which, in parts of Continental Europe, the witch kisses the Devil's backside as a show of allegiance. This illustration is, to my knowledge, the only depiction of fellatio in an English witchcraft pamphlet, and it appears to have been overlooked by historians. Despite its non-English origins (the engraver is Dutch) its inclusion on the frontispiece of an English witchcraft book from the late seventeenth century demonstrates that witchcraft was strongly associated with deviant, diabolical sex at this time and that this view of witchcraft was being circulated in English print.

Only three more early modern references to familiars sucking at witches' genitalia remain. In a 1690 pamphlet Margaret Landish, a witch accused of killing a child, confesses that 'her Imps did usually suck two Teats near the privy parts'.[79] Two of the other witches in this pamphlet, Susan and Rose, are also accused of having teats. Women searching Susan and Rose claim to have found 'several large Teates in the secret Parts of their Bodies', which both witches adamantly deny at trial.[80] For one last, far more graphic description of demonic cunnilingus, we need to venture into the eighteenth century. One witness, Mrs Evans, described how she was foolishly seduced into witchcraft by Elinor Shaw and Mary Phillips; but was then terrified when the moment for her conversion came. Mrs Evans deposed that Elinor and Mary had told her that 'she was a Fool to live so Miserable as she did, and therefore if she was willing, they would send something that Night that

Figure 4.1 A witch performing fellatio on the Devil and other scenes, depicted in Nathaniel Crouch, *The Kingdom of Darkness* (London: Printed for Nath. Crouch, 1688), frontispiece. © The British Library Board, C.118.b.3, engraved title page.

would Relieve her'.[81] Being a self-described 'ignorant woman' Mrs Evans agreed and that same night:

> Two little black Things, almost like Moles came into her Bed and sucked her lower Parts, repeating the same for two or three Nights after, till she was almost frighted out of her Sences, insomuch that she was forced to send for Mr. *Danks*, the Minster to Pray by her several Nights, before the said Imps would leave her.[82]

Mrs Evans is clearly terrified by her night-time encounter with these familiar spirits, so much so that she calls in the minister. In this encounter, demonic sex, specifically cunnilingus, is described as the entry into witchcraft, a key part of the relationship between witch and Devil.

Some acknowledgement needs to be made of the shape of the Devil during these encounters. In all of these interactions, the Devil was described as taking animal form. From 1533, bestiality was a crime punishable by death in England. But bestiality was not just condemned as an offence against the state. For early modern authors, bestiality was 'a sin against God, Nature and the Law' and an 'abominable and detestable Sin'.[83] Bestiality was ungodly, an offence against Christian morality. Erica Fudge has demonstrated that the sixteenth and seventeenth centuries witnessed increasing concern over human-animal relationships, and about the boundaries of being human.[84] Human-animal relations were increasingly viewed as monstrous and threatening, a concern evident in the early modern preoccupation with monstrous births.[85] These new early modern understandings of the dangers of human-animal relationships open up another way in which contemporaries may have interpreted witchcraft narratives. Not only were accused witches turning away from God and entering into pacts with the Devil, the Devil's animalistic form made their deviancy even more unnatural and disturbing.

Throughout the seventeenth century pamphlets highlighted a preoccupation with the idea that animalistic familiars could and did suck at teats within witches' genitalia, on their anus or on their thighs. Many of these cases are confined to the first half of the century, although there are several in the 1640s and a few in the decades following. Descriptions of familiars sucking at witches' genitalia, anuses and thighs demonstrate the increasing sexualisation in popular print of the relationships between witches and devils and of the demonic pact. These narratives generally depict witches as willing participants in sexual liaisons. In the decades following the 1640s, instances of sexual relations between witches and their devils become even more common in pamphlet narratives. Although instances of devils sucking at thighs and genitalia remain (as we have seen), from the 1640s onwards interactions between witches and devils were increasingly described as 'carnal intercourse'.

Sex with Devils: Intercourse and Pregnancy

From the 1640s onwards the focus of pamphlets shifts from non-penetrative sexual acts with animalistic familiars to accusations of witches sleeping with man-like devils. As noted above, a wide range of non-penetrative sexual practices were common during the seventeenth century. When describing early modern sexual practices, Patricia Crawford and Sara Mendelson have argued that during courtship, "bundling", 'a night of courting, fully clothed, which stopped short of intercourse' was 'widely practised', and as Kim Phillips and Barry Reay have reminded us, before the eighteenth century 'references to kissing, mutual fondling and groping suggest that many unmarried couples did possibly limit their sexual activity within that frame'.[86] These non-procreative acts may well have become the norm. But this emphasis on non-penetrative sex changed after the seventeenth century. Tim Hitchcock has argued that 'eighteenth-century England witnesses a "sexual revolution" which transformed attitudes, creating a phallocentric and increasingly heterosexual culture which saw forms of behaviour beyond the bounds of penetrative heterosexuality as "unnatural."'[87] Penetrative sex, therefore, became increasingly common throughout the eighteenth century.[88] This was obviously not a clean break; as Hitchcock himself has demonstrated, non-penetrative sexual practices persisted throughout the eighteenth century and the dominance of penetrative sex occurred only during the latter eighteenth century. However, the apparent increase in penetrative sex in eighteenth-century England cannot explain its sudden appearance in witchcraft pamphlets from the mid-seventeenth century onwards. I suggest that with the decline of censorship laws in the 1640s and the corresponding rise in printed pamphlets, pamphleteers were able to become more explicit in their descriptions of demonic sexual activity.[89] Even after the re-establishment of some censorship laws, references to penetrative sex in witchcraft pamphlets continued. It is possible that, once confessions or accusations of penetrative sex between witches and devils became a common element of witchcraft pamphlets, subsequent pamphleteers were more easily able to draw on this trope in their narratives.

On the 25th March 1645 Elizabeth Clarke, a woman who had been 'suspected for a Witch' confessed to Matthew Hopkins:

> [She] . . . had carnall copulation with the Devill six or seven yeares; and that he would appear to her three or four times in a weeke at her bed side, and goe to bed to her, and lye with her halfe a night together in the shape of a proper Gentleman . . . and would say to her, *Besse I must lye with you*, and shee did never deny him.[90]

An analysis of this passage, and the surrounding pages, provides an insight into the sexualisation of English witchcraft and the way in which this sexualisation was described in personal and emotional terms. As in Elizabeth's interactions with her familiars, who regularly visited her in her bed, this sexual relationship between Elizabeth and the Devil seems to have been a regular occurrence. Elizabeth's description of sex with the Devil is not forceful or aggressive; rather, it is almost affectionate. She relates what is evidently a routine that has continued for six or seven years and one that seems to be marked by mutual desire. The Devil's continual appearance at Elizabeth's bedside, and his statement that he 'must' lie with Elizabeth, suggests sexual desire. This is reciprocated by Elizabeth as she says that she 'never' denied the Devil, not that she 'couldn't.' She appears to respect her devilish partner, whom she describes as a 'proper Gentleman'. Similarly, the Devil's shortening of Elizabeth's name to 'Bess' is suggestive of affection or, at the very least, familiarity. What is unclear, however, is whether this devil is understood as a familiar. It seems not, as Elizabeth describes several animalistic spirits she owns as 'familiars', but refers to her sexual partner as 'the Devil'. Elizabeth sleeps with the Devil, and describes her familiars as her 'children'.[91] Elizabeth, a poor and lame woman, has constructed a demonic family in which she has a lover and children.

Elizabeth is not the only woman in this pamphlet who apparently had sexual relations with the Devil. In an echo of Elizabeth's description, Rebecca West describes the Devil as appearing to her 'in the likenesse of a proper young man, who desired of her, that he might have the same familiaritie with her, that others that appeared unto her before had had'.[92] This remark labels Rebecca as a woman of loose sexual morals. Rebecca later sleeps with the Devil, 'who lay with her as a man', so that he will agree to help her take revenge.[93] Uniquely among English witchcraft pamphlets, Rebecca does not just sleep with the Devil; she also marries him. This marriage provides a tantalising glimpse of how accused witches may have viewed their demonic lovers. Although we are not told what shape the Devil takes during his marriage to Rebecca (he has, throughout the pamphlet, variously appeared as a man, a kitten and a dog), we are presumably meant to assume that he is in the form of the 'proper young man' that Rebecca originally slept with. Rebecca describes her marriage in this way:

> the Devill appeared to her the said *Rebecca*, as shee was going to bed, and told her, he would marry her, and that shee could not deny him; she said he kissed her, but was as cold as clay, and married her that night, in this manner; He tooke her by the hand and lead her about the Chamber, and promised to be her loving husband till death, and to avenge her of her enemies; And that then shee promised him to be his obedient wife till death, and to deny God and Christ.[94]

This description is very useful in attempting to deconstruct the emotional overtones in the narrative.[95] Rebecca's promise of obedience draws directly on post-Reformation marriage vows, in which the woman swears the previously unused vow 'to obey'.[96] This vow of obedience was understood as a woman's way of demonstrating her love for her husband, since 'for women, loving behaviour was synonymous with obedience'.[97] The Devil also swears to love Rebecca, promising to be a 'loving husband till death'.[98] Here, the Devil is drawing on post-Reformation vows in which both parties vow 'to love and to cherish [each other], till death'.[99] These vows were not merely declarations of love but, as Katie Barclay has argued, highlighted the types of behaviour that both husband and wife used to demonstrate their love. Whereas women showed their love through obedience, men were expected to demonstrate their love by providing for and protecting their wives.[100] The Devil's promise to 'avenge' Rebecca of her enemies is a typical agreement between witch and Devil. However, read in the context of a marriage, it can be viewed as part of the demonic husband's promise to protect his wife. As a result of these gendered expectations, 'love reinforced male authority and female subordination'.[101] In the case of this demonic marriage ceremony, both Rebecca and her male devil are performing their traditional gender roles by expressing love and obedience and, in doing so, are confirming the importance of affection to their union.

Another accused, known only as Bush of Barton, also turned to the Devil for a husband-like figure. Although Bush did not marry the Devil, he came to her just three weeks after her husband's death:

> The Devill appeared to her in the Shape of a young black man, stand-ing by her bed side, which spoke to her with a hollow voice, and came into bed to her, and had the use of her body, and asked her to deny God and Christ and serve him, and then she should never want, but should be avenged of all her enemies, which she consented to, then she said he kissed her and asked her for bloud, which he drew out of her mouth . . . and that he us'd to have the use of her body two or three times a weeke, and then us'd to kisse her . . . but she said he was colder then man, and heavier, and could not performe nature as man.[102]

In this narrative this man-like Devil has replaced Bush's husband. Not only do Bush and the Devil regularly engage in sexual intercourse over the course of fifteen years, they also appear to have an affectionate bond. Bush empha-sises that the Devil kisses her during sex, thus stressing the intimacy of the encounter. The ongoing nature of this relationship also suggests that it is based on affection and mutual desire. As was the case with Rebecca West and her demonic lover, Bush's devil is cold, thus drawing attention to his inhuman nature and he also fails to ejaculate. Despite these shortcomings, Bush describes her relationship with the Devil as a long-term, loving part-nership: one that has existed for over a decade.

It is worth taking a step back here to consider the origins of these nar-ratives. As was made clear in the introduction, pamphlet narratives are made up of a myriad of different influences, including the witch's own confession, witness statements, editorial interference, pointed questioning and many, many others. It is impossible to say for sure how influenced these confessions were by interrogations and how much the confessions were changed when they were converted to print. But it does seem likely that elements of these narratives did stem from the witch and, in this case, it is possible that these stories of demonic copulation, love and marriage, were based on real relationships that the accused witches had experienced and then transformed at the point of confession into diabolical language. Although not without influence from legal personnel and pamphleteers, the accused witch's own experiences do seem to come through in these narratives.

Another example of demonic copulation comes from a 1645 pamphlet which describes the arraignment of eighteen witches and claims that there are '120 more suspected Witches in prison, at *St. Edmunds-bury*'.[103] Of these witches we are told:

> some have confessed that they have had carnall copulation with the Devill, one of which said that she had (before her husband dyed) conceived twice by him, but as soon as she was delivered of them they ran away in most horrid long and ugly shapes.[104]

This passage provides a sense of an ongoing relationship between witch and Devil, one that has progressed long enough to result in two, albeit misshapen, pregnancies. Deformed births were often markers of sin in early modern England. Monstrous births and wonders could be viewed as signs from God, which warned mankind to mend their sinful ways.[105] They could also be signs that the nation was in trouble, with deformities in newborns mirroring deformities in the body politic.[106] The deformed, monstrous children that this woman gave birth to are a physical reminder of her unnatural encounter with the Devil. The passage also allows an insight into how this witch viewed her demonic children. She describes them as 'horrid' and 'ugly', demonstrating an almost tangible repulsion for these deformed children. They are not described as animals, devils or humans, but simply as formless 'shapes'. The witch's description of these repulsive shapes running from her inverts traditional maternal feelings towards newborns and emphasises their inhuman nature.

Descriptions of witches falling pregnant to their demonic lovers opens up another way of understanding the emotional relationship between witches and devils and the particular emotions generated and sustained by them. Until the end of the seventeenth century, the majority of writers held that sexual pleasure was necessary for conception.[107] Some writers even stressed that for a child to be conceived quickly simultaneous orgasm was necessary.[108] Early modern authors advised husbands on how to arouse their wives, encouraging them to use 'wanton kisses [and] wanton words and speeches' and to handle 'her secret parts and dugs, that she may take fire and bee enflamed to venery'.[109] This understanding of sex urges us to understand relationships in which witches believed they conceived by the Devil as highly emotional, pleasurable interactions.

The above instance of demonic pregnancy is not an isolated example. Two other cases both demonstrate that the idea that witches could become pregnant by the Devil was circulating in English belief and, also, that this belief could be drawn upon in an attempt to avoid the executioner. As early as 1593, septuagenarian Alice Samuel tried to claim pregnancy to escape the death penalty. She was roundly mocked and it was decided 'that she was not with childe, unless (as some saide) it was with the divell.'[110] Another case, this time from 1652, concerned two accused witches who were keen to refute any suggestion that the Devil disgusted or hurt them. On the very first page of the pamphlet, Anne Ashby (alias Cobler) and Anne Martyn confessed 'that the Divell had known them carnally, and that they had no hurt by it'.[111] The mention of a lack of harm suggests that the questioner expects the witches to have been damaged by consorting with the Devil, and that both witches wish to correct this view. The judge then pronounces both witches guilty, and they react by pleading 'that they were with child pregnant, but confessed it was not by any man, but by the Divell'.[112] Patricia Crawford has argued that many women were aware of theories concerning conception and would have 'had reason to believe that any pleasurable heterosexual genital contact could lead to pregnancy'.[113] The fact that these women imagine that they are pregnant by the Devil suggests that they imagined their demonic liaisons as similar to other sexual relationships; that is, as pleasurable sexual interactions that could lead to pregnancy. Or, at the very least, believed it was possible that sex with the Devil could be believed to lead to pregnancy and, as such, spare them from execution.

Whether or not witches could fall pregnant by the Devil was a hotly debated topic in early modern Europe and one that seems to have found its way into popular witchcraft narratives. Jean Bodin, Nicholas Remy and Francesco Maria Guazzo, for example, all devoted substantial sections of their treatises to the subject, including whether demonic pregnancy was even possible.[114] Ideas of whether sex with the Devil was pleasurable or painful were also widely debated and could appear in English witchcraft narratives.[115] As Julia M. Garrett has recently noted, English witchcraft literature highlights an ongoing concern with women's erotic pleasure.[116] This has already become clear from Henry Goodcole's extraordinary example; he is determined to find out as much detail about Elizabeth's encounter as possible, paying particular attention to her willingness to engage in erotic encounters. Laura Gowing has argued that, even within marital, reproductive sex, female desire was characterised in a whole range of discourses as 'dangerous, grotesque and unsettling'.[117] In English witchcraft narratives, we see a preoccupation with the pleasurable or painful nature of erotic encounters, of the logistics of these demonic liaisons and a focus on the body of the accused. Depictions of witches as sexually deviant beings who engaged in sexual acts with devils positioned them as dangerous and gruesome, a threat to Christian morality. In many early modern narratives, the painful or pleasurable nature of demonic intercourse, and the witch's reaction to it, is emphasised.

We have only a small number of emotional descriptors that highlight the relationships between witches and their devils. However, by looking at all extant examples of these relationships, we are able to suggest what feelings may have been attached to them. A case from 1646 describes yet another demonic liaison between a witch and a human-like Devil and sheds light on the different uses of man-like and animal-like familiars. Elizabeth Weed, a widow of the County of Huntington, confessed that she had three spirits, 'one in the likenesse of a young man or boy, and the other two of two puppies'.[118] Soon after Elizabeth Weed made a covenant with the man-like spirit, 'he came to bed to her, and had the carnall knowledge of her, and so did divers times after'.[119] Here we see that the covenant or pact is becoming increasingly sexualised. A few lines after this confession, Elizabeth Weed explains:

> the office of [the white puppy] was to hurt man, woman, or coilde[child]; and the office of [the black puppy] was to hurt Cattell when she desired. And the office of the man-like Spirit was to lye with her carnally, when and as often as she desired, and that hee did lye with her in that manner very often.[120]

This description reminds us of Elizabeth Clarke, who slept with her man-like spirit but did not appear to sleep with her animalistic spirits. Elizabeth Weed has divided the functions of her spirits even more, by prescribing a specific role for each familiar. It is also clear here that Elizabeth Weed's demonic lover is actually a familiar, whereas this does not seem to be the case for Elizabeth Clarke. Elizabeth Weed depicts herself as very much in control of her demonic relationships. She is not forced to sleep with the man-like spirit; on the contrary she often 'desires' her devil to sleep with her. The Devil is also described as a willing participant, as he initiates the relationship by coming to bed with her. This type of sexual pleasure outside marriage and motherhood would have been viewed as highly deviant. As Crawford has argued, after the Reformation 'any woman whose sexual desires were not directed towards marriage and motherhood was labelled unnatural'.[121] Elizabeth Weed's admission that she desired this pleasure, not only outside of marriage and motherhood but also with the Devil, adds an extra layer of deviancy to her encounter.

Davenport's 1646 pamphlet contains another example of a witch who appears to feel sexual control over devils, but unlike in the case of Elizabeth Weed this woman refuses to enter into a sexual liaison. Jane Wallis, a spinster, recalls how she first met the Devil while she was 'making of her bedde in her Chamber'.[122] He appeared 'in the shape of a man in blacke cloaths . . . and bid her good-morrow'.[123] His name was Blackeman and he said that he would help her if she were poor. Jane, however, noticed that 'hee had ugly feete, and then she was very fearfull of him for that he would seem sometimes to be tall, and sometimes lesse, and suddenly vanished away'.[124] It is at this point in the narrative that the examiner interrupts Jane and asks whether the Devil 'lay with her'.[125] Jane replies that 'hee would have lain with her, but shee would not suffer him'.[126] Jane's repulsion here is almost tangible. She focuses on the Devil's physical characteristics, such as his shape and his 'ugly' feet. She is not just scared by his appearance, but repelled.

A similar revulsion is apparent, albeit less overtly, in John Stearne's 1648 pamphlet. Ellen Greenliefe, an accused witch from Suffolk, relates how 'the Devill had the use of her body, and used to come to bed to her, but was soft, cold and heavier, so heavie as she could not speake'.[127] Unlike Jane Wallis who actively rejects the Devil, or Rebecca West who embraces him, Ellen appears passive in this narrative. Although these women react differently to their encounter with the Devil, all three of these experiences are characterised by highly personal and sexual feelings. The phrase to have the 'use of' a woman's body was common in the law courts of the seventeenth century.[128] Crawford has argued that this language suggests that men sometimes saw sex as more of a need than a pleasure. Here, and in the above example concerning Bush of Barton, the Devil is described as having similar urges to a man. The Devil is very much defined as the initiator of this encounter and Ellen describes herself as literally unable to breathe under the weight of him, perhaps suggesting that she felt overwhelmed by the experience. Although Ellen has three imps, (a rat, a mole and a mouse), the Devil who sleeps with Ellen appears to be separate from these creatures.[129] John Stearne is very clear in differentiating 'imps' from 'the Devil', in this pamphlet, whereas other pamphlets (as we have seen) are far less explicit.[130]

Many historians have claimed that these accounts of sexual liaisons between witches and devils were only produced to any noteworthy degree during the 1640s.[131] This is part of a broader historiography that persists in seeing the witchcraft beliefs of the 1640s as an 'aberration'.[132] Walter Stephens, for example, has claimed that 'there was only one period when accusations of demonic copulation were prevalent in England: between 1644 and 1647'.[133] However, explicit sexual interactions between witches and devils were present in pamphlet literature from the early years of the seventeenth century and continued throughout the entire century and into the eighteenth. As was stated earlier, six of seven pre-1640 seventeenth-century witchcraft pamphlets describe sexual activity between witches and devils. I agree with Stephens that pamphlets from the 1640s do contain more references to sexual intercourse between witches and devils than pamphlets from previous decades. However, as this chapter has argued, a number of sexual practices such as cunnilingus and anilingus are visible in pamphlets from the first four decades of the seventeenth century. There is a divide between these earlier pamphlets, which showcase animalistic familiars engaging in non-penetrative sex with witches, and pamphlets from the 1640s and later which tend to focus on man-like devils engaging in penetrative sex with witches. Yet, these sexual practices, though varied, introduce the same element of sexualisation into English witchcraft narratives irrespective of the form they take. It does not seem helpful, therefore, to suggest that these references in the 1640s were atypical of the wider century. Sharpe has convincingly argued that during the 1640s 'in the actual content of the witch beliefs that surfaced . . . there was much more which was familiar than unfamiliar'.[134] The 1640s should be viewed not as an aberration but, rather, as an intensification of ideas that were already circulating. Ironically, Gaskill has argued that the increase in sexual accusations in the Hopkins' pamphlets may have actually increased scepticism in witchcraft and, in turn, encouraged the end of the witch-hunts.[135] Garrett has agreed with Gaskill, arguing that the emphasis on demonic sex 'clearly inspired' scepticism amongst key medical figures including John Cotta, John Webster, Thomas Ady and William Harvey.[136] As this chapter demonstrates, references to demonic sex are present throughout pamphlet literature across the entire seventeenth century and are not limited to one particular decade. As we shall see, pamphlets from the second half of the century continue to emphasise the sexual nature of the bond between witch and devil and often describe demonic copulation or intercourse, most typically between a witch and a man-like devil.

The first of these post 1640s narratives appears in a 1650 pamphlet in which Margaret White describes herself as 'the Divels servant':

> the Divell came to her in the likenes of a man in blew cloaths, in her owne house, and griped her fast by the hand, and told her she should never want, and gave her a nip on the shoulder, and another on her back . . . and that the Divell had carnall knowledge of her in her owne house two severall times.[137]

It is important to look at the context of this passage in order to properly understand it. The next line in the pamphlet is particularly helpful. Margaret claims:

> Mrs SWINOW, and her sister JANE, and her selfe were in the Divels company in her sister JANES house, where they did eate and drinke together (as by her conceived) and made merry.[138]

This statement presents the Devil as an ongoing sexual partner of Margaret who accompanies her to intimate social events and dinners.[139] The Devil here appears to be interested in entering into a relationship with Margaret that involves regular, ongoing sex, and is not one based on simply forcing or tricking her. The Devil's gripping of Margaret's hand could be interpreted as a reassuring gesture, particularly in the context of his assurance that she 'should never want'. In this context the 'nips' on Margaret's shoulder and back could also be interpreted as playful gestures. Although Margaret does not explicitly state how she feels towards the Devil, the above context would suggest that there is a mutual affection between witch and devil, and that Margaret is a willing participant in the liaison. Margaret's experience echoes that of Elizabeth Sawyer and Elizabeth Clarke, two witches who were described as experiencing sexual desire in their interactions with their devils. Although Margaret does not discuss desire for her devil, she does confess to being in a long-term partnership with him – one which involves pre-marital sex. In this pamphlet we see yet another example of sexual desire as a driving force behind succumbing to the Devil.

Further seventeenth-century examples of demonic sex appear in pamphlets from the 1680s. During this decade three highly sexualised pamphlets were published, all concerning the same three witches.[140] One of the witches in this group, Susanna Edwards described her sexual interaction with the Devil:

> she was suckt in her Breast several times by the Devil in the shape of a Boy lying by her in her Bed; and that it was very cold unto her. And further saith, that after she was suckt by him, the said Boy or Devil had the carnal knowledge of her body four several times.[141]

Susanna Edwards, Mary Trembles, alias Lloyd or Floyd and Temperance Floyd, alias Lloyd, commonly referred to as the Bideford witches, were all accused of sleeping with the Devil. In the above description, Susanna seems passive, saying that she 'was suckt' by the Devil. The description of the Devil as a 'boy' rather than a man adds to the unnaturalness of the encounter. The Devil sucks at Susanna's breasts, perhaps as part of a demonic pact, or perhaps to arouse her, in keeping with early modern advice about how to arouse one's wife. Susanna's description of the Devil as 'cold' suggests that this fails. The Devil could have been attempting, on the other hand, to arouse himself. Temperance does, though, seem seduced by the Devil. She confesses that the Devil sucked at her 'Paps' to 'Provoke her to Letchery'.[142] After the Devil aroused Temperance, he 'lay Carnally with her for Nine Nights together'.[143] As Kim Phillips and Barry Reay have illustrated, in premodern England the 'very act of sexual arousal was tainted by sin'.[144] As in the examples of Elizabeth Sawyer and Elizabeth Clarke, this pamphlet's emphasis on the witch's sexual arousal should perhaps be read as a further demonisation of an apparently immoral and sinful witch. Not only did Temperance engage in fornication, she also allowed herself to become sexually aroused. Temperance describes this Devil as a black man 'about the length of her Arm: and that his Eyes were very big; and that he hopt or leapt in the way before her'.[145] Although this devil takes the shape of a man, he is only as long as Temperance's arm, perhaps mirroring the unnaturalness of his relationship with Temperance. This deformed description represents a shift from descriptions by Elizabeth Clarke and Rebecca West in the 1640s of their Devil as a 'proper young man' or a 'Gentleman'.[146]

The third witch in the narrative, Mary Trembles, also confessed to sleeping with a devil, but in this case the Devil took the form of a lion rather than a tiny man.[147] Mary confesses:

> after the Devil had had [carnal] knowledge of her Body, that he did suck her Secret parts, and that his sucking was so hard, which caused her to cry out for the pain thereof.[148]

This is the only seventeenth-century printed reference to an animal familiar engaging in penetrative intercourse with its mistress. It is unclear from this passage whether this lion-like Devil is sucking Mary to arouse her or to access her blood as part of a demonic pact. The position of his sucking, however, combined with the Devil's similar behaviour towards Temperance, suggests that the Devil is attempting to arouse Mary, possibly as part of an increasingly sexualised demonic pact. Unlike Temperance's description of the Devil provoking her to 'letchery', this passage suggests that sexual interaction with the Devil could be painful and unnatural. Although Temperance appears to have enjoyed demonic sex, another example from the pamphlet shows that she too experienced pain. She relates how the misshapen devil 'did suck her again as she was lying down, and that his sucking was with a greate pain to her'.[149] In this pamphlet, therefore, it is not during sexual intercourse that the Devil hurts witches, but through his sucking of their private parts. However, as we have seen, other witches experienced pleasure rather than pain.[150] All three of the above witches seem to have had positive feelings towards their devils. Temperance and Mary appear to have tolerated the pain of the Devil's sucking and do not record any sort of revulsion, even when confronted with the misshapen Devil. Similarly, Susanna does not seem opposed to sleeping with the Devil in the shape of a boy.

One final example of demonic copulation comes from an early eighteenth-century pamphlet written by Ralph Davis in 1705. Elinor Shaw and Mary Phillips, both accused of witchcraft, confessed that they made a pact with the Devil in the form of a tall black man. After presenting Elinor and Mary each with three imps to 'be at their Service' the Devil:

> came to bed to them both, and had Carnal Knowledge of 'em, as if a Man, only with this difference instead of being Warm, his Embraces was very Cold and unpleasant.[151]

After this disagreeable experience, Elinor and Mary make full use of their imps to kill hogs, horses and a neighbour's child.[152] In this narrative Elinor and Mary are willing to endure unpleasant sex with the Devil in order to have the power to take revenge on their enemies.

This chapter has argued that English witchcraft pamphlets, in particular those from the seventeenth century, presented witchcraft as a sexualised activity. Nearly 50 per cent of all surviving pamphlets published in England during the seventeenth century depicted witches as sexual beings who sought out and enjoyed pleasurable sexual relationships with devils. These witches were not just believed to engage in intercourse; they also enjoyed illicit sexual practices such as fornication, cunnilingus and anilingus. The combination of illicit female sexuality with demonic power was instrumental in constructing the English witch as sinful, diabolical and sexualised. The female witch's illicit sexuality was inherently tied to her links with the Devil. In describing a witch's ability to fall pregnant to the Devil, her desire for sexual intercourse or illicit sexual acts with devils, and the pleasure she took in these interactions, pamphleteers helped to create an understanding of witches as sexually deviant, supernatural beings, whose deviancy was inherently tied to their links with the Devil. Although there are some ambiguous narratives which blur the lines between maternal and sexual affection, it seems clear that witchcraft narratives from the seventeenth century were far more sexualised than previous scholarship has suggested. This reading encourages us to readjust our ideas on the prevalence of sexual and diabolical ideas in English witchcraft beliefs.

Notes

1　A version of this chapter was originally published in Marcus Harmes and Victoria Bladen, eds., *Supernatural and Secular Power in Early Modern England* (Farnham: Ashgate, 2015). I am grateful to the editors and the publisher for permission to republish parts of this chapter.
2　Alan Macfarlane, "Witchcraft in Tudor and Stuart Essex," in *Articles on Witchcraft, Magic and Demonology: A Twelve Volume Anthology of Scholarly Articles: Volume Six: Witchcraft in England*, ed. Brian Levack (New York: Garland Publishing Inc., 1992), 10.
3　Keith Thomas, *Religion and the Decline of Magic* (London: Weidenfeld and Nicolson, 1971), 568.
4　Barry Reay, *Popular Cultures in England, 1550–1750* (London: Longman, 1998), 125. For an exploration of the links between sex and witchcraft in the 1640s, see Malcolm Gaskill, "Witchcraft, Emotion and Imagination in the English Civil War," in *Witchcraft and the Act of 1604*, eds. John Newton and Jo Bath (Leiden: Brill, 2008), especially pages 171–172.
5　John Phillips, *The Examination and Confession of Certaine Wytches at Chelmsforde in the Countie of Essex* (London: Willyam Powell for Willyam Pickeringe, 1566), sig. A6 v.
6　Ibid.
7　Ibid., sig. A7 r.
8　Ibid.
9　W.W., *A True and Just Recorde, of the Information, Examination and Confession of All the Witches* (London: Printed by Thomas Dawson, 1582), sigs. C1 r, D2 r, F2 v, F3 r and G5r.
10　Ibid., C6 r.
11　Anon., *The Apprehension and Confession of Three Notorious Witches* (London: E. Allde, 1589), A4 r.
12　James Sharpe, "Familiars," in *The Encyclopedia of Witchcraft: The Western Tradition*, ed. Richard M. Golden (Santa Barbara, California: ABC-CLIO, 2006), 347–348.

13 Philip Almond, *The Devil: A New Biography* (Ithaca: Cornell University Press, 2014), 138.
14 Julia M. Garrett, "Witchcraft and Sexual Knowledge in Early Modern England," *The Journal for Early Modern Cultural Studies* 1 (2013): 48.
15 Anon., *A True and Impartial Relation of the Informations Against Three Witches* (London: Printed by Freeman Collins, 1682), 31.
16 Ibid.
17 Walter Stephens, *Demon Lovers: Witchcraft, Sex and the Crisis of Belief* (Chicago: University of Chicago Press, 2002), 103.
18 O[liver] H[eywood], *Advice to an Only Child: or, Excellent Council to All Young Persons* (London: Printed for Tho. Parkhurst, 1693), 125.
19 Deborah Willis, *Malevolent Nurture: Witch-hunting and Maternal Power in Early Modern England* (Ithaca: Cornell University Press, 1995), 55.
20 Stephens, *Demon Lovers*, 103.
21 Diane Purkiss, "Women's Stories of Witchcraft in Early Modern England: The House, the Body, the Child," *Gender and History* 7 (1995): 420.
22 Willis, *Malevolent Nurture*; Purkiss, "Women's Stories of Witchcraft in Early Modern England." See also Lyndal Roper, *Oedipus and the Devil: Witchcraft, Sexuality and Religion in Early Modern Europe* (London: Routledge, 1994), especially chapter 9; Lyndal Roper, *The Witch in the Western Imagination* (Charlottesville; University of Virginia Press, 2012), especially chapter 4 and Frances Dolan, *Dangerous Familiars: Representations of Domestic Crime in England, 1550–1700* (Ithaca: Cornell University Press, 1994).
23 Francis Bragge, *A Full and Impartial Account of the Discovery of Sorcery and Witchcraft Practis'd by Jane Wenham of Walkerne in Hertfordshire* (London: Printed for E. Curll, 1712), 28; Anon., *A Full and True Account of the Tryal, Examination, and Condemnation of Mary Johnson, a Witch* (London: Printed by T. Bland, 1706), 1; and Anon., *A Tryal of Witches at the Assizes Held at Bury St. Edmonds for the County of Suffolk* (London: Printed for William Shrewsbery, 1682), 19.
24 Anon., *The Apprehension and Confession of Three Notorious Witches* (London: E. Allde, 1589), sig. B2 r.
25 Ibid., title page.
26 Thomas Potts, *The Wonderfull Discoverie of Witches in the Countie of Lancaster* (London: Printed by W. Stansby for John Barnes), sig. R3 v.
27 Ibid.
28 Ibid., sig. R4 r.
29 Anon., *The Wonderful Discoverie of the Witchcrafts of Margaret and Phillip Flower* (London: Printed by G. Eld for J. Barnes), sig. F4 v.
30 Ibid.
31 Ibid., sig. C3 v.
32 John Davenport, *The Witches of Huntingdon, Their Examinations and Confessions Exactly Taken by His Majesties Justices of Peace for That County* (London: Printed by W. Wilson for Richard Clutterbuck, 1646), 14.
33 Willis, *Malevolent Nurture*, 17–18.
34 Patricia Crawford, *Blood, Bodies and Families in Early Modern England* (Harlow: Longman, 2004), 149.
35 John Stearne, *A Confirmation and Discovery of Witch-craft* (London: Printed by William Wilson, 1648), 43 and 28.
36 B. Misodaimon, *The Devil's Delusions* (London: Printed for Richard Williams, 1649), sig. A4 r.
37 Anon., *A Tryal of Witches at the Assizes Held at Bury St. Edmunds* (London: Printed for William Shrewsbery, 1682), 36–37. This story is repeated in a later (extremely similar) version of this trial, see Anon., *A Tryal of Witches at the*

Assizes Held at Bury St. Edmonds for the County of Suffolk (London: Printed for D. Brown, J. Walthoe and M. Wotton, 1716).

38 For a similar case, see Anon., *The Most Strange and Admirable Discoverie of the Three Witches of Warboys* (London: Printed for Thomas Man and John Winnington, 1593) described in Philip Almond, *The Witches of Warboys*, 197–198. After she was hanged, convicted witch Alice Samuel was stripped naked and searched. The jailor found a lump of flesh, just near her genitals. When the teat was squeezed it first gave out yellow milk and water, then a clear, milk-like liquid and then, finally, blood.

39 Garrett, "Witchcraft and Sexual Knowledge in Early Modern England," 32.

40 The exception is Anon., *The Most Cruell and Bloody Murther* (London: Printed for William Firebrand, 1606).

41 W.W., *A True and Just Recorde, of the Information, Examination and Confession of All the Witches* (London: Printed by Thomas Dawson, 1582), sigs. B2 r and C3 r

42 Ibid., sig. D4 r.

43 Anon., *The Wonderful Discoverie of the Witchcrafts of Margaret and Phillip Flower*, sig. G1 r. For the definition of 'secrets' as a person's sex organs see the Oxford English Dictionary 'Secret, *adj.* and *n.*, Entry 1 j. Available [Online]: www.oed.com.ezp.lib.unimelb.edu.au/view/Entry/174537?rskey=vo7jEX&result=1&isAdvanced=false#eid [1 August, 2014].

44 G.R. Quaife, *Wanton Wenches and Wayward Wives: Peasants and Illicit Sex in Early Seventeenth-Century England* (London: Croom Helm, 1979), 169.

45 Ibid., 169–171.

46 J.L. Flandrin, "Repression and Change in the Sexual Life of Young People in Medieval and Early Modern Times," *Journal of Family History* 196 (1997): 203.

47 Quaife, *Wanton Wenches and Wayward Wives*, 38.

48 Ibid., 38, 41.

49 Ibid.

50 For further discussion of this pamphlet, see Garrett, "Witchcraft and Sexual Knowledge in Early Modern England," 52–56.

51 Goodcole, *The Wonderfull Discoverie of Elizabeth Sawyer a Witch* (London: Printed for William Butler, 1621), sig. C2 v.

52 Ibid., sig. C3 v.

53 Quaife, *Wanton Wenches and Wayward Wives*, 165.

54 Laura Gowing, *Common Bodies: Women, Sex and Reproduction in Seventeenth-Century England* (New Haven: Yale University Press, 2003), 103.

55 Flandrin, "Repression and Change in the Sexual Life of Young People in Medieval and Early Modern Times," 203; Edward Shorter, *A History of Women's Bodies* (New York: Basic Books, 1982), 11.

56 Richard Davenport-Hines, *Sex, Death and Punishment: Attitudes to Sex and Sexuality in Britain Since the Renaissance* (London: Collins, 1990), 79.

57 Quaife, *Wanton Wenches and Wayward Wives*, 165.

58 Tim Hitchcock, *English Sexualities, 1700–1800* (New York: St. Martin's Press, 1997), 32.

59 Goodcole, *The Wonderfull Discoverie of Elizabeth Sawyer a Witch*, sig. C3 v.

60 Shorter, *A History of Women's Bodies*, 9.

61 Quaife, *Wanton Wenches and Wayward Wives*, 59–88.

62 Keith Thomas, "The Puritans and Adultery: The Act of 1650 Reconsidered," in *Puritans and Revolutionaries: Essays in Seventeenth-Century History Presented to Christopher Hill*, eds. Donald Pennington and Keith Thomas (Oxford: Clarendon Press, 1978), 260.

63 Ibid.

64 Goodcole, *The Wonderfull Discoverie of Elizabeth Sawyer a Witch*, sig. C3 r.

65 Ibid., sigs. C3 r- C3 v.

66 For an analysis of how references to anilingus were circulating in early modern English literature, see James Bromley, "Rimming the Renaissance," in *Sex Before Sex: Figuring the Act in Early Modern England*, eds. James M. Bromley and Will Stockton (Minnesota: Universtiy of Minnesota Press, 2013), 171–194.

67 There is one other dimension that should be considered when discussing why familiars chose to suck at witches' genitalia. The familiar was believed to suck blood from the witch as part of the blood pact. It is possible, therefore, that familiars were believed to suck at witches' genitalia because of the greater amounts of blood present during menstruation. This concept is not mentioned in pamphlets and there is very little evidence to support it. However, given the links between suckling and blood, it seems an important point to mention. Any links between pleasurable sexual contact and menstruation would have been viewed as highly deviant and added to the sinful nature of these encounters.

68 Anon., *Witches Apprehended, Examined and Executed* (London: Printed for Edward Marchant, 1613), sig. C1 v.

69 Anon., *The Wonderful Discoverie of the Witchcrafts of Margaret and Phillip Flower*, sig. F2 v.

70 Anon., *Witchcrafts Strange and Wonderfull* (London: Printed by M.F. for Thomas Lambert, 1635), sig. C1 r.

71 H.F., *A True and Exact Relation of the Several Informations of the Several Informations, Examinations, and Confessions of the Late Witches, Arraigned and Executed in the County of Essex* (London: Printed by M.S. for Henry Overton and Benj. Allen, 1645), 6.

72 Ibid.

73 Dolan, *Dangerous Familiars*, 214.

74 These are spread across three pamphlets: H.F., *A True and Exact Relation of the Several Informations*; Anon., *The Lawes Against Witches, and Conivration* (London: Printed for R. W., 1645); Anon., *A True Relation of the Araignment of Eighteene Witches That Were Tried, Convicted, and Condemned, at a Sessions Holden at St. Edmunds-bury in Suffolke, and There by the Iudge and Iustices of the Said Sessions Condemned to Die, and So Were Executed the 27. Day of August 1645* (London: Printed by I.H., 1645).

75 See Anon., *A Declaration in Answer to Several Lying Pamphlets Concerning the Witch of Wapping* (London: 1652).

76 Anon., *Strange News from Shadwell* (London: printed by E. Mallet, 1684), 3.

77 Ibid.

78 Chapter 5, this volume, will explore these depictions of the sabbath. Although the sabbath is often viewed as a phenomenon more common in European witchcraft, there is compelling evidence for the presence of this belief in England. Until very recently most English witchcraft historians viewed the sabbath as a Continental phenomenon. For an alternative perspective, see Sharpe, "In Search of the English Sabbat: Popular Conceptions of Witches' Meetings in Early Modern England," *Journal of Early Modern Studies* 2 (2013): 161–183.

79 Anon., *The Full Tryals, Examination, and Condemation of Four Notorious Witches, at the Assizes Held at Worcester, on Tuesday the 4th of March* (London: Printed by J.W., 1690), 4.

80 Ibid., 6.

81 Ralph Davis, *An Account of the Tryals, Examination and Condemnation, of Elinor Shaw and Mary Phillip's* (London: Printed for F. Thorn near Fleet Street, 1705), 4.

82 Ibid.

83 Michael Dalton and Edward Coke quoted in Erica Fudge, "Monstrous Acts: Bestiality in Early Modern England," *History Today* 50 (2000): 21.

84 Fudge, "Monstrous Acts: Bestiality in Early Modern England," 20–25.

85 For a fascinating case study incorporating some of this issues, see chapter 1, "Agnes Bowker's Cat: Childbirth, Seduction, Bestiality, and Lies," in David Cressy, *Travesties and Transgressions in Tudor and Stuart England: Tales of Discord and Dissension* (Oxford: Oxford University Press, 2000), 9–28.

86 Patricia Crawford and Sara Mendelson, *Women in Early Modern England: 1550–1720* (Oxford: Clarendon Press, 1998), 118; Kim M. Phillips and Barry Reay, *Sex Before Sexuality: A Premodern History* (Cambridge: Polity Press, 2011), 52.

87 Hitchcock, *English Sexualities*, 2.

88 Ibid., 39–40.

89 For more on changes to censorship, see the introduction of this book.

90 H.F., *A True and Exact Relation of the Several Informations*, 2.

91 Ibid., 3–4.

92 Ibid., 11.

93 Ibid., 12.

94 Ibid., 14–15.

95 For an analysis of encounters in which witches marry the Devil, and an exploration of the pre- and post-Reformation marital rituals within these unions, see Charlotte-Rose Millar, "Rebecca West's Demonic Marriage: Exploring Emotions, Ritual and Women's Agency in Seventeenth-Century England," *Women's History* Spring (2016): 4–11.

96 David Cressy, *Birth, Marriage and Death: Ritual, Religion and the Life-Cycle in Tudor and Stuart England* (Oxford: Oxford University Press, 1997), 340.

97 Katie Barclay, *Love, Intimacy and Power: Marriage and Patriarchy in Scotland, 1650–1850* (Manchester: Manchester University Press, 2011), 103.

98 Cressy, *Birth, Marriage and Death*, 340 and H.F., *A True and Exact Relation of the Several Informations*, 15.

99 Cressy, *Birth, Marriage and Death*, 340 and H.F., *A True and Exact Relation of the Several Informations*, 15.

100 Barclay, *Love, Intimacy and Power*, 103.

101 Ibid.

102 Stearne, *A Confirmation and Discovery of Witchcraft*, 29.

103 Anon., *A True Relation of the Arraignment of Eighteene Witches*, 5.

104 Ibid.

105 For more on monstrous births, wonders and sin, see Jennifer Spinks, *Monstrous Births and Visual Culture in Sixteenth-Century Germany* (London: Pickering and Chatto, 2009), particularly pages 93–94, 97, 137 and 141.

106 Cressy, *Travesties and Transgressions in Tudor and Stuart England*, 23.

107 Crawford, *Blood, Bodies and Families*, 59.

108 Ibid., 58.

109 Ambrose Paré, *The Works of That Famous Chirurgion Ambrose Parey* (London: 1634), 889.

110 Anon., *The Most Strange and Admirable Discoverie of the Three Witches of Warboys*, sig. D2 v.

111 E.G. and H.F., *A Prodigious and Tragicall History of the Arraignment, Tryall, Confession, and Condemnation of Six Witches at Maidstone, in Kent* (London: Printed for Richard Harper, 1652), 3.

112 Ibid., 4. For more on 'pleading the belly', see Almond, *The Witches of Warboys*, 101.

113 Crawford, *Blood, Bodies and Families*, 64.
114 Jean Bodin, *On the Demon-Mania of Witches* (1580), Book 2.7, page 130, trans. Randy A. Scott, abridged and introduced by Jonathan Pearl (Toronto: Centre for Reformation and Renaissance Studies, 1995); Nicolas Remy, *Demonolatry*, trans. E.A. Ashwin, ed. Montague Summers (New York: University Books, 1974), xiii; Francesco Maria Guazzo, *Compendium Maleficarum*, Book I, Chapter xi, trans. E.A. Ashwin, ed. Montague Summers (New York: University Books, 1974), 30–31.
115 For an overview of learned debates about the pleasurable or painful nature of sex with the Devil, see Almond, *The Devil*, 104–108.
116 Garrett, "Witchcraft and Sexual Knowledge," 39.
117 Gowing, *Common Bodies*, 102.
118 Davenport, *The Witches of Huntingdon*, 1.
119 Ibid., 2.
120 Ibid.
121 Crawford, *Blood, Bodies and Families*, 84.
122 Davenport, *The Witches of Huntingdon*, 12.
123 Ibid.
124 Ibid.
125 Ibid.
126 Ibid.
127 Stearne, *A Confirmation and Discovery of Witchcraft*, 28.
128 Crawford, *Blood, Bodies, Families*, 70.
129 Stearne, *A Confirmation and Discovery of Witchcraft*, 28.
130 Ibid.
131 See, for example, Thomas, *Religion and the Decline of Magic*, 568, Reay, *Popular Cultures in England*, 125; Almond, *The Witches of Warboys*, 101.
132 Gaskill, "Witchcraft, Emotion and Imagination in the English Civil War," in *Witchcraft and the Act of 1604*, 164. Gaskill is summarising the traditional view of the Matthew Hopkins trials in the 1640s.
133 Stephens, *Demon Lovers*, 102.
134 James Sharpe, "The Devil in East Anglia: The Matthew Hopkins Trials Reconsidered," in *Witchcraft in Early Modern Europe: Studies in Culture and Belief*, eds. Jonathan Barry, Marianne Hester and Gareth Roberts (Cambridge: Cambridge University Press, 1996), 249.
135 Malcolm Gaskill, *Witchfinders: A Seventeenth-Century English Tragedy* (London: John Murray, 2005), 280.
136 Garrett, "Witchcraft and Sexual Knowledge," 63.
137 Mary Moore, *Wonderfull Newes from the North* (London: Printed by T.H., 1650), 24.
138 Ibid. Uniquely amongst English witchcraft pamphlets, this narrative was written by a woman, Mrs Mary Moore, the mother of the bewitched children who form the pamphlet's main basis. Although Mrs Moore succeeded in bringing an indictment against Mrs Swinow, evidence suggests that it is unlikely that she was apprehended, tried or convicted. This was partly because, as the wife of a colonel, Mrs Swinow was less socially vulnerable than most accused witches. Dolan, *Dangerous Familiars*, 232–233.
139 The conspiratorial aspects of this narrative will be discussed further in chapter 5, this volume.
140 Temperance Lloyd was also known as Temperance Floyd and Mary Trembles was also known as Mary Floyd. Anon., *A True and Impartial Relation of the Informations Against Three Witches*; Anon., *The Tryal, Condemnation, and*

Execution of Three Witches (London: Printed for J. Deacon, 1682); and Anon., *The Life and Conversation of Temperance Floyd, Mary Lloyd and Susanna Edwards* (London: Printed by J.W., 1687).

141 Anon., *A True and Impartial Relation of the Informations Against Three Witches*, 31.

142 Anon., *The Tryal, Condemnation, and Execution of Three Witches*, 4.

143 Ibid.

144 Phillips and Reay, *Sex Before Sexuality*, 19.

145 Anon., *A True and Impartial Relation of the Informations Against Three Witches*, 15.

146 Ibid., 12 and 2.

147 Ibid., 34.

148 Ibid.

149 Ibid., 15.

150 See, for example, Goodcole, *The Wonderfull Discoverie of Elizabeth Sawyer*, sig. C3 v and Anon., *The Examination, Confession, Trial and Execution of Joane Williford, Joan Cariden and Jane Hott* (London: Printed for J.G, 1645), 3.

151 Davis, *An Account of the Tryals, Examination and Condemnation, of Elinor Shaw and Mary Phillip's*, 6.

152 Ibid., 7.

5   The Witchcraft Conspiracy

Thus far, this book has focused on individual relationships between witches and devils.[1] In doing so, it has demonstrated that witches' activities were described in print in interpersonal terms. As we have seen, witches were believed to form strong bonds with their demonic familiars, bonds which could be purely pragmatic and used as a way of exacting revenge, or bonds that could turn into sexualised relationships. In this chapter, I turn to a consideration of witches as a group which inspired fear and anxiety amongst those affected by witchcraft. Unlike previous chapters which focused on a witch's relationship with the Devil, this chapter instead concentrates on the fear generated by printed descriptions of conspiring groups of witches. Many villagers feared witches' supposedly malicious natures and saw this malice made manifest in the often gruesome deaths of farm animals, children and neighbours. This chapter seeks to reconsider the historiographical tendency to view English witchcraft as a purely 'solitary' or 'irreligious' activity,[2] and to move away from the concept that the witches' sabbath or assembly was unknown in England, or simply a feature of the Hopkins' period of trials, born of Continental ideas.[3] Although witches could and did act alone in early modern England, they were also viewed as part of a dangerous underground group, one which was plotting to overthrow mainstream Protestant society. In the sixteenth century all but two (or 80 per cent) of witchcraft pamphlets describe witchcraft as a collaborative activity.[4] In the seventeenth century, thirty of forty-eight witchcraft pamphlets (or 62 per cent) also depicted witchcraft as a conspiratorial or group activity. These associations are most common in the early seventeenth century, with every seventeenth-century pamphlet up until 1645 depicting witchcraft as a demonic conspiracy. Although references to witchcraft as conspiracy continue throughout the seventeenth century, by the eighteenth these depictions are relatively few (two of eight pamphlets – 25 per cent – refer to collaborative witchcraft) and are confined to witches working together to spread evil and discord.[5]

Witchcraft as conspiracy was portrayed in print in three main ways: witches acting together to hurt their neighbours; witches working together as part of a hierarchical society (which often involved the Devil as leader);

and witches attending witches' sabbaths (or witches' assemblies, as they were often called in the English context). All three of these variations represented witches as dangerous and hidden threats to the community. While pamphleteers often described solitary witches as objects of fear, groups of witches were even more disturbing in their collective power, particularly when allied with a supposedly dangerous religious minority. Descriptions of hidden and threatening underground sects of witches appear designed to engender feelings of anxiety, fear and uncertainty in early modern readers. Depending on the time period, these acts could have different resonances. During the sixteenth century, witches were frequently associated with hidden Catholic practices, an association that reappeared at key moments of tension throughout the seventeenth century. In the mid-seventeenth century, a number of pamphlets were published which lend themselves more readily to an association with Quakerism. As will be argued later, this association was not at odds with fears of a Catholic conspiracy. In early modern England, any practice that did not conform to mainstream Protestantism could be labelled as threatening. Throughout this entire period, descriptions of witches plotting together to cause evil could be associated with fears of other minority groups who were also viewed as a threat.

In recent years, a number of scholars have agitated for a reassessment of the conspiratorial, anti-religious nature of English witchcraft belief, noting that although this concept may have been less developed in England than in a European context, it is still very worthy of study – perhaps even more worthy given its relative rarity.[6] Some have remarked that it was often the more 'exceptional' descriptions of meetings with the Devil that became the subject of sensational pamphlet accounts, thus allowing these ideas to circulate more easily.[7] In one of the most recent appraisals of the role of the sabbath in England, James Sharpe has argued that 'popular thinking [was] perfectly capable of envisaging meetings with the devil, although these were sometimes far removed from the sabbat proper'.[8] By studying all extant early modern English witchcraft pamphlets, I aim to reassess the importance of the Devil, conspiratorial witchcraft and the witch's sabbath in early modern England.

The Beginnings of the Conspiracy

In sixteenth-century England, witches were most commonly described as collaborative through their tendency to pass down magical secrets through the generations, to trade familiar spirits and to work together to harm their neighbours – all phenomena discussed in previous chapters. Pamphlets were commonly framed in collaborative terms, with names such as *The Apprehension and Confession of Three Notorious Witches*, *A Memorial of Certaine Most Notorious Witches* and *The Examination and Confession of Certaine Wytches at Chelmsford*, all implying a community of witches. In many of these pamphlets, readers were given the very strong impression that witches acted together in order to perform witchcraft. One pamphlet from 1579 creates a strong impressive of witchcraft as a collaborative activity. The pamphlet describes the witchcrafts of Elizabeth Stile, alias Rockingham, Mother Dutton, Mother Devell and Mother Margaret, all of whom work together to perform *maleficium*. Elizabeth Stile confessed that when she was arrested, Mother Margaret came to her and gave her money in return for her silence over their 'secrets'.[9] They also all conspired 'by their devillishe arte' to kill Master Galis.[10] All the accused confessed to owning familiar spirits, including 'a Sprite or feende in the likenesse of a Toade', a 'blacke Catte' called Gille, which 'aided [Mother Devell] in her Witchcrafte' and a 'ratte, beeyng in very deede a wicked Spirite, [who Elizabeth Stile named] Philip'.[11] Not only do these witches work together, they also have a leader: one accused confesses that Mother Seidre was the 'maistres Witche of all the reste, and she is now deade'.[12] The accused have also corrupted each other. The pamphlet records how 'Mother Dutton and Mother Devell did perswade [Elizabeth] to dooe as thei had doen, in forsakying God and his woorkes, and giving her self to the Devill'.[13] In this pamphlet, witches do not just collaborate with each other, but with the Devil through making a pact and owning familiar spirits. This is not a lone example. We have already seen how, in a 1582 pamphlet, witches traded their familiars in order to inflict harm on their neighbours. One 1566 pamphlet also depicts a belief in witches trading familiars between each other. In this narrative, Elizabeth Francis inherits her familiar from her grandmother and then trades it to her neighbour Agnes Waterhouse for a cake.[14] Sixteenth-century pamphlets are replete with references to witches working together and with the Devil to perform witchcraft. These acts of collaboration hint at a fear of a hidden conspiracy of witchcraft. Collaborative activities could, though, take on greater meanings and be tied to wider fears of underground sects. As such, in approximately a third of sixteenth-century pamphlets, witches were associated with Catholicism.

For many sixteenth-century Protestants, Catholicism was a serious threat, a hidden danger that needed to be stamped out. Although the 1559 religious settlement officially established Elizabeth's England as a Protestant country, in the early years of her reign Catholicism still flourished in numerous parishes.[15] Protestantism 'proved unattractive to the rural masses' and Catholic priests continued to provide Catholic ritual for those who preferred the old faith.[16] By the 1570s recusancy had become the 'hallmark of post-Reformation English Catholicism'[17] and, by the 1590s, one Jesuit contemporary, William Holt, estimated that there were still as many as forty or fifty recusant priests in England.[18] The widespread nature of this barely hidden recusancy, combined with a number of Catholic plots throughout Elizabeth's reign, created a deep mistrust of Catholicism in the minds of English Protestants.[19] As Nathan Johnstone has noted, the existence of recusants 'constituted a potential for diabolic activity which might be activated, as a spark might be put to gunpowder'.[20] Perhaps unsurprisingly, sixteenth-century witchcraft pamphlets were regularly used as a medium for anti-Catholic propaganda and, in doing so, created strong links between witchcraft and Catholicism in the minds of contemporaries.

It would be overly simplistic to argue for a straightforward link between witches, the Devil and Catholicism; and this reading would be completely wrong if we were only looking at the later seventeenth and eighteenth centuries. But the evidence from the sixteenth-century pamphlets is compelling, despite an older historiography which viewed witchcraft and anti-Catholic sentiment as separate phenomena in early modern England.[21] Recent works have explored the links between Catholicism, magic and the Devil, with many suggesting that links between witchcraft and Catholicism may have been more prevalent than previously thought.[22] But there is no clear consensus on this. As recently as 2013, Francis Young has rejected the idea that Catholics were persecuted as witches, focusing instead on how they were associated with the demonic.[23] Despite Young's concerns, it seems clear that ideas about the demonic, magic, ritual, Catholic worship and witchcraft could be quite fluid within the early modern period. These ideas, particularly in the sixteenth century, were often linked with the idea of witchcraft as conspiracy. This conflation would have had greater traction in the sixteenth-century than in later years given that many elderly witches would have been raised Catholic. Like the later pamphlets, sixteenth-century witchcraft pamphlets depict a preoccupation with the idea that witches were part of an underground, anti-religious sect, which was part of a larger conspiracy to overthrow mainstream Protestant society. These ideas were not as prevalent or as well-developed as those in seventeenth-century pamphlets but, nonetheless, were still present. By highlighting the links between witches, Catholicism and the Devil, I do not mean to argue that all Catholics were witches in the minds of all English Protestants, rather that the two were capable of being conflated in witchcraft print.

In one of the earliest witchcraft pamphlets from 1566, witchcraft and Catholicism were strongly linked. Mother Waterhouse, a sixty-four-year-old woman, told her examiner that Satan 'wolde at no tyme suffer her to say [her prayers] in englyshe, but at all times in laten'.[24] Further, she confessed that when she was commanding her familiar, ('an evyll favoured dogge with hornes on his head') she 'wolde say her Pater noster in laten' and he would do her bidding.[25] Finally, this same paternoster, when said in Latin, was said to have created her monstrous familiar who, before she recited the prayer, had been a domestic cat.[26] In this pamphlet Catholic ritual is perceived as having devilish power and the accused witch's alleged Catholicism and her witchcraft are seen as inextricably linked. A possession pamphlet from 1597 reinforces the link between Latin prayers and witchcraft by noting that accused witch Alice Gooderidge is asked to 'kneele down and pray for [the possessed boy, Thomas Darling] which she did, but so as nobody could understand what she sayd'.[27] It seems likely that sixty-year-old Alice is saying her prayers in the Latin that she would have memorised as a child.

Her mother, Elizabeth Wright, is also accused of saying these same 'divellish praiers', when she is found 'on her knees; praying (no doubt) to the divell,' thus furthering the link between Catholicism and the Devil.[28] Mother Waterhouse is also questioned about her praying practices, being asked what prayers she said (she tells her examiner that she says the Lord's Prayer). This question stresses the examiner's preoccupation with unorthodox religious practices. In the early years of Elizabeth's reign, the gap between unorthodox religious practices and Catholicism was extremely small in the Protestant imagination. Nor was this association confined to sixteenth-century pamphlets. In a wonderful image from the frontispiece of the 1658 play, *The Witch of Edmonton*, Elizabeth Sawyer is drawn with a speech bubble saying 'sanctabecetur nomen tuum' (see figure 3.1 in chapter 3). This mangled Latin prayer appears in the original 1621 pamphlet (in a non-mangled state). When describing the prayer, Elizabeth claims that 'The Divell taught me this prayer, Sanctificetur nomen tuum, Amen' and that she had never learned Latin before the Devil taught her.[29] The Devil tells Elizabeth that to pray like this is to pray to him.[30] As we can see, although links between Catholicism, witchcraft and the Devil are strongest in the sixteenth century, they continue to emerge at various points throughout the seventeenth.

Although witchcraft was punishable by state statute, in the minds of many it remained an essentially religious crime.[31] 'In Protestant thinking' as Malcolm Gaskill has argued, 'witchcraft was apostasy – idolatry even'.[32] One sixteenth-century pamphlet from 1582 makes this very clear:

> [Witches] . . . are mere blasphemers against the person of the most high God; and draw so neere to the nature of idolatrie (for they worshippe Sathan, unto whome they have sworne allegiance) that they are by no means to be exempted from the suspicion of that most accursed defection, nay rather they are guiltie of apparaunte apostasie, which is more heinous[33]

This pamphleteer identifies witches as part of an anti-religious sect. They are grouped together in their 'apparaunte apostaise'. The understanding of witchcraft as a religious crime is fundamental to how witches were portrayed in popular pamphlets, as engaged in a collaborative, underground activity that involved plotting with other witches and sometimes meeting the Devil at a formal gathering. At its core, this understanding of witchcraft identified the role of the Devil as paramount and, through the reference to 'idolatry', strongly tied it to Catholicism. Throughout the pamphlet there are many similar references to witchcraft as 'divillish idolaterie'.[34]

In attempting to link witchcraft and Catholicism, sixteenth-century witchcraft pamphleteers gave new meaning to old ideas. One example of this phenomenon was a witch's use of circle magic.[35] This phenomenon, believed in the Middle Ages to summon spirits, was criminalised by Henry VIII in *An Act against Conjurations, Witchcrafts, Sorcery, and Enchantments*, and remained a capital offence for the following two hundred years.[36] In 1566 accused witch John Walsh used 'a crosse of virgin mare' in his circle magic to 'raise the familiar spirit,' thus demonstrating the suspected devilish power of Catholic worship.[37] If he failed to perform this act his familiar would disappear. In 1589 Joan Cunny summoned her devils using a prayer taught to her by an older woman, who told her to 'make a Circle on the ground, and pray unto Sathan the cheefe of the Devills'.[38] Joan managed to summon two black frog familiars, which 'familiarly talke with her . . . in her owne language'.[39] The references to different languages and special prayers, while not overtly linking witchcraft with Catholicism, do imply unorthodox, religious practices, especially to a sixteenth-century Protestant reader. Finally, a possession pamphlet from 1600 describes how Edmond Hartley also engaged in circle magic. Although Edmond's ritual betrays no links with Catholic doctrine, the author is careful to place this reference to circle magic immediately after Edmond has been identified as a Catholic through his use of 'certaine popish charmes and hearbes'.[40]

As well as describing Latin prayers, unorthodox religious practices and circle magic, sixteenth-century pamphleteers also presented witchcraft as tied to Catholicism through descriptions of Catholic priests. Accused witch John Walsh claims to have learned 'Sorcerie and Witchcraft . . . of a certaine priest'.[41] These skills are labelled the 'fruites of papistes and papistrye'.[42] The pamphleteer goes on to claim that it is 'friers and idle, lusty Priestes . . . Popes, Cardinals, and Bishops [who are] chiefly and wholye given to the studye and exercise of these most wicked and divelish sciences'.[43] In one 1579 pamphlet the priest Father Rosimonde is not just implicated in teaching witchcraft but is denounced as a 'witche and Inchanter'.[44] Whereas the other four witches in the pamphlet are believed to possess familiars, Father Rosimonde is able to 'transforme himself by Devilishe meanes, into the shape and likenesse of any beaste whatsoever he will'.[45] Rather than simply being in a pact with a devilish animal, this priest takes on the form of the Devil himself. For this pamphleteer, priests are akin to devils.

Connections between witchcraft and Catholicism are strongest in the sixteenth century – an unsurprising finding given the religious turmoil that characterised Elizabeth's reign – but they are not confined to this century. In Thomas Potts' infamous account of the 1612 Lancashire witches, Catholic associations play a key role. There has been a tendency by historians to either dismiss the Pendle and Samlesbury witches (both of which are described in this pamphlet) as atypical of English witchcraft belief or to study them in isolation.[46] However, as Sharpe argues, the very fact that the collaborative, sabbath-like meetings described in this pamphlet are seen as atypical makes them even worthier of study.[47] Potts' descriptions of witches' collaboration and the sabbath can easily be integrated into a broader understanding of how conspiratorial witchcraft was described in popular narratives. The almost two-hundred-page pamphlet includes what is often referred to as the first sabbath in England.[48] The pamphlet is divided into two sections in which it accuses no less than twenty-eight men and women of witchcraft. The first and larger part is concerned with the Pendle witches and focuses on the activities of Elizabeth Sowtherns, alias Demdike, and Anne Whittle, alias Chattox, both elderly matriarchs of competing families. The second part describes witches in Samlesbury, Yorkshire and is about fourteen-year-old Grace Sowerbutts and the witchcraft supposedly inflicted upon her by Jennet Bierley, Ellen Bierley and Jane Southworth.

In the first section Elizabeth Sowtherns and Anne Whittle both confess to murdering men and to passing on witchcraft lore to younger generations. Potts is keen to explain the close relationships between the accused. The first witch questioned, Elizabeth Sowtherns, is said to have given her soul to the Devil 'twentie yeares past' and then gone on to corrupt those around her.[49] Anne Whittle, 'a very old withered, spent & decreped creature, her sight almost gone', claims that Elizabeth, whom she despises, has through 'wicked perswasions and counsell' seduced her into the 'abhominable profession of Witchcraft'.[50] The description of Anne as a 'creature' who is 'withered, spent and decreped' is designed to elicit disgust from the reader. Elizabeth's granddaughter Alizon Device claims that Elizabeth persuaded her to 'let a Devill or Familiar appeare unto her'.[51] This description marks both Elizabeth and Alizon as witches and reminds the reader of the links between witches and the Devil. The pamphlet continues to list those who have been corrupted by Elizabeth Sowtherns, including her daughter Elizabeth Device, her grandson James Device, and Anne Readfearne, the daughter of Anne Chattox. The tendency for witches to be related has been remarked upon in a number of studies.[52] This community of witches is said to live 'in the Forrest of *Pendle*' and is described as a 'wicked company of dangerous Witches'.[53] As Phil Withington has demonstrated, the word 'company', although broadly meaning an assembly of people, was often understood in the seventeenth century as a way for men and women to come together to learn a particular skill.[54] A 'company' was defined as a 'purposeful and deliberate association', particularly at the beginning and end of the seventeenth century.[55] Thus, as well as describing witches as a group, the use of the word 'company' in this narrative could imply a belief that witches came together to help each other learn evil arts. Potts is careful to use the word 'dangerous' in his attempts to make his readers fearful. Although individually these witches are sometimes described in grotesque terms (as is the case for Anne Whittle), as a 'company' they become more than disgusting or grotesque; they become objects of power and fear.

On their arrest, many of the Lancashire witches were imprisoned in Lancaster Castle.[56] According to Potts, after the arrests of their fellow witches, 'all the most dangerous, wicked, and damnable Witches in the County farre and neere' met together and plotted to free their comrades by blowing up Lancaster Castle.[57] This meeting, we are told, involved the 'Graund Witches of the Counties of Lancaster and Yorke', thus strongly hinting at a clear hierarchy among witches.[58] The 'speciall meeting' of the Pendle witches (also described as the 'great Assemblie') is referred to throughout the pamphlet.[59] It occurred on Good Friday and was conducted with 'great cheare, merry company, and much conference'.[60] At this meeting, the witches agree to blow up Lancaster Castle and kill several people. Potts also relates how the witches agreed to meet again on 'that day twelve-moneths' for a 'great Feast', thus suggesting to the reader an ongoing witchcraft conspiracy, rather than a one-off act of revenge.[61]

In this narrative, Potts reinforces the fact that these 'dangerous' witches have come together from two counties. Not only does this suggest that these witches will be more powerful as a group, it also implies that witches are communicating with each other across large areas. Potts then states that although some of the witches have been caught, others are determined to free them, suggesting that catching some witches is no assurance of safety, and that many more are lying in wait. In Potts' pamphlet, as we shall see in the following discussion, the links between Catholic plots and witches' plotting in secret are emphasised. Both are viewed as dangerous minority groups who aim to overthrow Protestant society.

The location of the Pendle witches is crucial to their Catholic associations. Lancaster was popularly viewed as 'one of Catholicism's strongholds' in Jacobean England.[62] This view was not wholly imagined; 6 to 7 per cent of the population of Lancashire was recusant or non-communicant in 1603, compared to an estimated 1 per cent of the English population.[63] Throughout both sections of the pamphlet Potts is keen to link witchcraft with Catholicism. In the first section he claims that the 'Countie of Lancaster . . . now may lawfully bee said to abound asmuch in Witches of divers kindes as Seminaries, Jesuites, and Papists', thus making a strong association between witchcraft and Catholicism.[64] These links are reinforced throughout the pamphlet. Many of the witches are said to say Latin prayers and to use these same Latin prayers as charms in their witchcraft, a practice reminiscent of some sixteenth-century narratives.[65] Through linking the Lancaster witches with Catholicism, Potts associates them with a dangerous threat. The idea that witches were coming together and plotting to destroy Lancaster Castle would have reminded a largely Protestant readership of the terror of the foiled Gunpowder Plot only eight years before. The publication date of the Lancashire pamphlet (1613), as well as its links with anti-Catholicism, and its focus on a plot to blow up a royal building, all suggest that this pamphlet is at least partly inspired by the events of 1605. Even more suggestive is the identity of the pamphlet's patron, Sir Thomas Knyvet, who caught and arrested Guy Fawkes.[66] The potent combination of witches and Catholics, both supposedly acting in secret to overthrow a Protestant world, would have no doubt been designed to arouse feelings of distress and fear in early modern readers. Not only were these witches supposedly plotting to destroy the castle, they are planning to do so on Good Friday, thus emphasising their complete inversion of Christian values.

Although Potts often mentions that the Pendle witches are in league with the Devil and that they own familiar spirits, the description of the 'Great Assemblie' does not mention the presence of the Devil.[67] The Devil is, however, emphasised in some later descriptions of English assemblies.[68] Potts' pamphlet should be viewed, therefore, as an early example of English belief in the sabbath, or, as we should perhaps call it, a witches' meeting or assembly. As Sharpe has argued, as 'the connection between the witch and the devil was slowly developing on a popular level, so too was the notion of the sabbat'.[69] Potts' pamphlet does not just demonstrate a belief in conspiratorial witchcraft, it also showcases how feelings of fear, anxiety and danger were provoked in readers through witchcraft literature. While unusual in its length, political motivations and level of detail, this pamphlet should be viewed as part of a genre of pamphlet literature that emphasised both the diabolical and the conspiratorial nature of English witchcraft.

The second and less famous part of Potts' pamphlet is even more sensational in its descriptions of witches' meetings. The main focus of this second section is on fourteen-year-old Grace Sowerbutts and the witchcraft supposedly inflicted upon her by Jennet Bierley, Ellen Bierley and Jane Southworth. The pamphlet describes how Ellen and Jennet took Grace out with them at night to retrieve the body of a child they had killed. They then boiled the child and used its fat to 'annoint themselves, that thereby they might sometimes change themselves into other shapes'.[70] This terrifying description of witches killing and boiling a child and then smearing themselves with its fat is clearly designed to elicit fear and repulsion in readers. Potts also records Grace's description of night-time meetings:

> [The witches] did meete at a place called Red banck, upon the North side of the water of Ribble, every Thursday and Sonday at night by the space of a fortnight, and at the waterside there came unto them, as they went thether, foure black things, going upright, and yet not like men in the face: which foure did carrie the said three women and this Examinate over the Water, and when they came to the said Red Banck they found some thing there which they did eate . . . After they had eaten, the said three Women and [Grace] danced, every one of them with one of the black things aforesaid, and after their dancing the said black things did pull downe the said three Women, and did as this Examinate thinketh, for shee saith, that the black thing that was with her, did abuse her bodie.[71]

This narrative describes witches coming together at night, eating, dancing and engaging in sexual relationships with disturbing black creatures that have strange faces. But there is a complication. Potts does not believe that the three women are guilty. Instead, he claims that Grace made up the accusation at the request of a Jesuit who wanted revenge on the three women, 'because they were once obstinate Papists and now came to [Protestant]

Church'.[72] Potts argues that the accusations are 'impossible' and even points out that the Jesuit, although he has concocted an elaborate story, 'forgot to devise a Spirit for [the witches]'.[73] Potts' disbelief provides a wonderful insight into the importance of familiar spirits in English witchcraft belief. For Potts, it is absurd that witches would boil babies for their fat or be abused by black creatures in the night, but he deems it necessary that they employ a demonic animal. It also highlights Potts' firm belief in the association between witchcraft and Catholicism; for Potts it can only be a Jesuit who introduces these fantastical ideas.

Potts' pamphlet suggests a very specific set of English witch beliefs which assume that witches' activities are conspiratorial. His commentary, however, suggests that there are conflicting beliefs about the activities of English witches. In his 2013 article, Sharpe uses this example as evidence of a popular, rather than a learned, belief in the sabbath. As Sharpe reminds us, both Potts and the presiding judge, Sir Edward Bromley, were sceptical of accounts of witches boiling children at night-time meetings.[74] The concept of night-time, sabbath-like meetings in this pamphlet were dismissed as popish and it is made clear that Grace's confession has been influenced by a Jesuit.[75] The English court dismisses these allegations yet has clear ideas about the importance of familiars in witchcraft narratives. Potts' pamphlet makes four things very clear: first, in 1612 it was believed possible that witches would conspire with each other to plot evil; second, that there were limits on this collaboration and descriptions of full-blown sabbaths were not readily believed; third, a familiar spirit was crucial to a witch's ability to perform *maleficium,* and fourth, that the links between witchcraft, the Devil and Catholicism were thought strong enough to be expanded upon in print.

Witchcraft and Conspiracy in Seventeenth-century England

References to conspiratorial witchcraft continued to evolve long after Potts' pamphlet. Another early seventeenth-century pamphlet also presents a distinctly English belief in the concept of conspiratorial witchcraft and the witches' sabbath. The 1612 title page depicts three female witches riding a gigantic sow (figure 5.1). This is apparently a monthly occurrence, in which the witches travel to meet a fellow witch at Ravensthorpe, Northamptonshire.[76] The pamphlet begins by describing witches as those 'who by the damnable practise of Witch-craft have sold themselves to the Devils service,' thus instantly reminding the reader of a witch's inherently diabolical nature.[77] The pamphlet focuses on the activities of five main witches: Agnes Browne, of 'poor parentage and poore education', who had 'an ill nature'; Joane Vaughan, her daughter, whom the pamphlet lewdly describes as 'a maide (or at least unmarried)'; Arthur Bill, 'a wretched poore Man, both in state and mind', who was 'begotten and borne of parents that were both Witches'; Helen Jenkenson, who had long been suspected of living an 'evill life'; and finally, Mary Barber, who had a 'barbarous nature'.[78] All five of

THE
WITCHES
OF
NORTHAMPTON-
SHIRE.

Agnes Browne. *Arthur Bill.*
Ioane Vaughan. *Hellen Ienkenson* Witches.
Mary Barber.

Who were all executed at *Northampton* the 22. of
Iuly last. 1612.

LONDON,
Printed by *Tho: Purfoot*, for *Arthur*
Iohnson. 1612.

Figure 5.1 Three witches riding a giant sow to a night-time meeting, depicted in Anon., *The Witches of Northampton-shire* (London: Printed by Tho: Parfoot, for Arthur Johnson, 1612), title page. © The Bodleian Libraries, The University of Oxford, Mal. 709 Tpage.

these witches, either through popular opinion or parentage, are viewed as having inherent connections with witchcraft. The dispositions of at least two of the witches are also described. Agnes is labelled as having 'an ill nature', and Mary is described as having a 'barbarous nature', suggesting that the dispositions of these women are directly linked to their descent into witch-craft.[79] They are also described as threatening. The pamphlet defines Joanne and Agnes as women whose 'rage' and desire for 'revenge . . . never rests', and who were therefore 'hated, and feared among [their] neighbours'.[80]

The author claims that Agnes Browne, as well as Ratherine [sic] Gardiner and Joane Lucas, who are 'all birds of a winge', rode 'all upon a Sowes backe, to see one Mother Rhoades'.[81] It seems hard to believe that the reader is meant to view this giant sow as anything other than unnatural and diabolical. Sharpe has recently commented on the belief that witches rode animals to sabbaths. He suggests that for these motifs to be included, there must have been 'an expectation that the readers of the pamphlet would find this narrative device familiar and convincing'.[82] In making this argument, Sharpe proposes that pamphlet readers had certain reference points for understanding sabbaths, and the motif of riding women was one such point. Although Mother Rhoades died before the three women arrived on the sow, she was heard to cry that she 'would meete with [the three women] in another place within a month after'.[83] This description not only hints at a greater conspiracy among a larger number of witches, but it also suggests that these witches meet regularly (presumably to plot evil) and, most strangely of all, that there may be some element of necromancy involved as Mother Rhoades' death does not seem to be a barrier to her attendance at the next meeting.

The next witches' meeting is not described in print until the 1640s, but this does not mean that witchcraft stopped being described as a conspiratorial activity. Pamphlets published in 1613, 1619 and 1635 also explore the idea of witchcraft as a group activity through describing witches taking on a family member as an apprentice.[84] One 1613 pamphleteer describes the crimes of Mother Sutton, a 'widow . . . of declining years', and her daughter Mary Sutton.[85] Mary lived with her mother, not as the townspeople thought 'as a stay and comfort to her age', but in fact 'as a furtherer to her divellish practises, nay indeed to make her a scholler to the Divell himselfe'.[86] Mary is portrayed as deceptive, presenting herself to her neighbours as a dutiful daughter, but actually acting as an agent of the Devil. In Potts' 1613 pamphlet, he describes older witches such as Elizabeth Sowtherns and Anne Whittle, as women who corrupt their younger family members. This anxiety is repeated here. The pamphleteer goes on to claim that Mother Sutton has spent 'one and twentie yeaers' teaching her daughter 'devillish charmes'.[87] We have already discussed the Suttons' revenge against Master Enger's young son Henry, an act that they performed together. Similarly, we have explored the 1619 pamphlet about Joane, Philippa and Margaret Flower who conspired together to practise evil magic against Henry Lord Rosse, son of the Earl of Rutland.[88] In the 1635 retelling of this pamphlet, the story of witches acting together to take revenge is repeated and, in the title of the pamphlet, the author alludes to a belief that witches have apprentices. He promises readers 'an approved triall how to finde out either Witch, or any Apprentise to Witch-craft'.[89] This statement implies that witchcraft was believed to be an activity that involved converting and teaching others. In both versions of the Flower pamphlet, Joane Willimot confesses that she met with Margaret and Philippa Flower and encountered 'two Spirits, one like a Rat, and the other like an Owle' who were shared among the witches.[90] From the very beginning of both retellings of this narrative, the three witches are believed to act in concert. The title pages of all three sources (both pamphlets and the ballad) depict an image of the Flower family (see figure 2.5 in chapter 2).[91] In the image the three women stand in a circle with numerous familiars, including a dog, an owl, a rat and a cat. They appear to be talking and consulting with each other. The four familiars complete the circle, adding a strong demonic tone to the meeting.

The idea of a witchcraft community circulated widely during the 1640s. Although there were very few witchcraft trials during the 1630s (and only one witchcraft pamphlet), this does not necessarily mean that witchcraft belief was declining. As Ian Bostridge has reminded us, 'witchcraft theory could thrive in periods of low-level prosecution'.[92] The devilish and conspiratorial themes of the 1635 pamphlet were reflected in both earlier and later print, suggesting that during this time of low prosecution rates, there was no significant change in the types of narratives that pamphlets related. A pamphlet from 1642 reinforces this argument. It claimed that accused witch John Lowes 'hath had the society and daily frequentation of divers others that are vehemently suspected for witches, and without doubt hath had the helpe of such to worke his intended purposes'.[93] The idea that John collaborated with other witches is in keeping with previous ideas of witchcraft as a group activity. A 1645 pamphlet introduces a new element. This pamphleteer explains that witches often 'meet together to Christen' their familiars.[94] This obvious inversion of Christian practices defines witches as members of a diabolical, anti-Christian sect. By the mid-1640s, during the Matthew Hopkins era of trials, the idea of witchcraft as a conspiracy appears frequently. Pamphlets from this decade describe witches as collaborative beings who meet with each other and with the Devil at secret meetings.

During the 1640s six pamphlets were published which described regular and secret meetings of witches who were in league with the Devil. The first of these (published in 1645) recorded how 'Goodwife Pantery did many times make meetings with Goodwife Williford and with Goodwife Hott'.[95] Joan Cariden described the most recent meeting:

> within these two daies that there was a great meeting at Goodwife *Panterys* house and that Goodwife *Dadson* was there, and that Goodwife *Gardner* should have been there, but did not come, and the Divell sat at the upper end of the Table.[96]

These meetings are apparently ongoing and involve a number of regular attendees as Joan remarks upon Goodwife Gardner's absence. The Devil is present and his authority is demonstrated through his position at the head of the table. Another 1645 pamphlet also emphasises the Devil's authority over witches:

> *Anne Leech, Elizabeth Gooding, Hellen Clark, Anne West*, and [Rebecca West], met all together at the house of the aforesaid *Elizabeth Clark* in *Mannyntree*, where together spent some time in praying unto their Familiars . . . and every one of them made their several Propositions to those Familiars.[97]

In this pamphlet witches meet together to pray to their familiars before asking them to fulfil their wishes. In the preceding narrative familiars very clearly perform the role of the Devil and are being prayed to as gods. This phenomenon is repeated in a pamphlet a year later. This 1646 pamphlet began by defining witches as inherently collaborative through its title, *The Witches of Huntington*. As in previous pamphlets, all ten accused witches confessed to being asked to 'renounce God and Christ' and to make a covenant with the Devil.[98] Only one witch, Elizabeth Chandler, claims she refused to do so. The others willingly renounced Christ, promised their familiars their souls and allowed them to suck their blood. Three of the witches went further than simply denying God. Instead they agreed, at the spirits' insistence, to 'take those spirits for [their] Gods'.[99] These witches did not just deny God; they replaced him with demonic spirits. In both this pamphlet and the one from 1645, the anti-religious nature of witches is emphasised and their meetings become places for them to renounce God and pray to the Devil.

References to witchcraft as a group activity become even more overt towards the end of this 1646 pamphlet. John Clarke Junior (whose 'Father and Mother were accused for Witches') was examined as a witch and denied that he 'had any [witch's] marks cut off, or that he had any place of meeting with any Witches, or that he had any consultation, or made any compact with the Devill'.[100] This examiner expects John, as a witch, to have made a pact with the Devil and to be in contact with other witches. In order to catch John, the court arranges for an informant, John Browne, to question him under the pretence of being a fellow witch. John Browne tells John Clarke that he was searched and his witch's marks were found. Clarke scoffs at Browne: 'had you no more wit but to have your marks found? I cut off mine three dayes before I was searched'.[101] This conversation suggests a community of witches sharing tips to avoid capture. John Clarke's growing scepticism over John Browne's true identity adds to this impression. He accuses the informant of subterfuge: 'I doe not beleeve you are a Witch, for I never saw you at our meetings'.[102] The overall impression that the reader of the pamphlet is left with is an unsettling sense that witches are working together in secret and are able to avoid detection.

Other pamphlets produced in the years following the Hopkins era of persecutions also present a belief in an underground conspiracy of witches. Hopkins' death in 1647 appears to have had no impact on the circulation of these ideas. One 1649 narrative details the crimes of John Palmer and Elizabeth Knott, *'two notorious* Witches'.[103] The pamphlet takes the form of a letter of warning by B. Misodaimon to his friend about all the witches working together secretly within his county. The author claims that Palmer has been a witch 'these 60 years' and confessed that 'Marsh of Dunstable' was the head of the *'College* of *Witches'*.[104] It is difficult here not to compare this college with a seminary, thus creating a parallel with the idea of an infiltrating and corrupting Catholic enemy. The college is apparently associated with 'the society of *Witches* in *England'*.[105] Withington has tracked how the word 'society' was used in early modern printed culture and has found that it was used 'to invoke and philosophize about shared ways of life and the structures and values underpinning them'.[106] When viewed in this light, 'the society of *Witches'* implies a group of likeminded men and women meeting together and emphasises the idea of witches as a group. Palmer also confessed that Marsh knew all the witches in the country, further highlighting the idea of witches as a group who come together regularly.[107] This pamphlet also hints at the idea of a hierarchy being present among witches. The pamphlet tells us that Palmer 'notoriously seduced Elizabeth Knott' into witchcraft and that she was 'but a novice, in comparison of him, and . . . had made no direct Covenant with the Divel, as *Palmer* had'.[108] The pamphlet ends with a list of sixteen witches (nearly all of whom are related in some way), whom Palmer claims are living on the other side of the county. B. Misodaimon hopes that his friend will be able to confront these witches. His letter serves as a call-to-arms against these hidden and dangerous individuals and shows a preoccupation with the need to seek out the underground sect of witches. These witches appear to be organised and in contact with each other, and they even seem to have a college and society where they are trained.[109]

Two pamphlets from the 1640s demonstrate a preoccupation with the links between witchcraft and Catholicism. A 1642 pamphlet describes how the accused witches:

> both daily have frequented the company of knowne Popish Recusants, entertained some of them, and lodged them, nay which is more, they have had the helpe, advice and assistance of Popish Recusants in many of their wild and abominable actions, and have had them for their chief and greatest confederates, agents and counsellors.[110]

The pamphlet also adds that the accused have been selling 'Popish wares'.[111] In a similar vein, John Stearne's 1648 pamphlet claims that 'where popery and prophanesse is, with contempt of Preaching or vile neglect thereof, there Witch-craft is most rife'.[112] He also links witchcraft with idolatry.[113]

Matthew Hopkins' *The Discovery of Witches* and John Stearne's *A Confirmation and Discovery of Witchcraft* (published in 1647 and 1648, respectively) both refer to witchcraft as conspiracy.[114] Both contain descriptions of conspiratorial witchcraft and witches' assemblies. Contrary to an older historiography of English witchcraft, these are not isolated references but, as this chapter demonstrates, appear in numerous English witchcraft accounts from the first half of the seventeenth century. This offers further evidence against the concept that 'the East Anglican witch-hunt [in the 1640s] . . . [was] . . . an aberration'.[115]

Hopkins' pamphlet, which attempts to defend his witch-finding methods, provides a detailed description of a witches' assembly:

> in *March* 1644 [Hopkins] had some seven or eight of that horrible sect of Witches living in the Towne where he lived, a Towne in *Essex* called *Manningtree*, with divers other adjacent Witches of other towns, who every six weeks in the night (being alwayes on the Friday night) had their meeting close by his house, and had their severall solemne sacrifices there offered to the *Devill*, one of which [Hopkins] heard speaking to her *Imps* one night, and bid them goe to another Witch, who was thereupon apprehended, and searched by women who had for many yeares knowne the Devills marks, and found to have three teats about her, which honest women have not.[116]

As we have seen, the suggestion that witches took part in devilish meetings on Friday nights was not new to the 1640s and was already circulating in popular print.[117] The Devil's Mark and familiar spirits were also well established concepts.[118] The only idea new to English popular pamphlets in Hopkins' description of the sabbath is that of 'sacrifices' to the Devil. The pamphlet also mentions that the 'Witch confessed severall other Witches, from whom she had her *Imps*', advancing the already established notion that witches were in contact with each other in pursuing their wicked purposes.[119] This passage also evokes similar emotions to those we have seen in the first half of the century. The witches are described as 'horrible' and dishonest, adjectives designed to provoke disgust and mistrust.[120] The reference to dishonesty evokes an image of secretive witches attempting to hide the physical proof of their contact with the Devil. Hopkins is portraying witches not only as repulsive, but as untrustworthy and difficult to detect. He simultaneously provokes fear in his readers, while claiming that he can protect them. But his image of witches is common in previous seventeenth-century pamphlets, and should by no means be viewed as a radical departure from English witchcraft beliefs.

John Stearne's 1648 pamphlet in which he also defends his witch-finding methods, presents a similar understanding of conspiratorial witchcraft and assemblies. Stearne makes passing reference to the idea that witches met with the Devil claiming that witches 'have been heard to speak of their transportation from home to certain places of their meetings with others there'.[121] He also notes that witches 'worshipped the Devil at their meetings'.[122] In one case, he describes how a woman was asked if 'she were willing to be entred into [the witches'] society'.[123] He also makes general mention of Satan's 'Assemblies and Sabbaths'[124] and, as we have seen, links witchcraft with Catholicism. As already noted, the idea of witches meeting together is not new to Stearne's pamphlet; pamphleteers have already referred to assemblies and sabbaths. Nor is the idea of a 'society' of witches the invention of this pamphlet, any more than Stearne's linking of witchcraft with Catholicism is breaking new ground. Like Hopkins, Stearne is not creating a new tradition of English witchcraft, but drawing on a number of pre-existing beliefs about witchcraft as a form of group activity. In the works of both Hopkins and Stearne as in all pamphlet literature, we see the broader circulation of ideas about conspiratorial witchcraft.

Other witchcraft pamphlets published during the 1640s do not concern themselves with witches' meetings or collaborative witchcraft. This decade has been grossly exaggerated as the time when ideas of conspiratorial witchcraft and the witches' sabbath entered into popular print. Instead, this period should be viewed as a time in which pamphleteers continued to depict witchcraft as a group or conspiratorial activity. Pamphlets from both before and after this decade describe witchcraft as an underground, conspiratorial activity. In some cases, witches were believed to meet with the Devil as part of this collaboration, at other times he was simply present in familiar form. Ideas about witchcraft as a group activity were a key part of English pamphlet literature throughout the sixteenth century and the entirety of the seventeenth.

Conspiracy After Hopkins – Some New Associations

For many, the tumultuous decades of the 1640s and 1650s, characterised by devastating Civil Wars, the beheading of a king and the interregnum, provided evidence for the Devil's increased power in the world and the coming of the Last Days. It was during this period that a number of non-Conformist sects sprung up, including the Quakers. From their very beginnings, Quakers were associated with witchcraft, diabolism and a desire to overthrow the godly Commonwealth.[125] As Peter Elmer has explained, Quakers were frequently accused of using diabolical witchcraft to promote their new heresy and subvert societal order.[126] The Quakers' methods of finding new converts, their fits, their trances and their night-time meetings all contributed to a fear of Quakers as a diabolical sect. For some contemporaries, just the Quakers' origins in the north, the established home of popery and witchcraft, was enough to label them as diabolical.[127] This is not to say that the threat of Quakerism in the mid-seventeenth century replaced the threat of Catholicism in the sixteenth and early seventeenth centuries. On the contrary, many elite, Protestant Englishmen saw a clear link between Catholicism and Quakerism and suggested that the Quaker movement was part of a Catholic-inspired plot designed to undermine the godly commonwealth.[128] Catholics were still very much viewed as a hidden threat, a threat heightened by the upheaval of the Civil Wars. For many, particularly for Puritans, Elizabeth's religious settlement had not gone far enough. As a compromise position, it allowed many elements of Catholic ritual to continue, enshrined in the Book of Common Prayer.[129] For the godly, Catholic ritual still held sway over the country. During the Civil War period, these fears appeared more relevant than ever before. As Peter Elmer has convincingly argued, in post-Revolution England 'all forms of opposition, recalcitrance, rebellion or apostasy were now susceptible to demonological explication'.[130] When reading witchcraft pamphlets from this period, we must remind ourselves of the importance of this context and how it could have informed readers' interpretations of witches' stories.

One 1650 pamphlet lends itself particularly well to an association between witchcraft, diabolism and Quakerism. This pamphlet, which describes the 'grievous torments Inflicted upon the Bodies of three Children', was, very unusually, written by a woman: the mother of the afflicted children, Mrs Mary Moore.[131] Three witches, Margaret White, Mrs Weinow and her sister Jane, confessed that they deliberately conspired together to kill two children, Margaret and Mary Muschamp.[132] As was the case in previous decades, these witches joined together to kill. As in the Flower pamphlets of 1619 and 1635, these witches are portrayed as particularly repellent through their attacks on a child. The pamphlet goes further than just looking at the notion of witchcraft as a group activity and describes a meeting with these three witches and the Devil. Margaret White claimed:

> Mrs SWINOW, and her sister JANE, and her selfe were in the Divels company in her sister JANES house, where they did eate and drinke together (as by her conceived) and made merry.[133]

These witches have met with the Devil, as a group, and are eating and drinking together. They are not, however, indulging in many of the more lurid trademarks found in some European sabbaths, such as eating babies or making unguents out of their fats, although they were apparently plotting to kill children. They appear to be enjoying themselves, as did the Pendle and Samlesbury witches of 1613. In 1650 it is hard to imagine that this cosy feast in one of the witch's homes would not have been associated with Quakerism in the minds of many readers. Whereas in the Pendle and Salmesbury case the feast is given Catholic undertones, almost forty years later, these associations have changed and become merged. In this diabolical activity, many associations can be read and, in all of them, the idea of witches as anti-religious members of a hidden sect working with the Devil to bring down social order, is paramount. Although this appears a rather tame description of a sabbath or assembly, it would have been deeply threatening for contemporaries.

This is the only pamphlet from the 1650s that refers to an assembly or feast, but witches do continue to be associated with conspiracy and diabolism throughout this decade. One pamphlet from 1652 refers to the Devil as the 'Grand-master' of witches, suggesting an association of witches with the Devil as their leader.[134] Another pamphlet, *The Witch of the Woodlands* (first printed in 1655 but reprinted three times over the next three decades) portrays the actions of four women who worked together to terrorise a man called Robin.[135] Robin has run away from his 'former evils' which involved getting 'three wenches with childe all in one night'.[136] The pamphlet presents Robin as a sinful man who is being punished for his behaviour. Of the four witches who attack Robin, three are described as the 'Disciples' of the 'grand Witch of the Companie', thus emphasising a hierarchical structure.[137] The four witches in this 1655 pamphlet act as an avenging group, transforming Robin into different animals in order to punish him for his 'Whore-hunting'.[138] Importantly, the pamphlet claims that it is through the spying of the witches' imps that they know of Robin's misdeeds. The role of the Devil in this conspiracy is crucial.

The title page of this pamphlet depicts three of the witches riding a horse (see figure 2.6 in chapter 2). This image is reminiscent of the three witches who, in 1612, rode a giant sow to Ravensthorpe (figure 5.1). The horse, as we learn later in the pamphlet, is actually Robin in animal form being punished by being ridden by witches.[139] Recently, Sharpe has commented on the seemingly popular belief, visible in depositions and plays, that witches bridled their victims and forced them to be ridden like horses.[140] The victim would often turn into a horse as soon as the bridle was applied. But there is one other association that can perhaps be read in this pamphlet. A 1659 pamphlet, written just four years after this pamphlet, describes how Quakers bewitched Mary Phillips 'in the shape of a Bay Mare' and rode her at night from Dinton towards the University, where she met a 'company of Quakers'.[141] In this 1659 pamphlet we see a clear echoing of the belief that witches bridled their victims – further evidence for the ongoing association between Quakers and witches in popular print – as well as the use of the word 'company' to describe their meetings, a word, as we have seen, sometimes used to describe groups of witches. Although it has been argued that most of the fears about Quakers as a diabolical sect came from elite sources, these fears do appear to be circulating in popular print.[142]

Returning to 1655 we find that, after Robin's ordeal (which also involved being transformed into a fox and a swan), the 'grand Witch consulting with the rest of the Witches' decided that Robin had been punished enough and could be turned back into a man.[143] The witches let Robin go but not before he was forced to 'kneele downe, and kisse every one of their fleshy parts'.[144] This demeaning inversion of the demonic pact highlights Robin's total humiliation and subservience to these women. The witches are depicted as members of a powerful sect strong enough to punish men and command homage. Robin was terrified by his ordeal:

> presently he fell into such a trembling condition, that his hands shooke, his pulses beat, his heart panted, his head aked, his nose dropt, his belly rumbled, and a certain parcell of melting teares dropt out of the lower ends of his breeches.[145]

Robin's distress actually occurs before he is punished; merely meeting the grand witch is enough for him to become physically distraught. He describes her as completely repulsive, 'long-nos'd, bleare-ey'd, crooked-neckt, way-mouth'd, crumy-shoulder'd, beetle-brow'd, thin-belly'd, bow-legg'd, and splay-footed'.[146] It is hard to imagine a description more designed to evoke disgust. Given this description, Robin's humiliating kiss becomes even more grotesque. At the time of meeting this witch, Robin also heard a voice coming from her chimney, chanting 'Robin the Cobler is mine'.[147] On hearing this voice and meeting the witch, Robin assumed that the Devil was coming for him.[148] Robin was terrified: a terror directly linked to his belief that witches worked with each other and the Devil in order to harm others. However, this pamphlet differs from others in so far as in this case the witches' role is to teach a valuable lesson to a naughty rogue. But despite the witches' good intentions, they are still described as repulsive, dangerous beings that are in league with each other and the Devil. It seems that even sympathetic witches are terrifying.

Ten years later, in the mid-1660s, the concept of witchcraft as a group activity emerges yet again, this time in a 1666 pamphlet *The Shee-Devil of Petticoat-Lane*. This pamphlet is primarily concerned with poltergeist activity, but it also discusses the existence of witchcraft:

> in their Magicall Assemblies, the Witches never fail to dance, and in their dances they sing these words: Har, har, Devil, devil, dance here, dance here, play here, play here, And whiles they sing and dance every one hath a broom in her hand.[149]

In this description, the author is not referring to any particular witches but is simply stating what all witches are believed to do. Witches and sabbath-like meetings are seen as the norm. This casual reference suggests that ideas of witches' assemblies were not by any means unknown to the English population. This is also not the first time that this quotation appeared in English print. In Reginald Scot's 1584 *Discoverie of Witchcraft,* he recounts 'Monsieur *Bodins* lies' and quotes the above passage. The passage, originally by Jean Bodin, has been quoted by Reginald Scot and picked up on almost one hundred years later by a pamphleteer writing a popular piece. This incident reminds us that ideas about witchcraft as a group conspiracy were circulating widely and were clearly not solely confined to popular pamphlets. Instead, popular pamphlets picked up on ideas about witchcraft as a conspiracy from treatises and tracts as well as from witches' confessions at trial and played an important role in the circulation of these ideas.

The 1680s and Beyond: Conspiratorial Witchcraft Illustrated

Malcolm Gaskill and Ian Bostridge have both viewed the 1680s as a turning point in witchcraft history, a time at which prosecutions declined yet belief remained.[150] When looking at witchcraft pamphlets, witchcraft belief appears to have remained very strong. More witchcraft pamphlets were published during the 1680s than in any other decade, including the 1640s.[151] In these pamphlets, witchcraft continues to be described as a conspiratorial activity, both visually and textually. Even in the face of fewer witchcraft trials, the belief in conspiratorial witchcraft remains.

During the 1680s, three pamphlets were published relating the witchcraft of Temperance Floyd, Mary Trembles and Susanna Edwards; witchcraft performed with 'the assistance of the Devil'.[152] These witches do not appear to take part in any form of witches' assembly but they do have a hierarchical structure. Temperance Floyd 'the eldest of the three' is labelled a 'grand *Witch*' who has 'debaucht the other two'.[153] In all three pamphlet accounts about these witches, it was their hierarchical relationship that was emphasised. Temperance has 'been in League with the Devil 20 years and upwards'.[145] She served the Devil and the two younger, less experienced witches served her. This was a formal hierarchy based on collaboration between the Devil, a senior witch and two junior witches. However, unlike previous pamphlets, in which meetings with the Devil are enjoyable, relaxed occasions, both Mary and Temperance claimed that they were frightened of the Devil because of his physical abuse. Temperance won't admit the location of a doll (used to inflict *maleficium*) because she fears the Devil will 'tear her in pieces' if she does.[155] Later in the pamphlet Temperance says that she refused to harm a woman, and so 'the Devil beat [her] about the Head grievously because [she] would not kill her'.[156] Although Temperance is portrayed throughout the pamphlet as a powerful witch, second only to the Devil in her hierarchy, here she is described as in danger herself, helpless in the face of the Devil's violence. Although the majority of witchcraft pamphlets focus on the fear engendered in readers by evil witches, this pamphlet reminds us of the complicated nature of emotions in witchcraft narratives. Although Temperance is in league with the Devil, she is subservient to him and appears to be just as afraid of him as any other man or woman might be.

The 1680s are marked by an increase in the number of witchcraft pamphlets that visually depict witches' meetings. Some of these images stand alone, while others have accompanying descriptions.[157] The first of these comes from a 1682 ballad which depicts a giant devil around whom witches and animals dance (figure 5.2). The Devil's prominence in this image cannot be denied.

The ballad also continually refers to how witches have 'joyned with Satan' and given their souls to the 'Prince of Hell'.[158] In the image, the Devil is holding a broomstick and a large, prominent candle and although the two are touching, the broomstick does not burn. The Devil, depicted in the form of a man with horns and cloven feet, is dancing. This woodcut appeared in other seventeenth-century print often with slight adjustments.[159] In one version, the Devil's large, erect penis is very obvious.[160] In the witchcraft version, the phallus is less distinct but still visible. It comes out through the fabric of his tunic, thus suggesting it is too large to be disguised. It is possible to read the candlestick and broomstick (both of which the Devil grasps prominently) as phallic objects designed to draw attention to the Devil's visible penis. When viewed in this light, both objects add a strong sexual element to this depiction of a witches' gathering. Although the ballad itself makes no mention of sabbaths or sexual activity, this image is being used as suggestive shorthand for the links between conspiratorial gatherings, sexual activity and the Devil.[161] As was argued in chapter 4, there are

Figure 5.2 Witches dancing around a Devil. Anon., *Witchcraft Discovered and Punished/Or, the Tryals and Condemnation of Three Notorious Witches, Who Were Tried/the Last Assizes, Holden at the Castle of Exeter, in the County of Devon: Where They Received Sentence/for Death, for Betwitching Several Persons, Destroying Ships at Sea, and Cattel by Land*, 1682. © The British Library Board, Rox.II.531.

many seventeenth-century cases of witches engaging in sex with the Devil. Yet, this ballad is one of only three seventeenth-century printed sources that link this deviant sexuality with a witches' meeting.[162] Even pamphlets that describe both sex with the Devil and the sabbath do not seem to combine the two.[163] These limited references reinforce just how far the English sabbath differs from its European equivalents. Far from being a fixed idea at the start of the century or one that evolved during the 1640s, it seems clear that despite their infrequency, depictions of the sabbath in English print continued to evolve and change throughout the entire early modern period.

As well as reading the large candle as a reflection of the Devil's erect penis, it is also possible to interpret it as a reference to Catholic practices. In the image the candle is held prominently by a dancing devil and is shining brightly. Before the Reformation holy candles were believed to protect Catholics from the Devil and, in some cases, from witchcraft.[164] They were also used for more mundane tasks such as protecting farm animals.[165] However, the 1547 Edwardian Injunctions forbade the use of 'blessing with the holy candle . . . to drive away devils'.[166] This change in attitude, brought on by the Reformation, led to holy candles being viewed as suspicious Popish objects with no protective purpose. Even before the Reformation, candles became associated with more than holy worship. For some, candles were a key object for conjuring spirits.[167] In the previous image a candle has been transformed from a holy, protective object to a demonic instrument, thus creating a potential link between Catholicism, witchcraft and the Devil. It is not surprising that this anti-Catholic imagery should appear in 1682 given the revival of fear and suspicion of Catholics engendered by the Popish Plot (1678–81). Although the link between witchcraft and Catholicism is not strong throughout seventeenth-century pamphlet literature, occasional associations remind us that these resonances still had traction in the late seventeenth century.

We could also, of course, read fears of Quakerism into this image. In this image, as in those to be discussed below, we see visual depictions of men and women meeting, dancing and feasting in remote locations. The tendency for Quakers to meet in isolated places, most commonly at night was remarked upon by their enemies, thus 'raising the spectre of nocturnal gatherings and that "Grand Quaker" the Devil'.[168] Each reader would have brought their own fears, associations and assumptions to these images; for some it may have been a warning about the dangers of popery, for others a reminder of the suspiciously remote outdoor meetings of Quakers. In all of these images, the community of witches is emphasised, as is their role as the Devil's servants.

Nathaniel Crouch's 1688 book, *The Kingdom of Darkness*, shows a particular preoccupation with visually depicting conspiratorial witchcraft. Crouch's book was one of his many histories. He claimed that his accounts of witchcraft were only collected from 'Authentick Records, Real Attestations, Credible Evidences, and asserted by Authors of Undoubted Verity'.[169]

His book includes three images depicting witchcraft as a group activity. The first image depicts a sabbath (see figure 4.1 in chapter 4) the second hints at witchcraft as a conspiracy (figure 5.3) and the third shows witches dancing with devils (figure 5.4).

Before analysing these images it is important to note some of the differing influences present in this work. Robert Mayer has suggested that Crouch's work represents a 'relatively rare and therefore highly significant meeting ground for high and low culture in England at the end of the seventeenth century'.[170] Throughout his work, Crouch includes references to both European and English witchcraft beliefs (discussed in the following paragraphs), thus reminding us that at least some English pamphleteers were aware of witchcraft beliefs circulating outside England and did incorporate them into their own works. The frontispiece of Crouch's book (figure 4.1), drawn by the Dutch engraver Jan Drapentier, also highlights the circulation of different ideas.

Figure 5.3 A witch and her apprentice and devils dancing in a circle, depicted in Nathaniel Crouch, *The Kingdom of Darkness* (London: Printed for Nath. Crouch, 1688), 11. © The British Library Board, C.118.b.3, Page 11.

Figure 5.4 Witches and devils dancing together in a circle, depicted in Nathaniel
Crouch, *The Kingdom of Darkness* (London: Printed for Nath. Crouch,
1688), 57. © The British Library Board, C.118.b.3, Page 57.

Some of the motifs depicted, such as the riders in the background, are reminiscent of earlier European depictions of the sabbath. At the same time,
however, other motifs, such as the woman sprinkling herbs in the forefront,
appear to refer to specific English cases of witchcraft described in the text.
Crouch's work demonstrates the differing influences present within some
witchcraft pamphlets and demonstrates the circulation of both European
and English ideas about witchcraft as a group activity in English print.

Drapentier's frontispiece, in a reversal of the 1682 ballad illustration,
depicts two witches standing inside a circle while devils dance outside
(figure 4.1). One witch sprinkles herbs and reads from a book. The second

image in this book also portrays two witches: again one of them is sprinkling herbs and reading from a book. However, this time the witches are outside the circle, while familiar spirits and devils dance within it (figure 5.3). The third is quite different and depicts devils and witches holding hands and dancing together in a circle (figure 5.4). It is likely that the first two images relate to the story of Anne Bodenham, an eighty-year-old woman accused of being an apprentice to the notorious witch Dr Lambe and also of recruiting an apprentice herself.[171] Figure 5.3 directly illustrates this story. As figure 4.1 is a frontispiece which shows a montage of different stories and beliefs, it is likely that part of this first image also represents this section of the book. Both images depict one witch as larger and more active than the second. The second witch stands behind the first and appears to be observing. But the second witch is not a mere bystander; in figure 4.1 she stands inside the circle with the first witch, and in figure 5.3, the smaller witch is just behind the larger. In both images it is possible to view the smaller witch as an apprentice who is learning from the more experienced witch. This suggestion is supported by the text which describes how 'the Witch [Anne Bodenham] earnestly desired the Maid to live with her, and told her if she would do so she would teach her to do as she did'.[172] This agreement was then sealed by Anne:

> [Anne] . . . pricked the forefinger of the Maid with a pin, and squeezed out the bloud which she put into a pen, and gave it the Maid holding her hand to write in a great Book.[173]

This description does not merely highlight a belief in a witch taking an apprentice; it suggests that this is a formal relationship sealed by a ritual. When comparing this image with the original story of Anne Bodenham's witchcraft from 1653, another conspiratorial element is added. In an echo of older, sixteenth-century pamphlets, Anne Bodenham is described as 'a woman much adicted to Popery, and to Papistical fancies'.[174] This description puts a different spin on Anne's ritualistic magic and her use of circles, both forms of activity commonly associated with witchcraft and Catholicism in the sixteenth century. Returning to the images, the interaction between the witch, her apprentice and the Devil becomes clear. In figure 4.1 the two witches are surrounded by happily dancing devils. The devils are naked and have horns and cloven feet. This hint of demonic sexuality is dramatically increased by the inclusion in the background of a Devil being fellated by a female witch (as discussed in chapter 4). As in the 1682 ballad, here we see one of the first links in popular pamphlets between sabbaths and illicit sexuality. The background of the image also depicts several witches feasting with naked Devils. Given the strong links between English witchcraft, the Devil and sex, it is not surprising that late images of the sabbath should include references to the sexual relationships between witches and the Devil. Figure 5.3 also depicts devils, but these are in the shape of young boys and familiar spirits. The young boys are all depicted with horns and are named Belzebub, Tormentor, Lucifer and Satan.[175] These spirits are clearly demonic. To add to this impression, the boys dance with a 'Dog and Cat of the Witches'.[176] Like the first image, this illustration depicts a clear belief in witches working together to consult devils.

The third image (figure 5.4) is used in three different places throughout the book.[177] The first description of the image poses a question about Fairy Circles:

> [What are] . . . the nature of those large dark Rings in the Grass, which they call Fairy Circles, whether they be the Randezvous of Witches, or the dancing places of those little Puppet Spirits which they call Elves or Fairies.[178]

The poser of this question goes on to describe how both men and women have admitted to dancing with 'cloven footed creatures' in the circles.[179] One man, John Michael, confessed to playing music for the dancers.[180] The author tells us that this occurred in 1590, almost one hundred years before *The Kingdom of Darkness* was published.[181] The second description of figure 5.4 identifies it as 'one of those Night Meetings where Witches Assemble and Meet the Devil'.[182] Crouch claims that this took place in Germany. The third description claims that the events took place in Scotland. However, the first description and the other popular print discussed throughout this chapter make it clear that the belief in witches meeting together and with the Devil was not one that was only circulating outside England. The fact that the same image was used to represent witchcraft in England, Scotland and Germany strengthens the argument that both England and parts of Europe shared a belief that witchcraft was a group activity. Although witchcraft generally took a very different form in England than in parts of mainland Europe, the core basis of the belief that witches joined with the Devil and with each other to disrupt social harmony appears to have been well integrated into popular depictions of English witchcraft by this time.

As has already been noted, eighteenth-century pamphleteers did not show the same preoccupation with witchcraft as a group activity as their forebears did. This could, perhaps, be due to the declining number of witches tried. As there were not as many witches brought to trial, there was less material for pamphleteers to draw on, especially when attempting to portray multiple witches acting in tandem. Instead, most eighteenth-century pamphlets focus on the malice and association with devils of individual witches. There are, though, two exceptions. In his pamphlet on the witchcrafts of Elinor Shaw and Mary Phillips, Ralph Davis makes sure to emphasise that these two accused worked together to kill women and children, and to recruit others to witchcraft.[183] They also entered into a contract with the Devil at the same time, and, subsequently, encountered the devil's imps together.[184] In a second case from

1716, the pamphleteer claims that Mrs Mary Hicks, accused for witchcraft, corrupted her nine-year-old daughter to give her body and soul to the Devil.[185] Although these references are few, they demonstrate that in cases where multiple witches are accused, they were frequently believed to be working together and with the Devil to spread evil and discord throughout the world.

English witchcraft is too often portrayed in secondary literature as a solitary activity. This chapter has demonstrated that English pamphlets frequently portrayed witchcraft as conspiratorial and diabolical. Witches were believed to work with each other and the Devil, and in some cases, were accused of attending sabbath-like meetings. In pamphlets from the entire early modern period these meetings and conspiracies were described in emotive terms, designed to unsettle, disgust and terrify the reader. They were also frequently linked to other perceived threats, such as Catholics or Quakers. Descriptions of conspiratorial witchcraft and sabbath-like meetings did not simply appear, as some have argued, in the 1640s, but were recorded in pamphlets from the very beginning of witchcraft prosecutions. They also continued to be referenced in popular pamphlets long after the Hopkins era of trials. This reading of the pamphlets demonstrates that far from being a solitary activity, English witchcraft was frequently imagined as a conspiratorial and demonic crime.

Notes

1 A version of this chapter was originally published in Michael Pickering and Julie Davies, eds., *The World Enchanted: Essays in Honour of Charles Zika* (Melbourne: The Melbourne Historical Journal Collective, 2014). I am grateful to the editors and the publisher for permission to republish this work.

2 For this view see Barbara Rosen, *Witchcraft* (London: Edward Arnold, 1969), 190 and Barbara Rosen, *Witchcraft in England 1558–1618*, 2nd edn. (Amherst: University of Massachusetts Press, 1991), 190.

3 Keith Thomas, *Religion and the Decline of Magic: Studies in Popular Beliefs in Sixteenth- and Seventeenth-Century England* (London: Weidenfeld and Nicolson, 1971), 444–445; Alan Macfarlane, *Witchcraft in Tudor and Stuart England: A Regional and Comparative Study*, 2nd edn. (London: Routledge, 1999), 10, 139.

4 The two that do not are: Anon., *The Severall Factes of Witchcraft* (1585) and G.B., *A Most Wicked Worke of a Wretched Witch* (London: Printed for R. Bourne by William Barley, 1592).

5 These two pamphlets are: Anon., *The Whole Trial and Examination of Mrs Mary Hicks and Her Daughter Elizabeth* (Printed by W. Matthews in Long-Acre, 1716) and Ralph Davis, *An Account of the Tryals, Examination and Condemnation of Elinor Shaw and Mary Phillip's (Two Notorious Witches)* (Printed for F. Thorn near Fleet Street, 1705).

6 Stuart Clark, *Thinking with Demons: The Idea of Witchcraft in Early Modern Europe* (Oxford: Clarendon Press, 1997), 15; Carlo Ginzburg, *Ecstasies: Deciphering the Witches' Sabbath* (New York: Pantheon Books, 1991), 4; James Sharpe, *Instruments of Darkness: Witchcraft in England* (London: Hamish Hamilton, 1996), 75–77; James Sharpe, "In Search of the English Sabbat: Popular Conceptions of Witches' Meetings in Early Modern England," *Journal of Early Modern Studies* 2 (2013): 161–183.

7 Andrew Pickering and David Pickering, *Witch-hunting in England* (Stroud, Gloucestershire: Amberley, 2010), 39.

8 Sharpe, "In Search of the English Sabbat," 168.

9 Anon., *A Rehearsal Both Straung and True, of Heinous and Horrible Actes Committed by Elizabeth Stile alias Rockingham, Mother Dutten, Mother Devell, Mother Margaret, Fower Notorious Witches* (London: Printed by J. Kingston for Edward White, 1579), sig. A6 v.

10 Ibid., sig. A7 r.

11 Ibid., sigs. A5 v and A6 r.

12 Ibid., B1 r.

13 Ibid., sig. A8 v.

14 John Phillips, *The Examination and Confession of Certaine Wytches at Chelmsforde* (London: Willyam Powell for Willyam Pickeringe, 1566), sigs. A7 r and v.

15 James Sharpe, *Witchcraft in Early Modern England* (Harlow: Longman, 2001), 232.

16 Christopher Haigh, "The Continuity of Catholicism in the English Reformation," *Past and Present* 93 (1981): 39, 41.

17 Alexandra Walsham, *Church Papists: Catholicism, Conformity and Confessional Polemic in Early Modern England* (New York: Boydell Press, 1993), 2.

18 William Holt quoted in Haigh, "The Continuity of Catholicism," 49.

19 The most significant of these dangers were the Revolt of the Northern Earls in 1569, the Ridolfi plot in 1571, the Throckmorton Plot in 1583, the Babington Plot in 1586 and a plot by the Essex Circle in 1599 to force Elizabeth I into naming James I as her successor. There was also a papal bull issued in 1570 delegitimizing Elizabeth's right to the throne and authorising English Catholics to rise up against her. All of these schemes, with the exception of the one in 1599, were formulated by Catholics to try to restore a Catholic monarch to the throne. Christopher Haigh, *Elizabeth I* (Harlow: Longman, 2001), 177.

20 Nathan Johnstone, *The Devil and Demonism in Early Modern England* (Cambridge: Cambridge University Press, 2006), 5.

21 Macfarlane, *Witchcraft in Tudor and Stuart England;* and Thomas, *Religion and the Decline of Magic.*

22 Johnstone, *The Devil and Demonism;* Emma Wilby, *Cunning Folk and Familiar Spirits: Shamanistic Visionary Traditions in Early Modern British Witchcraft and Magic* (Brighton: Sussex Academic Press, 2005); Owen Davies, *Popular Magic: Cunning Folk in English History* (London: Hambledon Continuum, 2007); Frederick Valletta, *Witchcraft, Magic and Superstition in England, 1640–70* (Ashgate: Aldershot, 2000).

23 Francis Young, *English Catholics and the Supernatural 1553–1829* (Farnham: Ashgate, 2013), especially 134–151.

24 Phillips, *The Examination and Confession of certaine Wytches at Chelmsforde,* sigs. 2A4 v. and 3A2 r.

25 Ibid., sigs. 1B4 r and 1B2 r.

26 Ibid., sig. 1B2 r.

27 I.D., *The Most Wonderfull and True Storie, of a Certaine Witch Named Alice Gooderige of Stapen Hill* (London: Printed for I.O, 1597), sig. B2 v.

28 Ibid., sigs. C1 r and D2 v.

29 Henry Goodcole, *The Wonderfull Discoverie of Elizabeth Sawyer, a Witch* (London: Printed for William Butler, 1621), sig. C4 v.

30 Ibid.

31 For more on the legal basis of witchcraft accusations, see the introduction, this volume.

32 Malcolm Gaskill, *Crime and Mentalities in Early Modern England* (Cambridge: Cambridge University Press, 2000), 42.

33 W.W., *A True and Just Recorde, of the Information, Examination and Confession of All the Witches* (London: Thomas Dawson, 1582), sig. A3 v. For other expressions of this view, see Richard Bernard, *A Guide to Grand Jury-men Divided into Two Bookes* (London: Printed by Felix Kingston for Ed. Blackmore, 1627), particularly chapters 8 and 9; Thomas Cooper, *The Mystery of Witch-craft* (London: Printed by Nicholas Okes,1617), 232 and 313–313.

34 W.W., *A True and Just Recorde*, sig. A3 v.

35 Circle magic, the act of creating a ceremonial circle, often by drawing it on the ground, was believed to summon spirits. Kathleen R. Sands, *Demon Possession in Elizabethan England* (London: Praeger, 2004), 149–150.

36 Ibid., 149–150 and Anon., *An Act Against Conjurations, Witchcrafts, Sorcery, and Enchantments 1541/2 33 Hen. VIII 8*, in Marion Gibson, *Witchcraft and Society in England and America, 1550–1750* (Ithaca: Cornell University Press, 2003), 1–2.

37 Anon., *The Examination of John Walsh Before Maister Thomas Williams* (London: Printed by John Awdely, 1566), sig. A7 v.

38 Anon., *The Apprehension and Confession of Three Notorious Witches* (London: Printed by E. Allde, 1589), sig. A3 r.

39 Anon., *The Apprehension and Confession of Three Notorious Witches*, sig. A3 v.

40 George More, *A True Discourse Concerning the Certaine Possession and Dispossession of 7 Persons in One Familie in Lancashire* (Middelburg, Printed by Richard Schilders, 1600), sig. A7 r.

41 Anon., *The Examination of John Walsh*, sig. A2 r.

42 Ibid., sig. A2 r.

43 Ibid., sig. A2 r.

44 Anon., *A Rehearsal Both Straung and True*, sig. A5 v.

45 Ibid., sig. A5 v.

46 There are several books that focus purely on the Lancashire witches rather than looking at them as part of a continuum of English belief. See, for example, Robert Poole, ed., *The Lancashire Witches: Histories and Stories* (Manchester: Manchester University Press, 2002) and Jonathan Lumby, *The Lancashire Witch-Craze: Jennet Preston and the Lancashire Witches, 1612* (Preston: Carnegie, 1995).

47 Sharpe, *Instruments of Darkness*, 76.

48 See, for example, Sharpe, *Instruments of Darkness*, 76.

49 Potts, *The Wonderfull Discoverie of Witches in the Countie of Lancaster* (London: Printed by W. Stansby for Iohn Barnes), sig. B2 v.

50 Ibid., sigs. D2 r and B4 r.

51 Ibid., sig. C1 r.

52 See for example, Rosen, *Witchcraft in England*, 2nd edn., 29; Barry Reay, *Popular Cultures in England 1550–1750* (London: Longman, 1998), 111–112 and Gaskill, *Crime and Mentalities*, 57–58.

53 Potts, *The Wonderfull Discoverie of Witches in the Countie of Lancaster*, sig. D2 r.

54 Phil Withington, *Society in Early Modern England: The Vernacular Origins of Some Powerful Ideas* (Cambridge: Polity Press, 2010), 108–109.

55 Ibid., 109, 112.

56 Potts, *The Wonderfull Discoverie of Witches in the Countie of Lancaster*, sig. C4 r.

57 Ibid., sig. C3 r.

58 Ibid., sig. F3 r.

59 Ibid., sig. C3 r.

60 Ibid.

61 Ibid., sig. G4 v

62 James Sharpe, "Introduction: The Lancashire Witches in Historical Context," in *The Lancashire Witches: Histories and Stories*, ed. Robert Poole (Manchester: Manchester University Press, 2002), 6.

63 James Sharpe, *Remember, Remember the Fifth of November: Guy Fawkes and the Gunpowder Plot* (London: Profile Book, 2005), 22 and 21.

64 Potts, *The Wonderfull Discoverie of Witches in the Countie of Lancaster*, sig. T2 r.

65 For examples, see Potts, *The Wonderfull Discoverie of Witches in the Countie of Lancaster*, sigs. E3 r, G4 r, K1 r and H3 r.

66 Marion Gibson, *Early Modern Witches: Witchcraft Cases in Contemporary Writing* (London: Routledge, 2000), 174.

67 Potts, *Wonderfull Discoverie of Witches in the Countie of Lancaster*, sig. C3 r.

68 Pamphlets which directly emphasise the diabolical elements of witches' assemblies include Anon., *The Wonderful Discoverie of the Witchcrafts of Margaret and Phillip Flower* (London: Printed by G. Eld for I. Barnes, 1619); Matthew Hopkins, *The Discovery of Witches* (London: Printed for R. Royston, 1647); Mary Moore, *Wonderfull Newes from the North* (London: Printed by T.H., 1650); and Anon., *The Shee-Devil of Petticoat Lane* (London: Printed by Peter Lillicrap, 1666).

69 James Sharpe, *Instruments of Darkness*, 75–76.

70 Potts, *The Wonderfull Discoverie of Witches in the Countie of Lancaster*, sig. L2 r.

71 Ibid., sig. L2 v.

72 Ibid., sig. M4 r.

73 Ibid., sigs. M2 v and M3 r.

74 Sharpe, "In Search of the English Sabbat," 166.

75 Potts, *The Wonderfull Discoverie of Witches in the Countie of Lancaster*, sigs. M1 v-M4 r

76 Anon., *The Witches of Northampton-shire* (London: Printed by Tho: Purfoot for Arthur Johnston, 1612), sig. C1 r.

77 Ibid., sig. A3 v.

78 Ibid., sigs. B2 r, C1 v, D1 v and D2 v.

79 See chapter 3, this volume, for a discussion of witches' malicious dispositions.

80 Anon., *The Witches of Northampton-shire*, sigs. B3 r and B2 r.

81 Ibid., sig. C1 r.

82 Sharpe, "In Search of the English Sabbat," 177.

83 Anon., *The Witches of Northamptonshire*, sig. C1 r.

84 Anon., *Witches Apprehended, Examined and Executed* (London: Printed by Edward Marchant, 1613); Anon., *The Wonderful Discoverie of the Witchcrafts of Margaret and Phillip Flower*; and Anon., *Witchcrafts, Strange and Wonderfull* (London: Printed by M.F. for Thomas Dawson, 1635), sig. A2 v.

85 Anon., *Witches Apprehended, Examined and Executed*, sig. A4 r.

86 Ibid.

87 Ibid.

88 Anon., *The Wonderful Discoverie of the Witchcrafts of Margaret and Phillip Flower*, 1619.

89 Anon., *Witchcrafts, Strange and Wonderfull*, title page.

90 Anon., *The Wonderful Discoverie of the Witchcrafts of Margaret and Phillip Flower*, sig. F1 r and Anon., *Witchcrafts, Strange and Wonderfull*, sig. B4 v.

91 This image is used in the 1619 pamphlet to represent both the Flower family and some other witches referred to in the pamphlet: Anne Baker, Joane Willimot and Ellen Greene. In the 1635 pamphlet and the 1619 ballad the image simply represents the Flower family.

92 Ian Bostridge, *Witchcraft and Its Transformations c.1650-c.1750* (Oxford: Clarendon Press, 1997), 3.

93 Anon., *A Magazine of Scandall* (London: Printed for R.H., 1642), sig. A3 v.

94 Anon., *The Lawes Against Witches, and Conjuration and Some Brief Notes and Observations for the Discovery of Witches* (London: Printed for R.W., 1645), sig. A2 v.

95 Anon., *The Examination, Confession, Trial and Execution of Joane Williford, Joan Cariden and Jane Hott* (London: Printed by J.G., 1645), 6.

96 Ibid., 3.

97 H.F., *A True and Exact Relation of the Several Informations, Examinations, and Confessions of the Late Witches, Arraigned and Executed in the County of Essex* (London: Printed by M.S. for Henry Overton and Benj. Allen, 1645), 12.

98 John Davenport, *The Witches of Huntington, Their Examinations and Confessions Exactly Taken by His Majesties Justices of Peace for That County* (London: Printed by W. Wilson for Richard Clutterbuck, 1646), 1.

99 Ibid., 9.

100 Ibid., 15 and 14.

101 Ibid., 15.

102 Ibid.

103 B. Misodaimon, *The Divels Delusions* (London: Printed for Richard Williams, 1649), title page.

104 B. Misodaimon, *The Divels Delusions*, 2.

105 Ibid.

106 Phil Withington, *Society in Early Modern England: The Vernacular Origins of Some Powerful Ideas* (Cambridge: Polity Press, 2010), 113.

107 B. Misodaimon, *The Divels Delusions*, 2.

108 Ibid., 4 and 5.

109 Ibid., 2.

110 Anon., *A Magazine of Scandall* (London: Printed for R.H., 1642), sig. A3 v.

111 Ibid., sig. A4 r.

112 John Stearne, *A Confirmation and Discovery of Witches* (London: Printed by William Wilson, 1648), sig A4 v.

113 Ibid., sigs. D1 v, and H4 r.

114 Hopkins, *The Discovery of Witches* and Stearne, *A Confirmation and Discovery of Witches*.

115 Gaskill suggests that to understand better the Hopkins era of witch-hunts more work needs to be done on the context surrounding them. Malcolm Gaskill, "Witchcraft, Emotion and Imagination," in *Witchcraft and the Act of 1604*, eds. John Newton and Jo Bath (Leiden: Brill, 2008), 164.

116 Hopkins, *The Discovery of Witches*, 2.

117 See, for example, Potts, *The Wonderfull Discoverie of Witches*; Anon., *The Witches of Northampton-shire*; Anon., *The Wonderful Discovery of the Witchcrafts of Margaret and Philip Flower*; and Anon., *Witchcrafts, Strange and Wonderfull*.

118 See chapter 2, this volume, for details.

119 Hopkins, *The Discovery of Witches*, 2.

120 Ibid., 2.

121 Stearne, *A Confirmation and Discovery of Witches*, 53.

122 Ibid., 16.

123 Ibid., 38.

124 Ibid., 52.

125 For more on the supposed links between Quakers and witches, see Barry Reay, *The Quakers and the English Revolution* (London: Temple Smith, 1985), 68–71 and Peter Elmer, " 'Saints or Sorcerers': Quakerism, Demonology and

the Decline of Witchcraft in Seventeenth-Century England," in *Witchcraft in Early Modern Europe: Studies in Culture and Belief*, eds. Jonathan Barry, Marianne Hester and Gareth Roberts (Cambridge: Cambridge University Press, 1998), 145–179.

126 Elmer, " 'Saints or Sorcerers,' " 145.
127 Ibid., 150.
128 Ibid., 160.
129 See Malcolm Gaskill, *Witchfinders: A Seventeenth-Century English Tragedy* (London: John Murray, 2006), 10.
130 Elmer, " 'Saints or Sorcerers,' " 174.
131 Moore, *Wonderfull Newes from the North*, title page.
132 Ibid., 25.
133 Ibid., 24.
134 E.G. and H.F., *A Prodigious and Tragicall History of the Arraignment, Tryall, Confession and Condemnation of Six Witches at Maidstone* (London: Printed for Richard Harper, 1652), 6.
135 L.P., *The Witch of the Woodlands* (London: Printed for John Stafford, 1655).
136 Ibid., title page and 3.
137 Ibid., 9 and 14.
138 Ibid., 9.
139 Ibid., 14.
140 Sharpe, "In Search of the English Sabbat," 161, 173.
141 Anon., *Strange & Terrible Newes from Cambridge, Being a True Relation of the Quakers Bewitching of Mary Philips Out of the Bed from Her Husband in the Night, and Transformed Her into the Shape of a Bay Mare, Riding Her from Dinton, Towards the University* (London: Printed for C. Brooks, and are to be sold at the Royal Exchange in Cornhill, 1659), title page and 4.
142 Reay, *The Quakers and the English Revolution*, 68–69; Elmer, " 'Saints or Sorcerers.' "
143 L.P., *The Witch of the Woodlands*, 14 and 15.
144 Ibid., 15.
145 Ibid., 7–8.
146 Ibid., 7.
147 Ibid.
148 Ibid.
149 Anon., *The Shee-Devil of Petticoat-Lane*, 8.
150 Gaskill, *Crime and Mentalities*, 79 and Bostridge, *Witchcraft and Its Transformations*, 3.
151 See Appendix B.
152 Anon., *The Tryal, Condemnation, and Execution of Three Witches* (London: Printed for J. Deacon, 1682), title page.
153 Anon., *The Tryal, Condemnation, and Execution of Three Witches*, 2; Anon., *The Life and Conversation of Temperance Floyd, Mary Lloyd and Susanna Edwards* (London: Printed by J. W., 1687), 6; and Anon., *A True and Impartial Relation of the Informations Against Three Witches* (London: Printed by Freeman Collins, 1642), 40.
154 Anon., *The Tryal, Condemnation, and Execution of Three Witches*, 2.
155 Anon., *A True and Impartial Relation of the Informations Against Three Witches*, 19.
156 Ibid., 38.
157 Images which stand alone without a description include: Anon., *Witchcraft Discovered and Punished/or, the Tryals and Condemnation of Three Notorious Witches, Who Were Tried/ the Last Assizes, Holden at the Castle of Exeter, in the County of Devon: Where They Received Sentence/for Death,*

for Bewitching Several Persons, Destroying Ships at Sea, and Cattel by Land (1682); and Balthasar Bekker, *The World Turn'd Upside Down, or, a Plain Detection of Errors, in the Common or Vulgar Belief, Relating to Spirits, Spectres or Ghosts, Daemons, Witches, &c. in a Due and Serious Examination of Their Nature, Power, Administration, and Operation* (London: Printed for Elizabeth Harris, 1700), 264.

158 Anon., *Witchcraft Discovered and Punished*, lines 11 and 32.

159 Anon., *The Merry Pranks of Robin Goodfellow* (London: Printed by and for W.Q), date unknown. This ballad appears in the Bagford Collection vols. I and II and the Roxburghe Collection, vol. I, 230. The image also appears in another version of this pamphlet: the Euing Collection of ballads, page 203. In the Euing version the Devil's penis appears more prominently. The Devil's penis is even clearer in yet another version of this image which appears in Anon., *The Rag Man: Or a Company That Fall at Oddes One Day, Which of Them Should Carry the Cunny Skins Away: They Strove Who Should Have It, but None of Them Wise, for the Usurer and the Divell Carry Away the Prize* (London: Printed for Fr. Grove, date unknown). This ballad can be found in the Roxburghe Collection, vol III, part I, 182–183.

160 See Anon., *The Rag Man*, Roxburghe Collection, vol III, part I, 182–183.

161 See chapter 4, this volume, for more on the sexual nature of English witchcraft.

162 See also Nathanial Crouch, *The Kingdom of Darkness* (London: Printed for Nath. Crouch, 1688), frontispiece, (discussed below) and Potts, *A Wonderful Discoverie*, sig. L2 v. (discussed above).

163 Pamphlets that describe both the English sabbath and diabolical sexuality are: Davenport, *The Witches of Huntington*; Stearne, *a Confirmation and Discoverie of Witchcraft*; and Moore, *Wonderful News from the North*. There are many other pamphlets that allude to loose or immoral sexuality and the Devil, but these are the only three that mention both the physical sabbath and sexuality associated with the diabolical.

164 Thomas, *Religion and the Decline of Magic*, 1st edn., 493.

165 Ibid., 32.

166 Ibid., 53.

167 Ibid., 229.

168 Elmer, " 'Saints or Sorcerers,' " 150; Reay, *The Quakers and the English Revolution*, 70.

169 Nathanial Crouch, *The Kingdom of Darkness: Or the History of Daemons, Specters, Witches, Apparitions, Possessions, Disturbances, and Other Wonderful and Supernatural Delusions, Mischievous Feats, and Malicious Impostures of the Devil* (London: Printed for Nathanial Crouch, 1688), title page. For more on Crouch's life as a celebrated historian and bookseller, see Robert Mayer, "Nathaniel Crouch, Bookseller and Historian: Popular Historiography and Cultural Power in Late Seventeenth-Century England," *Eighteenth-Century Studies* 27 (1994): 391–419.

170 Mayer, "Nathanial Crouch, Bookseller and Historian," 393.

171 For the story of Anne Bodenham, see Crouch, *The Kingdom of Darkness*, 10. It is also described in two pamphlets from 1653: Edmond Bower, *Doctor Lamb Revived, or, Witchcraft Condemned in Anne Bodenham* (London: Printed by T.W. for Richard Best and John Place, 1653); James Bower, *Doctor Lamb's Darling* (London: Printed for G. Horton, 1653). For a description of the life of Dr. Lambe, see Anon., *A Briefe Description of the Notorious Life of John Lambe, Otherwise Called Doctor Lambe, Together with His Ignominious Death* (London, Amsterdam: G.E. Miller, 1628).

172 Crouch, *The Kingdom of Darkness*, 14.
173 Ibid., 14.
174 Bower, *Dr. Lambe Revived*, 1.
175 Crouch, *The Kingdom of Darkness*, 11.
176 Ibid., 12.
177 Ibid., 57, 115 and 128.
178 Ibid., 56.
179 Ibid., 58.
180 Ibid.
181 Ibid.
182 Ibid., 115.
183 Davis, *An Account of the Tryals, Examination and Condemnation*, 4, 6 and 7.
184 Ibid., 6 and 7.
185 Anon., *The Whole Trial and Examination*, 5.

Conclusion

This book began with the claim that English witchcraft has for too long been viewed as a predominantly malefic crime. To re-evaluate the role of the Devil in English witchcraft, I analysed all sixty-six extant early modern English witchcraft pamphlets. This is the first time that these sources have been analysed as a group and also the first time that they have been used to explore how witches were believed to interact with the Devil in early modern England. These pamphlets clearly demonstrate that English witchcraft narratives emphasised the centrality of the Devil in witchcraft beliefs. They also demonstrate a preoccupation with the emotional character of the relationships between witches and their devils. Emotions were of critical importance in witchcraft narratives. Anger, hatred, a desire for revenge, malice, love and lust were viewed as key drivers of witchcraft acts and accusations. From a study of pamphlet literature, I have argued that English witchcraft was understood as a diabolical crime that was motivated by strong emotions.

In attempting to re-evaluate the role of the Devil in English witchcraft beliefs, this book has argued that witchcraft pamphlets did not present one clear concept of the Devil. The new post-Reformation emphasis on the Devil as an omnipresent force for evil and a dangerous tempter is visible in the prologues to many witchcraft pamphlets. These epistles often emphasised that the Devil was most dangerous as an incorporeal source of mental temptations. At the same time, the Devil most commonly appeared in witchcraft narratives as a small, physical domestic animal such as a cat, dog or ferret. As a result, witchcraft narratives present a set of varied and ambiguous understandings of the Devil. The Devil was a common feature in witchcraft pamphlets throughout the entire early modern period, with only three pamphlets not tying witchcraft to diabolical power. In studying the role of the Devil in English witchcraft narratives, we can shed further light on the types of beliefs about the Devil circulating in post-Reformation England. The presence of the Devil in witchcraft pamphlets across the entire early modern period is suggestive of a strong ongoing belief in the Devil even in the face of rising scepticism and declining trials.

The Devil's appearance as a familiar spirit has been of the utmost importance to this book. The omnipresence of this diabolical creature as a companion to the witch, as an entry into witchcraft, as an emotional conduit, as a powerfully magical demonic creature and as a demonic tempter, all encourage us to reassess the importance of diabolical ideas to English witchcraft narratives. As we have seen, the familiar spirit was crucial in tempting a man or woman into making a pact with the Devil. Familiar spirits were believed to convince potential witches to join with them through appearing when they were particularly desirous of revenge, money or love. Familiars also appeared to men and women at times when they had lost control of their emotions and had given in to violent, angry outbursts. Familiar spirits played on witches' emotions in order to draw them away from God and into Satan's clutches. More than this, familiars were often described as physical manifestations of a witch's anger, malice or vengeance. Through the familiar spirit, witches were able to act on their desires; without him, they were powerless.

The relationship between witch and familiar could, as has been discussed, take a variety of different forms. In sixteenth-century pamphlets, witches were often described as lewd or of loose sexual morality and in almost 50 per cent of seventeenth-century pamphlets, female witches were described as engaging in sexual relationships with their devils. These relationships were often well established, having existed for many years, and were described as being based on mutual love, sexual desire and affection. Through familiar spirits, witches created personal bonds with the Devil that often involved illicit sexual activities such as fornication, cunnilingus and anilingus. In portraying female witches as sexual beings who engaged in sexual relationships with devils, pamphlets created an understanding of witchcraft as a diabolical and sexualised crime. This pamphlet evidence contrasts starkly with the long-held view that witchcraft in England was a predominantly asexual and non-diabolical crime.

Witchcraft was portrayed in English pamphlets as a personal crime. Witches formed close bonds with their familiars and then relied on these spirits to injure those who had angered them. However, witches were also believed to work together to carry out vengeful acts. In the majority of early modern pamphlets, witches were believed to act together and with the Devil to spread evil and discord. In the religiously unstable climate of early modern England, descriptions of witches plotting together and with the Devil to do evil were sometimes linked with minority groups such as Catholics or Quakers. These associations made the threat of witchcraft even more palpable. In presenting witchcraft as a conspiratorial rather than solitary activity, pamphlets amplified the fear of witchcraft to that of a group working secretly against society. In this way, witches were even further demonised and identified as part of a terrifying, underground conspiracy.

As well as emphasising the role of the Devil, this book has also focused on the role of emotions in witchcraft acts and accusations and has explored how emotions "work" in witchcraft pamphlets. It has highlighted the role of witches, victims, accusers, witnesses and pamphleteers in creating a genre that presents witchcraft as a crime motivated by strong emotions. It has, I hope, reminded readers of the many different influences that make up a witchcraft pamphlet and also shown the difficulties in separating these influences. This book has highlighted both how pamphleteers may have manipulated witchcraft narratives but also suggested that we can hear the voice of the witch in many of these stories. Although subject to many differing influences, in some pamphlets it is possible to see the witch as an agent who helped contribute to the diabolical narrative. Witchcraft pamphlets help us understand the specific forms of emotional expression that were believed to drive interactions between witches and devils, witches and accusers or victims, and also witches and readers. In this way, pamphlets created a framework for how early modern people reacted to and experienced witchcraft stories.

In covering such a broad period, this book has been able to highlight continuity and change across the entire one hundred and seventy year period of state-sanctioned witchcraft prosecutions. It has demonstrated how pamphlets published before 1645 labelled witches as vengeful, and often malicious, but how during the 1650s and 1660s these descriptors were largely absent. It has also highlighted the differences in the types of sexual activity female witches were believed to engage in with the Devil: pre-1640 witches were more likely to engage in non-penetrative sex with animalistic devils, whereas during the 1640s and later, witches were more often described as engaging in penetrative sex with man-like devils. It has shown how sixteenth-century pamphlets placed a greater emphasis on Catholic associations than later pamphlets as well as demonstrating how this association continued sporadically throughout the centuries and how new religious groups came to be associated with witchcraft in different periods. As a whole though, I have been surprised by the strong continuities that come through in witchcraft pamphlets. In reading one pamphlet from the 1570s and another from the 1710s, it is extremely difficult to date them based purely on the beliefs expressed within. Pamphlets from both the very beginning and the end of witchcraft prosecutions depict witches as malicious, vengeful men and women who collaborate with each other and with the Devil to act on their desires. The way in which the making of the pact is described and witches' motivations for entering into it are remarkably similar across the early modern period, and witches are routinely presented as figures of fear in their communities. Even pamphlets from the 1640s do not depict beliefs that were not already visible in witchcraft print. This decade represents an intensification of witchcraft belief but not, as has too often been suggested, a reinvention. Although there are notable differences across the early modern period, the continuity of witchcraft beliefs across a period of such significant change, both political and religious, is striking and points to pamphlets as a genre which depicted a very specific idea of what a witch was.

This book has argued that the role of the Devil was of paramount importance in early modern English witchcraft pamphlets. In exploring the different ways in which the Devil appeared in these narratives, it has suggested that the paradigm of English witches as those who primarily practised non-diabolical *maleficium* has been overdrawn and needs to be revisited. The primary aim of this book has been to analyse all extant early modern witchcraft pamphlets. This is just the first, crucial step in understanding the role of the Devil in English witchcraft. In writing this book, I have attempted to set the scene for further study on the broader context of these beliefs. Future research on trial records and learned demonologies might also help broaden the findings of this study. A consideration of these sources may allow us to further explore the key role of the Devil in early modern English witchcraft; a role that, as this book has demonstrated, was of crucial importance to witchcraft narratives.

Appendix A: The Core Group of Witchcraft Pamphlets

Arranged in Chronological Order

1 Anon. *The examination of John Walsh before Maister Thomas Williams, Commissary to the Reverend father in God William bishop of Excester, upon certayne interrogatories touchyng Wytchcrafte and Sorcerye, in the presence of divers ge[n]tlemen and others: The. xxiii. of August. 1566.* London: Printed by John Awdely, 1566.

2 Phillips, John. *The examination and confession of certaine wytches at Chelmsford in the countie of Essex: Before the Quenes Majesties judges, the xxvi daye of July, anno 1566, at the Assise holden there as then, and one of them put to death for the same offence, as their examination declareth more at large.* London: Printed by Willyam Powell for Willyam Pickeringe, 1566.

3 Anon. *A detection of damnable driftes, practized by three witches arraigned at Chelmisforde in Essex at the last Assizes there holden, whiche were executed in Aprill, 1579: Set forthe to discover the ambushementes of Sathan, whereby he would surprise us lulled in securitie, and hardened with contempte of Gods vengeance threatened for our offences.* London: Printed by J. Kingston for Edward White, 1579.

4 Anon. *A rehearsal both straung and true, of heinous and horrible actes committed by Elizabeth Stile alias Rockingham, Mother Dutten, Mother Devell, Mother Margaret, fower notorious Witches, apprehended at Winsore in the countie of Barks: And at Abbington arraigned, condemned, and executed, on the 26 daye of Februarie laste Anno. 1579.* London: Printed by J. Kingston for Edward White, 1579.

5 Galis, Richard. *A brief treatise conteyning the most strange and horrible crueltye of Elizabeth Stile alias Rockingham & hir confederates executed at Abington upon Richard Galis.* London: 1579.

6 W.W. *A true and just Recorde, of the information, examination and confession of all the witches, taken at S. Oses in the countie of Essex whereof some were executed, and other some entreated according to the determination of lawe: Wherein all men may see what a pestilent*

people witches are, and how unworthy to lyve in a Christian Common-wealth: Written orderly, as the cases were tried by evidence, by W.W. London: Printed by Thomas Dawson, 1582.

7   Anon. *The severall factes of Witch-craft.* 1585.

8   Anon. *The apprehension and confession of three notorious witches: Arreigned and by Justice condemned and executed at Chemes-forde, in the Countye of Essex, the 5. Day of Julye, last past, 1589 with the manner of their divelish practices and keeping of their spirits, whose fourmes are herein truelye proportioned.* London: E. Allde, 1589.

9   B., G. *A most wicked worke of a wretched witch (the like whereof none can record these manie yeeres in England): Wrought on the person of one Richard Burt, servant to Maister Edling of Woodhall in the parrish of Pinner in the Countie of Myddlesex, a myle beyond Harrow: Latelie committed in March last, An. 1592 and newly recognised according to the truth: By G. B. maister of Arts.* London: Printed by R. Bourne for William Barley, 1592.

10 I., T. "A memorial of certaine most notorious witches, and of their deal-ings." In *a World of Wonders, a MASSE of Murthers, a COVIE of Cosenages: Containing many of the moste notable wonders, horrible Murthers and detestable Cosonages that have been within this Land.* London: Printed for William Barley, 1595.

11 Anon. *The most cruell and bloody murther committed by an inkeepers wife, called Annis Dell, and her Sonne George Dell, four yeares since: On the bodie of a childe, called Anthony James in bishops Hatfield in the Countie of Hartford, and now most miraculously revealed by the Sister of the said Anthony, who at the time of the murther had her tongue cut out, and foure yeeres remained dumme and speechlesse, and now perfectly speaketh, revealing the murther, having no tongue to be seen: With the severall witchcrafts, and most damnable practices of one Johane Harrison and her daughter upon severall persons, men and women at Royston, who were all executed at Hartford the 4 of August last past, 1606.* London: Printed for William Firebrand and John Wright, 1606.

12 Anon. *The witches of Northampton-shire: Agnes Browne: Joane Vaughan: Arthur Bill: Hellen Jenkenson: Mary Barber: Witches: Who were all executed at Northampton the 22. of July last, 1612.* London: Printed by Tho: Parfoot, for Arthur Johnson, 1612.

13 Potts, Thomas. *The wonderfull discoverie of witches in the countie of Lancaster with the arraignement and triall of nineteene notorious witches, at the assizes and general gaole deliuerie, holden at the castle of Lancaster, vpon Munday, the seuenteenth of August last, 1612: Before Sir Iames Altham, and Sir Edward Bromley, Knights; barons of his Maiesties Court of Exchequer: and iustices of assize, oyer and terminor, and generall gaole deliuerie in the circuit of the north parts: Together with the arraignement and triall of Iennet Preston, at the assizes holden*

at the castle of Yorke, the seuen and twentieth day of Iulie last past,
with her execution for the murther of Master Lister by witchcraft:
Published and set forth by commandement of his Maiesties iustices of
assize in the north parts: By Thomas Potts Esquier. London: Printed by
W. Stansby for Iohn Barnes, 1613.

14 Anon. *Witches apprehended, examined and executed, for notable vil-*
lanies by then committed both by land and water: With a strange and
most true trial how to know whether a woman be a witch or not. London: Printed for Edward Marchant, 1613.

15 Anon. *The wonderful discoverie of the witchcrafts of Margaret and*
Phillip Flower, daughters of Joan Flower neere Bever Castle: Executed
at Lincolne, March 11. 1618: Who were specially arraigned and con-
demned before Sir Henry Hobart, and Sir Edward Bromley, Judges of
Assise, for confessing themselves actors in the destruction of Henry
Lord Rosse, with their damnable practices against others the children
of the Right Honourable FRANCIS Earle of Rutland: Together with the
severall examinations and confessions of Anne Baker, Joan Willimot,
and Ellen Greene, Witches in Leicestershire. London: Printed by G. Eld
for I. Barnes, 1619.

16 Goodcole, Henry. *The wonderfull discoverie of Elizabeth Sawyer a*
witch, late of Edmonton, her conviction and condemnation and death:
Together with the relation of the Divels accesse to her, and their con-
ference together: Written by Henry Goodcole Minister of the Word of
God, and her continuall visitor in the Gaole of Newgate: Published by
Authority. London: Printed for William Butler, 1621.

17 Anon. *Witchcrafts strange and wonderfull: Discovering the damnable*
practices of seven witches, against the lives of certaine Noble Personages,
and others of this Kingdome, as shall appeare in this lamentable History:
With an approved trial how to find out either witch, or any apprentise
to witch-craft. London: Printed by M.F. for Thomas Lambert, 1635.

18 Anon. *A Magazine of scandall, or, a heape of wickednesse of two infa-*
mous ministers, consorts, one named Thomas Fowkes of Earle Soham
in Suffolk, convicted by law for killing a man, and the other named
John Lowes of Brandeston, who hath beene arraigned for witchcraft,
and convicted by law for a common barrettor together with the manner
how my Lord of Canterbury would put and keep them in the minis-
tery: Not withstanding the many petitions and certificates from their
parishioners and others, presented to him, they being the head and most
notorious of the scandalous ministers within the county of Suffolke,
and well may be said of all England : And against whom as chiefe of
the scandalous ministers the county of Suffolke have petitioned to the
Parliament : and desired to bee seene by Parliament because herein is
something mentioned which is conceived, that one of these scandalous
ministers have abused the authority of the Lords in Parliament. London: Printed for R.H., 1642.

19 Anon. *A most certain, strange and true discovery of a witch: Being taken by some Parliament Forces, as she was standing on a small planck board and sayling on it over the River of Newbury: Together with the strange and true manner of her death, with the propheticall words and speeches she used at the time.* Printed by John Hammond, 1643.

20 Anon. *The examination, confession, triall, and execution, of Joane Williford, Joan Cariden, and Jane Hott: Who were executed at Feversham in Kent, for being witches, on Munday the 29 of September, 1645: Being a true copy of their evill lives and wicked deeds, taken by the Major of Feversham and jurors for the said inquest: With the examination and confession of Elizabeth Harris, not yet executed: All attested under the hand of Robert Greenstreet, major of Feversham.* London: Printed for J.G., 1645.

21 Anon. *Signes and wonders from heaven: With a true relation of a monster borne in Ratcliffe Highway, at the signe of the three Arrows, Mistris Bullock the midwife delivering here thereof: Also shewing how a cat kitned a monster in Lombard street in London: Likewise a new discovery of witches in Stepney parish: And how 20. witches more were executed in Suffoke this last assise: Also how the divell came to Soffam to a farmers house in the habit of a gentlewoman on horse-backe: With divers other strange remarkable passages.* London: Printed by I. H., 1645.

22 F., H. *A true and exact relation of the several informations, examinations, and confessions of the late witches, arraigned and executed in the County of Essex: Who were arraigned and condemned at the late Sessions, holden at Chelmesford before the Right Honorable Robert, Earle of Warwicke, and severall of his Majesties Justices of Peace, the 29 of July, 1645: Wherin the severall murthers, and devilish witchcrafts, committed on the bodies of men, women, and children, and divers cattell, are fully discovered: Published by Authority.* London: Printed by M.S. for Henry Overton, and Benj. Allen, 1645.

23 Anon. *A true relation of the araignment of eighteene vvitches: That were tried, convicted, and condemned, at a sessions holden at St. Edmundsbury in Suffolke, and there by the iudge and iustices of the said sessions condemned to die, and so were executed the 27. day of August 1645: As also a list of the names of those that were executed, and their severall confessions before their executions: VVith a true relation of the manner how they find them out: The names of those that were executed. Mr. Lowes parson of Branson: Thomas Evered a cooper with Mary his wife: Mary Bacon: Anne Alderman: Rebecca Morris: Mary Fuller: Mary Clowes: Margery Sparham Katherine Tooley: Sarah Spinlow: Iane Limstead: Anne Wright: Mary Smith: Iane Rivert: Susan Manners: Mary Skipper: Anne Leech.* London. Printed by I. H., 1645.

24 Anon. *The lawes against vvitches, and conivration and some brief notes and observations for the discovery of witches: Being very usefull for*

these times, wherein the Devil reignes and prevailes over the soules of poore creatures, in drawing them to that crying sin of witch-craft: Also, the confession of Mother Lakeland, who was arraigned and condemned for a witch, at Ipswich in Suffolke: Published by authority. London: Printed for R.W., 1645.

25 Davenport, John. *The witches of huntingdon, their examinations and confessions exactly taken by his Majesties Justices of Peace for that County: Whereby will appeare how craftily and dangerously the Devill tempteth and seizeth on poore soules: The reader may make use hereof against hypocrisie, anger, malice, swearing, idolatry, lust, covertousnesse, and other grievous sins, which occasioned this their downfall.* London: Printed by W. Wilson for Richard Clutterbuck, 1646.

26 Hopkins, Matthew. *The discovery of witches: In answer to severall queries, lately delieved to the Judges of Assize for the County of Norfolk: And now published by Matthew Hopkins, Witch-finder: For the benefit of the whole Kingdome.* London: Printed for R. Royston, 1647.

27 Stearne, John. *A confirmation and discovery of witch-craft, containing these severall particulars; that there are witches called bad witches, and witches untruely called good or white witches, and what manner of people they be, and how they may bee knowne, with many particulars thereunto tending: Together with the confessions of many of those executed since May 1645 in the severall Counties hereafter mentioned. As also some objections Answered.* London: Printed by William Wilson, 1648.

28 Misodaimon, B. *The Divels delusions or a faithfull relation of John Palmer and Elizabeth Knott two notorious witches lately condemned at the Sessions of Oyer and Terminer in St. Albans: Together with the confession of the aforesaid John Palmer and Elizabeth Knott, executed July 16. Also their accusations of severall witches in Hitchen, Norton, and other places in the County of Hartford.* London: Printed for Richard Williams, 1649.

29 Moore, Mary. *Wonderfull news from the North: Or, a true relation of the sad and grievous torments, inflicted upon the bodies of three children of Mr. George Muschamp, late of the County of Northumberland, by witch-craft: And how miraculously it pleased God to strengthen them, and to deliver them: As also the prosecution of the sayd witches, as by oaths, and their own confessions will appear, and by the indictment found by the Jury against one of them, at the Sessions of the Peace held at Alnwick, the 24, day of April, 1650.* London: Printed by T.H., 1650.

30 Magomastix, Hieronymus. *The strange witch at Greenwich, (Ghost, Spirit, or Hobgoblin) haunting a wench, later servant to a miser, suspected a murtherer of his late wife: With curious discussions of walking spirits and spectars of dead men departed, for rare and mysticall knowledge and discourse.* London: Printed by Thomas Harper, 1650.

31 Vicars, John. *Against William LI-LIE (alias) Lillie, that most audacious atheisticall rayling rabscheca, that impious witch or wizzard, and most abhominable sorcerer, or star-gazer of London, and all his odious almanacks, and others.* London: 1652.

32 G., E. and F., H. *A prodigious and tragicall history of the arraignment, tryall, confession, and condemnation of six witches at Maidstone, in Kent, at the Assizes there held in July, Fryday 30: This present Year: 1652: Before the Right Honorable, Peter Warburton, one of the Justices of the Common Please: Collected from the observations of E.G. Gent (a learned person, present at their Conviction and Condemnation) and digested by H.F. Gent: To which is added a true elation of one Mrs. Atkins, a mercers wife in Warwick, who was strangely carried away from her house in July last, and hath not been heard of since.* London: Printed for Richard Harper, 1652.

33 Anon. *The witch of wapping: Or an exact and perfect relation, of the life and devilish practices of Joan Peterson, that dwelt in Spruce Island, near Wapping; Who was condemned for practicing witch-craft, and sentenced to be hanged at Tyburn on Monday the 11th of April, 1652: Shewing, how she bewitch'd a child, and roch'd the cradle in the likenesse of a cat; how she frighted a baker; and how the Devil often came to suck her, sometimes in the likeness of a Dog, and at other times like a Squirrel. Together, with the confession of Prudence Lee, who was burnt in Smithfield on Saturday the 10th: Of this instant for the murthering her husband; and her admonition and counsel to all her sex in general.* London: Printed for Th. Spring, 1652.

34 Anon. *A declaration in answer to several lying Pamphlets concerning the Witch of Wapping: Being a more perfect relation of the arraignment, condemnation, and suffering of Jone Peterson, who was put to death on Munday the 12 of April, 1652: Serving the bloudy plot and wicked conspiracy of one Abraham Vandenbernde, Thomas Crompton, Thomas Collet, and others.* London: 1652.

35 Anon. *The tryall and examination of Mrs. Joan Peterson, before the Honorable Bench, at the Sessions house in the Old-Bayley, yesterday; for her supposed witchcraft, and poisoning of the Lady Powel at Chelsey: Together with her confession at the Bar: Also, the tryal, examination, and confession, of Giles Fenderlyn, who had made a covenant with the Devil for 14 years, written with the bloud of his two fore fingers, & afterwards kill'd his wife: With the strange apparitions that appeared unto him in prison and how the Devil saluted him in the likeness of a Lawyer: Likewise, the manner how he was enchanted, and made shot-free; and by the power and efficacy of a ring which the Devil gave him, could find out any monies that was hid, and escape undiscover'd from his enemies; but his covenant being expir'd, he was apprehended, and (according to Law) sentenc'd to be hang'd in Chaines.* London: Printed for G. Horton, 1652.

36 Bower, James. *Doctor Lamb's darling: Or, strange and terrible news from Salisbury; being a true, exact, and perfect relation, of the great and wonderful contract and engagement made between the Devil, and Mistris Anne Bodenham; with the manner how she could transform her self into the shape of a mastive dog, a black lyon, a white bear, a woolf, a bull, and a cat; and by her charms and spels, send either man or woman 40 miles an hour in the Ayr: The trial, examination, and confession of the said Mistris Bodenham, before the Lord chief Baron Wild, & the Sentence of Death pronounc'd against her, for betwitching of An Stiles, and forcing her to write her name in the Devils "Book with her own blood; so that for five dayes she lay in cruel and bitter torments; sometimes the Devil appearing all in black without a head, renting her cloaths, tearing her skin, and tossing her up and down the chamber, to the great astonishment of the spectators.* London: Printed for G. Horton, 1653.

37 Bower, Edmond. *Doctor Lamb revived, or, witchcraft condemned in Anne Bodenham.* London: Printed by T.W. for Richard Best and John Place, 1653.

38 P., L. *The witch of the Woodlands: Or, the coblers new translation; written by L.P: Here Robin the Cobler for his former evils, was punisht worst then Faustus was with devils.* London: Printed for John Stafford, 1655.

39 Anon. *The snare of the devil discovered: Or, a true and perfect Relation of the sad and deplorable condition of Lydia the wife of John Rogers house-carpernter, living in Greenbank in Pumpe alley in Wappin; how she wanting money the Devil appered to her in the shape of a man, on Monday night the 22th of March last and brought her money, and caused her to Cut a Vein in her right hand, and a contract was made between them: Also her examination by Mr. Johnson the Minister of Wappin, and her Confession: As also in what a sad condition she continues: Likewise a brief relation of her former life and conversation.* London: Printed for Edward Thomas, 1658.

40 Anon. *The power of witchcraft, being a most strange but true relation of the most miraculous and wonderful deliverance of one Mr. William Harrison, of Cambden in the County of Glocester, steward to the Lady Nowel: Who was supposed to have been murthered by his own servant, and his servants mother and brother: But to the amazement of all people that lived neard the said place, the truth is now brought to light; and Mr. Harrison after above two years absence is returned into his own country and place of above in Cambden: The manner how he was bewitched away, and the manner of his safe return back again into his own Countrey you shall hear in this following discourse.* London: Printed for Charls Tyns, 1662.

41 Anon. *The Shee-Devil of Petticoat-Lane, or, a true and perfect relation of a sad accident which befel Mr. Freeland at the Kings-head in*

Petticoat-Lane near White-Chappel-Bars on Friday last, Jully 20, 1666 occasioned (as it is supposed) by a maid servant living in the house, who upon cause therof was searched by the neighbour women, and what was the effects thereof. London: Printed by Peter Lillicrap, 1666.

42   Anon. *A full and true relation of the tryal, condemnation, and execution of Ann Foster, (Who was arrained for a witch) on Saturday the 22th of this instant August, at the place of execution of Northampton: With the manner how she by her malice and witchcraft set all the barns and corn on fire belonging to one Joseph Weeden living in Eastcoat, and bewitched a whole flock of sheep in a most lamentable manner, and betwiching [sic] all his horses, with his other cattle, to the utter ruin and undoing of the said Joseph Weeden: And also in what likeness the Devil appeared to her while she was in prison, and the manner of her deportment at her tryal.* London: Printed for D.M., 1674.

43   Anon. *Relation of the most remarkable Proceedings at the late Assizes at Northampton: Conteyning truly and fully, the tryals, confessions, and executions of a most mischievous witch, notorious hugh-way-man, barbarous murderers: The first being Mary Forster, who by witchcraft destroyed above 30 sheep belonging to one Joseph Weedon, and afterwards burned to the ground his dwelling-house, and two large barns, full of corn and hay: To his damage above 300l: With her confession of the fact, how, and why she did it: and asking him forgiveness for the same: And a wodnerful experiment of her devilish skill shewed in the gaol, after she was condemned: The second a high-way-man, who had been 14 times in Gaol, and before his death discovered several others: The third a young wench that killed her child, with the strange means how the same was discovered, and her penitent behaviour at the execution: Who all suffered at Northampton aforesaid, Saturday, Aug. 22. 1674.* London: Printed for Nathaniel Savegde, 1674.

44   Anon. *Strange and wonderful news from Yowel in Surry; giving a true and just account of one Elizabeth Burgiss, who was most strangely bewitched and tortured at a sad rate, having several great lumps of clay pulled forth from her back, full of pins and thorns, which pricked so extreamly, that she cry'd and roar'd in a vehement and out-ragious manner, to the great amazement of all the beholders. As also, how great Stones as abig as a mans fist, were thrown at her in the dwelling house of Mr. Tuers, which came flying into the house in a most strange and amazing manner, the doors being shut and windows, so that it could not be imagined how they should be conveyed into the house, and that none of the family was any ways hurt, byt this maid; also how the bellows was thrown at her: Mr. Tuers her master, finding his house thus troubled, after some time, sent her home to her mothers house at Asteed, about three miles off from Yowel, where by the way she was most strangely assaulted with stones as before; and after she came to her fathers house, the throwing of the pewter-dishes, candlesticks, and other clattering of*

household-goods at her, besides the displacing of a musical instrument, hanging up her grand-fathers breeches on the top of the sealling: With many more strange and miraculous things, filling the spectators with wonder and amazement. London: Printed for F. Clarke, Seignior, 1681.

45 Anon. *An account of the tryal and examination of Joan Buts, for being a common witch and inchantress, before the Right Honourable Sir Francis Pemberton, Lord Chief Justice, at the Assizes holden for the Burrough of Southwark and County of Surrey, on Monday, March 27. 1682.* London: Printed for S. Gardener, 1682.

46 Anon. *A full and true account of the Proceedings at the Sessions of Oyer and Terminer, Holdern for the City of London, County of Middlesex, and Goal-Delivery of Newgate; which began at the Sessions-House in the Old-Bayly, on Thursday, June 1st. and ended on Fryday, June 2d, 1682: Wherein is contained the tryal of many notorious malefactors, for murders, fellonies, burglary, and other misdemeanours, but more especially the tryal of Jane Kent for witch-Craft: Together, with the names of those that received sentence of death, the number of those burn'd in the hand, transported, and whip'd: As likewise some Proceedings in relation to the persons that violently took the lady out of the coach on Hounslow-Heath.* London: Printed for T. Benskin, 1682.

47 Anon. *A tryal of witches at the Assizes held at Bury St. Edmonds for the County of Suffolk; on the Tenth day of March, 1664: Before Sir Matthew Hale Kt: Then Lord Chief Baron of His Majesties Court of Exchequer: Taken by a person then attending the court.* London: Printed for William Shrewsbery, 1682.

48 Anon. *The tryal, condemnation, and execution of three witches viz.: Temperace Floyd, Mary Floyd, and Susanna Edwards: Who were arraigned at Exeter on the 18th. of August, 1682: And how being prov'd guilty of witch-craft, were condemn'd to be hang'd which was accordingly executed in the view of many spectators, whose strange and much to be lamented impudence, is never to be forgotten: Also, how they confessed what mischiefs they had done, by the assistance of the Devil, who lay with the above-named Temperance Floyd nine nights together. Also, how they squeezed one Hannah Thomas to death in the arms; how they also caused several ships to be cast away, causing a boy to fall from the top of a main mast into the sea: With many wonderful things, worth your reading.* London: Printed for J. Deacon, 1682.

49 Anon. *A true and impartial relation of the informations against three witches, viz., Temperance Lloyd, Mary Trembles, and Susanna Edwards, who were indicted, arraigned and convicted at the assizes holden for the county of Devon, at the castle of Exon, Aug. 14, 1682: With their several confessions, taken before Thomas Gist Mayor, and John Davie Alderman of Biddiford in the said County, where they were inhabitants: As also their speeches, confessions, and behaviour, at the time and place*

of execution on the Twenty fifth of the said month. London: Printed by Freeman Collins, 1682.

50 Anon. *Strange news from Shadwell, being a true and just relation of the death of Alice Fowler, who had for many years been accounted a witch; together the manner how she was found dead with both her great Toes Ty'd together, and laid out on the Floor having a Blanket flung over her: She being left lock'd up alone by her nurse, with a discovery of what markes or teats were found about her, when she was searched by the neighbours*. London: Printed by E. Mallet, 1684.

51 Anon. *Strange and dreadful news from the town of Deptford in the County of Kent: Being the full, true, and sad relation of one Anne Arthur, who according to her own report, had divers discourses with the Devil, on the third of this Instant March 1685: Who offered her Gold and Silver; telling her many strange and wonderfull things; and, in the end, carried her in the air a quarter of a furlong, &c: Together, with the life and conversation of the said party; and directions to the place of her abode: And a particular relation of the sad distractions she fell into, upon that occasion; and divers other circumstances relating thereto*. London: Printed for D.W., 1685.

52 Jenken, Peter and John Geofe. *A true account of a strange and wonderful relation of one John Tonken, of Pensans in Cornwall, said to be bewitched by some women; two of which on suspition are committed to prison: He Vomiting up several pins, pieces of walnut-shels, an ear of rye, with a straw to it half a yard long and rushes of the same length; which are kept to be shown at the next Assizes for the said County*. London: Printed by George Croom, 1686.

53 Anon. *The life and conversation of Temperance Floyd, Mary Lloyd, and Susanna Edwards three eminent witches, lately condemed at Exeter Assizes; together with a full account of their first agreement with the Devil: With the manner how they prosecuted their devillish sorceries: Also a full Account of their tryal, examination, condemnation, and confession, at the place of execution: With many other things remarkable, and worthy observation*. London: Printed by J.W., 1687.

54 Crouch, Nathaniel. *The kingdom of darkness: or the history of daemons, specters, witches, apparitions, possessions, disturbances, and other wonderful and supernatural delusions, mischievous feats, and malicious impostures of the Devil: Containing near Fourscore memorable relations, forreign and demestick, both antient and Modern. Collected from authentick records, real attestations, credible evidences, and asserted by authors of undoubted verity: Together with a Preface obviating the common objections and allegations of the Sadduces and Athiests of the Age, who deny the being of spirits, witches, &c: With pictures of several memorable accidents*. London: Printed for Nath. Crouch, 1688.

55 Anon. *Great news from the West of England: Being a true account of two young persons lately betwitch'd in the Town of Beckenton in*

Somerset-shire: Shewing the sad condition they are in, by vomiting, or throwing out of their bodies, the abundance of pins, nails, pewter, brass, lead, iron, and tin, to the admiration of all beholders: And of the old witch being carried several times to a great river; into which, her legs being tied, she was thrice thrown in; but each time she swam like a cork: Afterwards, by order from a Justice of Peace, she was search'd by a Jury of Women, and such signs and marks being found about her, positive oath was given in against her; so that she is committed to Jayl, until the next Assizes. London: Printed by T.M., 1689.

56 Anon. *The full tryals, examination, and condemation of four notorious witches, at the Assizes held at Worcester, on Tuesday the 4th of March: As also, their confessions, and last dying speeches at the place of execution; with other amazing particulars concerning the said witch-craft: Printed according to order.* London: Printed by J.W., 1690.

57 Petto, Samuel. *A faithful narrative of the wonderful and extraordinary fits which Mr. Tho. Spatchet (Late of Dunwich and Cookly) was under by witchcraft: Or, a mysterious providence in his even unparallel'd fits: With an account of his first falling into, behaviour under, and (in part) deliverance out of them: Wherein are several remarkable instances of the gracious effects of fervent prayer.* London: Printed for John Harris, 1693.

58 Hale, Matthew, ed. Edward Stephens. *A collection of modern relations of matter of fact, concerning witches and witchcraft upon the persons of people: To which is prefixed a meditation concerning the mercy of God, in preserving us from the malice and power of evil angels: Written by the Late Lord Chief Justice Hale, upon occasion of a tryal of serveral witches before him: Part I.* London: Printed for John Harris, 1693.

59 Anon. *A full and true account of the apprehending and taking of Mrs Sarah Moordike, who is accused for a witch: Being taken near Paul's Wharf, on Thursday the 24th of this instant, for having bewitch'd one Richard Hetheway, near the Faulken-Stairs in Southwark.* London: Printed for John Alkin near Fleet-street, 1701.

60 Greenwel, Thomas. *A full and true account of the discovering, apprehending and taking of a notorious witch, who was carried before Justice Bateman in Well-Close, on Sunday, July the 23: Together with her examination and commitment to Bridewel, Clerkenwell.* London: Printed by H. Hill in [. . .] near the Waterside, 1704.

61 Davis, Ralph. *An account of the tryals, examination and condemnation of Elinor Shaw and Mary Phillip's (two notorious witches) at Northampton Assizes, on Wednesday the 7th of March 1705, for bewitching a woman, and two children, tormenting them in a sad and lamentable manner till they dyed: With an account of their strange confessions, about their familiarity with the Devil, and how they made a wicked contract with him to be revenged on several persons, by bewitching their cattel to death, &c and several other strange and amazing particulars.* London: Printed for F. Thorn near Fleet Street, 1705.

62 Anon. *A full and true account of the tryal, examination, and condemnation of Mary Johnson a witch: At the Assizes held at Coventry on Saturday July the 27th, by the honourable J. Trevors and Baron Prise, for bewitching several men, women, children and cattle, of which several died, through her hellish malice, the most unaccountable, violentest and strangest deaths as ever was known, and also committing her devilish envy on her husband and two of her own children who for fourteen days lay under most intollerable pains and great misery, and then departed this life.* London: Printed by T. Bland, 1706.

63 Bragge, Francis. *A full and impartial account of the discovery of sorcery and witchcraft, practis'd by Jane Wenham of Walkerne in Hertfordshire, upon the bodies of Anne Thorn, Anne Street, &c: The Proceedings against her from her being first apprehended, till she was commited to Goal by Sir Henry Chauncy: Also her tryal at the Assizes at Hertford before Mr Justice Powell, where she was found guilty of felony and witchcraft and receiv'd sentence of death for the same, March 4. 1711–12.* London: Printed for E. Curll, 1712.

64 Bragge, Francis. *Witchcraft farther display'd: Containing I: An account of the witchcraft practis'd by Jane Wenham of Walkerne, Hertfordshire, since her condemnation, upon the bodies of Anne Thorn and Anne Street, and the deplorable condition in which they still remain: II: An answer to the most general objections against the being and power of witches: With some remarks upon the case of Jane Wenham in particular and Justice Powell's Procedure therein: To which are added, the tryals of Florence Newton, a famous Irish Witch, at the Assizes held at Cork, Anno 1661; as also of two witches at the Assizes held at Bury St. Edmonds in Suffolk, Anno 1664, before Sir Matthew Hale (the Lord Chief Baron of the Exchequer) who were found guilty and executed.* London: Printed for E. Curll, 1712.

65 Anon. *The whole trial and examination of Mrs Mary Hicks and her daughter Elizabeth, but of nine years of age, who were condemn'd the last Assizes held at Huntington for witchcraft: and there executed on Saturday the 28th of July, 1716.* London: Printed by W. Matthews in Long-Acre, 1716.

66 Anon. *A tryal of witches at the Assizes held at Bury St. Edmonds for the County of Suffolk; on the Tenth Day of March, 1664: Before Sir Matthew Hale, K$^{t.}$ then Lord Chief Baron of His Majesty's Court of Exchequer: Taken by a person then attending the Court.* London: Printed for D. Brown, J. Walthoe, and M. Wotton, 1716.

Appendix B: Chronological Spread of English Witchcraft Pamphlets

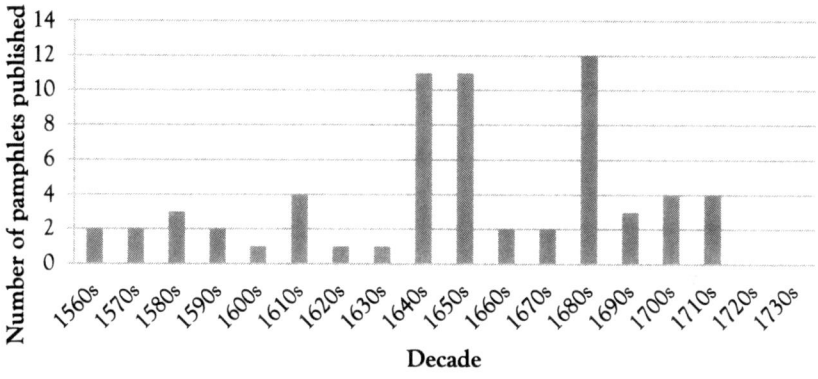

Bibliography

Primary Sources

For the core group of sixty-six pamphlets see Appendix A.

Additional Primary Sources

Abernethy, John. "The Poysonous Tongue." In *A Christian and Heavenly Treatise Containing Physicke for the Soule: Very Necessary for All That Would Enjoy True Soundnesse of Minde, and Peace of Conscience*, newly corrected and inlarged by the author, M. I. Abernethy, now Bishop of Cathnes, 463–485. London: Printed by Felix Kyngston for John Budge, 1622.

Anon. *Tales and Quicke Answers Very Merry, and Pleasant to Rede*. London: Printed in the house of Thomas Bethelet, 1532.

Anon. *The Most Strange and Admirable Discoverie of the Three Witches of Warboys Arraigned, Convicted and Executed at the Last Assises at Huntington, for the Bewitching of the Five Daughters of Robert Throckmorton Esquier, and Divers Other Persons, with Sundrie Divelish and Grievous Torments : And Also for the Bewitching to Death of the Lady Crumwell, the Like Hath Not Bene Heard of in This Age*. London: Printed for Thomas Man and John Winnington, 1593.

Anon. *Damnable Practices/of Three Lincolne-shire Witches, Joane Flower, and Her Two Daughters,/Margret and Phillip Flower, Against Henry Lord Rosse, with Others the Children of the Right/Honourable the Earle of Rutland, at Beauer Castle, who for the Same were Executed at Lincolne the 11. of/ March Last*. Printed by G. Eld for John Barnes, 1619.

Anon. *A Briefe Description of the Notorious Life of John Lambe, Otherwise called Doctor Lambe, Together with His Ignominious Death*. Amsterdam, London: G.E. Miller, 1628.

Anon. *An Ould Play, with Some New Scenes, Doctor Lambe and the Witches, to Salisbury Courte, the 16th Ausgust 1634*. 1634.

Anon. *Doctor Lambe and the Witches*. Published between 1628 and 1634.

Anon. [*The Sal]isbury Assizes. [. . .] ard of Witchcraft: Being a True Relation of One Mistris Bodnan Living in Fisherton, Next House but One to the Gallowes, Who Being [a] Witch Seduced a Maid, Called by Name, Anne Stiles, to the Same Abominable and Detested Action of Vvitchcraft; Which VVitch for that Action was Executed the 19 day of March 1653: To the Tune of Bragandary*. London: 1653.

Anon. *The English Devil: Or, Cromwel and His Monstrous Witch. Discover'd at White-Hall: With the Strange and Damnable Speech of This Hellish Monster, by Way of Revelation Touching King and Kingdom; and a Narrative of the Infernal Plots, Inhumane Actings, and Barbarous Conspiracies of this Grand Impostor, and Most Audacious Rebel, That Durst Aspire from a Brew-house to the Throne, Washing His Accursed Hands in the Blood of his Royal Soveraign; and Trampling over the Heads of the Most Loyal Subjects, Making a Foot-ball of a Crown, and Endeavouring Utterly to Extirpate the ROYAL PROGENY, Root and Kinde, Stem and Stock*. London: Printed by Robert Wood, 1660.

Anon. *Witchcraft Discovered and Punished/Or, the Tryals and Condemnation of Three Notorious Witches, Who Were Tried/ the Last Assizes, Holden at the Castle of Exeter, in the County of Devon: Where They Received Sentence/for Death, for Bewitching Several Persons, Destroying Ships at Sea, and Cattel by Land*. 1682.

Anon. *The History of the Most Remarkable Tryals in Great Britain and Ireland in Capital Cases, viz. Heresy, Treason, Felony, Incest, Poisoning, Adultery, Rape, Sodomy, Witchcraft, Pyracy, Robbery, Murder &c. Both by the unusual methods of ORDEAL, COMBAT and ATTAINDER, and by the Ecclesiastical, Civil and Common Laws of these Realms*. London: A. Bell; J. Pemberton; J. Brown, 1715.

Anon. *The Errores Gazariorum*. In *Witchcraft in Europe 400–1700: A Documentary History*, 2nd edn, edited by Alan Charles Kors and Edward Peters, 159–162. Philadelphia: University of Pennsylvania Press, 2001.

Anon. "An Act Against Conjurations, Enchantments and Witchcrafts 1563 5 Eliz I c. 16." In *Witchcraft and Society in England and America 1550–1750*, edited by Marion Gibson, 3–5. New York: Cornell University Press, 2003.

Anon. "An Act Against Conjuration, Witchcraft and Dealing with Evil and Wicked Spirits 1604 1 Jas. 1 c. 12." In *Witchcraft and Society in England and America 1550–1750*, edited by Marion Gibson, 5–7. New York: Cornell University Press, 2003.

Anon. "An Act Against Conjurations, Witchcrafts, Sorcery, and Enchantments 1541/42 33 Hen. VIII 8." In *Witchcraft and Society in England and America 1550–1750*, edited by Marion Gibson, 1–2. New York: Cornell University Press, 2003.

Anon. *The Merry Pranks of Robin Goodfellow*. London: Printed by and for W.Q.

Anon. *The Rag Man: Or a Company That Fall at Oddes One Day, Which of Them Should Carry the Cunny Skins Away: They Strove Who Should Have It, But None of Them Wise, for the Usurer and the Divell Carry Away the Prize*. London: Printed for Fr. Grove.

Bacon, Francis. *The Essays, or Councils, Civil and Moral*. London, 1718.

Becon, Thomas. *The Worckes of Thomas Becon Whiche He Hath Hitherto Made and Published, with Diverse Other Newe Books Added to the Same, Heretofore Never Set Forth in Print, Divided into Thre Tomes or Parts And Amended This Present [sic] of Our Lord 1564; Perused and Allowed, Accordyng to Thorder Appointed in the Quenes Majesties Injunctions*. London: Printed by John Day, 1564.

Bekker, Balthasar. *The World Turn'd Upside Down: Or, a Plain Detection of Errors, in the Common or Vulgar Belief, Relating to Spirits, Spectres or Ghosts, Daemons, Witches, &c. In a Due and Serious Examination of Their Nature, Power, Administration, and Operation. In What Forms or Shape Incorporeal*

Spirits Appear to Men, by What Means, and of What Elements They Take to Themselves, and Form Appearances of Bodies, Visible to Mortal Eyes; Why They Appear, and What Frights and Force of Imagination Often Delude Us into the Apprehension of Supposed Phantasms, Through the Intimidation of the Mind, &c. Also What Evil Tongues Have Power to Produce of Hurt to Mankind, or Irational Creatures and the Effects Men and Women are Able to Produce by Their Communication with Good or Evil Spirits, &c: Written at the Request of a Person of Honour, by B. B., a Protestant Minister for Publick Information. London: Printed for E. Harris, 1700.

Bernard, Richard. *A Guide to Grand Jury-Men Divided into Two Bookes: In the First, Is the Authors Best Advice to Them What to Doe, Before They Bring in a Billa vera in Cases of Witchcraft, with a Christian Direction to such as Are Too Much Given upon Every Crosse to Thinke Themselves Bewitched: In the Second, Is a Treatise Touching Witches Good and Bad, How They May be Knowne, Evicted, Condemned, with Many Particulars Tending Thereunto: By Rich. Bernard.* London: Printed by Felix Kingston for Ed. Blackmore, 1627.

Blackburne, Lancelot. *The Unreasonableness of Anger.* London: Printed by Tho. Warren for Thomas Bennet, 1694.

Bodin, Jean. *On the Demon-Mania of Witches*, translated by Randy A. Scott, edited by Jonathan Pearl. Toronto: Centre for Reformation and Renaissance Studies, 1995.

Boulton, Richard. *A Compleat History of Magick, Sorcery, and Witchcraft: Volume I.* London: E. Curll, 1715.

Boulton, Richard. *A Compleat History of Magick, Sorcery, and Witchcraft: Volume II.* London: E. Curll, 1715.

Bradford, John. *A Godlye Medytacyon Composed by the Faithfull and Constant Servant of God J.B., Latlye Burnte in Smytfelde.* London: Printed by Wyllyam Coplande, 1559.

Caussin, Nicolas. *The Holy Court: The Command of Reason over the Passions*, translated by T. H. Rouen. Printed by John Cousturier, 1638.

Cooper, Thomas. *The Mystery of Witch-craft: Discovering the Truth, Nature, Occasions, Growth and Power Thereof: Together with the Detection and Punishment of the Same: As Also, the Severall Stratagems of Sathan, Ensnaring the Poore Soule by This Desperate Practize of Annoying the Bodie: With the Severall Uses Therof to the Church of Christ: Very Necessary for the Redeeming of these Atheisticall and Secure Times: By Thomas Cooper.* London: Printed by Nicholas Okes, 1617.

Crooke, Helkiah. *Microcosmographia.* London: Printed by William Jaggard, 1615.

D., I. *The Most Wonderfull and True Storie, of a Certaine Witch Named Also Gooderige of Stapen hill, Who Was Arraigned and Convicted at Darbie at the Assises There as also a True Report of the Strange Torments of Thomas Darling, a Boy of Thirteene Yeres of Age, That Was Possessed by the Devil, with His Horrible Fittes and Apparitions by Him Uttered at Burton upon Trent in the Countie of Stafford, and of His Marvellous Deliverance.* London: Printed for I.O., 1597.

Eugenius IV. *A Letter to All Inquisitors of Heretical Depravity* (1437). In *Witchcraft in Europe 400–1700: A Documentary History*, 2nd edn., edited by Alan Charles Kors and Edward Peters, 154–155. Philadelphia: University of Pennsylvania Press, 2001.

Fairfax, Edward. *Daemonologia: A Discourse on Witchcraft as It Was Acted in the Family of Mr Edward Fairfax, of Fuyston, in the County of York, in the Year 1621*, edited by William Grainge. Harrogate: R. Ackrill, 1882.

Heer, Henry de. *The Most True and Wonderfull Narration of Two Women Betwitched in Yorkshire: Who Coming to the Assizes at York to Give in Evidence Against the Witch After a Most Horrible Noise to the Terror and Amazement of All the Beholders, Did Vomit Forth Before the Judges, Pins, Wool, and Hasts of Knoves, &c: All Which Was Done (to Make the Wonder More Wonderfull) Without the Least Drop of Bloud or Moisture from Their Mouths: Also a Most True Relation of a Young Maid Not Far From Luyck, Who Being Bewitched in the Same Manner Did (Almost Incredibly) Vomit Forth Wads of Straw, with Pins a Crosse in Them, Iron Nails, Needles, Points, and Whatsoever, She Had Seen in the Basket of the Witch That Did Bewitch Her: As It Is Attested Under the Hand of That Most Famous Phisitian Doctor Henry Heer: Together, How it Pleased God That She was Afterwards Recovered by the Art of Physick, and the Names of the Ingredients and the Manner How To Make That Rare Receipt That Cured Her.* Printed for Tho. Vere and W. Gilberfox, 1658.

Gifford, George. *A Dialogue Between a Papist and a Protestant Applied to the Capacitie of the Unlearned: Made by G. Gifford, Preacher in the Towne of Maldon: Seene and Allowed According to the Order Appointed.* London: Thomas Dawson for Tobie Cooke, 1582.

———. *A Discourse of the Subtill Practises of Devilles by Witches and Sorcerers: By Which Men Are and Have Bin Greatly Deluded: The Antiquitie of Them: Their Divers Sorts and Names: With an Aunswer unto Divers Frivolous Reasons Which Some Doe Make to Proove That the Devils Did Not Make Those Aperations in Any Bodily Shape: By G. Gyfford.* London: By T. Orwin for Toby Cooke, 1587.

———. *A Dialogue Concerning Witches and Witchcraftes: In Which Is Laide Open How Crafely the Divell Deceiveth Not Onely the Witches but Many Other and So Leadeth Them Awrie into Many Great Errours: By George Gifford Minister of Gods Word in Maldon.* London: Printed by John Windet for Tobie Cooke and Mihil Hart, 1593.

Gouge, William. *The Whole Armour of God: Or a Christians Spirituall Furniture, to Keep Him Safe From All the Assaults of Satan: The Second Edition Corrected & Inlarged: Whereunto Is Added a Treatise of the Sin Against the Holy Ghost.* London: John Beale, 1619.

Granada, Luis de. *Guia de pecadores.* 1556.

Guazzo, Francesco Maria. *Compendium Maleficarum* (1608), translated by E. A. Ashwin, edited by Montague Summers. New York: University Books, 1974.

H[eywood], O[liver]. *Advice to an Only Child: or, Excellent Councils to All Young Persons Containing, the Summ and Substance of Experimental and Practical Divinity/Written by an Eminent and Judicious Divine, for the Private Use of an Only Child, Now Made Publick for the Benefit of All.* London: Printed for Tho. Parkhurst, 1693.

Hutchinson, Francis. *An Historical Essay Concerning Witchcraft: With Observations upon Matters of Fact: Tending to Clear the Texts of the Sacred Scriptures, and Confute the Vulgar Errors About That Point.* London: R. Knaplock, 1718.

Institoris, Henricus and Jacobus Sprenger. *Malleus Maleficarum,* edited and translated by Christopher S. Mackay. Cambridge: Cambridge University Press, 2006.

James VI and I, King of Scotland and England. *Daemonologie* (1597), edited by G. B. Harrison. London: John Lane, 1924.

Jonson, Ben. *The Staple of News,* edited by Anthony Parr. Manchester: Manchester University Press, 1988.

————. *The Devil is an Ass*, edited by Peter Happé. Manchester: Manchester University Press, 1994.

Juxon, Joseph. *A Sermon upon Witchcraft: Occasion'd by a Late Illegal Attempt to Discover Witches by Swimming: Preach'd at Twyford in the Count of Leicester, July 11, 1736*. London: H. Woodfall, 1736.

Kramer, Heinrich. "The Malleus Maleficarum." In *Witchcraft in Europe 400–1700: A Documentary History*, 2nd edn., edited by Alan Charles Kors and Edward Peters, 180–229. Philadelphia: University of Pennsylvania Press, 2001.

Marconville, Jean de. *A Treatise of the Good and Euell Tounge with the Vnstablenesse of the Same, and Also with the Abuses Thereof: With a Discourse of the Punishment Which the Lord Hath Shewed on Al Those Which Through Swearing and Perjuring Themselues, haue Broken Gods Commandementes: As by This Treatise Most Plainely Appeareth: Made by John of Marconville Gentleman*. London: By J. Wolfe for John Perin, 1592.

Marlowe, Christopher. *Doctor Faustus: A Two-Text Edition (A-Text, 1604; B-Text, 1616), Contexts and Sources, Criticism*, edited by David Scott Kastan. New York: W. Norton, 2005.

More, George. *A True Discourse Concerning the Certaine Possession and Dispossession of 7 Persons in One Familie in Lancashire Which Also May Serve as Part of an Answere to a Fayned and False Discoverie Which Speaketh Very Much Evill, as well as this, as of the Rest of Those Great and Mightie Works of God Which Be of the like Excellent Nature*. Middelburg: Printed by Richard Schilders, 1600.

N., W. *The Second Part of Merry Drollery, or, a Collection of Jovial Poems, Merry Songs, Witty Drolleries, Intermix'd with Pleasant Cathces Collected by W.N., C.B., R.S., J.G., Lovers of Wit*. London: Printed by J.W. for P.H., 1661.

Nider, Johannes. "The Formicarius." In *Witchcraft in Europe 400–1700: A Documentary History*, 2nd edn., edited by Alan Charles Kors and Edward Peters, 155–159. Philadelphia: University of Pennsylvania Press, 2001.

Olde, John. *A Short Description of Antichrist unto the Nobilitie of Englande, and to All My Brethren and Contreymen Borne and Dwelling Therin, with a Warnynge to See to, That They Be Not Deceaved by the Hyposcrise and Crafty Conveyance of the Clergie*. 1555.

Paradin, Claude. *The Heroicall Devises of M. Claudius Paradin Canon of Beauieu: Whereunto Are Added the Lord Gabriel Symeons and Others: Translated out of Latin into English by P.S.* London: Imprinted by William Kerney, 1591.

Paré, Ambrose. *The Works of That Famous Chirurgion Ambrose Parey*. London: 1634.

Parker, Martin. *The Tragedy of Doctor Lambe/The Great Suposed Coniurer, Who Was Wounded to Death by Saylers/and Other Lads, on Fryday the 14. of Iune, 1628: And Dyed in the/Poultry Counter, Neere Cheap-side, on the Saturday Morning Followin*. London: Printed for H.G., 1628.

Perkins, William. *A Direction for the Government of the Tongue According to Gods Word*. Edinburgh: Printed by Robert Waldegrave, 1593.

————. *A Discourse of the Dammed Art of Witchcraft so Farre Forth as It Is Revealed in the Scriptures, and Manifest by True Experience: Framed and Delivered by M. William Perkins, in His Ordinarie Course of Preaching, and Now Published by Tho. Pickering Batchelour of Divinitie, and Minister of Finchingfield in Essex: Whereunto is Adjoined a Twofold Table; One of the*

Order and Heades of the Treatise; Another of the Texts of Scripture Explaned, or Vindicated from the Corrupt Interpretation of the Adversarie. Cambridge: Cantrel Legge, 1608.

———. *A Direction for the Government of the Tongue According to Gods Word.* London: Printed by John Legate, 1611.

Rémy, Nicolas. *Demonolatry: An Account of the Historical Practice of Witchcraft* (1595), translated by E. A. Ashwin, edited by Montague Summers. London: J. Rodker, 1930.

———. *Demonolatry* (1595), translated by E. A. Ashwin, edited by Montague Summers. New York: University Books, 1974.

Reyner, Edward. *Rules for the Government of the Tongue: Together, with Directions in Six Particular Cases Added as a Supplement to the Rules for Governing the Thoughts, the Affections in the Precepts for Christian Practice, or, the Rule of the New Creature, New Molded, by Edward Reyner.* London: Printed by R. I. for T. N, 1658.

Rio, Martin del. *Investigations into Magic* (1600), translated by P. G. Maxwell Stuart. Manchester: Manchester University Press, 2000.

Roberts, Alexander. *A Treatise of Witchcraft: Wherein Sundry Propositions Are Laid Downe, Plainely Discouering the Wickednesse of That Damnable Art, with Diuerse Other Speciall Points Annexed, Not Impertinent to the Same, such as Ought Diligently of Euery Christian to be Considered: With a True Narration of the Witchcrafts Which Mary Smith, Wife of Henry Smith Glouer, Did Practise: Of Her Contract Vocally Made Between the Deuill and Her, in Solemne Termes, by Whose Meanes She Hurt Sundry Persons Whom She Envied: Which Is Confirmed by Her Owne Confession, and Also From the Publique Records of the Examination of Diuerse vpon THEIR oathes: And Lastly, of Her Death and Execution, for the Same; Which Was on the Twelfth Day of Ianuarie Last Past: By Alexander Roberts B.D. and Preacher of Gods Word at Kings-Linne in Norffolke.* London: Printed by Nicholas Okes for Samuel Man, 1616.

Rowley, William, Thomas Dekker and John Ford. *The Witch of Edmonton: A Known True Story.* London: Printed by J. Cottrel for Edward Blackmore, 1658.

Scot, Reginald. *The Discovery of Witchcraft, Wherein the Lewde Dealing of Witches and Witchmongers Is Notablie Detected, the Knaverie of Conjurors, the Impietie of Inchantors, the Follie of Soothsaiers, the Impudent Falshood of Cousenors, the Infidelitie of Astheists, the Pestilent Practises of Pythonists, the Curiosite of Figurecasters, the Vanitie of Dreamers, the Beggerlie Art of Alcumystrie, the Abhomination of Idolatrie, the Horrible Art of Poisioning, the Vertue and Power of Natural Magike, and All the Conveiances of Legierdemaine and Juggling Are Deciphered: And Many Other Things Opened, Which Have Long Been Hidden, Howbeit Verie Necessarie to be Knowne: Heereunto Is Added a Treatise upon the Nature and Substance of Spirits and Divels, &: All Latelie Written by Reginald Scot, Esquire.* London: by Henry Denham for William Brome, 1584.

Stephens, Edward. *Phinehas, or, the Common Duty of All Men, and the Special Duty of Magistrates, to Be Zealous and Active in the Execution of Laws Against Scandalous Sins and Debauchery: And of That in Particular Against Prophane Cursing and Swearing.* London: Printed for Richard Smith, 1695.

Taylor, John. *A Juniper Lecture: With the Description of All Sorts of Women, Good, and Bad: From the Modest to the Maddest, from The Most Civil, to the Scold Rampant, Their Praise and Dispraise Compendiously Related: Also the*

Authors Advice How to Tame a Shrew, or Vexe Her. London: by Iohn Okes for William Ley, 1639.

Tholosan, Claude. "Ut Magnorum et Maleficiorum Errores." In *Witchcraft in Europe 400–1700: A Documentary History*, 2nd edn., edited by Alan Charles Kors and Edward Peters, 162–166. Philadelphia: University of Pennsylvania Press, 2001.

Webbe, George. *The Araignement of an Unruly Tongue: Wherein the Faults of an Evill Tongue are Opened, the Danger Discovered, the Remedies Prescribed, for the Taming of a Bad Tongue, the Right Ordering of the Tongue, and the Pacifying of a Troubled Minde Against the Wrongs of an Evill Tongue: By George Web, Preacher of Gods Word at Stepleashton in Wiltshire*. London: Printed by G. Purslowe for John Budge, 1619.

Webster, John. "The Faire Maide of the Inne." In *The Complete Works of John Webster*, edited by F. L. Lucas, 157–224. New York: Gordian Press, 1966.

Wright, Thomas. *The Passions of the Minde in Generall*. London: 1601.

Secondary Sources

Adair, Richard. *Courtship, Illegitimacy, and Marriage in Early Modern England*. Manchester: Manchester University Press, 1996.

Almond, Philip C. *The Witches of Warboys: An Extraordinary Story of Sorcery, Sadism and Satanic Possession*. London: I.B. Tauris, 2008.

———. *The Devil: A New Biography*. Ithaca: Cornell University Press, 2014.

———. "Science, Witchcraft and Demonology: The 'Saducismus Triumphatus' of Joseph Glanvill and Henry More." *In Umbra* 5 (2016): 185–202.

Amundsen, Karin. "The Duke's Devil and Doctor Lambe's Darling: A Case Study of the Male Witch in Early Modern England." *Psi Sigma Journal* (2004): 29–60.

Anderson, Flemming G. *Ballad as Narrative: Studies in the Ballad Tradition of England, Scotland, Germany and Denmark*. Odense: Odense University Press, 1982.

Anderson, Jennifer and Elizabeth Sauer, eds. *Books and Readers in Early Modern England: Material Studies*. Philadelphia: University of Pennsylvania Press, 2002.

Ankarloo, Bengt and Gustav Henningsen, eds. *Early Modern European Witchcraft: Centres and Peripheries*. Oxford: Clarendon Press, 1990.

Ankarloo, Bengt and Stuart Clark, eds. *Witchcraft and Magic in Europe: Six Volumes*. London: Athlone, 1999–2002.

Apps, Lara and Andrew Gow. *Male Witches in Early Modern Europe*. Manchester: Manchester University Press, 2003.

Arcangeli, Alessandro. *Cultural History: A Concise Introduction*. London: Routledge, 2012.

Astbury, Raymond. "The Renewal of the Licensing Act in 1693 and its Lapse in 1695." *The Library* s5 – XXXIII 4 (1978): 296–322.

Bailey, Michael D. "The Medieval Concept of the Witches' Sabbath." *Exemplaria* 8 (1996): 419–439.

———. *Battling Demons: Witchcraft, Heresy, and Reform in the Late Middle Ages*. Philadelphia: The Pennsylvania State University Press, 2003.

———. *Historical Dictionary of Witchcraft*. Maryland: The Scarecrow Press, Inc., 2003.

———. *Fearful Spirits, Reasoned Follies: The Boundaries of Superstition in Late Medieval Europe*. Ithaca: Cornell University Press, 2013.

Baldwin, Martha R. "Toads and Plague: Amulet Therapy in Seventeenth-Century Medicine." *Bulletin of the History of Medicine* 67 (1993): 227–247.

Barclay, Katie. *Love, Intimacy and Power: Marriage and Patriarchy in Scotland, 1650–1850.* Manchester: Manchester University Press, 2011.

Baron, Sabrina A. "Licensing Readers, Licensing Authorities in Seventeenth-Century England." In *Books and Readers in Early Modern England: Material Studies*, edited by Jennifer Andersen and Elizabeth Sauer. Philadelphia: University of Pennsylvania Press, 2002.

Barry, Jonathan, Marianne Hester and Gareth Roberts, eds. *Witchcraft in Early Modern Europe: Studies in Culture and Belief.* Cambridge: Cambridge University Press, 1996.

Baumann, Gerd. *The Written Word: Literacy in Transition: Wolfson College Lectures 1985.* Oxford: Clarendon, 1986.

Behringer, Wolfgang. *Witchcraft Persecutions in Bavaria: Popular Magic, Religious Zealotry and Reason of State in Early Modern Europe*, translated by J. C. Grayson and David Lederer. Cambridge: Cambridge University Press, 1997.

Beier, A. L. *The Problem of the Poor in Tudor and Early Stuart England.* London: Methuen, 1983.

Bellany, Alistair. "The Murder of John Lambe: Crowd Violence, Court Scandal and Popular Politics in Early Seventeenth-Century England." *Past and Present* 200 (2008): 37–76.

Bernard, G. W. and S. J. Gunn, eds. *Authority and Consent in Tudor England: Essays Presented to C.S.L. Davies.* Aldershot: Ashgate, 2002.

Berry, Herbert. "The Globe Bewitched and 'El Hombre Fiel'." *Medieval and Renaissance Drama in England* 1 (1984): 211–230.

Bever, Edward. "Magic, Learned." In *Encyclopedia of Witchcraft: The Western Tradition*, edited by Richard M. Golden, 700–703. Santa Barbara: ABC-CLIO, 2006.

Bierma, Lyle D. "The Role of Covenant Theology in Early Reformed Orthodoxy." *The Sixteenth Century Journal* 20 (1990): 453–462.

Black, Jeremy. "The Eighteenth-Century British Press." In *The Encyclopedia of the British Press, 1422–1992*, edited by Dennis Griffiths, 13–23. Basingstoke: MacMillan Press, 1992.

Blécourt, Willem de. "The Making of the Female Witch: Reflections on Witchcraft and Gender in the Early Modern Period." *Gender and History* 12 (2000): 287–309.

———. "Sabbath Stories." In *The Oxford Handbook of Witchcraft in Early Modern Europe and Colonial America*, edited by Brian Levack. Oxford: Oxford University Press, 2013.

Borman, Tracy. *Witches: James I and the English Witch-Hunts.* London: Vintage Books, 2014.

Bostridge, Ian. *Witchcraft and Its Transformations c.1650-c.1750.* Oxford: Clarendon Press, 1997.

Brady, Andrea. "Dying with Honour: Literary Propaganda and the Second English Civil War." *The Journal of Military History* 70 (2006): 9–30.

Brayman Hackel, Heidi. *Reading Material in Early Modern England: Print, Gender, and Literacy.* Cambridge: Cambridge University Press, 2005.

Briggs, Robin. *Witches and Neighbours: The Social and Cultural Context of European Witchcraft.* London: HarperCollins, 1996.

Broedel, Hans Peter. *The Malleus Maleficarum and the Construction of Witchcraft: Theology and Popular Belief*. Manchester: Manchester University Press, 2003.

Bromley, James M. "Rimming the Renaissance." In *Sex Before Sex: Figuring the Act in Early Modern England*, edited by James M. Bromley and Will Stockton, 171–194. Minnesota: University of Minnesota Press, 2013.

Bromley, James M. and Will Stockton, eds. *Sex Before Sex: Figuring the Act in Early Modern England*. Minneapolis: University of Minnesota Press, 2013.

Broomhall, Susan, ed. *Emotions in the Household, 1200–1900*. Basingstoke: Palgrave Macmillan, 2008.

Bryson, Norman, Michael Holly and Keith Moxey, eds. *Visual Culture: Images and Interpretations*. Hanover: University Press of New England, 1994.

Burke, Peter. *Popular Culture in Early Modern Europe*. London: T. Smith, 1978.

———. "A Civil Tongue: Language and Politeness in Early Modern Europe." In *Civil Histories: Essays Presented to Sir Keith Thomas*, edited by Peter Burke, Brian Harrison and Paul Slack, 31–48. Oxford: Oxford University Press, 2000.

———. *What Is Cultural History?* Cambridge: Polity Press, 2004.

———. *What Is Cultural History?* 2nd edn. Cambridge: Polity Press, 2008.

Carlson, Eric Josef. *Marriage and the English Reformation*. Oxford: Blackwell, 1994.

Carlton, Charles, ed. *State, Sovereigns & Society in Early Modern England: Essays in Honour of A.J. Slavin*. London: Sutton, 1998.

Carnochan, W. B. "Witch-Hunting and Belief in 1751: The Case of Thomas Colley and Ruth Osborne." *Journal of Social History* 4 (1971): 389–403.

Chartier, Roger. *Cultural History: Between Practices and Representations*, translated by Lydia G. Cochrane. Cambridge: Polity in association with Blackwell, 1988.

———, ed. *The Culture of Print: Power and the Uses of Print in Early Modern Europe*, translated by Lydia G. Cochrane. Cambridge: Polity, 1989.

Clark, Sandra. *The Elizabethan Pamphleteers: Popular Moralistic Pamphlets 1580–1640*. London: Athlone Press, 1983.

Clark, Stuart. *Thinking with Demons: The Idea of Witchcraft in Early Modern Europe*. Oxford: Clarendon Press, 1997.

———, ed. *Languages of Witchcraft: Narrative, Ideology and Meaning in Early Modern Culture*. Houndmills: Macmillan Press, 2001.

Clayton, John A. *The Lancashire Witch Conspiracy: A History of Pendle Forest and the Pendle Witch Trials*, 2nd edn. Barrowford: Barrowford Press, 2007.

Cohn, Norman. *Europe's Inner Demons: The Demonization of Christians in Medieval Christendom*. London: Pimlico, 1975.

Combs, Josiah Henry. "Sympathetic Magic in the Kentucky Mountains: Some Curious Folk Survivals." *The Journal of American Folklore* 27 (1914): 328–330.

Coontz, Stephanie. *Marriage, a History: From Obedience to Intimacy or How Love Conquered Marriage*. New York: Viking, 2005.

Corthell, Ronald, Frances E. Dolan, Christopher Highley and Arthur F. Marotti, eds. *Catholic Culture in Early Modern England*. Notre Dame: University of Notre Dame Press, 2007.

Crawford, Patricia. *Blood, Bodies and Families in Early Modern England*. Harlow: Longman, 2004.

Creager, A. N. H. and W. C. Jordan, eds. *The Human/Animal Boundary*. Rochester: University of Rochester Press, 2002.

Cressy, David. *Literacy and the Social Order: Reading and Writing in Tudor and Stuart England.* Cambridge: Cambridge University Press, 1980.

———. *Bonfires and Bells: National Memory and the Protestant Calendar in Elizabethan and Stuart England.* London: Weidenfeld and Nicolson, 1989.

———. *Birth, Marriage, and Death: Ritual, Religion, and the Life-Cycle in Tudor and Stuart England.* Oxford: Oxford University Press, 1997.

———. *Travesties and Transgressions in Tudor and Stuart England: Tales of Discord and Dissension.* Oxford: Oxford University Press, 2000.

———. *Society and Culture in Early Modern England.* Aldershot: Ashgate, 2003.

———. *Dangerous Talk: Scandalous, Seditious and Treasonable Speech in Pre-Modern England.* Oxford: Oxford University Press, 2010.

Crump, Marty. *Eye of Newt and Toe of Frog, Adder's Fork and Lizard's Leg: The Lore and Mythology of Amphibians and Reptiles.* Chicago: University of Chicago Press, 2015.

Darnton, Robert. "The Great Cat Massacre." *History Today* August (1984): 7–15.

Darr, Orna Alyagon. *Marks of an Absolute Witch: Evidentiary Dilemmas in Early Modern England.* Farnham: Ashgate, 2011.

Davenport-Hines, Richard. *Sex, Death and Punishment: Attitudes to Sex and Sexuality in Britain Since the Renaissance.* London: Collins, 1990.

Davies, Owen. *Popular Magic: Cunning Folk in English History.* London: Hambledon Continuum, 2007.

———. "Talk of the Devil: Crime and Satanic Inspiration in Eighteenth-Century England." (2007): 1–25.

Davis, Lloyd, ed. *Sexuality and Gender in the English Renaissance: An Annotated Edition of Contemporary Documents.* New York: Garland Publishing, 1998.

Davis, Natalie. *Fiction in the Archives: Pardon Tales and Their Tellers in Sixteenth-Century France.* Stanford: Stanford University Press, 1987.

Day, Geoffrey, ed. *The Pepys Ballads, Volumes 1–5.* Cambridge: Brewer, 1987.

Delumeau, Jean. *Sin and Fear: The Emergence of a Western Guilt Culture, 13th – 18th Centuries.* New York: St. Martin's Press, 1990.

Dillinger, Johannes. "Terrorists and Witches: Popular Ideas of Evil in the Early Modern Period." *History of European Ideas* 30 (2004): 167–182.

Dinzelbacher, Peter. "Swimming Test." In *Encyclopedia of Witchcraft: The Western Tradition*, edited by Richard M. Golden, 1097–1099. Santa Barbara: ABC-CLIO, 2006.

Dixon, Thomas. *From Passions to Emotions: The Creation of a Secular Psychological Category.* Cambridge: Cambridge University Press, 2003.

Doelman, James. *King James I and the Religious Culture of England.* Cambridge: D.S. Brewer, 2000.

Dolan, Frances E. *Dangerous Familiars: Representations of Domestic Crime in England, 1550–1700.* Ithaca: Cornell University Press, 1994.

———. *True Relations: Reading, Literature and Evidence in Seventeenth-Century England.* Philadelphia: University of Pennsylvania Press, 2013.

Driver, Martha W. *The Image in Print: Book Illustration in Late Medieval England and its Sources.* London: British Library, 2004.

Duby, Georges. *Love and Marriage in the Middle Ages*, translated by Jane Dunnett. Cambridge: Polity, 1994.

Duffy, Eamon. *The Stripping of the Altars: Traditional Religion in England, c.1400-c.1580.* New Haven: Yale University Press, 1992.

Dures, Alan. *English Catholicism, 1558–1642: Continuity and Change*. Harlow: Longman, 1983.

Eales, Jacqueline. *Women in Early Modern England, 1500–1700*. London: UCL Press, 1998.

Edwards, Robert R. and Stephen Spector, eds. *The Olde Daunce: Love, Friendship, Sex and Marriage in the Medieval World*. Albany: State University of New York Press, 1991.

Elliott, Dyan. *Fallen Bodies: Pollution, Sexuality and Demonology in the Middle Ages*. Philadelphia: University of Pennsylvania Press, 1999.

Elmer, Peter. " 'Saints or Sorcerers': Quakerism, Demonology and the Decline of Witchcraft in Seventeenth-Century England." In *Witchcraft in Early Modern Europe: Studies in Culture and Belief*, edited by Jonathan Barry, Marianne Hester and Gareth Roberts. Cambridge: Cambridge University Press, 1998.

———. Elmer, Peter, ed. *Challenges to Authority*. New Haven: Yale University Press in association with the Open University, 2000.

———, ed. *The Later English Trial Pamphlets: Volume Five, English Witchcraft 1560–1736*. edited by James Sharpe and Richard Golden. London: Pickering and Chatto, 2003.

———. *Witchcraft, Witch-Hunting and Politics in Early Modern England*. Oxford: Oxford University Press, 2016.

Eustace, Nicole, Eugenia Lean, Julie Livingston, Jan Plamper, William M. Reddy and Barbara H. Rosenwein. "AHR Conversation: The Historical Study of Emotions." *American Historical Review* 117 (2012): 1487–1531.

Ewen, Cecil L'Estrange. *Witch Hunting and Witch Trials: The Indictments for Witchcraft from the Records of 1373 Assizes held for the Home Circuit A.D. 1559–1736*. London: Kegan Paul, Trench, Trubner & Co., Ltd, 1929.

———. *Witchcraft and Demonism: A Concise Account Derived from Sworn Depositions and Confession Obtained in the Courts of England and Wales*. London: Heath Cranton Limted, 1933.

Ferber, Sarah. *Demonic Possession and Exorcism in Early Modern France*. London: Routledge, 2004.

———. "Body of the Witch." In *Encyclopedia of Witchcraft: The Western Tradition*, edited by Richard M. Golden, 131–133. Santa Barbara: ABC-CLIO, 2006.

Fildes, Valerie, ed. *Women as Mothers in Pre-Industrial England: Essays in Memory of Dorothy McLaren*. London: Routledge, 1990.

Fincham, Kenneth and Nicholas Tyacke. *Altars Restored: The Changing Face of English Religious Worship, c.1547–1700*. Oxford: Oxford University Press, 2007.

Finlay, Anthony. *Demons: The Devil, Possession and Exorcism*. London: Blandford, 1999.

Flandrin, Jean Louis. *Families in Former Times: Kinship, Household and Sexuality*, translated by Richard Southern. Cambridge: Cambridge University Press, 1979.

———. "Repression and Change in the Sexual Life of Young People in Medieval and Early Modern Times." *Journal of Family History* 196 (1997): 196–210.

Fletcher, Anthony. *Gender, Sex, and Subordination in England, 1500–1800*. New Haven: Yale University Press, 1995.

Flynn, Maureen. "Blasphemy and the Play of Anger in Sixteenth-Century Spain." *Past and Present* 149 (1995): 29–56.

Fox, Adam. *Oral and Literate Culture in England, 1500–1700*. Oxford: Clarendon Press, 2000.

Foyster, Elizabeth. "Boys will be Boys?: Manhood and Aggression, 1660–1800." In *English Masculinities, 1660–1800*, edited by Tim Hitchcock and Michèle Cohen. London: Longman, 1999.

———. *Manhood in Early Modern England: Honour, Sex and Marriage*. London: Longman, 1999.

Frevert, Ute. *Emotions in History: Lost and Found*. Budapest: Central European University Press, 2011.

Friedman, Jerome. *Miracles and the Pulp Press During the English Revolution: The Battle of the Frogs and Fairford's Flies*. London: UCL Press, 1993.

Fudge, Erica. "Monstrous Acts: Bestiality in Early Modern England." *History Today* 50 (2000): 20–25.

Fumerton, Patricia, Anita Guerrini and Kris McAbee. *Ballads and Broadsides in Britain, 1500–1800*. Farnham: Ashgate, 2010.

Garrett, Julia M. "Witchcraft and Sexual Knowledge in Early Modern England." *The Journal for Early Modern Cultural Studies* 13 (2013): 32–72.

Gaskill, Malcolm. "Witchcraft and Power in Early Modern England: The Case of Margaret Moore." In *Women, Crime and the Courts in Early Modern England*, edited by Jenny Kermode and Garthine Walker, 125–145. London: UCL Press, 1994.

———. "The Devil in the Shape of a Man: Witchcraft, Conflict and Belief in Jacobean England." *Historical Research* 71 (1998): 142–171.

———. *Crime and Mentalities in Early Modern England*. Cambridge: Cambridge University Press, 2000.

———. *Witchfinders: A Seventeenth-Century English Tragedy*. London: John Murray, 2006.

———. "Witchcraft, Politics, and Memory in Seventeenth-Century England." *The Historical Journal* 50 (2007): 289–308.

———. "Witchcraft, Emotion and Imagination in the English Civil War." In *Witchcraft and the Act of 1604*, edited by John Newton and Jo Bath, 161–178. Leiden: Brill, 2008.

———. "Masculinity and Witchcraft in Seventeenth-Century England." In *Witchcraft and Masculinities in Early Modern Europe*, edited by Alison Rowlands, 171–190. Basingstoke: Palgrave Macmillan, 2009.

———. "Witchcraft Trials in England." In *The Oxford Handbook of Witchcraft in Early Modern Europe and Colonial America*, edited by Brian Levack, 283–299. Oxford: Oxford University Press, 2013.

Gaukroger, Stephen, ed. *The Soft Underbelly of Reason: The Passions in the Seventeenth Century*. London: Routledge, 1998.

Geis, Gilbert and Joan Bunn. *A Trial of Witches: A Seventeenth-Century Witchcraft Prosecution*. London: Routledge, 1997.

Geneva, Ann. *Astrology and the Seventeenth Century Mind: William Lilly and the Language of the Stars*. Manchester: Manchester University Press, 1995.

Gibson, Joyce. *Hanged for Witchcraft: Elizabeth Lowys and Her Successors*. Canberra: Tudor Press, 1988.

Gibson, Marion. "Mother Arnold: A Lost Witchcraft Pamphlet Rediscovered." *Notes and Queries* 243 (1998): 296–300.

———. *Reading Witchcraft: Stories of Early English Witches*. London: Routledge, 1999.

———, ed. *Early Modern Witches: Witchcraft Cases in Contemporary Writing*. London: Routledge, 2000.

———. *Witchcraft and Society in England and America, 1550–1750*. Ithaca: Cornell University Press, 2003.

———, ed. *Women and Witchcraft in Popular Literature, c.1560–1715*. Aldershot: Ashgate, 2007.

Gijswijt-Hofstra, Marijke, Brian Levack and Roy Porter, eds. "Volume Five, The Eighteenth and Nineteenth Centuries." In *Witchcraft and Magic in Europe: Six Volumes*, edited by Bengt Ankarloo and Stuart Clark. London: Athlone, 1999–2002.

Ginzburg, Carlo. "The Witches' Sabbat: Popular Cult or Inquisitorial Stereotype?" In *Understanding Popular Culture: Europe from the Middle Ages to the Nineteenth Century*, edited by Steven Kaplan, 39–52. Berlin: Mouton, 1984.

———. *Ecstasies: Deciphering the Witches' Sabbath*. New York: Pantheon Books, 1991.

Goldstein, Leba. "The Life and Death of John Lambe." *Guildhall Studies in London History* 4 (1979): 19–32.

Goodare, Julian, ed. *The Scottish Witch-Hunt in Context*. Manchester: Manchester University Press, 2002.

Gourlay, Kristi. "A Pugnacious Pagan Princess: Aggressive Female Anger and Violence in Fierabras." In *The Representation of Women's Emotions in Medieval and Early Modern England*, edited by Lisa Perfetti. Gainesville: University Press of Florida, 2005.

Gowing, Laura. *Domestic Dangers: Women, Words, and Sex in Early Modern London*. Oxford: Oxford University Press, 1996.

———. *Common Bodies: Women, Sex, and Reproduction in Seventeenth Century England*. New Haven: Yale University Press, 2003.

Grafton, Anthony, and Ann Blair, eds. *The Transmission of Culture in Early Modern Europe*. Philadelphia: University of Pennsylvania Press, 1990.

Graves, Robert. *The English Ballad: A Short Critical Survey*. London: Ernest Benn Ltd, 1927.

———, ed. *English and Scottish Ballads. Edited with an Introduction and Critical Notes by R. Graves*. London: William Heinemann, 1957.

Green, Anna. *Cultural History*. Basingstoke: Palgrave Macmillan, 2008.

Greenblatt, Stephen. *Learning to Curse: Essays in Early Modern Culture*. London: Routledge, 1990.

———. *Renaissance Self-Fashioning: From More to Shakespeare*, 2nd edn. Chicago: University of Chicago Press, 2005.

Gunther, Karl. "The Origins of English Puritanism." *History Compass* 4 (2006): 235–240.

Guskin, Phyllis J. "The Context of Witchcraft: The Case of Jane Wenham (1712)." *Eighteenth-Century Studies* 15 (1981): 48–71.

Haigh, Christopher. "The Continuity of Catholicism in the English Reformation." *Past and Present* 93 (1981): 39, 41.

Hall, S. C. *The Book of British Ballads*. London: George Routledge and Sons, 1879.

Harris, Jonathan Gill. *Foreign Bodies and the Body Politic: Discourses of Social Pathology in Early Modern England*. Cambridge: Cambridge University Press, 1998.

Haskell, Yasmin. "Early Modern Anger Management: Seneca, Ovid, and Lieven De Meyere's *De Ira libri* tres (Antwerp, 1694)." *International Journal of the Classical Tradition* 18 (2011): 36–65.

Hawkes, Gail. *Sex and Pleasure in Western Culture*. Malden: Polity Press, 2004.

Haynes, Alan. *Sex in Elizabethan England*. Gloucester: Sutton, 1997.

Herbert, Henry, and N. W. Bawcutt. *The Control and Censorship of Caroline Drama: The Records of Sir Henry Herbert, Master of the Revels, 1623–73*. Oxford: Oxford University Press, 1996.

Hester, Marianne. *Lewd Women and Wicked Witches: A Study of the Dynamics of Male Domination*. London: Routledge, 1992.

Hibbert, Christopher. *Cavaliers & Roundheads: The English at War, 1642–1649*. London: HarperCollins, 1993.

Hill, Christopher. *Antichrist in Seventeenth-Century England*. London: Oxford University Press, 1971.

———. *Some Intellectual Consequences of the English Revolution*. Madison: University of Wisconsin Press, 1980.

Hitchcock, Tim, and Michéle Cohen. *English Masculinities, 1660–1800*. London: Longman, 1999.

Hodgart, Matthew John Caldwell, ed. *The Faber Book of Ballads*. London: Faber & Faber, 1965.

Holmes, Clive. "Popular Culture? Witches, Magistrates and Divines in Early Modern England." In *Understanding Popular Culture: Europe from the Middle Ages to the Nineteenth Century*, edited by Steven Kaplan, 85–112. Berlin: Mouton, 1984.

———. "Women: Witnesses and Witches." *Past and Present* 140 (1993): 45–78.

Honeybone, Michael. *Wicked Practise and Sorcerye: The Belvoir Witchcraft Case of 1619*. Buckingham: Baron, 2008.

Houlbrooke, Ralph, ed. *English Family Life, 1576–1716: An Anthology from Diaries*. New York: Blackwell, 1989.

Housman, John E, ed. *British Popular Ballads*. London: Harrap, 1952.

Hsia, Po-Chia and R. W. Scribner, eds. *Problems in the Historical Anthropology of Early Modern Europe*. Wiesbaden: Harrassowitz, 1997.

Hutton, Ronald. *The Witch*. Forthcoming with Yale University Press.

Ingram, Martin. *Church Courts, Sex and Marriage in England, 1570–1640*. Cambridge: Cambridge University Press, 1987.

———. " 'Scolding Women Cucked or Washed': A Crisis in Gender Relations in Early Modern England?" In *Women, Crime and the Courts in Early Modern England*, edited by Jenny Kermode and Garthine Walker, 48–80. London: UCL Press, 1994.

Jackson, Louise. "Witches, Wives and Mothers: Witchcraft Persecution and Women's Confessions in Seventeenth-century England." *Women's History Review* 4 (1995): 63–83.

Jacquart, Danielle and Claude Thomasset, eds. *Sexuality and Medicine in the Middle Ages*, translated by Matthew Adamson. Cambridge: Polity Press, 1988.

Jagodzinski, Cecile M. *Privacy and Print: Reading and Writing in Seventeenth-Century England*. Charlottesville: University Press of Virginia, 1999.

James, Susan. *Passion and Action: The Emotions in Seventeenth-Century Philosophy*. Oxford: Clarendon Press, 1997.

Johnstone, Nathan. *The Devil and Demonism in Early Modern England.* Cambridge: Cambridge University Press, 2006.

Jones, David Martin. *Conscience and Allegiance in Seventeenth Century England: The Political Significance of Oaths and Engagements.* New York: University of Rochester Press, 1999.

Jones, Norman. "Defining Superstitions: Treasonous Catholics and the Act Against Witchcraft of 1563." In *State, Sovereigns & Society in Early Modern England: Essays in Honour of A.J. Slavin*, edited by Charles Carlton, 187–203. London: Sutton, 1998.

Joseph, John Earl. *Language and Politics.* Edinburgh: Edinburgh University Press, 2006.

Julius, Anthony. *Trials of the Diaspora: A History of Anti-Semitism in England.* Oxford: Oxford University Press, 2010.

Kaplan, Steven, ed. *Understanding Popular Culture: Europe from the Middle Ages to the Nineteenth Century.* Berlin: Mouton, 1984.

Karant-Nunn, Susan C. *The Reformation of Feeling: Shaping the Religious Emotions in Early Modern Germany.* New York: Oxford University Press, 2009.

Karlsen, Carol F. *The Devil in the Shape of a Woman: Witchcraft in Colonial New England*, 2nd edn. London: Norton, 1998.

Kennedy, Gwynne. *Just Anger: Representing Women's Anger in Early Modern England.* Carbondale: Southern Illinois University Press, 2000.

Kent, E. J. "Masculinity and Male Witches in Old and New England, 1593–1680." *History Workshop Journal* 60 (2005): 69–92.

———. "Turning off the Witch." In *Hearing Places: Sound, Place, Time and Culture*, edited by Ros Bandt, Michelle Duffy and Dolly MacKinnon. Newcastle: Cambridge Scholars Publishing, 2007.

———. *Cases of Male Witchcraft in Old and New England, 1592–1692.* Turnhout: Brepols, 2013.

Kermode, Jenny and Garthine Walker, eds. *Women, Crime and the Courts in Early Modern England.* London: UCL Press, 1994.

Kieckhefer, Richard. *Magic in the Middle Ages.* Cambridge: Cambridge University Press, 1989.

———. "Mythologies of Witchcraft in the Fifteenth Century." *Magic, Ritual and Witchcraft* 1 (2006): 79–108.

———. "The First Wave of Trials for Diabolical Witchcraft." In *The Oxford Handbook of Witchcraft in Early Modern Europe and Colonial America*, edited by Brian Levack, 159–178. Oxford: Oxford University Press, 2013.

Kittredge, George Lyman. *Witchcraft in Old and New England*, 3rd edn. New York: Atheneum, 1972.

Koopmans, Joop W, ed. *News and Politics in Early Modern Europe (1500–1800).* Leuven: Peeters, 2005.

Kors, Alan Charles and Edward Peters, eds. *Witchcraft in Europe 400–1700: A Documentary History*, 2nd edn. Philadelphia: University of Pennsylvania Press, 2001.

Kounine, Laura. "The Gendering of Witchcraft: Defence Strategies of Men and Women in German Witchcraft Trials." *German History* 31 (2013): 295–317.

Kwan, Natalie. "Woodcuts and Witches: Ulrich Molitor's 'De lamiis et pythonicis mulieribus', 1489–1669." *German History* 30 (2012): 493–527.

Lacquer, Thomas. *Making Sex: Body and Gender from the Greeks to Freud.* Cambridge: Harvard University Press, 1990.

Larner, Christina. *Enemies of God: The Witch-hunt in Scotland.* London: Chatto and Windus, 1981.

———. *Witchcraft and Religion: The Politics of Popular Belief.* New York: Blackwell, 1984.

———. "Was Witch Hunting Women Hunting?" *New Society* 58 (1991): 11–12.

Lavenia, Vincenzo. "Witch's Mark." In *Encyclopedia of Witchcraft: The Western Tradition,* edited by Richard M. Golden, 1220–1221. Santa Barbara: ABC-CLIO, 2006.

Leach, MacEdward. *The Ballad Book.* New York: Barnes, 1955.

Lemon, Rebecca. *Treason by Words: Literature, Law, and Rebellion in Shakespeare's England.* Ithaca: Cornell University Press, 2006.

Levack, Brian P, ed. *Articles on Witchcraft, Magic and Demonology: A Twelve Volume Anthology of Scholarly Articles.* New York: Garland Publishing Inc., 1992.

———. "The Decline and End of Witchcraft Prosecutions." In *Witchcraft and Magic in Europe,* edited by Bengt Ankarloo and Stuart Clark. *Volume Five, The Eighteenth and Nineteenth Centuries,* edited by Marijke Gijswijt-Hofstra, Brian Levack and Roy Porter. London: Athlone, 1999.

———. *The Witch-Hunt in Early Modern Europe,* 3rd edn. Harlow: Longman, 2006.

———. *Witch-Hunting in Scotland: Law, Politics and Religion.* London: Routledge, 2008.

———, ed. *The Oxford Handbook of Witchcraft in Early Modern Europe and Colonial America.* Oxford: Oxford University Press, 2013.

———. *The Devil Within: Possession and Exorcism in the Christian West.* New Haven: Yale University Press, 2013.

Lindley, Keith. *Popular Politics and Religion in Civil War London.* Aldershot: Scolar Press, 1997.

Lockyer, Roger. *Buckingham, the Life and Political Career of George Villiers, First Duke of Buckingham, 1592–1628.* New York: Longman, 1981.

Lumby, Jonathan. *The Lancashire Witch Craze: Jennet Preston and the Lancashire Witches, 1612.* Preston: Carnegie, 1995.

Lutz, Catherine A. and Lila Abu-Lughod, eds. *Language and the Politics of Emotion.* Cambridge: Cambridge University Press; Paris: Editions de la Maison des Sciences de L'homme, 1990.

MacDonald, Michael. *Mystical Bedlam: Madness, Anxiety and Healing in Seventeenth-Century England.* Cambridge: Cambridge University Press, 1983.

Macfarlane, Alan. *Witchcraft in Tudor and Stuart England: A Regional and Comparative Study.* London: Routledge and K. Paul, 1970.

———. *Witchcraft in Tudor and Stuart England: A Regional and Comparative Study.* 2nd edn. London: Routledge, 1999.

———. "Witchcraft in Tudor and Stuart Essex." In *Articles on Witchcraft, Magic and Demonology: A Twelve Volume Anthology of Scholarly Articles: Volume Six: Witchcraft in England,* edited by Brian Levack. New York: Garland Publishing Inc., 1992.

———. *Marriage and Love in England: Modes of Reproduction, 1300–1840.* New York: B. Blackwell, 1986.

McShane, Angela. *Political Broadside Ballads of Seventeenth-Century England: A Critical Bibliography*. London: Pickering & Chatto, 2011.

McShane, Angela, and Garthine Walker, eds. *The Extraordinary and the Everyday in Early Modern England: Essays in Celebration of the Work of Bernard Capp*. New York: Palgrave Macmillan, 2010.

Mair, Lucy. *Witchcraft*. London: Weidenfeld and Nicolson, 1969.

Marsh, Christopher. *Popular Religion in Sixteenth-Century England: Holding Their Peace*. New York: St. Martin's Press, 1998.

Marshall, Peter. "Protestants and Fairies in Early-Modern England." In *Living with Religious Diversity in Early-Modern Europe*, edited by Scott Dixon, Dagmar Freist and Mark Greengrass. Farnham: Ashgate, 2009.

Marshburn, Joseph H. *Murder and Witchcraft in England, 1550–1640: As Recounted in Pamphlets, Ballads, Broadsides, and Plays*. Norman: University of Oklahoma Press, 1971.

Maxwell-Stuart, P. G. *Satan: A Biography*. Stroud: Amberley Publishing, 2008.

Mayer, Robert. "Nathaniel Crouch, Bookseller and Historian: Popular Historiography and Cultural Power in Late Seventeenth-Century England." *Eighteenth-Century Studies* 27 (1994): 391–419.

Mendelson, Sara and Patricia Crawford. *Women in Early Modern England, 1550–1720*. Oxford: Clarendon Press, 1998.

Messadié, Gérald. *A History of the Devil*, translated by Marc Romano. New York: Kodansha International, 1996.

Midelfort, Eric H. C. *Witch Hunting in Southwestern German, 1562–1684: The Social and Intellectual Foundations*. Stanford: Stanford University Press, 1972.

———. *Witchcraft, Madness, Society and Religion in Early Modern Germany: A Ship of Fools*. Farnham: Ashgate, 2013.

Millar, Charlotte-Rose. "The Witch's Familiar in Sixteenth-Century England." *Melbourne Historical Journal* 38 (2010): 119–136.

———. "Witchcraft and Deviant Sexuality: A Case Study of Dr Lambe." In *The British World: Religion, Memory, Society, Culture*, edited by Marcus Harmes, Lindsay Henderson, Barbara Harmes and Amy Antonio, 51–62. Toowoomba: University of Southern Queensland, 2012.

———. "The Witchcraft Confederacy." In *A World Enchanted: Magic and the Margins*, edited by Michael Pickering and Julie Davies, 115–156. Parkville: Melbourne Historical Journal Collective, 2014.

———. "Sleeping with Devils: The Sexual Witch in Seventeenth-Century England." In *Supernatural and Secular Power in Early Modern England*, edited by Victoria Bladen and Marcus Harmes, 207–231. Farnham: Ashgate, 2015.

———. "Rebecca West's Demonic Marriage: Exploring Emotions, Ritual and Women's Agency in Seventeenth-Century England." *Women's History* Spring (2016): 4–11.

———. "Church and Parish Records." In *Emotions in Early Modern Europe: An Introduction*, edited by Susan Broomhall. London: Routledge, 2017.

———. "Familiar Spirits." In *Emotions in Early Modern Europe: An Introduction*, edited by Susan Broomhall. London: Routledge, 2017.

———. "Over-Familiar Spirits: Seventeenth Century English Witches and Their Devils." In *Emotions in the History of Witchcraft*, edited by Laura Kounine and Michael Ostling. London: Palgrave Studies in the History of Emotions, 2017.

Monter, E. William. *Witchcraft in France and Switzerland: The Borderlands During the Reformation.* New York: Cornell University Press, 1976.

———. "Toads and Eucharists: The Male Witches of Normandy, 1564–1660." *French Historical Studies* 20 (1997): 563–595.

———. "Devil's Mark." In *Encyclopedia of Witchcraft: The Western Tradition,* edited by Richard M. Golden, 275–277. Santa Barbara: ABC-CLIO, 2006.

Muchembled, Robert. *A History of the Devil: From the Middle Ages to the Present,* translated by Jean Birrell. Cambridge: Polity Press, 2003.

———. *Orgasm and the West: A History of Pleasure from the 16th Century to the Present,* translated by Jean Birrell. Cambridge: Polity Press, 2008.

Murray, Jacqueline and Konrad Eisenbichler, eds. *Desire and Discipline: Sex and Sexuality in the Premodern West.* Toronto: University of Toronto Press, 1996.

Newton, John and Jo Bath, eds. *Witchcraft and the Act of 1604.* Leiden: Brill, 2008.

Normand, Lawrence and Gareth Roberts, eds. *Witchcraft in Early Modern Scotland: James VI's Demonology and the North Berwick Witches.* Exeter: University of Exeter Press, 2000.

Notestein, Wallace. *A History of Witchcraft in England from 1558 to 1718.* Washington: The American Historical Association, 1911.

Oldridge, Darren. *The Devil in Early Modern England.* Stroud: Sutton, 2000.

———. *The Devil in Tudor and Stuart England.* Stroud: The History Press, 2010.

———. "Fairies and Devils in Early Modern England." *The Seventeenth Century* (2016): 1–15.

Osling, Michael and Richard Forest. " 'Goblins, Owles and Spirites': Discerning Early Modern English Preternatural Beliefs Through Collocational Analysis." *Religion* 44 (2014): 547–572.

Pagels, Elaine. *The Origin of Satan.* New York: Random House, 1995.

Partridge, Eric. *A Dictionary of Slang and Unconventional English,* edited by Paul Beale. Oxford: Routledge, 2000.

Paster, Gail Kern, Katherine Rowe and Mary-Floyd Wilson, eds. *Reading the Early Modern Passions: Essays in the Cultural History of Emotion.* Philadelphia: University of Pennsylvania Press, 2004.

Pendergast, John S. *Religion, Allegory, and Literacy in Early Modern England, 1560–1640: The Control of the Word.* Aldershot: Ashgate, 2006.

Pennington, Donald and Keith Thomas, eds. *Puritans and Revolutionaries: Essays in Seventeenth-Century History Presented to Christopher Hill.* Oxford: Clarendon Press, 1978.

Perfetti, Lisa, ed. *The Representation of Women's Emotions in Medieval and Early Modern England.* Gainesville: University Press of Florida, 2005.

Peters, Greg. *Reforming the Monastery: Protestant Theologies of the Religious Life.* Oregon: Cascade Books, 2014.

Phillips, Kim M. and Barry Reay. *Sex Before Sexuality: A Premodern History.* Cambridge: Polity, 2011.

Phipps, Christine. *Buckingham, Public and Private Man: The Prose, Poems, and Commonplace Book of George Villiers, Second Duke of Buckingham (1628–1687).* New York: Garland Publishing, 1985.

Pickering, Andrew and David Pickering. *Witch-hunting in England.* Stroud: Amberley, 2010.

Pollock, Linda A. "Anger and the Negotiation of Relationships in Early Modern England." *The Historical Journal* 47 (2004): 567–590.

Poole, Robert, ed. *The Lancashire Witches: Histories and Stories.* Manchester: Manchester University Press, 2002.

Pumfrey, Stephen. "Potts, Plots and Politics: James I's 'Daemonologie' and 'The Wonderfull Discoverie of Witches'." In *The Lancashire Witches: Histories and Stories,* edited by Robert Poole, 19–41. Manchester: Manchester University Press, 2002.

Purkiss, Diane. "Women's Stories of Witchcraft in Early Modern England: The House, the Body, the Child." *Gender and History* 7 (1995): 408–432.

———. *The Witch in History: Early Modern and Twentieth-century Representations.* London: Routledge, 1996.

———. "Desire and Its Deformities: Fantasies of Witchcraft in the English Civil War." *Journal of Medieval and Early Modern Studies* 27 (1997): 103–132.

———. *At the Bottom of the Garden: A Dark History of Fairies, Hobgoblins and Other Troublesome Things.* New York: New York University Press, 2000.

———. "Fairies." In *Encyclopedia of Witchcraft: The Western Tradition,* edited by Richard M. Golden, 345–347. Santa Barbara: ABC-CLIO, 2006.

———. *The English Civil War: Papists, Gentlewomen, Soldiers, and Witchfinders in the Birth of Modern Britain.* New York: Basic Books, 2006.

———. *Fairies and Fairy Stories: A History.* Stroud: Tempus, 2007.

Quaife, G. R. *Wanton Wenches and Wayward Wives: Peasants and Illicit Sex in Early Seventeenth-Century England.* London: Croom Helm, 1979.

———. *Godly Zeal and Furious Rage: The Witch in Early Modern Europe.* London: Croom Helm, 1987.

Questier, Michael C. *Catholicism and Community in Early Modern England: Politics, Aristocratic Patronage and Religion, c.1550–1640.* Cambridge: Cambridge University Press, 2006.

Raymond, Joad. *The Invention of the Newspaper: English Newsbooks, 1641–1649.* Oxford: Oxford University Press, 1996.

———. *Pamphlets and Pamphleteering in Early Modern Britain.* Cambridge: Cambridge University Press, 2003.

———, ed. *Cheap Print in Britain and Ireland to 1660.* Oxford: Oxford University Press, 2011.

Reay, Barry. *The Quakers and the English Revolution.* London: Temple Smith, 1985.

———. *Popular Cultures in England 1550–1750.* London: Longman, 1998.

Reddy, William M. "Against Constructionism: The Historical Ethnography of Emotions." *Current Anthropology* 38 (1997): 327–351.

———. *The Navigation of Feeling: A Framework for the History of Emotions.* Cambridge: Cambridge University Press, 2001.

———. *The Making of Romantic Love: Longing and Sexuality in Europe, South Asia and Japan, 900–1200 CE.* Chicago: University of Chicago Press, 2012.

Richardson, R. C., and Geoffrey M. Ridden. *Freedom and the English Revolution: Essays in History and Literature.* Manchester: Manchester University Press, 1986.

Robbins, Caroline. "Selden's Pills: State Oaths in in England 1558–1714." *Huntington Library Quarterly* 35 (1972): 303–321.

Roper, Lyndal. *Oedipus and the Devil: Witchcraft, Sexuality and Religion in Early Modern Europe.* London: Routledge, 1994.

———. *Witch Craze: Terror and Fantasy in Baroque Germany.* New Haven: Yale University Press, 2004.

———. *The Witch in the Western Imagination.* Charlottesville: University of Virginia Press, 2012.

Roper, Lyndal, Alon Confino, Ute Frevert, Uffa Jensen, Lyndal Roper and Daniela Saxer. "Forum: History of Emotions." *German History* 28 (2012): 67–80.

Rosen, Barbara. *Witchcraft.* London: Edward Arnold, 1969.

———. *Witchcraft in England, 1558–1618*, 2nd edn. Amherst: University of Massachusetts Press, 1991.

Rosenwein, Barbara H. *Anger's Past: The Social Uses of an Emotion in the Middle Ages.* Ithaca: Cornell University Press, 1998.

———. "Worrying About Emotions in History." *American Historical Review* 107 (2002): 821–45.

———. *Emotional Communities in the Early Middle Ages.* Ithaca: Cornell University Press, 2006.

Rowlands, Alison. "'Not the "Usual Suspects?' Male Witches, Witchcraft and Masculinities in Early Modern Europe." In *Witchcraft and Masculinities in Early Modern Europe*, edited by Alison Rowlands, 1–30. Basingstoke: Palgrave Macmillan, 2009.

———, ed. *Witchcraft and Masculinities in Early Modern Europe.* Basingstoke: Palgrave Macmillan, 2009.

———. "Witchcraft and Gender in Early Modern Europe." In *The Oxford Handbook of Witchcraft in Early Modern Europe and Colonial America*, edited by Brian Levack, 449–467. Oxford: Oxford University Press, 2013.

Rublack, Ulinka. "Fluxes: The Early Modern Body and the Emotions." *History Workshop Journal* 53 (2002): 1–16.

Russell, Jeffrey Burton. *Witchcraft in the Middle Ages.* Ithaca: Cornell University Press, 1972.

———. *Lucifer: The Devil in the Middle Ages.* Ithaca: Cornell University Press, 1984.

———. *Mephistopheles: The Devil in the Modern World.* Ithaca: Cornell University Press, 1986.

Sabean, David Warren. *Power in the Blood: Popular Culture and Village Discourse in Early Modern Germany.* Cambridge: Cambridge University Press, 1984.

Sands, Kathleen R. *Demon Possession in Elizabethan England.* London: Praeger, 2004.

Schulte, Rolf. *Man as Witch: Male Witches in Central Europe*, translated by Linda Froome-Döring. Basingstoke: Palgrave Macmillan, 2009.

Serpell, James A. "Guardian Spirits or Demonic Pets: The Concept of the Witch's Familiar in Early Modern England, 1530–1712." In *The Animal-Human Boundary: Historical Perspectives*, edited by Angela Creager and William Chester Jordan, 157–190. Woodbridge: University of Rochester Press, 2002.

Shachar, Isaiah. *The Judensau: A Medieval Anti-Jewish Motif and Its History.* London: Warburg Institute, 1974.

Sharpe, James. "Witchcraft and Women in Seventeenth-Century England: Some Northern Evidence." *Continuity and Change* 6 (1991): 179–199.

———. "The Devil in East Anglia: The Matthew Hopkins Trials Reconsidered." In *Witchcraft in Early Modern Europe: Studies in Culture and Belief*, edited by Jonathan Barry, Marianne Hester and Gareth Roberts, 237–254. Cambridge: Cambridge University Press, 1996.

———. *Instruments of Darkness: Witchcraft in England 1550–1750.* London: Hamish Hamilton, 1996.

————. *Instruments of Darkness: Witchcraft in Early Modern England*, Paperback edn. Philadelphia: University of Pennsylvania Press, 1997.

————. "Introduction." In *Witchcraft in Tudor and Stuart England: A Regional and Comparative Study*, 2nd edn., edited by Alan Macfarlane, xi–xxvi. London: Routledge, 1999.

————. *Witchcraft in Early Modern England*. Harlow: Longman, 2001.

————. "Introduction: The Lancashire Witches in Historical Context." In *The Lancashire Witches: Histories and Stories*, edited by Robert Poole, 1–18. Manchester: Manchester University Press, 2002.

————. "The Witch's Familiar in Early Modern England." In *Authority and Consent in Tudor England: Essays Presented to C.S.L. Davies*, edited by G. W. Bernard and S. J. Gunn, 219–232. Aldershot: Ashgate, 2002.

————, and Richard Golden, eds. *English Witchcraft 1560–1736, Six Volumes*. London: Pickering and Chatto, 2003.

————. *Remember, Remember the Fifth of November: Guy Fawkes and the Gunpowder Plot*. London: Profile Book, 2005.

————. "Familiars." In *The Encyclopedia of Witchcraft: The Western Tradition*, edited by Richard M. Golden, 347–349. Santa Barbara: ABC-CLIO, 2006.

————. "In Search of the English Sabbat: Popular Conceptions of Witches' Meetings in Early Modern England." *Journal of Early Modern Studies* 2 (2013): 161–183.

Sharpe, Kevin and Peter Lake. *Culture and Politics in Early Stuart England*. Basingstoke: Macmillan, 1994.

Shepard, Alexandra. *Meanings of Manhood in Early Modern England*. Oxford: Oxford University Press, 2003.

Shephard, Simon. *The Women's Sharp Revenge: Five Women's Pamphlets from the Renaissance*. London: Fourth Estate, 1985.

Shoemaker, Robert, B. *Gender in English Society, 1650–1850: The Emergence of Separate Spheres?* New York: Longman, 1998.

Shorter, Edward. *A History of Women's Bodies*. New York: Basic Books, 1982.

————. *Written in the Flesh: A History of Desire*. Toronto: University of Toronto Press, 2005.

Simons, Patricia. *The Sex of Men in Premodern Europe: A Cultural History*. Cambridge: Cambridge University Press, 2011.

Skelton, John. "Against Venomous Tongues." In *The Complete Poems of John Skelton, Laureate*, edited by Philip Henderson. London: J.M. Dent, 1959.

Skerpan, Elizabeth Penley. *The Rhetoric of Politics in the English Revolution, 1642–1660*. Columbia: University of Missouri Press, 1992.

Slack, Paul. *The English Poor Law 1531–1782*. Houndmills: Macmillan, 1990.

Smyth, Adam. *"Profit and Delight": Printed Miscellanies in England, 1640–1682*. Detroit: Wayne State University Press, 2004.

Spinks, Jennifer. *Monstrous Births and Visual Culture in Sixteenth-Century Germany*. London: Pickering and Chatto, 2009.

Spufford, Margaret. *Small Books and Pleasant Histories: Popular Fiction and Its Readership in Seventeenth-century England*. London: Methuen, 1981.

Spurr, John. "Perjury, Profanity and Politics." *The Seventeenth Century* 8 (1993): 37–63.

Stanford, Peter. *The Devil: A Biography*. London: Heinemann, 1996.

Stavreva, Kirilka. "Fighting Words: Witch-Speak in Late Elizabethan Docu-Fiction." *Journal of Medieval and Early Modern Studies* 30 (2000): 309–338.

Stearns, Carol Zisowitz and Peter N. Stearns. "Emotionology: Clarifying the History of Emotions and Emotional Standards." *American Historical Review* 90 (1985): 813–836.

———. *Anger: The Struggle for Emotional Control in America's History*. Chicago: The University of Chicago Press, 1986.

Steenberg, Kristine. "Emotions and Gender: The Case of Anger in Early Modern English Revenge Tragedies." In *A History of Emotions 1200–1800*, edited by Jonas Liliequist, 119–133. London: Taylor and Francis, 2012.

Stephens, Walter. *Demon Lovers: Witchcraft, Sex and the Crisis of Belief*. Chicago: University of Chicago Press, 2002.

Stone, Lawrence. *The Family, Sex and Marriage in England 1500–1800*. New York: Harper and Row, 1979.

Stoyle, Mark. *The Black Legend of Prince Rupert's Dog: Witchcraft and Propaganda During the English Civil War*. Exeter: University of Exeter Press, 2011.

Suhr, Carla. *Publishing for the Masses: Early Modern English Witchcraft Pamphlets*. Helsinki : Société Néophilologique, 2011.

Thomas, Keith. *Religion and the Decline of Magic: Studies in Popular Beliefs in Sixteenth and Seventeenth Century England*. London: Weidenfeld and Nicolson, 1971.

———. "The Puritans and Adultery: The Act of 1650 Reconsidered." In *Puritans and Revolutionaries: Essays in Seventeenth-Century History Presented to Christopher Hill*, edited by Donald Pennington and Keith Thomas, 257–282. Oxford: Clarendon Press, 1978.

———. "The Meaning of Literacy in Early Modern England." In *The Written Word: Literacy in Translation*, edited by Gerd Baumann, 97–131. Oxford: Oxford University Press, 1986.

———. *Religion and the Decline of Magic: Studies in Popular Beliefs in Sixteenth and Seventeenth Century England*, 2nd edn. London: Penguin Books, 1991.

———. *Man and the Natural World: Changing Attitudes in England, 1500–1800*, 2nd edn. Oxford: Oxford University Press, 1996.

Thompson, Janet A. *Wives, Widows, Witches & Bitches: Women in Seventeenth-Century Devon*. New York: P. Lang, 1993.

Trevor-Roper, Hugh. *The European Witch-craze of the Sixteenth and Seventeenth Centuries*. Harmondsworth: Penguin, 1969.

Trinterud, Leonard J. "The Origins of Puritanism." *Church History* 20 (1951): 37–57.

Turner, David M. *Fashioning Adultery: Gender, Sex and Civility in England, 1660–1740*. New York: Cambridge University Press, 2002.

Underdown, David. "The Taming of the Scold: The Enforcement of Patriarchal Authority in Early Modern England." In *Order and Disorder in Early Modern England*, edited by Anthony Fletcher and John Stevenson. Cambridge: Cambridge University Press, 1985.

———. *A Freeborn People: Politics and the Nation in Seventeenth-Century England*. Oxford: Clarendon Press, 1996.

Valletta, Frederick. *Witchcraft, Magic and Superstition in England, 1640–70*. Aldershot: Ashgate, 2000.

Vienne-Guerrin, Nathalie, ed. *The Unruly Tongue in Early Modern England: Three Treatises*. Madison: Fairleigh Dickinson University Press, 2012.

Walker, Garthine. *Crime, Gender, and Social Order in Early Modern England*. Cambridge: Cambridge University Press, 2003.

———. "The Strangeness of the Familiar: Witchcraft and the Law in Early Modern England." In *The Extraordinary and the Everyday in Early Modern England: Essays in Celebration of the Work of Bernard Capp*, edited by Angela McShane and Garthine Walker, 105–124. New York: Palgrave Macmillan, 2010.

Walsham, Alexandra. *Church Papists: Catholicism, Conformity and Confessional Polemic in Early Modern England*. Woodbridge: Boydell Press, 1993.

———. "'The Fatall Vesper': Providentialism and Anti-Popery in Late Jacobean London." *Past and Present* 144 (1994): 36–87.

———. *Providence in Early Modern England*. Oxford: Oxford University Press, 1999.

———. "The Reformation and 'The Disenchantment of the World' Reassessed." *The Historical Journal* 51 (2008): 497–528.

Warburton, Greg. "Gender, Supernatural Power, Agency and the Metamorphoses of the Familiar in Early Modern Pamphlet Accounts of English Witchcraft." *Parergon* 20 (2003): 95–118.

Warren, F. E., trans. *The Sarum Missal in English*. London: Alexander Moring Ltd., 1911.

Watt, Tessa. *Cheap Print and Popular Piety, 1550–1640*. Cambridge: Cambridge University Press, 1991.

Weir, David. *The Origins of the Federal Theology in Sixteenth Century Reformation Thought*. Oxford: Clarendon Press, 1990.

Wilby, Emma. "The Witch's Familiar and the Fairy in Early Modern England and Scotland." *Folklore* 111 (2000): 283–305.

———. *Cunning Folk and Familiar Spirits: Shamanistic Visionary Traditions in Early Modern British Witchcraft and Magic*. Brighton: Sussex Academic Press, 2005.

Willis, Arthur J. *Church Life in Kent Being Church Court Records of the Canterbury Diocese, 1559–1565*. London: Phillimore and Co. Ltd, 1975.

Willis, Deborah. *Malevolent Nurture: Witch-Hunting and Maternal Power in Early Modern England*. Ithaca: Cornell University Press, 1995.

Wimberly, Lowry Charles. *Folklore in the English and Scottish Ballads*. New York: Frederick Ungar Publishing Co., 1959.

Withington, Phil. *Society in Early Modern England: The Vernacular Origins of Some Powerful Ideas*. Cambridge: Polity Press, 2010.

Wolfram, Sybil. *In-Laws and Outlaws: Kinship and Marriage in England*. London: Croom Helm, 1987.

Worden, Blair. *The English Civil Wars: 1640–1660*. London: Weidenfeld & Nicolson, 2009.

Young, Francis. *English Catholics and the Supernatural 1553–1829*. Farnham: Ashgate, 2013.

Zika, Charles. *Exorcising our Demons: Magic, Witchcraft and Visual Culture in Early Modern Europe*. Leiden: Brill, 2003.

———. *The Appearance of Witchcraft: Print and Visual Culture in Sixteenth-century Europe*. London: Routledge, 2007.

———. "Images of Witchcraft in Early Modern Europe." In *The Oxford Handbook of Witchcraft in Early Modern Europe and Colonial America*, edited by Brian Levack, 141–156. Oxford: Oxford University Press, 2013.

Zika, Charles and Elizabeth Kent. *Witches and Witch-Hunting in European Societies: A Working Bibliography and Guide to Materials in Melbourne Libraries*. Melbourne: University of Melbourne History Department, 1998.

Index